THE SOCIOBIOLOGICAL IMAGINATION

SUNY Series in Philosophy and Biology

David Edward Shaner, Editor

THE SOCIOBIOLOGICAL IMAGINATION

Edited by

MARY MAXWELL

State University of New York Press

"Three Male Chimp startle while on patrol" p. 236. Reprinted by permission of the publisher from *The Chimpanzees of Gombe* by Jane Goodall, Cambridge, Mass.: Harvard University Press. Copyright 1986 by the President and Fellows of Harvard College.

Published by
State University of New York Press, Albany

© 1991 State University of New York

For information, address the State University of New York Press,
State University Plaza, Albany, NY 12246

Production by Christine M. Lynch
Marketing by Theresa A. Swierzowski

Library of Congress Cataloging-in-Publication Data

The Sociobiological imagination / edited by Mary Maxwell.
    p.   cm — (SUNY series in philosophy and biology)
    Includes bibliographical references and index.
    ISBN 0-7914-0767-5 (alk. paper). — ISBN 0-7914-0768-3 (pbk. :
alk. paper)
    1. Sociobiology. I. Maxwell, Mary. II. Series.
GN365.9.S58   1991
304.5—dc20   90-10336
                                                           CIP

10 9 8 7 6 5 4 3 2 1

CONTENTS

Acknowledgments

I thank, first and foremost, the twenty-one contributors to this volume, who have skillfully carried out the assignment of describing, in succinct form, the ways in which sociobiology affects their particular academic disciplines. During the time this volume was growing (from its original plan of eight-or-so chapters), it was exciting every day to see what would arrive in the mailbag. The manuscripts kept surprising me, and there was hardly any repetition among them. I lived in the Middle East during the preparation of this book and therefore had no chance to meet the authors face to face (except John Chandler, during a short trip to Australia). Nor did the authors have much opportunity to consult one another. Yet a balanced whole seemed to emerge from their several efforts.

I especially want to pay respects to the first five members of this project—Charles Lumsden, Pierre van den Berghe, Jack Beckstrom, Vernon Reynolds, and Roger Masters. Beckstrom clued me in on the background of several developments in sociobiology. He cajoled me into attending the 1987 Evolution and Human Behavior Conference at Ann Arbor, Michigan, where I learned that there was indeed sociobiological research "west of the Charles River," to use Van den Berghe's phrase. Lumsden talked me into keeping the format simple (I, in turn, talked him out of using any equations in his chapter). Reynolds advised me on artwork. Masters insisted that we include a chapter on economics. I thank these scholars for their camaraderie.

Early encouragement came from nonparticipants as well, including Lionel Tiger, Helen Fisher, Jack Hirshleifer, and Sarah Hrdy. Karen Lanphear acted as Independent Reader of the first draft and made valuable suggestions, such as to include a "biosketch" of each author at the end of the book. The text was typed to perfection by the Santos brothers: Tony on keyboard,

Delfin on "mouse." Susan Moran designed the tables; Margaret Heiss Moustafa proofread the galleys. The faculty and students of the medical school of the University of the United Arab Emirates gave me moral support. All of this was greatly appreciated.

Several authors in this volume, myself included, have, in the past, garnered numerous "pink slips" from publishers when trying to place manuscripts that had a sociobiological theme. For this reason, I am especially pleased that our book is to be published by one of the early, daring leaders in the sociobiological field, State University of New York Press. Bill Eastman, director of that press, has given the manuscript extra care. Christine Lynch, Production editor, solved all my technical problems and never made me feel like a pest—well, hardly ever. I send her my affectionate thanks. Others at SUNY assisted us also.

I am grateful to at-home editor George Maxwell for helping with the bibliography, and for shouting me to a fax machine, not to mention for making my life worth living. I thank Napoleon Chagnon for the use of his photograph of Yanamamo warriors and Nancy De Vore of Anthropophoto for searching for primate photos. Lastly, I am indebted to E. O. Wilson for teaching me, *inter alia,* the difference between "that" and "which."

Grateful acknowledgment is made for permission to reprint previously published material as follows: Longman, London and the authors gave us permission to use, in chapter 12, several paragraphs, a table, and four of Penelope Dell's illustrations from Vernon Reynolds and R. E. S. Tanner's *The Biology of Religion* (1983). Plenum Press allowed us to reprint, as chapter 16, a revised version of Pierre L. van den Berghe's "Why Most Sociologists Don't (and Won't) Think Evolutionarily" published in *Sociological Forum,* vol. 5, June, 1990. The first cartoon in the Introduction appears by permission of Don Addis and Creators Syndicate. The Far Side Cartoon by Gary Larson in the Glossary is reprinted by permission of Chronicle Features, San Francisco, California. We have permission from The University of Illinois Press to reprint, as chapter 2, part of a chapter from John Beckstrom's *Evolutionary Jurisprudence* (1989) Copyright (c) 1989 by the Board of Trustees of the University of Illinois. McGraw-

Hill, Inc., New York allowed us to use as Table 1, in chapter 3, a table from Rensis Likert's *Human Organization* (1967).

The figure entitled "Complexity," in Chapter 15, first appeared in Gerda Smets's *Aesthetic Judgement and Arousal* (1973), Leuven University Press, Belgium. The drawing of the stirrup jar and the sword in Chapter 15 was done by Netia Piercy, and was previously published in the *American Journal of Archaelogy,* volume 92, 1988. Figure 1 in the Introduction was reprinted by permission of the publishers from *Sociobiology— the New Synthesis* by Edward O. Wilson, Cambridge, Mass.: Harvard University Press, Copyright (c) 1975 by the President and Fellows of Harvard College. The American Psychological Association holds the copyright for Figure 1 in Chapter 18. Cambridge University permitted us to use Figure 4 in Chapter 15. Table 3, in chapter 3, is published by permission of Transaction Publishers from Trans-action/Society, vol. 1 no. 5, Copyright (c) by Transaction Publishers. Addison-Wesley Publishing Co., Inc. gave permission to reprint Table 4, in chapter 3, from William Ouchi's *Theory Z,* Copyright (c) 1981 by William Ouchi.

I also thank W. W. Norton and Company, New York for permission to use, in chapter 5, a table, three figures, and excerpts, from Robert Frank's *Passions within Reason* (1988); Oxford University Press, New York, for permission to use, in chapter 7, eight lines of Edward Muir's "The Wheel" from his *Collected Poems* (1960); Kluwer Academic Publishers, Dordrecht, The Netherlands for permission to use, in chapter 11, several paragraphs from Michael Ruse's "Evolutionary Epistemology: Can Sociobiology Help?" that appeared in *Sociobiology and Epistemology,* edited by James Fetzer (1986); John Wiley and Sons, Inc., New York for permission to reprint Table 3, in chapter 3, from Chris Argyris's *Integrating the Individual and the Organization* (c) 1964 by John Wiley and Sons, Inc.; *The New Yorker* for permission to reprint the cartoon by Lee Lorenz (1989); and Sage Publications, Inc. for permission to reprint Table 1 in Chapter 8, from Lanzetta et al., "Emotional and Cognitive Responses to Televised Images of Political Leaders," in *Mass Media and Political Thought,* edited by Sidney Kraus and Richard E. Perloff, Sage, Beverley Hills, California (c) 1985 by Sage Publications, Inc.

Introduction

Mary Maxwell

The title of this book, *The Sociobiological Imagination,* recalls the title of C. Wright Mills's book, *The Sociological Imagination.* Mills claimed, in 1959, that the academic subject of sociology had caught on with the public. A few decades after sociology's arrival on university campuses, he said, the sociological imagination was part of everyday thinking. Journalists, for example, had begun to report the phenomenon of unemployment as a sociological trend, as having to do with broad social and economic forces rather than with particular workers or factories. No doubt a similar book could have been written around the same time, entitled "The Psychological Imagination," concerning the popular acceptance of theories of psychology. The academic terms *repression, conditioning, neurosis,* and *sublimation,* for example, had come into ordinary lay usage.

The book at hand deals with the rapid spread of the ideas of sociobiology. Unlike Mills's *Sociological Imagination,* though, this book will not be concerned with the way those ideas have reached the general public. The public understanding—or, more often, misunderstanding—of sociobiology is not, I ween, worthy of a celebratory volume. Instead, it is my plan here to demonstrate the wide influence sociobiology has had on other *academic* disciplines. In eighteen chapters, scholars from such fields as philosophy, psychology, anthropology, and political science discuss how their areas of knowledge have been illuminated by, or challenged by, the new ideas of sociobiology.

The purpose of this book is threefold. First, it is meant to acknowledge that the proliferation of sociobiological ideas is

1

a remarkable phenomenon in itself. It would be hard to think of another example in which one major new theory has had such extensive intellectual ramifications. Second, this book is intended to show that the majority of the developments in human sociobiology have in fact taken place in various disciplines outside of biology. The reader will see that, for the most part, sociobiologists have not personally invaded other academic areas. Rather, qualified scholars in those other areas have taken the basic theory of sociobiology and used it, and developed it, with respect to their own subject matter, their own theoretical concerns. If one were to ask today, Where is the corpus of human sociobiological research?, the reply would have to be that it is located in these disparate places. (Note: in this book, each chapter—with the exception of those on aesthetics and history— has been written by a member of the respective discipline.)

Third, by presenting the multifaceted discipline of socio-biology in this way, this book should stand as a useful introduction to the major principles of sociobiology. It is by no means meant to serve as a textbook; readers will be referred elsewhere for technical discussions. Nor is it meant to be a complete record of developments within each field. Some of the chapters in fact cover only one or two issues—enough to give the reader a sense of how the work is done. Nevertheless, a reasonable picture of contemporary sociobiological research, and the direction of future research, should emerge from these pages.

Let me now give a brief sketch of the field of human sociobiology, which can be said to have become "reified" in 1975 upon the publication of E. O. Wilson's *Sociobiology: The New Synthesis*. I shall outline its two major stages, which I see as centering on two theories—the theory of genetic altruism, also known as "inclusive fitness," and the theory of gene–culture coevolution, sometimes known as "evolved constraints." Before getting to that, however, I must backtrack to the late 1960s and early 1970s when human ethology was coming into bloom.

ETHOLOGY

Ethology—the scientific study of animal behavior—had been developed since the 1930s, mainly in Europe, as the study of instincts—for example, how an animal deals with predators, how it finds food, and so forth. Whereas it had been appreciated since Darwin's time that anatomical features were genetically inherited, it now became apparent that behaviors were likewise genetically inherited. And whereas it had been realized that anatomical features could be accounted for by natural selection—that is, these functions were adaptations to the environment that helped their owners to be "selected" in evolution—it now became realized that behaviors, too, are adaptations. Suddenly, animal behaviors that had been curiosities (say, the mating dance of the fly, or migratory patterns in ungulates) now came in for Darwinian analysis.

In cases where the animal behavior in question happened to resemble a human behavior, it seemed logical to suggest that the human behaviors, too, were based on instinct. Human ethology received widespread notice by way of several popular books. Konrad Lorenz, an ethologist who had become known for his theory of "imprinting" in geese, wrote provocatively about the human propensity for violence in his 1967 book, *On Aggression.* Robert Ardrey, who was a playwright rather than a scientist, took up the hypothesis that territorial behavior in humans was the same preprogrammed phenomenon as seen in animals. He published this idea in 1971, titling his book, *The Territorial Imperative,* to refer to this instinct. Desmond Morris, a zoologist, pointed out numerous points of comparison between human and animal behavior in *The Naked Ape* (1969)—notably in regard to sexual activity. (Accordingly, this book reached a large audience by being serialized in tabloid newspapers.)

Around the same time, in 1971, Jane Goodall published *In the Shadow of Man.* Her mission was not to show that humans were like chimpanzees, but to show that many chimpanzee behaviors were astonishingly humanlike. In any case, her book added to the general idea that some of our human behaviors may be genetically given rather than invented by culture. The anthropologists Lionel Tiger and Robin Fox took up specifically the problem of how cultures come to invent the very things for which people are already genetically predisposed. The rituals of courtship, for example, which anthropologists had always assumed to be "invented," were now hypothesized by Tiger and Fox to be based on the "biogram" of our species, and to be similar in some ways to animal rituals of courtship. The same could be said of, say, political leadership. The cover of the paperback edition of their 1971 book, *The Imperial Animal,* featured an ape wearing ermine and a crown and holding a sceptre.

It is not now possible—and I suspect will never be possible— for us to measure precisely the contribution these human ethological studies made to the sociobiological imagination. Clearly they were widely disseminated and discussed, and given time, they perhaps would have led to many developments in the academic disciplines represented in this book. In their day, however, they were generally not considered academically respectable. This was partly due to a moral objection—the popular ethologists played up many of mankind's less desirable traits and implied that these traits were insurmountable. It was also due to an intellectual objection—the way in which "instincts" actually translated into human behavior remained a mystery. There was no way to show whether humans were performing certain actions because they freely chose to do so, or because they were "genetically determined" to do so. Hence, it seemed that the two alternative explanations—nature and nurture—were equally valid; intellectuals could hold one opinion or the other, more or less according to taste, since science could not offer a ruling.

SOCIOBIOLOGY

This situation changed, beginning in 1975 with the publication of *Sociobiology* by the entomologist (insect specialist) E. O. Wilson. Wilson's book had been "in the works" to synthesize certain major theoretical developments in biology, quite apart from the human ethology studies just mentioned (though those studies obviously contributed to Wilson's speculations about the human species in the final chapter of his book). *Sociobiology* is a large and unquestionably scientific book concerned mainly with the sociobiology of animals. "Sociobiology" does not mean "the biology of people," as is often assumed; it means "the biology of society." Societies are found in many nonhuman species; the new discipline of sociobiology studies how these societies first evolved, and how patterns of the animals' social behavior continue to be governed by genes. Needless to say, this part of the work is uncontroversial: no one seems to mind when a biologist points out how the food-sharing practices of ants, for instance, is an inherited trait.

The principal theory on which the science of sociobiology is based is one that was put forth by another entomologist, William D. Hamilton, in 1964. It is known as the theory of genetic altruism, or kin altruism, or kin selection, or inclusive fitness. This theory shows how it is biologically possible for an individual animal to have a genetic trait that causes it to perform some unselfish action—some action that favors the survival of another individual at expense to itself. This was no small discovery in biology—many great minds had been working on it for years. The "Darwinian synthesis" of the 1930s had linked Darwin's theory of natural selection to the science of genetics and the science of ecology, but further developments were held up by "the problem of altruism." Biologists were frustrated by the lack of a theoretical explanation for many of the social behaviors that were easily observed in nature.

Hamilton's (1964) solution to the problem of altruism—which came to him through his study of bees—was that an individual, Ego, can perform an altruistic act if it helps another member of the family, since that member of the family possesses some of Ego's genes (that is, copies of the same genes as Ego possesses). By helping that member in some way to survive and thus reproduce, Ego is thereby helping its own genes to proliferate in the next generation. This is true even if Ego's altruistic act causes Ego's premature death or Ego's failure to leave direct descendants. As long as Ego's genes get included in the next generation through "collateral descendants," the altruistic trait can be passed on. Altruistic behavior is thus no longer a biological mystery. It is not always the *individual* that is selected for, as in the traditional theory of natural selection— the *family* with the trait can be selected for, hence Hamilton's theory is sometimes known as "kin selection."

Hamilton's theory is simple—so simple, Wilson says, that a person could work it out on the back of an envelope in three minutes—but one that, Wilson admits, he would probably never have thought of (1985, 478). The essence of Hamilton's theory is "genetic selfishness," or, as Richard Dawkins (1976, revised

1989) calls it, "the selfish gene." The key point is that altruism is not "really" performed for the good of others, it is performed for the good of the gene that selfishly "wants" to be included in future generations. Thus, biological altruism always has a payoff for the donor—in the long run (as long as we think of the well-proliferated gene as being the winner, even after the altruistic individual's death).

This is quite a different perspective from trying to account for an altruistic act in terms of its more obvious effects, namely, the beneficial effects it has on the recipient. For decades, biologists had tried to figure out why certain behaviors contribute to "the good of the group." It is now widely accepted, following the insights of Hamilton and of George C. Williams (1966) that evolution does not occur for the good of the group. It occurs only for the good of the individual or the good of the genes. There are enormous—and largely unexpected—ramifications of this basic sociobiological theory for human life. Most of the chapters in the first half of this book discuss these ramifications. The chapters in the second half of the book mostly discuss the ramifications of a "second stage" of sociobiological theory, namely gene-culture theory—which deals exclusively with the human species.

GENE–CULTURE THEORY

I stated earlier that the human ethology ideas of the late 1960s and early 1970s led to polarity over nature-nurture, which, I hinted, was "resolved" by the arrival of sociobiology. Of course, that resolution was appreciated at first by only a few scholars; sociobiology hardly swept through the groves of Academe. Indeed, for a few years after its publication, Wilson's *Sociobiology* was more or less taboo among scholars of the humanities and social sciences, and Wilson himself was thought to be the new personification of social Darwinism. Much of this reaction was purely ideological—genetics as applied to humans had earned a bad name and was automatically associated with certain political policies. However, there were also the same grounds for rejecting human sociobiology as there had been for rejecting human ethology, namely, that it did not account for the mind. Despite sociobiology's finding the key to the genetics of social behavior—at least in animals—it still failed to show how culture came about, or how individuals exercise free choice in the face of genetic constraints.

Various biologists began to put together some ideas about the relationship between genes and culture. Early writers in this field were William Durham (1978), L. L. Cavalli-Sforza and M. W. Feldman (1981) and Robert Boyd and Peter J. Richardson (1985). In 1978, Charles Lumsden initiated a collaboration with E. O. Wilson that led to the theory of gene-culture coevolution (Lumsden and Wilson 1981, 1983). Culture evolves, they said, through genes that design the human mind. In evolutionary time, some individuals had certain "mental mutations"—so to speak—that made them able to invent, or imitate, some cultural artifact or cultural behavior. These individuals may have survived better than others who did not possess such mutations (that is, such genes). Thus, to oversimplify greatly, genes and culture *coevolve:* the genes help the cultural items (known as "culturgens") to proliferate, and the cultural items (warm clothing, fish hooks) help their bearers to survive.

The essence of this theory is that the inherited mental traits consist mainly of *preferences* for one thing over another, and thus lead to a similarity of cultural forms that people eventually invent (thus solving the riddle of the universality of certain cultural institutions). In the Lumsden-Wilson theory, inherited mental traits also lead to "semantic" understanding, such that words and concepts conjure up roughly the same thing to all users of a particular language.

Throughout the 1980s, much work was done by psychologists in an effort to explain how evolved "rules" in the brain lead to preferential, or constrained, learning of certain things over others. Indeed, psychologists now attempt to find out how genes can (if they can) govern *thought.* Leda Cosmides and John Tooby (1989) have come up with the idea that different types of thinking, or mental "computations," evolved to deal with different social and environmental events. Thus, we may have a set of cognitive operations that gets switched on when we are faced with threat, or cheating, or finding a mate. This is quite different from the traditional view of the mind as receiving all its thoughts through learning—in fact, it is almost reminiscent of the pre-Lockean notion of innate ideas. This research is sometimes known as the study of "evolved constraints."

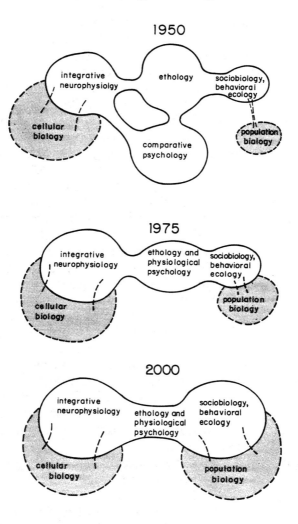

Figure 1. E. O. Wilson's projection, for the year 1950 to the year 2000, of the relative number of ideas from various disciplines in and adjacent to behavioral biology. (Reprinted from Wilson, 1975, with permission.)

In 1975, E. O. Wilson drew what he called a "subjective conception of the relative number of ideas in various disciplines" that bore on behavioral biology (see fig. 1). He showed how they had changed from 1950 to 1975 and projected how they might change from 1975 to 2000. As we draw closer to the turn of the century, it appears that the middle of the "dogbone" in the future picture should probably be thicker, to account for the increasing work by psychologists. Of course, it must be remembered that Wilson's conceptualization has more to do with animal sociobiology than with humans.

PLAN OF THIS BOOK

As stated earlier, the purpose of this book is threefold—to acknowledge the remarkably wide influence of a central idea, to demonstrate that the research of human sociobiology takes place in disparate fields, and to introduce the major principles of sociobiology. In regard to the first item, this book acknowledges the influence of a central idea simply by presenting evidence that the sociobiological idea *has* spread to many other fields. There has been no attempt by myself or the other authors to chronicle how the idea got spread, that is, to trace the particular pathways of knowledge. That would be an interesting topic, and one which historians of science will no doubt undertake, but is not something we could accomplish in these pages.

In regard to the second item, the demonstration that the research of human sociobiology takes place in disparate fields, it will not be surprising to find that the fields that have been most involved, to date, are psychology and anthropology. Crawford's chapter on psychology, Kenrick and Hogan's chapter on cognitive psychology, Nesse's chapter on psychiatry, and Iron's chapter on anthropology all make strong claims as to the importance of sociobiological theory for guiding new research in their fields. Masters's chapter on political science outlines experiments that could yield new knowledge about politics; Beckstrom's chapter on law suggests one way in which sociobiology could inspire new empirical research. Betzig's chapter on history contends that historians have missed out on a radical new (sociobiological) perspective on human history, and presents new problems for historians to solve.

As mentioned, the first half of the book emphasizes the theory of altruism, the second half emphasizes gene–culture theory. Ruse's chapter on epistemology and Lumden's chapter on aesthetics discuss ways in which gene–culture theory illuminates science and art, respectively. Van der Dennen's chapter on conflict studies mentions one way in which the study of war could be aided by gene–culture considerations. Two chapters are critical of gene–culture theory: Reynolds's on the socioecology of religion, and Karpinskaya's on Marxist thought (the latter, from an angle one might not expect!) Two earlier chapters incorporate criticism of the theory of altruism: Chandler's on ethical philosophy, and Galdikas and Vasey's on primatology.

Three chapters have to do with the influence (or potential influence) of general evolutionary theory, rather than specifically sociobiological theory, on their fields. They are Frank's chapter on economics, Hurford's chapter on linguistics, and Bernhard and Glantz's chapter on management theory. One chapter has mainly to do with the *non*influence of sociobiological theory on a given field, namely van den Berghe's chapter on sociology (although its author is a prominent user of that theory in regard to sociology).

In regard to the third purpose of this book, to introduce the major principles of sociobiology, I have attended to this in two ways. The first consists of appending a glossary to this introduction. Although it is perhaps not customary for readers to imbibe glossary items in alphabetical order, this particular glossary was written with just that in mind. The easy sociobiological definitions (by some quirk of fate or editorial meddling) come at the beginning of the alphabet, and the more complex ones later. ("Natural selection," for example, moved its way up by being renamed "Darwin-Wallace theory of natural selection.") The glossary items also direct the reader to particular chapters; thus, for example, the entry *Reproductive Success* directs the reader to discussions of this in chapters 4 and 7; the entry *Epigenetic Rules* directs the reader to chapters 11, 15, and 17.

The second way of introducing the major principles of sociobiology consists of having each chapter author say as much as she or he needs to say—about reciprocal altruism, the theory of differential parental investment, or whatever— to be able to argue her or his case. This has resulted in some repetition, but repetition is no doubt needed by the novice and should make the old pro feel—well, like an old pro. Also, authors have also been asked to resist the temptation to write in the way they normally write for colleagues, and to concentrate on things of interest to the lay reader. (And who is not a lay reader, when a book involves eighteen disciplines?)

OTHER SOURCES

Breathes there a student who never before has delved into sociobiology, he might begin by reading the book of that name (or at least Wilson's 1980 *Sociobiology: The Abridged Edition*), or Robert Trivers's highly illustrated *Social Evolution* (1985). He might equally well begin by trying a work of "applied sociobiology" that also contains basic theory, such as Pierre van den Berghe's *The Ethnic Phenomenon* (1981) or Richard Alexander's *The Biology of Moral Systems* (1987). To locate other works, he may thumb through the combined bibliography of the volume at hand, or may peruse a lengthier catalogue such as *A Bibliography of Biosocial Science* by Hiram Caton and Frank Salter.

Journals in which articles on human sociobiology appear regularly are easy to list because they are very few. *Behavioral and Brain Sciences* is one; it often covers a new aspect of sociobiology in depth, with numerous authors proffering "peer commentary." *Politics and the Life Sciences* does the same, particularly—but not exclusively—for books in political science. *The Journal of Social and Biological Structures* carries original articles and sometimes publishes symposia on sociobiology. *Ethology and Sociobiology* is the meeting place for those in the front line of sociobiological research; it occasionally publishes retrospectives and hosts heated debates. *Human Nature* is a new journal, aiming for the general reader; *Biology and Philosophy* aims at philosophically minded scientists and scientifically minded philosophers. As one can see from citations at the end of this book, there are also mainstream journals that carry occasional sociobiological articles, for example, *Current Anthropology, Primates, American Anthropologist, the Journal of Human Evolution, Philosophy, Perspectives in Biology and Medicine,* and *Zygon: Journal of Science and Religion.*

As well, there are societies that have annual meetings and send out regular newsletters, often with very up-to-date reviews of books on sociobiological topics. These include the Human Behavior and Evolution Society, the European Sociobiological Society, the Human Ethology Society, the International Society of Human Ecology, and the Association of Politics and the Life Sciences.

GLOSSARY

Altruism. In common parlance, the word *altruism* means generosity or a particularly selfless act or attitude. In biology, altruism likewise means an act that helps another, but since the 1964 work of W. D. Hamilton, the term means "an act by which one individual helps another in a way that benefits the (altruistic) individual's genes" (see *kin altruism* below). Since the 1971 work of Robert Trivers, it also means "an act by which one individual helps another in expectation that an equal or greater favor will be returned" (see *reciprocal altruism* below). For a philosophical discussion of the problematical definition of altruism, see chapter 9.

Balance of power. Why did hominids or early humans form larger and larger groups? Such agglomerations require more altruism of individuals than does living in small family groups, and so appear costly and unadaptive. Richard Alexander (1979) hypothesizes that the explanation for group living among hominids is defense of one group against another. Hominids cooperated in order to balance the power of rivals. See chapter 13 for discussion of the origin of warfare.

Cultural selection. This term refers not to a biological but to an historical process. In the Darwin-Wallace theory of natural selection (see below) one speaks of a trait—or its possessor—being "selected for" or "selected against," meaning that the pressures of the environment cause certain biological traits to survive over others. In human history, a culture may be selected against, for example, if its technology is unable to compete with that of a more advanced culture. Cultural selection may, but does not necessarily, involve the disappearance of the people who practice the culture, as in the case of the genocide of Tasmanian aboriginals by European settlers. For comparison of cultural selection with other modes of change, see chapter 12.

Darwin-Wallace theory of natural selection. This is the theory explaining the evolution of life (both plants and animals) over eons, and thus explaining the multiplicity of species. It was independently arrived at in the middle of the nineteenth century by Charles Darwin and Alfred Russell Wallace. Its major premises are as follows: (1) There is an abundance of young born in most species (sometimes thousands of offspring born to one parent). (2) Only a fraction of these can survive to reproductive age. (3) There is variation among individuals as to characteristics (later recognized to be based on assortment of genes, and occasional mutations in genes). (4) The most "fit" individuals, that is, the ones with characteristics best suited to the environment, will survive and reproduce, passing on those traits to progeny.

Darwinian algorithm. An algorithm is a recurring computation or a logical process in which a particular choice gives rise to another sequence of choices. A physician can arrive at a medical diagnosis algorithmically, for example, by narrowing down the possibility of certain diseases according to the presence or absence of key symptoms. The term *Darwinian algorithm,* coined in 1985 by Leda Cosmides, refers to the idea that certain mental processes (and the physiology supporting them) evolved by natural selection. For example, there may be an algorithm that people (or animals) automatically use to compute the seriousness of a threat by a predator. This work by Cosmides and Tooby is discussed in chapters 1, 10, 13, and 18.

Epigenesis. The word *genesis* means "origin," *epi* means "after." The biological theory of epigenesis holds that what happens after the origin of a new life at conception is the carrying out of instructions that are present in the first cell—but that this process is at least partly dependent on the environment. The first environment of the embryo for a mammal is the womb; the later environment is outside.

Epigenetic rules. Why do we learn certain things and not others? Why do most people "see" things the same way? It may be that we inherit genes for mental processes that cause us to take in information from the environment in more or less prescribed ways. E. O. Wilson (1978) suggested that we inherit "learning rules." Lumsden and Wilson (1981) refer to these as "epigenetic rules." See chapters 11, 15, and 17 for theory and examples.

Ethology. Ethology is the study of animal behavior with particular reference to the evolutionary explanation of the behavior. A related field, behavioral ecology, emphasizes the environmental factors—such as types of food resources, or predators—that make certain behaviors adaptive in evolution. For a study in human ethology, see chapter 8.

Fitness. This term does not refer to trimness of figure obtained by exercise! Fitness is a measure of one's ability, relative to other members of the same species, to survive and leave progeny. Evolutionary biologists frequently refer to this as "Darwinian fitness" or "reproductive fitness," emphasizing that one is not fit unless one reproduces. The word *fitness* can also be used to indicate one's fitness to a particular environment. The "survival of the fittest" means that those who are fit in their environment (giraffes with long necks to reach high foliage) will survive. In the sense mentioned above, in which fitness is an actual measure of survival, the phrase *survival of the fittest"* is rather circular.

Gene. The gene is the basic unit of heredity. Genes recombine differently in each generation, in species with sexual reproduction. Such recombination accounts for most diversity, while mutations account for evolutionary change. Genes are contained in every living cell. Gregor Mendel "knew about" genes indirectly from his experiments with garden peas in 1866. James Watson and Francis Crick, in 1953, found the actual mode by which a gene gives out instructions for development.

Gene–culture coevolution. It used to be thought that humans had some general capacity for culture—a receptor, or blank state—that allowed them to absorb whatever their culture offered them. That, however, does not explain how cultures get started in the first place, or why very distant cultures often bear much resemblance to one another. Various sociobiologists have now put forth models to show how culture could have evolved biologically, in the sense that there could be brain mechanisms that influence the adoption of certain cultural practices or artifacts. See the Introduction for the Lumsden-Wilson theory of coevolution; see chapters 11 and 15 for applications of it, chapter 12 for comparison to other theories of cultural evolution, and chapters 12 and 14 for criticism of it.

"Hey, man. What's happening?"

© *The New Yorker*

Group selection. Within sociobiological circles, belief in this phenomenon marks you as a member of the out-group. The theory of group selection is viewed as one of the great mistakes made by earlier biologists—notably, by Wynne-Edwards (1962). It holds that traits (particularly altruistic traits) that make Group A more fit than Group B (as a group) can proliferate because Group A will survive and Group B will die out. For instance, a group or population of animals that limits its birthrate would avoid overconsumption of resources and consequent famine, hence it would do better than a group of prolific profligate individuals. The flaw in group-selectionist thinking is that there is no way to explain how the *early* mutants with this self-sacrificing trait would survive—they would obviously be out-reproduced by their fellow group-members. For the most part, it has now been shown (by George C. Williams [1966] and others) that the illusion of group selection can usually be explained by individual selection or by kin selection (see below). As applied to the human species, however, group selection may be possible, since one group of humans can consciously organize their altruistic behaviors and wipe out a rival group. See chapter 13.

Inclusive fitness. This is a measure of how many of Ego's genes are *included* in future generations. An individual's inclusive fitness refers to both her own reproductive fitness (how many offspring she has) and the extent to which she influences the fitness of other relatives (such as indirect descendants). An altruist may have low reproductive fitness yet still have high inclusive fitness, if her altruism is "well-aimed." That is, it should be aimed only at relatives and only at helping them in ways that enhance their reproductive fitness. The notion of inclusive fitness as formulated by William D. Hamilton (1964) is the basis of sociobiological theory. See references to this in chapters 1, 2, 4, 6, 7, 8, 9, and 18.

Is-ought. One of the early philosophical complaints about sociobiology, or earlier about Darwinism, was that the study of how a thing "is" in nature is tantamount to an appraisal that that is how it "ought" to be. Aggressive behavior is one famous example, as is the more abstract principle of "struggle for existence." The logic goes something like this: if nature (God) has mandated that there be a struggle in which the aggressive win, then civilization (modern humans) should not go against this by legislating gentleness, welfare assistance, and so forth. Most sociobiologists now tread a careful path in this area. See chapter 2 for the distinction between using sociobiological research in a facultative way rather than in a norm-setting or goal-setting way.

Kin altruism. Altruism performed toward kin. See also *reciprocal altruism.* Discussions appear in chapters 2, 6, 9, and 18.

Kin selection. John Maynard Smith (1976) coined the term *kin selection* to account for the evolutionary phenomenon that takes place according to Hamilton's formula of inclusive fitness. Instead of the individual undergoing selection, it is the family or kin group that undergoes selection. Note that kin selection is thus a type of group selection (see above), but it is a "correct" type. It does not encounter the difficulty of the "early mutants." Early mutants who help family members may die, but their mutant altruistic traits can live on through the collateral descendants whom they help.

Lamarckism and Lysenkoism. Named after a great, if mistaken, biologist, Lamarck, *Lamarckism* is a convenient term for what modern biologists do not believe in: they do not believe that acquired traits are passed on to progeny. One cannot improve one's genetic stock by exercise; giraffes who stretch their necks do not give birth to giraffes with longer necks. Lamarckism had a revival as Lysenkoism in Russia, with disastrous consequences for agriculture. The Soviet biologist Trofim Lysenko in the 1930s, in line with the Marxist doctrine of environmental influence, believed that acquired characteristics (for example, in plant species) could improve the genetic stock. See chapter 14 for Marxist commentary on this.

Learning. The theory of learning has changed greatly since the behaviorist heyday of the 1960s. Psychologists now look at the costs and benefits of learning (see chapter 18) and at learning that is situation-specific (see chapter 10). See also *epigenetic rules,* above.

Level of selection. Sociobiologists are very keen on distinguishing between levels of selection: group, kin, individual, and even selection at the level of the gene, that is, genetic selection (see *selfish gene,* below). After reading, say, chapter 4 or chapter 7 of this book, the novice may try her luck at identifying the level of selection that was most discussed in that chapter. Hint: in chapter 9 it is genetic selection; in chapter 5 it is individual; in chapter 6 it is kin; in (part of) chapter 13 it is group. A case can be made, though, that it is always genetic selection.

Life histories. Every animal has a life to lead that may include various stages, calling for different behaviors. Ethologists, sociobiologists, and now evolutionary psychologists are interested in explaining the range of behaviors involved throughout an individual's lifetime. What is an adaptive behavior for an infant may be maladaptive for an adolescent. See chapters 1, 10, and 18 for psychologists' use of the life-histories concept.

Mating strategy. A human individual can consciously work out a mating strategy—by planning, for example, to marry a wealthy person or a person who does not already have children. Such strategies could increase his or her inclusive fitness. Sociobiologists believe that most animals, including humans, have inherited predispositions for engaging in particular mating strategies that will increase their inclusive fitness. These predispositions operate below the conscious level of awareness, as though the genes were demanding that the individual maximize her or his number (and quality) of offspring. It is possible that such behavioral predispositions result in the human invention of certain cultural customs about marriage choice. See chapters 4, 7, 10, and 18.

Maximize. This term, as in "maximizing one's fitness," and *optimal,* as in "seeking optimal strategies," are terms used by biologists in the tradition of economics or game theory. They typify the level of abstraction at which sociobiologists frequently operate. These words almost never refer to conscious planning by individuals; rather, the impulse to maximize is deduced from the successful results.

Monogamy. Among mammals, monogamy (having a sole mate) is unusual, for reasons having to do with sexual selection (see below). Humans are mammals, and therefore human monogamy is a peculiarity that needs to be accounted for. See chapter 7.

Nepotism. This word came into the English language through the Italian word *nepotismo,* meaning "favoring nephews" (by sixteenth-century prelates). It generally conjures up a shady practice. Yet it is only a cultural belief in "fair treatment" that gives us the idea that nepotism is wrong. Throughout the animal kingdom nepotism is the norm for social species. I go further: the practice of nepotism *defines* social species. Moreover, as shown above, the ability of altruism to be passed on genetically depended in the first instance on its being a practice directed exclusively toward relatives. See chapters 4, 7, 13, and 18. Concerning nepotism in the courtroom, see chapter 2.

Parent–offspring conflict. Every child "has words" now and then with his parents—or vice versa. Why is this so? According to Robert Trivers's 1974 theory of parent-offspring conflict, it is because a parent and his children have somewhat conflicting interests. The parent *is* interested in helping his child, because that will make the child grow to maturity and help the parent's reproductive fitness. But the parent also has an interest in turning his attention away from that particular child and investing in reproducing and raising others. See chapter 6 for application of this theory in primates, chapter 1 for humans.

Parental investment theory. To a sociobiologist, *parental investment* means something more fundamental than saving for college tuition, and it is more complicated. Robert Trivers's theory of parental investment (1972) builds on Darwin's theory of sexual selection (see below). It is also called "differential parental investment" to indicate that a female parent has reason to invest in offspring in a different way than the male. Very often in nature, the female invests a lot, and the male invests little or nothing—beyond the act of mating. This dictates that the female may use very different criteria than the male for choosing a mate. See chapters 1, 4, 7, and 10.

Reciprocal altruism. "You pick my lice, I'll pick yours." Grooming among monkeys is an example of altruistic behavior that is often done on behalf of kin (see *kin altruism* above), but it is also done on behalf of non-kin. In the latter case, it is probably a manifestation of reciprocal altruism. Robert Trivers's 1971 theory of reciprocal altruism holds that some species have evolved the trait for performing favors in expectation of a returned favor. This has probably been of enormous significance in the invention of human morality (see Maxwell 1990, 1991). It is not known how reciprocal altruism got started. See chapter 5 for discussion of the way cooperators can beat cheaters. See also chapters 1, 4, 6, 8, 9, and 18.

Reproductive success. This is simply a measure of the number of an individual's surviving offspring; it is abbreviated "RS." At social gatherings, sociobiologists are heard to ask one another What's your RS? (instead of "How many kids have you got?"). See chapters 4 and 7.

Selection pressure. Natural selection occurs when the pressures of the environment (such as difficulty of access to food or to mates, or hot climate, or the activity of predators) cause individuals with certain traits (including new mutations) to survive over others. One can say that the trait "responded" to the particular selection pressure. Ethologists and socio-biologists like to look at an evolved trait (such as territorial behavior or a mating strategy) and try to guess the selection pressure that brought it about.

Selective retention. Human societies may selectively retain certain cultural practices or may abandon them over time. Sociobiologists want to know why and how certain ones get retained. See chapter 12 for discussion, and chapters 11, 13, and 15 for examples.

Selfish gene. No gene—which is a mere collection of DNA molecules—can be said to have a selfish attitude or to make selfish plans, since these things require a brain. Nevertheless, it is useful to pretend, as Richard Dawkins (1976) has done, that a gene thinks about its desire to survive, and that it can do so only by causing its bearer to perform actions that will result in reproduction of the gene in future generations. This heuristic device allows sociobiologists to "predict" the evolution of things that would otherwise seem impossible—notably, altruism. Dawkins (1989) admits that there is a tension between thinking of the gene and thinking of the individual. In the first image we see "independent DNA replicators, skipping...down the generations, temporarily brought together in throwaway survival machines, immortal coils shuffling off an endless succession of mortal ones..." (234). In the second image, each individual body appears to consist of an obviously "coherent, integrated, immensely complicated machine, with a conspicuous unity of purpose" (234). Sociobiology employs both of these images.

Sexual selection. There is natural selection and there is sexual selection (which, also, is "natural"). For natural selection to occur, the selection pressure can be anything in the environment. For sexual selection to occur, the environmental pressure has specifically to do with the opposite sex. Charles Darwin (1871) identified two kinds of sexual selection. The first is epigamic. Here the female, say, has a preference for some visible characteristic of the male (such as colorful feathers). Males with that trait will be more successful than others in winning mates, and so the trait will proliferate—even if it is not an adaptive trait in any other practical sense.

The second type of sexual selection is inter-sexual competition. Where male mates are the "limiting resource," females have to fight with one another to establish a hierarchy of privilege for access to the males. Most often it works the other way. Among mammals, females are the limiting resource because a pregnancy "ties them up" for several months. Hence, males fight each other—not always for the immediate privilege of mating, but in general to establish their hierarchy of priority. One obvious indicator that sexual selection has taken place in a given species is *sexual dimorphism*—that is, differences in the bodies of the male and female. The male orangutan, for example, is twice the size of the female. See chapters 1, 4, 6, 7, 10, 13, and 18.

"Don't encourage him, Sylvia."

Sociobiology. Called "so-so biology" by its detractors, sociobiology is defined as the systematic study of the biological basis of all social behavior whether human or animal. It relies on the theory of altruism, described above, but in its study of particular species it must take much more information into consideration; for example, from ecology and ethology. E. O. Wilson says of sociobiology, "I believe that the subject has an adequate richness of detail and aggregate of self-sufficient concepts to be ranked as coordinate with such disciplines as molecular biology and developmental biology" (1980, 4). Not all scholars find the name for the new discipline, *sociobiology,* satisfactory. Richard Alexander (1987) points out that the word seems to exclude some important nonsocial topics such as life histories. He also observes that "the attachment of labels like sociobiology to advances in evolutionary thinking that explicitly concern human behavior tends to create 'ideologies'" (5). Jerome Barkow (1989) notes that some consider the term *sociobiology* a retronym—a renaming of work originally done as "human ethology," "behavioral socioecology," or "biosocial anthropology." (8).

Ultimate causation. The reason why sociobiological ideas often strike people as odd, especially when it is *human* sociobiology that is being discussed, is that the explanations given for current behavior are very remote in time. Ultimate causes in evolution are the environmental factors that made a certain behavior (or anatomical modification) adaptive originally. For example, as noted above, the ultimate cause of human mating strategies may be the selection pressure of mate competition that has been characteristic of mammals. Scholars in disciplines such as psychology, political science, and even ethology have been more accustomed to identifying the *proximate* causes of behavior; these are the immediate cues from the environment, or the specific mechanisms of one's physiology, that trigger the behavior. Ernst Mayr (1961) differentiated proximate causation that asks How? from ultimate causation that asks Why? See chapters 1, 4, 9, 10, and 18.

1

Psychiatry

Randolph M. Nesse

Psychiatry is the speciality of medicine devoted to the diagnosis and treatment of mental and behavioral disorders. These disorders range widely: from chronic schizophrenia to temporary insomnia, from infantile autism to geriatric dementia, from inherited defects to normal reactions to stress. Psychiatric treatments are accordingly diverse and include psychoanalysis, psychotherapy, behavior therapy, medications, and electroconvulsive therapy. In contrast to psychologists, whose extensive education emphasizes the study of cognition, psychodynamics, learning, and behavior, psychiatrists first prepare for the practice of general medicine and then take four or more years of residency training to learn to diagnose mental disorders. In decades past, we psychiatrists were pitied by colleagues in other areas of medicine who felt we could do little to help our patients. Now, psychiatrists and their new thera-peutic powers are increasingly envied by other medical specialists.

Psychiatry in the 1960s, just emerging from the dominance of psychoanalytic ideology and unrealistic hopes for changing society, was scrambling to reestablish itself as a respectable specialty of medicine. It sought not only increased effectiveness and scientific acceptance, but also to establish psychiatric disorders as medical diseases eligible for insurance reimbursements. These goals were strongly advanced by the discovery of effective drug treatments, first for psychoses and depression, later for anxiety and mania, and most recently for obsessive compulsive disorder and panic disorder. They were further advanced by new diagnostic nomenclatures and the development of new research methodologies, including radio-immunoassay, advances in molecular biology, and exotic techniques of looking inside the functioning brain, such as positron emission tomography.

Federal funding grew rapidly for research in these areas. In fact, in academic psychiatry, research on the biology of the brain has so prospered that it has largely displaced the study of psychological conflicts and adaptations. These changes in mainstream psychiatry help to explain, for reasons to be discussed later, psychiatry's slowness to incorporate recent advances in evolutionary biology.

ADVANCES IN EVOLUTIONARY BIOLOGY THAT BENEFIT PSYCHIATRY

The greatest contribution an evolutionary perspective can offer to psychiatry is to show how the functions of psychological traits can be scientifically studied, and thus to begin to provide, for psychiatry, what physiology provides for the rest of medicine. In the rest of medicine, the search for evolutionary explanations based on function is intrinsic to everyday practice and research. The physiologist demarcates the respiratory, circulatory, and immune systems, not by their anatomy, but by their functions. The surgeon knows the functions of the gallbladder, and therefore the consequences of removing it. When a patient presents with renal failure, the internist knows the functions of the kidneys and thus how to compensate for renal insufficiency even if its etiology is not known.

The psychiatrist has, however, no comparable body of knowledge. The psychiatrist does not know the normal functions of the systems disrupted by mental disorders, except in the most general terms. For example, when a patient presents with depression, the psychiatrist does not know the normal functions of the capacity for mood and therefore has difficulty in distinguishing between normal and pathological sadness. When a patient presents with extreme jealousy, few psychiatrists understand its evolutionary origins and functions. Evolutionary biology offers psychiatry the conceptual tools needed to construct a framework for understanding normal mental function akin to that which physiology provides for understanding the normal functions of other bodily systems.

Attention to the "adaptive" significance of behavior is not a new aspect of psychiatry. Adolf Meyer, the founder of the Phipps Clinic, in 1913, at Johns Hopkins, was the first to advocate the term *psychobiology* and one of the first to base psychiatric evaluation and practice on a systematic assessment of the patient's adaptation to life. Strongly influenced by Darwin, he emphasized the relationship between symptoms and disruptions of a person's current adaptive strategies (Willmuth 1986). More recently, psychoanalysts and marital and family therapists have studied the adaptiveness of certain symptoms. Most of them, however, have studied psychological adaptation. Biological adaptation, the focus of evolutionary studies, is a different concept; it refers to the ways in which a trait increases reproductive success.

Darwin's great achievement was to explain the origins of adaptations as the products of natural selection, gradually shaped to give their bearers some advantage in the desperate competition for survival and reproduction. The additional advance that gave rise to sociobiology was the discovery that the struggle is not among species but, ultimately, among genes (Hamilton 1964; Williams 1966; Wilson 1975; Dawkins 1976). Before sociobiology, behaviors were usually explained by vague reference to their benefits for the species. Now the task is more exacting—to demonstrate how the genes that code for a trait increase their own representations in future generations.

This insight has turned many assumptions about behavior topsy-turvy. Altruistic behaviors that were previously easy to explain in terms of their benefits to the species, such as cessation of reproduction in response to overcrowding, became mysteries. Apparently pathological behaviors that were previously inexplicable, such as killing of infants by male langur monkeys who take over a harem, became expected strategies. And some apparently maladaptive psychiatric symptoms appear markedly different in the light of sociobiology. Normality can no longer be defined by happiness and social harmony; instead, capacities for sadness and tendencies for self-serving behavior may be biologically "normal," if they increase fitness.

The task of evolutionary psychiatry, one just getting underway, is to explain the functional significance of psychopathology. In this chapter, it is not possible to mention all the relevant papers, or even all the areas of current work, so I will limit my review to a summary of progess in several areas where sociobiology is influencing the understanding of psychopathology, with emphasis on those in which further advances can soon be anticipated. For inclusive reviews, see Wenegrat's *Sociobiological Psychiatry* (1990); McGuire's article "Sociobiology: Its Potential Contributions to Psychiatry" (1979); Feierman's symposium "The Ethology of Psychiatric Populations" (1987); "The Overlapping Territories of Psychiatry and Ethology," by Kramer and McKinney, Jr. (1979); and works by Gilbert (1989), Thayer (1989), and Marks (1987).

KINSHIP RELATIONS

Attachment

Just before the main advances in evolutionary behavioral biology were recognized, John Bowlby, in his 1969 book *Attachment and Loss,* made a strong case for the biological importance of attachment for the survival of infants. Harry Harlow (1971), with his famous studies of "surrogate mothers" in rhesus monkeys, had likewise demonstrated that attachment is not a derivative of other impulses, but an independent capacity with adaptive significance (1971). Newer studies of attachment by Hinde (1974); Ainsworth, McBlehar, and Waters (1978); and Emde and Gaensbauer (1981) are explicitly based on the evolutionary paradigm and have documented the ontogeny and characteristics of separation anxiety in its various forms. Nonetheless, they are presociobiological in that they do not incorporate the discovery that selection acts mainly at the level of the individual. For instance, patterns of attachment characterized as "abnormal" might, in fact, be highly adaptive when viewed from the point of view of an infant trying to get investments from an unengaged mother (Barbara Smuts, personal communication). And abnormalities of mothering that are socially unacceptable may, nonetheless, be expected responses when the mother's fitness is best served by abandoning her baby.

Child Abuse

Not investing in an offspring can, in certain circumstances, increase a mother's Darwinian fitness. For example, the cessation of ovulation in women with anorexia nervosa may result from a mechanism shaped by natural selection for preventing pregnancy in times of famine (Surbey 1987). The inhibition of ovulation caused by lactation serves the related function of spacing births to minimize the number of children who are born while an older sibling still requires all the milk the mother can provide.

That natural selection acts to benefit genes and individuals instead of species is gruesomely illustrated by the actions of a male langur monkey that takes over a harem. He usually kills any existing offspring that are still nursing (Hrdy 1977). The females try to prevent this, but when they fail they quickly come into estrus and mate with the new male, thus increasing their reproductive success and that of the male, who then protects his own offspring. Although no such automatic mechanism explains the behavior of humans, children living with step-parents are much more likely to be abused than children living with both natural parents. In fact, as Martin Daly and Margo Wilson have shown in their recent book, *Homicide* (1988a), children of stepparents are a hundred times more likely to be killed than others. It appears that the psychological mechanisms that usually protect children from such violence when both natural parents are present are less effective in reconstituted families. The implications of these findings are just being considered by child protection agencies.

Marriage

Marriage is as close to a universal as there is in human cultures. The most common pattern of human marriage has been polygyny, while a minority of cultures practice something close to monogamy. An evolutionary analysis of marital relationships reveals intense commitment and cooperation between spouses to produce and raise offspring, but also intrinsic conflicts that arise from the differences in male and female reproductive interests (Symons 1979, Buss 1989). This difference consists primarily in the fact that women can have only a limited number of children and their reproductive success is restricted mainly by the availability of resources and protection. Men can have many children, even in a single year, and their reproduction is restricted mainly by the availability and cooperation of sexual partners. Women and men must cooperate to succeed, but the different strategies available to them inevitably also cause conflict.

These insights have had remarkably little impact on marital therapy, where harmony is often assumed to be elusive only because of distorted perceptions, imperfect communication, and individual psychopathology. This false belief makes many people feel dissatisfied with marriages that are, in fact, better than average. People interpret their urges to act in ways that are in their reproductive interests, but not in their spouse's interests, as arising from psychopathology, instead of as expected impulses that must, for the most part, be inhibited for the sake of the marriage. I believe that when the intrinsic nature of conflict in sexual relationships are finally acknowledged, the impact will be far-reaching and might conceivably decrease the vicissitudes of marriage.

RECIPROCITY AND RELATIONSHIPS

One of the most powerful subtheories to emerge from socio-biology analyzes relationships as reciprocal exchanges. People benefit from relationships not only with those who have genes in common (Hamilton 1964) but also with those who can exchange favors in ways that result in a net gain (Trivers 1971, Axelrod and Hamilton 1981, Axelrod 1984). The negotiation of such relationships is the key to human social success, and social success is crucial to reproductive success (Cosmides and Tooby 1989; Tooby and Cosmides 1989; Alexander 1979, 1987). The patterns of social exchange are enormously complicated because deception and defection are ever-present strategies. When is it wise to cooperate, when to defect, and when to deceive? How can one tell that the other is going to continue to cooperate, to be loyal, to defect, or to cheat? From such difficulties come many of the problems people bring to psychiatrists. Many psychiatrists try to help people to improve their capacity to negotiate such difficulties in relationships, but only a few know that a new theory exists to analyze the adaptive significance of such situations. Attempts to apply reciprocity theory to psychiatry are just beginning (Essock-Vitale and Fairbanks 1979, Littlefield and Lumsden 1987, Glantz and Pearce 1989, Lloyd 1990).

Neurosis, Character Disorder, and Reciprocity

A reciprocity framework offers insights into the relationship between neuroses and character disorders (Nesse 1990a, Nesse and Lloyd 1991). The neurotic cooperates even when it is senseless to do so. Guilt and obligation motivate excessive altruistic behavior that is rarely fully reciprocated. This tends to attracts exploiters, who soon justify the neurotic's sour view of human nature. The neurotic expects too much from people, continually hoping that they will offer him a benevolent relationship like a parent once did, and continually being disappointed.

In contrast, the person with a character disorder either expects too much in return for a small investment, or expects nothing at all. Those who feel entitled to help without having to reciprocate are called "narcissistic," while those who have lost all hope for secure and mutual relationships are described as schizoidal isolates or sociopathic manipulators. An evolutionary approach does not explain these disorders or their etiology, but it does suggest that we could understand them better by studying how the innate capacities for negotiating relationships interact with individual experience to shape personalities. For example, children who grow up in small, isolated, nuclear families may come to have very different, and often idiosyncratic, expectations about relationships, compared to those who must early negotiate relationships with many other children.

EMOTIONS

Psychiatrists treat emotional disorders, so one might expect that they would be intensely interested in theories of normal functions of emotions. But such theories are still developing and are just coming to the point of clinical utility. The promulgation of evolutionary approaches to emotions has especially been assisted by the efforts of R. Plutchik (1980) and the contributors to the series *Theories of Emotions,* which Plutchik edited with H. Kellerman in the 1980s. Most of these theorists now view the emotions as useful states that have been shaped by natural selection, and a number go further to suggest the specific ways in which different emotions contribute to fitness. To date, this foundation for a scientific understanding of emotions and emotional disorders is little known in clinical psychiatry.

The functions of different emotions—fear, love, anger, and others—may be analyzed by considering them to be akin to computer programs that adjust the organism to cope with different situations (Nesse 1990a). For instance, the diverse components of panic and agoraphobia—physiological arousal, concentration on escape routes, flight, avoidance of closed places, staying close to home—make sense as a pattern shaped to facilitate escape from, or avoidance of, mortal danger (Nesse 1988). An evolutionary explanation of mood may at first seem unlikely. Sadness just doesn't seem useful. But sadness may serve functions in hierarchy negotiations (Gardner 1982, Raleigh et al. 1983, Sloman and Price 1987) regulation of arousal (Thayer 1989) or alternation of broad life strategies (Gut, 1989). Also, mood might be explained as a mechanism that allocates resources as a function of the propitiousness of the social environment (Nesse 1990a). Low energy and pessimism can be useful if they conserve resources for a time when they will offer a better return on investment. An adequate theory of mood awaits progress in measuring social resources and discovering how they contribute to reproduction, how they are tallied in the mind, and how their changes influence mood.

The main problems that people bring to psychiatrists are emotions— anxiety, sadness, anger, guilt, and all the rest. It is painful emotions that people most want to change. The first principle of an evolutionary view of emotions is that *uncomfortable feelings do not necessarily indicate the presence of an abnormality.* Like pain and nausea, anxiety and sadness seem to be capacities shaped by natural selection to counter threats to fitness. The next step, one just now being taken, is to specify the exact functions of each emotion in the situations for which it was shaped. Such an understanding of the function of emotions is crucial for psychiatry, which has so far tried to bypass this step and has thus studied the mechanisms of the mind/ brain without a deep understanding of what they are for.

PSYCHODYNAMICS

Psychodynamics is the field that studies high-level mental processes, especially those that are unconscious. Psycho-analysts have explored the unconscious mind for nearly a century, with only rough maps of the territory. Back on the level of conscious thinking, they compare notes and argue about fine points, even as they agree on certain core features of the landscape—conflicts between impulses and inhibitions, ego defenses, Oedipal wishes, castration anxiety, and penis envy. Other scholars, many of whom have never visited this realm, are skeptical of the whole enterprise. Psychoanalysts have not spent their time trying to convert such skeptics, but have more often argued amongst themselves in institutes increasingly divorced from academic psychiatry.

Psychoanalysis may conceivably find, in evolutionary psychology, an opportunity to join the mainstream of science. If the patterns of the unconscious mind are considered to be traits shaped by natural selection that serve specific adaptive functions, then it should be possible to analyze them, just like other biological traits (Leak and Christopher 1982, Badcock 1986, Rancour-LaFerrier 1985).

The unconscious is itself an excellent target for evolutionary explanation. It first seems odd that natural selection would shape mental mechanisms specifically to keep us unaware of our own impulses, until we realize that the mind is shaped not for accuracy, but for fitness. If distortion and self-deception have increased fitness, then their presence in the human mind is an expected adaptation, not a mistake. Hence their absence must be recognized as a disorder. Some kinds of obsessive disorders could conceivably result from just such a lack of subjectivity. Such ideas profoundly challenge the rationalist foundations of psychiatry. Psychiatrists generally believe, in accord with the larger culture, that rationality and self-knowledge are normal and good. Indeed, psychopathology is said to result from being out of touch with oneself, and overcoming self-deception is a goal of psychotherapy. No doubt it will be difficult to dispassionately assess the possibility that objective self-knowledge is sometimes toxic.

Alexander (1979) and Trivers (1976) suggest that the ability to deceive oneself may be adaptive because it increases one's ability to deceive others. They think the unconscious might have evolved to allow people to appear cooperative while nonetheless seeking personal advantage without even knowing it (Lockard 1980, Slavin 1985). This suggestion seems to me profound but too narrow. I have argued (Nesse 1990b, Nesse and Lloyd 1991) that while self-deception can facilitate manipulation, it can also offer profound benefits in the maintenance of good relationships. Robert Frank (1988) has persuasively marshaled the evidence for this position in a book that analyzes emotions from the viewpoint of economics (see chapter 5, "Economics," this volume).

Other psychodynamic phenomena are also susceptible to evolutionary explanation. Slavin (1985) explains regression as a strategy children use to elicit resources from parents by appearing to be younger than they really are. Badcock (1990) interprets the Oedipal complex as a strategy in which children use precocious sexual signals to manipulate parents into providing extra resources. Efforts have also been made to explain castration anxiety, penis envy, and many other psychodynamic phenomena (Badcock 1986, 1990; Rancour-LaFerrier 1985). Only a few people are pursuing this radical endeavor, but they may eventually provide psychodynamics with a biological foundation, and evolutionary psychobiology with access to the insights of psychodynamics.

Trivers's (1974) recognition of parent–offspring conflict is another advance with special applications in psychiatry. Psychiatry has usually expected normal maternal love to be pure and unambivalent. But Trivers notes that the reproductive interests of mother and offspring are congruent only early in infancy. The time soon comes when the mother's fitness would be maximized by having another child, while the existing child's fitness is best served if the mother waits. The child manipulates the parent mainly by deception. This deception takes the form of the child's appearing to be less mature (and thus more needy) than is actually the case, so as to make the parent believe that its interests are best served by continued high investment. This pattern may explain not only the "terrible twos" but the general phenomenon of regression (Slavin 1985, Trivers 1985). Why do we find regressive behavior so annoying? Perhaps because we intuitively know that it is often a deceptive manipulation designed to get us to provide more resources than we otherwise would.

PERSONALITY

Different kinds of personality may be understood as individual characteristic emotional and cognitive strategies for negotiating interpersonal relationships (Buss 1987, Kofoed 1988). The social emotions are excellent candidates for "Darwinian algorithms," the term used by Tooby and Cosmides (1989) to describe the innate rules that regulate mind and behavior. Friendship and love maintain good relationships, even through rough periods. Anger prevents exploitation and may, paradoxically, help to preserve relationships. Anxiety and guilt, those most common, most aversive, and most socializing of emotions, motivate people to fulfill their commitments, to abide by the social contract, and to stay loyal to their friends. Because socially unacceptable desires (such as the desire to cheat) are especially likely to remain unconscious, it is not surprising that we often find it hard to say why we are anxious. Such anxiety is uncomfortable and unaccountable, but not abnormal.

We know that many personality attributes are strongly heritable, and it is thus tempting to interpret personality types as alternative strategies for getting along in the social world. Tooby and Cosmides (in press) have recently shown, however, that this is most unlikely. They argue that the multiple aspects of personality are almost certainly controlled by different genes, and constellations of genes that constitute a particularly good strategy would be split up by genetic recombination in every generation. Individual differences caused by genetic variation will usually, they argue, turn out to be of relatively small adaptive significance. This strikes me as one of the more profound insights evolutionary psychology has offered psychology and psychiatry.

SUBSTANCE ABUSE

Substance abuse is one of the more thorny problems faced by psychiatry. Is it a disease or just a behavior pattern? Is it a medical issue, a moral issue, or something else? Research efforts are unraveling the brain mechanisms by which drugs give pleasure and relieve mental pain, but a broader, evolutionary understanding of the functions of pleasure and pain is needed, I believe, to answer our questions about substance use.

The adaptationist approach I have been outlining assumes that the capacities for mental suffering are products of evolution that are usually useful. Therefore, using drugs that block these capacities should generally make individuals less fit. Of course, mental suffering is not *always* a part of the organism's solution to a problem. Some anxiety and depression is caused by brain abnormalities, and many bad feelings are no longer useful in our current environment. Deciding which bad feelings are useful, and which are not, becomes an urgent practical issue as we develop drugs that relieve them without dangerous side-effects or physiological dependency. A sensible debate about how such drugs should be used will be possible only when we have a solid theory of the evolutionary origins and functions of the emotions.

NEUROSCIENCE AND PSYCHIATRIC RESEARCH

Psychiatric research now mainly studies neurophysiological mechanisms, in hopes of finding chemical abnormalities that cause mental disorders. While some mental disorders are certainly caused by brain defects, it is my guess that many neurophysiological "abnormalities" are merely aspects of the operation of evolved mechanisms that mediate normal anxiety and sadness. Thus, searching for the causes of anxiety in the anatomy and chemistry of brain centers that mediate anxiety may turn out to be like searching for the cause of cough in the brain centers that cause cough. If anxiety and sadness, like cough and pain, are defenses shaped by natural selection, then understanding the proximate mechanisms that mediate them is a worthy goal but is no substitute for understanding how they defend us, and the cues and algorithms that regulate them.

PSYCHIATRIC DIAGNOSIS

Psychiatric diagnosis has changed drastically in the past twenty years, starting with the subjective interpretation of symptoms in the context of various theories, and culminating in categories based on observation and induction, as free from theory as possible. This change has been a great advance for research. Psychiatric diagnosis, especially when based on a structured interview, is now fairly reliable. Researchers at different centers can now report their findings with reasonable confidence that they will also apply to patients who receive the same diagnosis elsewhere.

The cost of this reliability, however, is a diagnostic system that is well characterized as "mindless," not only because it is not based on any theory of etiology, but also because it focuses attention on objective, observable, and measurable aspects of psychiatric conditions, at the expense of attention to cognitive, psychodynamic, and experiential factors. A more insidious consequence of the new diagnostic system is its tendency to encourage psychiatrists to think of diagnostic categories as if they were diseases. If such carefully defined, objective, and reliable categories are approved by the American Psychiatric Association and required by insurance companies, and if researchers use them to search for etiology and better treatments, then it is difficult for the clinician to resist the unjustified belief that each is a distinct disease with a specific cause.

An evolutionary perspective may help to prevent this logical leap. By providing a way to distinguish those aspects of disease that are manifestations of *defects of the body's machinery* from those that are *adaptive responses to a threat,* an evolutionary approach decreases the tendency to confuse diseases and symptoms. In the general medical clinic, cough, fever, and high white blood cell count are recognized as signs and symptoms of lung infection that are defensive responses, not the disease itself. At one time, physicians argued about how to define the subtypes of "cough disorder" just as we now do for the anxiety disorders, dividing them inductively on the basis of onset, family history, course, and associated findings. For cough, such nomenclatures have been replaced by diagnoses based on etiology.

For anxiety, however, comparable diagnostic categories remain elusive. This is, at least in part, because the etiologic factors that elicit anxiety are less specific than those that elicit cough. Anxiety is not primarily a defense against threats as simple as a pathogen or even loss of homeostasis, but against the loss of reproductive resources, loss of status, and loss of strategies that have previously been effective. Because the significance of such losses depends on the individual person, it is extraordinarily difficult to show the relationship of life events to mental symptoms.

Categories of mental disorders based on their adaptive significance are no substitute for understanding the specific causes of psychopathology, but they may help to broadly conceptualize the causes of mental disorders (see table 1).

Table 1

CATEGORIES OF MENTAL DISORDERS
BASED ON EVOLUTIONARY PSYCHOBIOLOGY

1. Primary brain abnormalities (caused by genetic abnormalities, infection, toxins, developmental factors, etc.) that result in malfunction either in basic mental processing (for example, schizophrenia), or in regulation of the expression of adaptive responses (for example, manic-depressive disorder).

2. Maladaptive behavior patterns that arise from normal brain mechanisms, as a result of exposure to novel environmental circumstances or idiosyncratic learning histories (for example, addictions, some anxiety states, fetishes), or the imperfection of the evolved programs of the mind.

3. Patterns of emotion or behavior that are painful or socially unacceptable, but nonetheless adaptive (for example, failure to fully attach to an adopted baby, wishes for illicit sex, shyness).

LIFE-HISTORY ANALYSIS
AND PSYCHIATRIC EVALUATION

Behavioral ecologists have developed sophisticated methods of analyzing "life histories" based on the adaptive significance of behavior patterns in different life stages and different environments (Krebs and Davies 1989). For instance, the death of salmon after spawning is not an accident, but the best strategy for maximizing the number of offspring. Those salmon that reserve resources to go back out to sea are so unlikely to make it back to the spawning grounds again that they end up (on average) having fewer offspring than those that exhaust all their resources in a single reproductive effort.

The concepts developed by behavioral ecology should be useful for human psychology. The conflicts faced by a single woman in her late thirties, for instance, can be conceptualized as difficult choices between career success without having children, versus having children with a partner who might be less than ideal while sacrificing financial status and independence. The main alternatives available to a young girl from a ghetto may be a poorly paid, boring job, a marriage to someone who will likely leave her or be unable to support her, or association with wealthy but dangerous men such as drug dealers. Many other dilemmas are characteristic of certain life situations: men who have families but are attracted to younger women, married women who become successful and find they are courted by wealthy men, parents who must split their investments between their children and their aging parents, teenagers who must choose between social and academic success. Such conflicts, especially those between parents and children and between spouses, can be interpreted in a life-history framework.

An evolutionary psychiatrist approaches a problem by systematic analysis of the patient's goals, strategies, and resources (tangible, personal, social, and kin). From this perspective, a "life crisis" can often be understood as a situation in which a threat to current adaptation is looming, or in which a current strategy is not working and must be changed. Such an evolutionary approach to psychiatry deemphasizes the explanation of psychopathology in terms of the individual's personality idiosyncrasies, and instead focuses attention on his or her current life situation, dilemmas, and coping strategies.

Standards of Evidence

Sociobiology is still in an early stage of development, which partly explains why it has so little influenced psychiatry. There is much disagreement about how hypotheses are best formulated and even about what are legitimate and illegitimate objects of explanation. There is disagreement also as to what evidence most powerfully tests evolutionary hypotheses. At this early stage, it is not surprising that even among psychiatrists who appreciate sociobiology there has been an appeal for stricter standards of evidence (Lane and Luchins 1988).

It is tempting to hope that we just need to be more careful and explicit about our hypotheses and to gather more data to test them, but I doubt that this will prove sufficient. As Donald Symons (1987) has pointed out, as long as we lack agreement on fundamental conceptual issues, continued arguments about theory and general problems in the field will be a painful and tedious stage that we cannot bypass. As consensus emerges from the current debates, evolutionary psychobiology should begin to make incremental progress in which advance builds on advance to build a coherent whole.

Conclusion

A quarter of a century ago, the recognition of kin selection (Hamilton 1964) and the demise of group selection as a theoretical emphasis in evolutionary biology (Williams 1966) initiated a revolution in our understanding of behavior. Over a decade ago, these advances were applied systematically to animal behavior and social structures (Wilson 1975, Alcock 1984), and the implications for human psychology were recognized (Wilson 1978, Alexander 1979, Konner 1982). But psychiatry is still just beginning to change.

Why has psychiatry been so slow to incorporate the advances of evolutionary psychobiology? Conceptual and historical issues both appear to be responsible. The first conceptual difficulty is that evolution offers insights mainly about adaptation, while psychiatry's concern with pathology seems, at first glance, to be quite different. Second, by trying to understand the functions of traits, evolutionary psycho- biologists undertake an enterprise that is viewed with suspicion by those who are unaware of advances in basic biology (Mayr 1988) and especially by those who believe psychiatry should disassociate itself from all but the "hardest" sciences. Third, the research methods of evolutionary psychobiologists lack specificity and elegance, and firm findings are few.

Historical and political factors also offer important explanations. Sociobiology has arisen at the very moment when its insights are least welcome in psychiatry. Just as psychiatrists are returning to their medical identities and searching for the physical causes of diseases, sociobiology suggests that many psychiatric disorders may not be diseases at all. Just as psychiatry has gained the capacity to relate various aspects of brain function to mental disorders, sociobiology suggests that brain abnormalities may be unrelated to the etiology of many psychiatric disorders. Just as research funding has become available for physiological research, sociobiology suggests that we need to understand the adaptive functions of psychological mechanisms. It is really not surprising that psychiatry has been largely unreceptive to sociobiology.

How much acceptance has there been? J. A. Talbott's 1989 book, *Future Directions for Psychiatry,* which surveys leading authorities about the future of psychiatry makes no mention of sociobiology or even evolution. Nevertheless, there are many hopeful signs. A chapter on sociobiology (Barash and Lipton 1985) was published in the widely respected *Comprehensive Textbook of Psychiatry,* and the newest edition of this text has a chapter on Anthropology based on evolutionary principles (Konner 1989). B. Wenegrat's promising overview of evolutionary psychiatry published in 1989, has now been completely reworked (Wenegrat 1990), and several similar works are in preparation. A 1987 conference on evolutionary psychology and psychiatry at the University of Michigan drew 150 participants (Low and Nesse 1989), and several symposia and a course were devoted to evolutionary psychiatry at the 1990 meeting of the American Psychiatric Association. There now seems to be a critical mass of psychiatrists applying evolutionary psychobiology to problems of psychopathology, and enthusiasm for their work is rapidly growing, especially among young psychiatrists, many of whom learned the fundamentals of sociobiology in college and who expect that psychiatry will be based on this foundation.

The first practical consequences of this change will be seen, I would guess, in the consulting room, at the step where the clinician assesses and tries to conceptualize the patient's problem. Currently, clinicians try to integrate psychodynamics, learning factors, life situations, personality, and organic factors to understand how an individual has come to have a particular problem. The task is daunting, and the temptation is always to simplify by considering only one or two kinds of causes. But clinicians keep being forced, by clinical necessity, to try to find a way to make a coherent fabric from this mixed bag of yarn. The theory of evolution offers a well-tested loom.

The goal of such integration is widely accepted in psychiatry and has been the subject of innumerable publications. The vast majority of these either advocate an eclectic view of psychopathology that incorporates perspectives from various schools, or else propose some specific scientific framework such as systems theory or process theory. But eclecticism cannot integrate psychiatry, and no new theory is needed. As the editors of a conference on evolution and behavior said over 30 years ago:

> It is so universally accepted as not to need explicit statement that the theory of morphology is evolution, with its various concomitants such as homology, analogy, adaptive radiation and progression and so on. It should by now be equally obvious that there is, indeed, a general theory of behavior and that theory is again, evolution, to just the same extent and in almost the same ways in which evolution is the general theory of morphology. (Roe and Simpson 1958, 1-2)

May this perspective soon come to psychiatry.

2

Law

John H. Beckstrom

PRESENT AND FUTURE LEGAL USES
OF SOCIOBIOLOGY

In the past when I have suggested to scientists that socio-biology might be used in the legal process, they have usually assumed I meant "goal-establishment normative uses"—uses implementing the idea that if evolution has given humans predispositions or tendencies toward certain types of behavior, then the law should aim to promote that behavior because it is "natural." There are deep philosophical problems with that idea—with moving from reportorial observations of behavioral tendencies to suggestions that they should be endorsed by society. Most thinkers, including sociobiologists, shy away from such uses of natural history (see discussion in Beckstrom, 1989, Chap.3). In this chapter, I shall assume that sociobiology can have little or no goal-establishment normative use in lawmaking. Nevertheless, it does have considerable impressive potential for contributing to the legal process.

We are just beginning to uncover ways in which socio-biological knowledge might aid the legal process, though several people have already written in this field.[1] At the present time it appears to me that the most promising way sociobiology may assist lawmakers is to help them achieve goals they have decided upon as being appropriate for their society—that is, the science could be *facilitative*. For example, sociobiology could help in the effort to regulate criminal activity of various sorts when deterrence is the announced goal (Beckstrom 1985a, 127-34. Similarly, see Alexander 1987, 220-21; Thornhill and Thornhill 1983, 137; Daly and Wilson 1988a). It could help to decide child custody disputes when the law attempts to serve the best interests of the children (Beckstrom 1985a, 75-92, 134-36), and it could assist in efforts to reform marriage prohibition laws after it has been decided that such efforts should be made (Beckstrom 1985a, 117-23).

When one analyzes these and a large proportion of the other instances where sociobiology appears to have potential for assisting lawmakers, an interesting pattern emerges: legal authorities have made an assessment of average or *typical behavior* of some part of a population an important part of the solution of many legal problems. Scientists unfamiliar with the legal process have often been puzzled when I have said that sociobiologists and lawmakers have a mutual interest in "typical behavior." They may understand that an important focus of sociobiology is assessment of average or typical behavior in a population given various environmental circumstances, but when I say that an assessment of typical behavior is often instrumental in lawmaking, I am met by disbelief. I think this is due to the layperson's impression—or hope—that justice is individualized. I suppose we all would like to hear that when a legal decision involving us is made, it is based upon our *personal* actions, intentions, or whatever is relevant, and not on the attributes of someone else—even an hypothesized average or typical member of the population.

The law does strive for individualized justice—laypeople can be reasonably assured of that. But the search for information on such things as a particular individual's behavior and intentions, in order to provide individualized justice, is frequently thwarted by practical limitations. In such circumstances lawmakers, of necessity, turn to an assessment of typical behavior of the population in the relevant locality. I can illustrate this with a subject that I have treated in detail elsewhere— intestate succession (Beckstrom 1985a, 7-59; 1981). In this area legislatures have had to deal with the question of what to do with the property of people who die without wills (intestate). In respect to any particular deceased person, the authorities would like to know what the deceased intended—or would have intended—in that regard. Of course, the deceased is not available to testify, and any other evidence on the question (short of a duly executed will, which obviously does not exist in this case) is generally unacceptable. Lawmakers have solved this dilemma by creating schemes of distribution that purport to reflect what the *typical* decedent who did not write a will would have done with her or his property if she or he had.

Dilemmas like this have peppered the law with now-institutionalized instances of lawmakers attempting to detect or predict typical behavior patterns in a population in order to help solve legal problems. Let me use, as another example, an area of the law that I have also treated more fully elsewhere (Beckstrom 1989, 96-111). There is a substantial body of cases in United States law reports, under the heading of contracts, in which litigants have approached the courts seeking compensation for services provided to another. It is agreed that the service was provided, but that there was no explicit contract for the service; the parties more or less drifted into the arrangement. Nevertheless, the courts in these cases apply the general rule of thumb used in contract disputes—they seek to carry out what the parties intended at the time they entered into the arrangement.

When these cases get into the courtroom and the parties give evidence as to their earlier intentions, the party who provided the service routinely says he expected to be compensated. The recipient of the service says he did not expect to have to pay for it. Both parties appear to be telling the truth. What is the court to do? If the court washes its hands of the matter and turns the parties away, it will, in effect, be deciding the case against the party asking for compensation. The courts have solved the dilemma by applying a tiebreaker derived from what they presume to be the *typical* expectations of parties under these circumstances.

The law of evidence can provide us with a third example of how "typical behavior" is important in lawmaking and adjudication. When weighing the evidence that a witness gives on the stand on behalf of a party to litigation, U.S. legal authorities have decided that it is important to consider the relationship of the witness to the party in whose favor the testimony is given. As the veracity of a witness is usually difficult, if not impossible, to determine from the witness's words and demeanor, authorities have, as a corrective device, resorted to assumptions that people who bear various close relationship to one another are more inclined to stretch or forget the truth for each other's benefit than if they were comparative strangers to one another,[2] and it is permissible to point out this probable bias during the course of a trial. (3A Wigmore, Evidence, §949 Chadbourn, rev. 1970). Those assumptions of testimonial bias are based on the lawmakers' impressions of typical or average behavior.

The illustrations I have given of how typical behavior is important in legal processes are just some of the many that have occurred to me from my particular vantage point. With the concerted effort of experts in all the various areas of the law, I suspect that up to a hundred, maybe more, similar examples could be located.

Lawmakers, in their attempts to describe typical behavior when it is important to their tasks, have historically relied almost entirely on their own observations, reflective intuition, or plain gut feelings. Thoughtful lawmakers most certainly would be willing to admit that frequently they could have been off the mark. But they do not have the luxury that pure scientists have of waiting to report their impressions or theories for practical consumption until hard confirming evidence is available. Lawmakers have been forced to do the best they can by their own lights, because they are called upon to make prompt decisions. I believe that most lawmakers would welcome any creditable help that became available.

In many, if not all, of the instances where typical behavior is or will be important to a legal task, social scientists with empirical research skills could doubtless provide lawmakers with comparatively hard evidence of actual typical behavior. But individualized empirical research on every type of legally significant typical behavior in relevant subsets of the population would require an ambitious, expensive, and time-consuming effort. It seems unlikely that such comprehensive assistance will be available to lawmakers. On the other hand, selective modest amounts of empirical research prompted by a knowledge of sociobiological theory is feasible. In what areas should such research be done? How should priorities be determined? Here is where I think sociobiology can help lawmakers *today*.

It seems reasonable to assume that a major portion of surmises or predictions that lawmakers have made and will make about typical behavior patterns will agree with what sociobiologists predict. In those cases, if sociobiology is to have any immediate use for lawmakers, it might merely be to give them some comfort from an outside source that the observations or predictions they have arrived at independently are close to the mark. But in the areas where typical behavior is important to the law, and impressionistic legal conclusions *differ* from sociobiological theory, that theory can serve a more active, advisory role. Knowledge of the conflicting theory could prompt lawmakers to commission empirical studies of actual behavior to discover whether their impressions or the sociobiologists' predictions are closest to the facts of actual typical behavior.

This potential for immediate use of sociobiology by legal systems calls for illustrations. I will draw one from American tort law and a second from the law of the Netherlands regarding the disqualification of witnesses in lawsuits.

EMPIRICAL BEHAVIORAL RESEARCH
FOLLOWING SOCIOBIOLOGICAL LEADS

United States: Torts

In recent years courts have been struggling with the question of whether to permit bystanders who observe an accident, such as an automobile striking a pedestrian, to recover compensation for alleged emotional damages the bystanders suffered as a result of their observation, (for example, Leibson 1976-77, 163; Simons 1976). Some courts have been reluctant to extend the liability of the party accountable for the accident (the tortfeasor) in this way because of the difficulties of disproving alleged emotional or psychological damage to the bystander. When monetary recovery for such damages has been permitted, it generally has been limited to relatives of the victim of the physical impact. In an attempt to put some bounds on a tortfeasor's liabilities in this regard and help ensure the genuineness of claims, the Iowa Supreme Court circumscribed the relatives permitted to recover for such damages in its jurisdiction. (Barnhill v. Davis, 300 NW 2d 104, Iowa, 1981.)

The line drawn by the court represented a judgment that the relatives permitted to recover were more likely, typically, to suffer emotional damages from observing the impact than those who were not permitted to recover; mothers, fathers, sons, daughters, siblings, and other close relatives were permitted to recover, but cousins, for example, were not. Sociobiologists will feel reasonably comfortable with such gross categorizations in large population samples—such as all people who will appear as bystander litigants in Iowa courts in the next several decades. Here is why.

Common experience, as well as documented research, teaches us that we can be subject to severe neurophysiological repercussions from being personally endangered (Bourne 1970, 486; Buck, Parke, and Buck 1970). The lingering effects (Cohen 1980) may have an evolutionary adaptive function of impressing on us the need for taking avoidance action when faced with similar dangers in the future. Furthermore, sociobiologists hypothesize that we are programmed to be particularly concerned for not only our own welfare and survival, but also for that of others who bear a close genetic relationship to us: the closer the genetic relationship, the more solicitude we should have for those others (Beckstrom 1985a, 107-12).

It should follow that the typical mother, for instance, who observes her child being endangered would react in much the same manner as if she herself were endangered. The reaction should be similar in character but probably not as severe, inasmuch as the child does not carry all of the mother's "familial" genes—only one-half. The other family members who are also related to the impact victim by "one-half" (to use the shorthand terms of population genetics)—the father and siblings—may be typically expected to react not much differently from the mother. At least they all could be expected to have a more severe emotional reaction than the typical cousin of an impact victim, who is related by one-eighth. Thus the Iowa scheme that permits recovery by those related by one-half to the impact victim but not by cousins and others related by one-eighth or less seems sociobiologically sound if lines must be drawn.

However, there is one aspect of the Iowa scheme that should raise sociobiologists' eyebrows. Bystanders may recover when their grandparents are impact victims, but not when their uncles, aunts, nieces, or nephews are the victims (Beckstrom 1985a, 102-3). From the evolutionary biologist's viewpoint this categorization is highly suspect—all of the named relatives are related to the bystanders by one-fourth. However, aunts/uncles and nephews/nieces are, on the average, one and three generations younger, respectively, than grandparents. The younger people, therefore, have more remaining reproductive and nurturing potential. On that basis sociobiologists would suspect that the typical bystander would be more solicitous toward the niece/ nephew or aunt/uncle than toward the grandparent and would have corresponding emotional reactions when observing them endangered. Therefore, if bystanders are permitted to recover compensation when their grandparents are the impact victims, sociobiologists would expect that recovery should also be permitted when their uncles and aunts and, yet more clearly, their nieces and nephews, are the impact victims (primarily focusing on relatedness and "reproductive value").

Of course, sociobiologists would observe that other operative factors, such as local environment and culture or generalized reciprocal altruism patterns, may alter the basic picture just outlined and justify this aspect of the Iowa scheme. But sociobiological theory generates a suspicion that the Iowa court was wrong in this particular, in view of its announced purposes for line drawing. The suspicion is sufficient to warrant a study by empirical researchers. They could, for example, administer a questionnaire giving grandmother, aunt, and niece as paired alternatives and ask interviewees which one they would be most disturbed to see hit by an automobile.[3] The answers from a representative sample of the population in Iowa ought to be of interest to lawmakers there. And similar studies prompted by a knowledge of sociobiological theory could provide useful information to lawmakers in other states who are contemplating the question of circumscribing bystander-relatives permitted to recover for emotional distress.

Netherlands Law: Evidence

The examples I have thus far given of the potential for use of sociobiology in the solution of legal problems have focused on U.S. legal systems or at least those systems with origins in English common law. This merely reflects the limitations of my own experience. Undoubtedly whatever sociobiology has to offer legal systems has applicability outside the Anglo-American sphere. As an illustration of that, let us venture onto the European continent and into the Roman-influenced civil law sphere for our second example of how sociobiological theory might prompt empirical research that could assist in the solution of legal problems.

The statutory laws of the Netherlands contain a provision[4] that generally disqualifies people from testifying in certain lawsuits when they are lineal relatives of a party to the action, that is, a party's parents, grandparents, etc., or children, grandchildren, etc. (Fruin 1986; Pitlo 1981, 169).[5] This disqualification does not apply to other genetic relatives of the parties—although spouses and linear in-laws are also disqualified (Fruin 1986).

Commentators have suggested that there are two aspects to the disqualification of relatives. On the one hand, if the relative's testimony were to disfavor the party, it might create disharmony in the family—an occurence that lawmakers were anxious to avoid, even at the cost of foregoing pertinent evidence (Asser 1953). On the other hand—and most important for our purposes—if the relative's testimony were to favor the party, it would be unreliable because of the closeness of the relationship (Asser 1953; Pitlo 1981, 90). In other words, the lawmakers were fearful that the disqualified relatives would shade the truth, tell half-truths, and the like, to favor the party. Presumably this judgment by the lawmakers was based upon an impression of typical conduct among close relatives.

Notice again that collateral (nonlineal) relatives of a party, such as siblings, aunts/uncles, and nephews/nieces, are not disqualified by The Netherlands' provision. Sociobiological hypotheses suggest that the Netherlands' categorizations of those relatives disqualified and those qualified to testify may not be artfully drawn, given the goal of excluding unreliable testimony.

The principal relevant sociobiological hypothesis here is related to the one regarding patterns of solicitude for others that I mentioned in the last section—it concerns aid-giving patterns. The proposition is that humans are genetically predisposed to aid close genetic relatives before aiding strangers, everything else being equal; and the greater the genetic overlap, the greater the propensity to render aid (Beckstrom 1985a, 8-14). Humans are also hypothesized to be more inclined to render aid to younger than to older relatives, everything else being equal (Beckstrom 1985a, 13-14). Such aid-giving propensities in large population samples, such as all people appearing in the Netherlands' courts as witnesses, presumably would translate into testimonial manipulation of facts in order to favor close relatives.

If this sociobiological hypothesis about aid giving is true, then the Netherlands' related-witness disqualification list may be either underinclusive or overinclusive. If a person's grandson, for example, cannot testify in the person's behalf, then that person's sister probably should not be permitted to so testify either. Or *both* should be permitted to testify, inasmuch as, typically, everything else being equal, a sister (one-half related) would be predicted to aid her sibling to the same or a greater degree as a grandson (one-fourth related) would be predicted to aid his grandparent.

Again, however, local environment and culture, including generalized reciprocal altruism patterns, may be acting in such a way as to justify the Netherlands' categorizations. But there is enough of a discrepancy indicated here between what lawmakers in the Netherlands seem to have presumed about typical behavior of people appearing in their courts, and what sociobiologists would predict about that behavior, to justify an empirical study of what that behavior really is. It is not as easy to visualize a research design here as it was in the previous example regarding emotional disturbance resulting from observing a tortious impact to a relative. I suspect, however, that empiricists could devise ways to measure willingness to shade the truth in behalf of various relatives without violating ground rules governing experimentation with human subjects. If not, then this legal problem area would be a candidate not for immediate assistance from sociobiology, but for long-range assistance from sociobiology, of the sort I will discuss shortly.

Simultaneous Testing of Behavioral Hypotheses

At this point, we should note something that has probably already occurred to many readers who are scientists. Empirical research following sociobiological leads could not only give lawmakers useful information concerning typical behavior important for their purposes, but the *same research,* if properly tailored, could also serve as tests of the behavioral hypotheses that prompt the research: two birds could be killed with one stone. Furthermore, funding for this work could be sought from two directions—from law and from science-oriented sources. Thus a fertile ground would appear to exist here for mutually beneficial cooperative research between scientists and lawyers (Beckstrom 1985b, 33-35).

DIRECT USE OF SOCIOBIOLOGY BY LAWMAKERS IN ASSESSING TYPICAL BEHAVIOR

It is important to observe that the potential we have just explored—for immediate use of sociobiology *to prompt empirical research* on actual typical behavior important to the law—does not entail the direct use of sociobiological theory to inform lawmakers on such matters. The theory would only be used only as a signal, in a given case, that a study of actual behavior should be commissioned. However, I do not mean to suggest by this that sociobiological theory, when and if it becomes well settled and substantiated, should not be directly employed by lawmakers searching for typical behavior.

Differences in detail now exist among sociobiologists in their hypotheses concerning typical behavior. With time, consensus is likely to develop on an ever-increasing number of concepts. Again, with time, those concepts may be confirmed by ongoing empirical testing, including empirical testing in fields like anthropology and psychology.

When sociobiological theory is thus firmed up, responsible authorities should study the structure and decide whether some aspects of the total pattern could be used as an additive or corrective to lawmakers' impressions of typical behavior. Such an application might be particularly useful in an area like the intestate succession laws, where lawmakers are attempting to reflect what sort of property disposition the typical person dying without a will would have made if he or she had written one. That behavioral question is imagined—it never happens, so it cannot be observed. Thus it would be fruitless for lawmakers to employ empirical researchers to discover actual behavior in those instances where the impressions of lawmakers and sociobiological theory differ regarding the people to whom typical intestate decedents would have disposed their property. If sociobiology were to assist the law here, it would have to be used in a direct manner on the assumption that sociobiological predictions as to typical aid-giving behavior are a better representation of what dead people would have done than any other information lawmakers could gather.

We could expect initial resistance to such direct use of substantiated sociobiology to come from members of the legal profession who have had experience in dealing with witnesses expert in what one might call "soft" science. Lawyers have found, for example, that expert opinions as to when someone should be considered insane and thus legally irresponsible have been based on shifting sands (Schwartz 1983, 17-18). From this and similar experiences, judges, in particular, have become wary of the social sciences, often preferring to rely on their own impressions or those of lay jurors. For good reason, they have generally been more receptive to information from "hard" sciences like mathematics and physics. Sociobiology is social science in that it addresses human interactive behavior; however, its foundations are in genetics, mathematics, and the economic logic of natural processes. Its way of looking at the world is congenial to those trained, as lawyers are, in logical analysis starting from factual premises.

The few lawyers I know who have taken the time to look deeply into evolutionary biology have all been favorably impressed. I suspect that as growing numbers of lawyers learn sociobiology, the problem will not be to convince them to use it in their profession, but rather to convince them to wait until it has been well tested. There is no need to wait, however, to engage in empirical research on *actual* behavior when sociobiological theory differs from what lawmakers have presumed to be typical behavior. That can be done immediately.

Notes

1. See, for example, J. Hirshleifer, "Privacy: Its Origin, Function, and Future" (1980); W. Rodgers, "Bringing People Back: Toward a Comprehensive Theory of Taking in Natural Resources Law" (1982); R. Posner, *The Economics of Justice* (1983, 186-87); E. Elliot, "The Evolutionary Tradition in Jurisprudence" (1985); M. Wilson, "Impact of the Uncertainty of Paternity on Family Law" (1987); M. Daly and M. Wilson, *Homicide* (1988).

2. I have elsewhere explored the message that sociobiology might hold for the law in regard to handling the testimony of one identical twin offered on behalf of the other (Beckstrom 1985b, 33-35).

3. An unpublished paper by H. Ginsburg, read to the Psychonomic Society in Washington, D.C., in November 1977, concerned an empirical survey of this type. Grandparents were asked to choose between saving children or saving grandchildren. The children prevailed except when they were beyond their reproductive years. After that point there was a tendency to save the potentially reproductive grandchildren (Freedman 1979, 115).

4. I wish to acknowledge the translation assistance of Martine De Proost-Ford and Philip Hinnekens.

5. A bill to revise the relevant provision was reported to be pending (Pitlo 1981, 169). Other European countries have had similar provisions that appear to have origins in the Napoleonic code and perhaps Roman law. Essentially the same provision in Italy was held unconstitutional as against the general right to be heard (Certoma 1985, 205).

3

Management Theory

J. Gary Bernhard and Kalman Glantz

The academic study of organization theory and management theory, an important part of the curriculum of business schools, is of fairly recent origin. In the United States, competition to produce and be efficient in industry encouraged a "scientific" approach to studying how organizations are structured and how people behave in them. In the early twentieth century, Fredrick Taylor developed a theory of industrial production that influenced American industry for decades. His idea was that each manufacturing task could be broken down into smaller and smaller tasks that could be analyzed and standardized. Each worker would then have to be responsible for completing only a specific number of tasks in a specific amount of time. The manufacturing process would become more efficient, and the product's quality would be more consistent. What is called "classical" management theory emphasized the goals of the organization and relegated its individual members to "units of labor."

In the 1930s and 1940s the assumptions of classical management theory were called into question. Elton Mayo, in his 1945 book, *The Social Problems of an Industrial Civilization*, rejected the notions that society is made up of atomized individuals, each maximizing his or her own individual self-interest, and that labor could thus be considered a commodity. Employees, said Mayo, are not content to function as units of labor even if their basic needs are satisfied. The new line of thought begun by Mayo became the Human Relations school, the largest and most influential division of management theory.

As we shall show in this chapter, the Human Relations school of management theory has, without knowing it, produced a theory that accords with evolutionary theory. In addition, some of the most vehement critics of that school have also, inadvertently, come up with "evolutionary" ideas. Their insights have been based on intuition and observation of everyday behavior in the workplace—including specific studies carried out by interview and experimentation. However, management theory has never been able to offer a clear idea of *why* organizations operate as they do and why members are motivated to participate in teamwork. It is our contention that insights derived from the theory of human evolution provide this "why." Also, as we shall demonstrate below, an evolutionary model can be used to judge the strengths and limitations of the views put forward by various organizational theorists. Indeed, the immense and confusing literature of organizational theory literally organizes itself when seen through the evolutionary lens.

THE NATURAL "ORGANIZATION":
THE BAND OF HUNTER-GATHERERS

Let us first offer a very brief overview of some evolutionary insights into human group behavior. These are taken from anthropologists' descriptions of the hunter-gatherer way of life. Our species lived in small groups, or bands, for the majority of its history, that is, from human origins up until the development of agriculture ten thousand years ago. Thus, the hunting and gathering band was the first human "organization." The environment of the band shaped the evolution of the human species. The foraging way of life formed emotional responses that helped emerging humans survive and reproduce.

A key feature of the social organization of the band was reciprocal altruism. Males probably exchanged meat for the food gathered by females. Meat was distributed on the basis of kinship and past favors. Tools, gifts, and favors were "lent" and exchanged. Everybody in a band owed and was owed by virtually all other members of the band. One could always count on a friend or relative for assistance, because friends and relatives knew that if they gave to you, they could eventually go to you in time of need.

Various evolved human emotions helped to ensure reciprocity. Gratitude, sympathy, empathy, and guilt induced people to pay their debts. Envy may have facilitated the redistribution of the few possessions that existed. Righteous anger served to intimidate those who were tempted to cheat. Intellectual capacity grew to keep track of ever more complex obligations and entitlements. These traits served to mitigate the selfishness inherent in any organism, thereby promoting cooperation and collaboration in an environment where all individuals were generally dependent on close relatives for their survival.

We shall not attempt to present the relevant sociobiological theories in this chapter, since they are covered elsewhere in this volume. It is sufficient for our purposes to note that humans are adapted to life in hunting and gathering bands. Of course, they are able to live in other types of social environments, too; notably they are able to adjust to life in large organizations. But when they do so, they develop characteristic problems. These are the problems that management and organizational theorists address over and over again. We will outline these problems below. First, however, let us list some of the salient features of the band's organization, as it existed for hundreds of thousands of years. (This picture is largely derived from hunter-gatherer societies that persisted into the twentieth century.)

1. *Belonging and connection.* The foraging way of life depended on kinship, cooperation, and loyalty. People belonged to the group they were part of, and knew they could count on others in the group.

2. *Recognition.* At the same time everyone was recognized individually and accorded respect for his or her abilities and achievements.

3. *Self-reliance and communal loyalty.* Everyone in a band was self-reliant and had a range of skills that enabled survival and social well-being. At the same time, individuals could not survive without the band and so were willing to work for the group's benefit.

4. *Reciprocity.* Hunter-gatherer bands survived on the strength of the reciprocal ties among individual members. Gift exchange, formalized "partnerships," and traditions of food

distribution established in the species feelings about "fairness" and "owing" and "being owed."

5. *Meaningful activity.* Hunting, gathering, singing, healing, tool making, storytelling—all were essential to survival and well-being in bands. One's effort was thus valuable and meaningful.

6. *Leadership and authority.* People with influence in bands were those who demonstrated competence, had experience, could draw consensus from the group, and were willing to assume responsibility. The reward of effective leadership consisted largely of the respect of one's fellows, since material goods had no value and there were few special privileges.

7. *Communication and say.* In a band everyone knew just about everything that was going on, and everyone could voice an opinion about anything. Decisions were usually made collectively; disputes were public.

With the advent of sedentary living, a mere ten thousand years ago, the hunting and gathering way of life was gradually replaced by a more "organized" type of life, and eventually the organizational way of doing things came to be seen as the human way. It is only in the last fifty years that scholars have begun to grope toward a vision of human interaction that is closer to our nature. However, in most cases, those theorists attempting to close the gap between organizational life and human needs were unaware of the importance of the band. Indeed, when evolution was invoked it was usually to justify the "survival of the fittest," not to demonstrate the collaborative nature of human beings.

THE HUMAN RELATIONS SCHOOL

The Human Relations or Human Development school is the most significant movement in the history of organizational studies. Before it arose, the theory of management was based on the idea that people wouldn't work unless they were coerced or bribed. Managers were taught to give explicit orders, to keep the lines of authority clear, and to make sure that employees knew their places. Centralized authority was the ideal. Rules and regulations were drafted to cover every eventuality. Basically, the boss was the top dog—the "alpha"—keeping all the others in their places and running the show.

The Human Relations theorists offered a vision of management that was more democratic. Employees should be consulted.
Bureaucracy was out; flexibility was in. The structure of an
organization, they argued, should be flexible and responsive to
human needs. Place should be made for spontaneity and
creativity. Authority should be shared, employees should be
autonomous as far as possible. Trust and openness should be
the rule.

The Human Relations school began with the work of Chester
Barnard in the 1940s. Among its most important theorists are
Douglas McGregor, Rensis Likert, Chris Argyris, Michael
Maccoby, and William Ouchi. Each one's vision, we argue here,
was shaped by the invisible presence of the band.

Chester Barnard

Chester Barnard, a top executive at AT&T and author, in 1948,
of *The Functions of the Executive* (1968), was one of the principal
founders of the Human Relations school. Barnard saw clearly
that human beings had a deep need to cooperate and work
together toward a common goal. He wrote:

> The most intangible and subtle of incentives is that which I
> have called the condition of communion. . . . It is the feeling
> of personal comfort in social relations that is sometimes called
> solidarity, social integration. . . . The need for communion is
> a basis of informal organization that is essential to the
> operation of every formal organization (Barnard 1968, 148).

The key phrase here is *informal organization,* by which
Barnard meant that humans naturally associated with one
another. Formal organizations couldn't exist without that that
tendency. Now what could that mean? Isn't it his way of saying
that we humans have a predisposition to live in bands?

Barnard understood that people are by nature willing to
work for the common good, but if they can't identify with the
organization's goals they can destroy the organization. Thus
the organizational leader (the executive) is charged with the
responsibility of creating an environment in which "the
capacity, development, and state of mind of employees as
individuals must be the focal point of all policy and practice

relating to personnel" (1968, 20). The state of mind of individuals included, of course, their tendency toward informal organization, that is, their need to be in a band. The intersection of individual goals and organizational goals, Barnard said, creates the best kind of organization—one in which individuals can grow and develop by contributing to the organization's efficiency and effectiveness.

Douglas McGregor

Douglas McGregor, long the bright light of the Sloan School of Industrial Administration at MIT, is the author of a book aptly named *The Human Side of Enterprise* (1966, first published in 1957). His enduring fame rests on the distinction he made between "Theory X" and "Theory Y" (the latter being his own theory). What he called Theory X was the early theory of management that stated that people have to be coerced into working because they are greedy, self-interested, and lazy. McGregor realized that this theory was based on "a faulty conception of human behavior and human motivation" (McGregor 1966, 45), so he created "Theory Y."

His assumptions were similar to those of Chester Barnard:

> People are not by nature passive or resistant to organizational needs. They have become so as a result of experience in organizations. . . .The *motivation, the potential for development, the capacity for assuming responsibility, the readiness to direct behavior toward organizational goals are all present in people.* Management does not put them there. It is a responsibility of management to make it possible for people to recognize and develop these human characteristics for themselves. (McGregor 1966, 15) (emphasis added)

The key idea here is that the readiness to direct behavior toward organizational goals is "present in people." McGregor seems never to have asked himself how it got there, what it is doing there, what purpose it is designed to serve. He would probably not have liked the idea that it is "in the genes." Nevertheless, he correctly identified the tendency.

Like Barnard, McGregor believed that if the organization took care of people, people would be inclined to take care of the organization: The essential task of management, he wrote, is "to arrange organizational conditions and methods of operation so that people can achieve their own goals *best* by directing *their own* efforts towards organizational objectives" (McGregor 1966, 15).

In a band, you don't need a manager to "arrange the conditions." There *is* no difference between the goals of the band and those of its members. Thus, it seems, McGregor wants the manager to recreate the band.

Rensis Likert

Rensis Likert, author of *The Human Organization* (1967), was for many years the head of the Institute for Social Research at the University of Michigan. He believed he could arrange management styles on a continuum ranging from authoritarian to participative. He described four separate approaches, from "System 1" (the most authoritarian) to "System 4" (the most participative). He developed long questionnaires designed to measure management effectiveness, and submitted these questionnaires to thousands of managers at different levels in various organizations. An example from one seven-page questionnaire is found in table 1.

Likert's major conclusion was that

> the highest productivity, best performance, and highest earnings appear at present to be achieved by System 4 organizations. These organizations mobilize both the non-economic motives and and economic needs so that all available motivational forces create cooperaive behavior focused on achieving the organization's objectives (Likert 1967, 106).

In other words, Likert recommends that an organization should be more like a band, a place where everyone is involved in decisions in some way and where there are explicit links between the success of individuals and the success of the organization. Such an organization will be more productive than those that threaten or punish employees.

Chris Argyris

Let's move on to the current scene. Harvard Business School's Chris Argyris, author of many influential books on management,

COMPARISON OF AUTHORITATIVE AND PARTICIPATIVE
SYSTEMS OF MANAGEMENT

Operating Characteristics	Authoritative Systems		Participative Systems	
	Exploitive authoritative	Benevolent authoritative	Consultive	Participative Group
Level at which decisions are made	Bulk of decisions at top of organization	Policy at top, many decisions within prescribed framework made at lower levels	Broad policy and general decisions at top, more specific decisions at lower levels	Decision making done throughout organization, integrated through overlapping groups
Adequacy and accuracy of information	Partial and often inaccurate information is available	Moderately adequate and accurate information available	Reasonably adequate and accurate information available	Relatively complete and accurate information available
Extent to which decision makers are aware of problems	Often unaware or only partially aware	Aware of some, unaware of others	Moderately aware of problems	Generally quite well aware of problems
Extent to which technical and professional knowledge is used in decision making	Used only if possessed at higher levels	Much of what is available in higher and middle levels is used	Much of what is available in higher, middle, and lower levels is used	Most of what is available anywhere in the organization is used

Table 1. Adapted from Table 3–1, Likert (1967) with permission.

is squarely in the Human Relations tradition. One of his major concerns is the gap between "being human and being organized" (this phrase is the title of an article he published in *Transaction* in July, 1968). Argyris doesn't get his ideas about being human from evolution or biology, he invents them or borrows them from psychologists like Freud and Maslow; but we think he gets closer to the band than almost anyone else. Look at table 2, a diagram in which he lays out seven "lines of development".

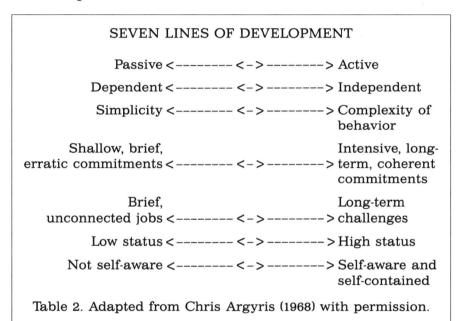

Table 2. Adapted from Chris Argyris (1968) with permission.

The right-hand side of the diagram is where most people would feel better—most truly human, he thinks. And lo and behold, the right side is much more like a band than the left. One might think that the simplicity/complexity continuum is backward. Isn't life in a band simple? But what Argyris means by "simple" is the one-dimensional relationship between boss and subordinate where the subordinate blindly obeys. Life in a band is much more complex. Most organizations, Argyris argues, are structured in ways that bring out the left-hand side, so they aren't good for people. In other words, organizations aren't good because they aren't very much like bands.

In his 1964 book *Integrating the Individual and the Organization,* Argyris describes what he thinks are the "essential properties" of good management. Again, he presents a series of continuums with the "bad" side on the left and the "good" side on the right (see table 3). Note that in every case, the "essential properties" side of the continuum is closer to the kind of interpersonal, group processes that are characteristic of the band.

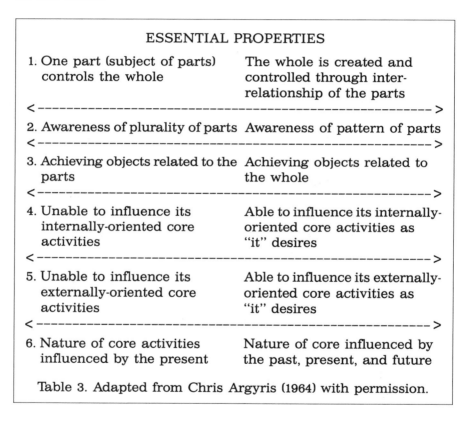

ESSENTIAL PROPERTIES

1. One part (subject of parts) controls the whole — The whole is created and controlled through inter-relationship of the parts

< -- >

2. Awareness of plurality of parts — Awareness of pattern of parts

< -- >

3. Achieving objects related to the parts — Achieving objects related to the whole

< -- >

4. Unable to influence its internally-oriented core activities — Able to influence its internally-oriented core activities as "it" desires

< -- >

5. Unable to influence its externally-oriented core activities — Able to influence its externally-oriented core activities as "it" desires

< -- >

6. Nature of core activities influenced by the present — Nature of core influenced by the past, present, and future

Table 3. Adapted from Chris Argyris (1964) with permission.

Michael Maccoby

Michael Maccoby, author of such works as *The Leader* (1981) and the best selling *The Gamesman* (1976), is particularly interested in the characteristics of effective leadership. In *The Gamesman,* Maccoby described "the hero of the 1970s" as "the risk-taking, fast-talking entrepreneur who had the aura of a winner" (xiv). But the leaders of the 1980s, according to Maccoby, would be "developers," people who "invite partici- pation in developing new ideas and . . . encourage subordinates to share power" (xv). Among other things, the new leaders

- must demonstrate a leadership style that builds relationships and inspires trust.
- are flexible, yet principled.
- are consultative, yet courageous.
- are participative, but persuasive.

Does this sound familiar? At this point it is worth quoting anthropologist Asen Balikci's (1970) description of how an Eskimo Inhumataq (leader) used to operate.

All [the Inhumataq's] decisions were taken informally and gently, in consultation with the other adult members of the extended family, involving long discussions when everyone present could freely express his opinions. In a sense, the headman's task was to achieve consensus without hurting the feelings and designs of the other hunters, whose autonomy he respected (116).

Maccoby's "new leader" is as old as the human species. The characteristics of true leadership haven't changed in thousands of years.

William Ouchi

William Ouchi, author of the best-selling book *Theory Z* (1981), is primarily interested in how to make organizations more productive. What does he say? "Involved workers are the key to increased productivity" (4). "Productivity is a problem of social organization" (4). And what is the key feature of social organization? "Productivity and trust go hand in hand, strange as it may seem" (5).

If Ouchi had an evolutionary perspective it wouldn't seem strange at all. Ouchi bases his theory on Japanese manage- ment practices, but what he emphasizes about the Japanese style is precisely its band-like features. For example, he stresses the willingness of the Japanese to sacrifice short-term personal goals in the interests of their company:

Japanese employees want to get ahead just like Americans. . . .
They want to make deals beneficial to both their departments
and themselves. . . . But sometimes personal success must be
sacrificed for the good of the company. . . .The success of the
trading company depends critically upon the willingness of
individual officers and employees to make these sacrifices. (5)

Table 4 shows how Ouchi contrasts Japanese and American
management styles. In every case, the feature he selects from
Japanese society is closer to the band than the contrasting
American feature. In a band:

- Your membership is for life
- You are evaluated slowly and rise with age and experience
- There is little specialization
- There are few if any formal rules
- Decision-making is by consensus
- The notion of individual responsibility is not dominant: everyone is responsible
- Concern for the welfare of the whole is central.

EMPLOYMENT CHARACTERISTICS OF
AMERICAN AND JAPANESE COMPANIES

AMERICAN	JAPANESE
Short-term employment	Lifetime employment
Rapid evaluation and promotion	Slow evaluation and promotion
Specialized career paths	Non-specialized career paths
Explicit control mechanisms	Implicit control mechanisms
Individual decision-making	Collective decision-making
Individual responsibility	Collective responsibility
Segmented concerns	Holistic concerns

Table 4. Adapted from William Ouchi (1981) with permission.

Here is Ouchi's description of an ideal organization:

[It] is one that has no organizational chart, no divisions, no
visible structure at all. In a sense, a basketball team that
plays well together fits this description. . . . Each person

understands his task and its relationship to other tasks so well that the coordination is unspoken....In a less cooperative team, however, the players attempt to hog the ball, to take as many shots for themselves as possible....The coach responds to this human frailty by asserting the hierarchical right to monitor each player closely, forcing them to stick to their job descriptions.... Such a team can never perform with the same grace, the same satisfaction, nor the same productivity as the one that operates as a *clan.* (1981, 91, emphasis added)

A clan? That's as close as anyone has come to saying *a band.*

In summary, the Human Relations school has been trying to define what kind of organization would be good for human beings—without really having a clear idea of what human beings were about. They deserve credit for the insights they were able to develop, but their task would have been considerably easier if they had thought to look at human evolution.

SOME CRITICISMS OF THE HUMAN RELATIONS APPROACH

These thinkers who almost rediscovered the band through observation and imagination did a good job, but because they weren't looking at the original model they made some mistakes. Knowing about real hunter-gatherer bands enables us to see some gaps in their thinking. Even persons without knowledge of the band have identified some of these gaps in their criticisms of the Human Relations school.

Charles Perrow, one of the most influential of today's organizational theorists, is the author of *Complex Organization* (1981). He contends that the reforms of the Human Relations school are often nothing more than cynical attempts to fool people. Their so-called reforms are little more than attempts by management to give employees the *illusion* of participation so that they will become more productive. After all, how interesting can you make a job on an assembly line in an auto plant? How much influence can a line worker have in important decisions?

The Human Relations school has also been subjected to attack because one of its fundamental assumptions—that better human relations, more participation, better communication will increase the organization's productivity—is simply not borne out by research. Or rather, sometimes it is borne out and sometimes it is not. Why not always? No one has been able to solve the mystery.

We believe that people will make an extra effort only if they feel that the organization is truly theirs, that is, only if they respond to it as if it were really their band. It follows from this that genuine reforms will work better than phony ones. Increased productivity will depend on whether the reforms are perceived by the workers as cosmetic or real.

Human nature is complicated. Reforms probably work only as long as they make people believe that the organization is becoming *more like their band than before.* As long as people are getting *more* respect, *more* recognition, and *more* status, they will probably increase productivity. Even then, productivity will not rise forever. Once people are getting plenty—of food, respect, status, security, etc.—their motivation to work harder begins to decline.

Evolution forces us to confront a basic truth. Happy workers don't necessarily work harder. Hunter-gatherers don't drive themselves. They forage when necessary, they relax when they have a chance. There will always be people who begin to ease up once they feel comfortable. People who run the organizations of the future will need to take this into account.

WORK TEAMS

There is another group of management theorists we should like to mention here, as their work is extremely popular at the moment. They often consider themselves too hard-nosed for the Human Relations school, but they, also, have "discovered" the band; they call it the "work team." There is a veritable mountain of literature on work teams, and everybody is running experiments with them. In high-tech industries, work teams are actually taking over. Some of the most influential organizational theorists now place the work team at the center of what Rosabeth Moss Kanter, author of the 1983 book,

The Change Masters, calls the "corporate renaissance." Robert Reich goes so far as to say that the work team is the hero of modern industry: "If we are to compete in today's world, we must begin to celebrate collective entrepreneurship, endeavors in which the whole of the effort is greater than the sum of individual contributions. We need to honor our teams more, our aggressive leaders and maverick geniuses less" (Reich 1987, 78).

In his 1988 book *Thriving on Chaos,* Tom Peters suggests that "multifunction teams [be used] for *all* development activities" (210) and that every function should be organized "into ten- to thirty-person, largely self-managing teams" (296). The acknowledged goal of this restructuring is to "compete in today's world." New ways of working and thinking about work, Peters says, are crucial to organizational survival. But these "new" ways, the reader will now appreciate, are as old as Maccoby's "new" leader. And when Reich calls for groups "in which the whole of the effort is greater than the sum of individual contributions" he is calling for the band.

In virtually every study and experiment, it's clear that the closer a work team is to a band, the more effective it is. For example, in *Improving Productivity and the Quality of Work Life* (1977), T. G. Cummings and E. S. Molloy identify six "action levers"—their fancy term for motivators. Here are the six: autonomy, technical-physical features (new equipment, different space), task variety, information or feedback, rewards and recognition, and interpersonal interventions. Cummings and Molloy don't say *why* these "action levers" are present in effective work groups. But the answer is clear. Bands were autonomous, people had variety in their daily activities, information was shared, everyone was recognized as an individual, and there was no bureaucratic authority. These conditions allow people to work effectively because people are predisposed to work under such conditions.

This is not to say that the work team is always a perfect solution. When work teams are less like bands, they don't work well. Sometimes they don't produce as much as the organization expects, sometimes they simply fall apart, and sometimes they actively oppose the organization with what Argyris (1985) calls "defensive routines." In the same way that humanistic reformers expected individuals to become more productive as soon as their needs are satisfied, work team advocates often expect groups to explode with energy as soon as they are given a space and told that they are a "team."

The modern organization, however, is not a natural environment for bands. While the opportunity to work in teams generally calls forth deep-seated inclinations to cooperate and take responsibility, these inclinations can easily be blocked. If, for example, the organization only pretends to take the team's work seriously, or greatly limits the group's autonomy, interest in the team and in the task will rapidly fade. By the same token, many workers—especially industrial workers—have learned to just "do the job and not ask questions." The level of responsibility required of each member on an effective team is hard for a wary worker to accept—even when the organization genuinely offers to share power and profits.

What is usually missing when work teams don't work is mutual trust. This view of the effectiveness of teams makes it possible to understand something about the remarkable success of Japanese organizations, to which we now turn as our final presentation.

THE SECRET OF JAPANESE SUCCESS

Although large Japanese organizations are, obviously, not bands, they have managed to preserve one of the most salient characteristics of the band: reciprocity. Japanese workers can count on the organization to stand by them—even in hard times. A Japanese secretary or an assembly-line worker with personal problems won't be cut adrift. In fact, the company will provide assistance in time of need. In the same way, the worker is expected to come to the company's aid when necessary. If overtime is required, employees are obligated to keep working past the regular shift. But "obligation" isn't seen as negative. Neither the threat of reprisal nor the reward of time-and-a-half motivates the employees' behavior. Rather they are holding up their end of a reciprocal relationship with the organization.

It is true that Japanese reciprocity is feudal rather than band-like. People acknowlege differences in rank and prestige as well as personal responsibility to one another. Japanese organizations are clearly hierarchical even though they sustain complex give-and-take relationships, and the concern of the chief executive for his workers is really a form of noblesse oblige. This makes the Japanese company very different from a band. Nevertheless, when it comes to reciprocity, the Japanese company is closer to the band than the American company. And this sort of reciprocity feels much better to most people than the abstracted reciprocity of wage labor. Feudal reciprocity is a way in which specialization and hierarchy can coexist with cooperation and trust. But it can work only if the high-ranking leaders continue to merit the respect of the low-ranking workers.

In conclusion, the Japanese have been able to create organizational stability, motivate employees, and maintain quality within a rather strict hierarchy. In an effort to imitate the Japanese and thus obtain similar benefits in the American workplace, many American reformers advocate, without knowing it, a kind of modern feudalism in which enlightened bosses concern themselves with their subordinates' thoughts and feelings, while enlightened subordinates are enthusiastic partners in a common enterprise.

We believe, however, that American society's history of individualism, freedom, and mobility makes it nearly impossible to establish feudal relationships within an already existing organization. "Quality circles" never work as well in the United States as they do in Japan. American managers are generally not as serious about their responsibilities as are their Japanese counterparts. Western organizations cannot just simply imitate the Japanese. They will have to find their own way back to the band.

4

Anthropology

William Irons

Anthropology focuses on culture and cultural diversity. It takes as its starting point the observation that human beings are never just human beings. Rather they are Frenchmen, Chinese, Hopi, Yanomamo, Samoans, or members of some other society and bearers of its shared tradition. Anthropology seeks both to describe and to explain the total range of cultural diversity. It takes as its purview all of human experience since the origin of a distinctly human line of descent approximately two million years ago. Thus anthropology is concerned with the cultural developments of prehistory and with human evolution. Anthropology has been mainly concerned with simpler preliterate societies, including hunting and gathering societies, and simple horticultural and pastoral societies that lack writing and centralized governmental hierarchies.

Anthropologists are especially interested in those institutions of more traditional societies that are exotic from the point of view of our modern, urban, industrial society—for example, the phenomena of dowry, bridewealth, and exogamous lineages. They are interested in the fact that some societies emphasize the female line in kinship by forming matrilineal descent groups and having property and high office pass from a man to his sister's son on his death. Anthropologists endeavor to *explain* institutions of this sort.

THE PLACE OF BIOLOGY IN
ANTHROPOLOGY'S VIEW OF HUMANITY

The main unifying element in anthropology is its focus on
culture. For anthropologists, culture is a unique feature of the
human species consisting of the learned and shared systems
of beliefs, knowledge, and values that form a sort of blueprint
around which each human society organizes its life. Because
of their emphasis on culture and the learned nature of culture,
most anthropologists see biological evolution as irrelevant to
their subject matter. They believe that, in contrast to animals,
human beings do not have an elaborate set of genetically
shaped behavioral propensities that are products of past
natural selection. Rather, human beings are like blank slates
on which a cultural tradition can write whatever behavioral
instructions it might happen to contain. The only evolved
behavioral propensity of humans is a propensity to learn a
cultural tradition and live their lives according to this learned
tradition.

During the 1950s and 1960s, a few anthropologists, such as
Count, Freeman, Tiger, and Fox, argued that evolved behavioral
propensities do play a role in human life. However, these
individuals had relatively little success in convincing other
anthropologists that they should incorporate some element of
biology into their thinking. For the majority of anthropologists,
the effect of biology on culture was not an issue worth
considering.

This situation changed sharply with the publication of E.
O. Wilson's *Sociobiology* in 1975. Wilson's book received both
extreme praise and extreme condemnation and unleashed a
heated controversy. In many ways, the division of anthropologists—into a majority who reject the relevance of evolution
and a minority who do not—remained the same, but the issue
was in effect moved to the forefront of discussion.

THE EARLY NEGATIVE RESPONSE

Very soon after the publication of Wilson's *Sociobiology*,
Marshall Sahlins's book *The Use and Abuse of Biology* (1976)
appeared. In the introduction, Sahlins states that he has

written his book hurriedly because of the extensive attention given to sociobiology after the appearance of Wilson's book and because sociobiology will probably soon disapper as science and remain only as a part of popular culture (xv). Sahlins appears to believe that once the obvious flaws of sociobiology have been pointed out, no credible scholar or scientist will take it seriously.

Sahlins emphasized the widespread belief among anthropologists that culture shapes human thought and behavior but not the reverse. This is the traditional anthropological idea that culture is superorganic, or as Sahlins says, an "autonomous phenomenon." This means that cultural phenomena can only be explained by referring to other cultural phenomena. The fact of its autonomy stems, he says, from its meaningful and symbolic character. Since culture is acquired symbolically and shapes the basic goals for which humans strive in a profound way, it is obvious that evolved behavioral propensities cannot influence behavior. Culture orders human nature rather than the reverse.

Sahlins presents anthropological evidence to demonstrate that human beings frequently behave in ways that do not maximize inclusive fitness. Instead, they pursue culturally defined goals. One example of this type of behavior is adoption in Polynesia. If people were acting so as to maximize their inclusive fitness they clearly would want to invest their parental effort in their own children, but in some areas of Polynesia the majority of children are given in adoption to other people to raise. This clearly is an act based on symbolically conveyed values and not on a propensity to maximize inclusive fitness. As other further examples of behaviors that cannot be explained in evolutionary terms, Sahlins points to the fact that most systems of classifying kin lump relatives who are both genealogically close with relatives who are distant, and that the composition of households and other social groups similarly includes both genealogically close and distant relatives as well as unrelated individuals. He further suggests that the fact that most human languages do not have words for fractions makes it unlikely that human beings could maximize their inclusive fitness, since inclusive fitness can only be explained by the use of fractions. He adds that the assumption that animals can maximize their inclusive fitness is even more unlikely in view of the fact that it would require a knowledge of fractions.

Sahlins then addresses the question of why anyone would support such an illogical theory as sociobiology. Here he emphasizes the idea that bourgeois culture has created sociobiology as a form of self-justification. All cultures, he notes, have a tendency to preserve themselves by creating self-justifying ideologies. In the case of sociobiology, first the competitive markets of capitalist society are projected into nature in the form of a competitive struggle among life forms to reproduce. This makes them natural. The second step is then to perceive the same competitive struggle in society, specifically in the markets of bourgeois society, and to conclude that since it parallels what is found in nature, it is natural and inevitable. Thus Sahlins concludes that the negative reaction of the political left to sociobiology is justified: "Hence the response by men of the Left becomes intelligible, as does the interest of the public at large. What is inscribed in the theory of sociobiology is the entrenched ideology of the Western society. . . ." (101). In one form or another, similar political arguments were made in a number of sources (Kitcher 1985 is a recent example).

Sahlins has a few other criticisms. He points out that sociobiology is equivalent to totemism (a common belief in various preliterate societies that members of a particular clan have a particular animal as their ancestor). He states that sociobiology, if taken seriously, will cause us to lose our best hope of understanding ourselves because we would "have to abandon all understanding of the human world as meaningfully constituted" (107). He also notes that, beyond political reasons, there is another reason why some anthropologists are interested in sociobiology: dabbling in sociobiology represents a fascinating "descent in the kingdom of tabu" (106).

My own impression from discussions over many years with a wide range of anthropological colleagues is that Sahlins's book had the immediate effect of assuring anthropologists who accepted the majority view that there was no reason to take sociobiology seriously. I also have the impression that it further reinforced the widespread belief that anthropologists who took sociobiology seriously were morally and politically suspect.

Anyone who would take sociobiology seriously despite its obvious flaws must do so because of some political agenda of questionable character.

Let me note here that Sahlins's argument is basically literary in quality, and anthropologists who are more scientific in orientation often find it frustrating because of its vagueness and easy presumption that plausible-sounding phrases are as good as any careful attempt to formulate theoretical predictions and test them against careful observation. For these anthropologists, the idea that culture was autonomous needed to be put into falsifiable form and evaluated empirically. A few qualitative ethnographic facts cannot resolve definitively the question of the role of evolved behavioral tendencies in shaping culture and human behavior.

Some of us who felt that evolutionary theory had more to offer anthropology were convinced the issue could only be resolved by much more elaborate analyses of existing data and by the collection of new data (Chagnon and Irons 1979, 509-510). Note that many of the evolutionary anthropological studies cited below are based on analyses of either quantitative data from the Human Relations Area File or quantitative data on the effects of behavior on reproduction in specific ethnographic contexts. Also, many of these studies involve a more detailed examination of the qualitative ethnographic data of particular societies than characterized Sahlins's presentation of evidence. Importantly, many of these studies are organized in terms of specific *hypotheses* that specify what kinds of data will disconfirm and what kind will confirm the existence of a particular evolutionary influence on behavior or culture.

Anthropologists who wish to explore the applicability of evolutionary models to human social behavior have also found Sahlins's sympathy for the political criticism of sociobiology especially irritating. The assertion that their interest in sociobiology would somehow lend support to the politics of the Right was false, unfair, and amounted to obscuring with political innuendo what should be a scientific debate. The argument that sociobiology supported right-wing views was not, of course, invented by Sahlins: it seems to have sprung up quickly in many places, reflecting a long-standing commitment by many intellectuals to combat social Darwinism, combined with the misimpression that sociobiology incorporated assumptions of genetic determinism. This view took very deep root in the popular mind (cf. Alexander 1987, 4–6). On several occasions I had anthropological colleagues tell me that they hated sociobiology because it supported racist and sexist positions. It is interesting that this (quite inaccurate) view still persists in some quarters, despite the fact that the literature produced by evolutionary, or sociobiological anthropologists is almost totally devoid of any political statements.

THE POSITIVE RESPONSE

Despite the initial strong negative reaction of many anthropologists to sociobiology, a small group was convinced that evolutionary theory had the potential of providing anthropology, as well as the other social and behavioral sciences, with a basic theory. In contrast to the natural sciences, the social sciences lack a basic theory, and these anthropologists felt this was one of the reasons that the social sciences had made so little progress. For these anthropologists the most important task was to find ways to evaluate empirically the applicability of evolutionary theory to human social behavior and culture.

The theoretical view of human social behavior and culture these researchers sought to test can be summarized as follows (see Alexander 1979, Irons 1979b). The human psychological apparatus—emotions, basic motivations, learning and decision-making abilities—are products of past evolution. They have been selected to maximize the reproduction of the individual's genes by guiding behavior toward forms that best promoted that goal in past environments. Maximizing the reproduction of the individual's genes is usually referred to with phrases like *pursuing, or serving, reproductive interests.*

Human beings have extensive abilities to learn and to process large amounts of information about their environments. This is an evolved adaptation for changing behavior as environments change and molding behavior to what best promotes the individual's reproductive interests. The psychological mechanisms that guide behavior, however, do not take the form of conscious awareness of, and striving for, reproductive ends. Rather they take the form of a conscious striving for *intermediate goals,* such as getting enough to eat, gaining prestige and a good reputation with one's associates, gaining mates, and nurturing children. These goals actually cause the individual to behave in ways that best suit reproductive interests if the individual's environment is sufficiently similar to the environments of evolution.

This theoretical view leads to two broad predictions that anthropologists can test in traditional societies. The first is simply the prediction that *individuals will behave in ways that best suit their reproductive interests.* The second is the prediction that people will *try to influence the social rules* and other aspects of their culture in such a way as to promote their reproductive interests. Thus, the rules governing behavior in a particular society will tend to assume a form that serves the reproductive interests of those who are best able to influence the continual renegotiation of rules.

Since 1975, anthropologists who accepted this view have produced an extensive literature. Much of this consists of explicit hypothesis testing. The underlying methodology of this work is basically the same as that employed by biologists, psychologists, and primatologists who study animal social behavior in evolutionary terms. This is a methodology not shared by many of the anthropologists who initially had a strong negative reaction to sociobiology. For extensive reviews of this literature see Betzig et al. 1988, Borgerhoff Mulder, in press, Cronk in press b, Irons in press, and Gray 1985. In a recent brief assessment, Monique Borgerhoff Mulder (1988b) attempted to count up all the empirical studies found in this literature. She limited her count to empirical quantitative studies that address hypotheses derived from evolutionary theory with data from traditional societies—that is, the types of societies usually studied by anthropologists. The total count came to 163. This was in 1988; since then, the number of studies of this sort has continued to grow.

Of course, the quantity of studies by itself proves relatively little. What is more important is the *quality* of these studies. How rigorous are they? How strong is the support they provide for the idea that human behavior and culture are influenced in important ways by evolved behavioral propensities? What sort of new insight do these studies offer? To provide an answer to these questions, I review below a representative sample of empirical studies. I will begin with studies focused on a very simple hypothesis that addresses the question of reproductive strivings in a very direct way.

CULTURAL AND BIOLOGICAL SUCCESS

In all human societies, there are culturally defined goals for which people strive. Common examples of these things are wealth, status, and reputation. Exactly what is defined as worth striving for varies from society to society, but nevertheless in any society some such culturally defined goals are conspicuous. People who accomplish these goals are defined in terms of the local culture as successful. A straightforward prediction from "selection thinking" is that whatever is defined as worth striving for, in a particular society, should be a resource for reproductive success in that society.

This was first suggested as a general hypothesis in 1976 and tested in a series of papers that analyze the effect of wealth on reproduction among the Yomut Turkmen of northern Iran (Irons 1976, 1979a, 1980). The Yomut Turkmen are an ethnic minority who until recently were not effectively controlled by the Iranian government. They live traditionally by raising sheep and goats and cultivating wheat and barley. Until recently most of them spoke only their own language, Turkmen, and literacy was limited to about 1 to 2 percent of the population who were religious teachers.

The general method of analysis suggested was to identify in a particular society some goal—wealth, status, or whatever—that was seen as worth striving for in that society. Then an attempt should be made to demonstrate empirically that accomplishing this goal would, on average, enhance on individual's reproductive success. In the case of the Yomut Turkmen, the goal identified was the accumulation of wealth in agricultural land and livestock. The prediction was that wealthier people would have higher reproductive success. Reproductive success means not just having many children, but also having children who survive at a higher rate. Survey data collected in 1973-74 were used to test this prediction. The families in the survey were ranked according to the monetary value of their total wealth in land and livestock. Using this ranking list, I divided the population into the "wealthy half" and the "poor half."

The author, Bill Irons, and Turkmen friend, in front of the latter's home, in 1970.

Birthrates were calculated for men and women in both halves of the population. Both wealthier men and wealthier women were shown to have higher birthrates, although the difference was much greater for men, owing to the fact that more wealthy men were polygynous. Next, rates of survival of children born in each half of the population were calculated, and it was shown that both boys and girls had a higher chance of surviving to adulthood in the wealthier half of the population. The overall effect of these differences in birth and death rates was that the men in the wealthier half of the population were reproducing at a rate 1.75 times that of their poorer counterparts. Wealthier women were reproducing at 1.12 times the rate of poorer women. Thus the initial prediction was confirmed. (At this point, I wish to emphasize that this research result has no "eugenic" implications. It does not say that it is good that wealthier Turkmen reproduce at a higher rate. Nor does it say that they are reproducing at a higher rate because they have "better genes." Rather the question is simply: are they striving for things that will enhance their reproduction or not?)

I grant that the association between reproductive success and culturally defined success does not prove definitively that striving for wealth causes higher reproductive success. Research of this sort does not strive for proof in the sense of banishing all possible doubt. Rather, the goal is to formulate predictions that can be falsified or confirmed and then to use appropriate data to test these predictions. If many such tests are carried out, and a high proportion of these tests confirm a hypothesis, then one can infer that the hypothesis is probably correct. The more numerous the tests, the more carefully they are done, and the greater the proportion of confirming results, the more probable the correctness of the hypothesis.

The above test was only a first step. Of course, more tests were necessary before much could be said. There are many reasons why the above associations could occur other that the one suggested by the hypothesis that people choose goals that serve their fitness interests. Maybe Yomut who happen to have many children become wealthy because child labor is an important source of wealth. Maybe the culturally defined goals of traditional societies vary randomly with respect to their effect on reproduction, and the Yomut happen by chance to be one of the societies where cultural goals do serve reproductive interests.

In later work, I ruled out the first possibility (Irons 1980). As to the second possibility, studies done in a number of other traditional societies make it seem highly unlikely (Barkow 1977; Borgerhoff Mulder 1987; Chagnon, Flinn, and Melancon 1979, 1988; Cronk in press a; Flinn 1986; Kaplan and Hill 1985; Turke and Betzig 1985). All of these tested the same basic hypothesis. They analyzed ways in which birth and death rates are affected by achieving such goals as wealth, high status, or some other culturally defined form of success. In each case the demographic and other data used were gathered by the researchers themselves and analyzed in some depth in terms of the ethnographer's knowledge of a society they studied first-hand. Thus, these were all in-depth studies within single societies. In addition there is a cross-cultural study that supports this hypothesis. Laura Betzig (1986) used the Human Relations Area File to test the hypothesis that in more stratified societies—societies in which power and wealth are more unequally distributed—powerful men will have larger harems. (The Human Relations Area File is a file that organizes the data contained in several hundred ethnographies so that it can be readily analyzed for statistical associations among the variables that commonly are recorded in such ethnographies.) Her sample included 104 societies and showed a consistent cross-cultural tendency in traditional societies for powerful men to monopolize access to large numbers of women. (See Chapter 7, "History," this volume.)

As is often the case, research does as much to raise new questions as it does to answer old ones. The above hypothesis has been tested in more modern societies as well, and here the results are less consistently supportive of the above hypotheses. (See Irons, in press, for references to these studies.) These less consistent results suggest that modern environments are less similar to those of human evolution in terms of the variables relevant to cultural goals and reproduction, and that the result is that behavior is less consistently reproductively advantageous (compare Irons 1979, 272). It should be noted, however, that even here most studies yielded a positive correlation between cultural success and reproductive success. Some of the anthropologists involved in the above research are looking into the precise nature of the environmental changes that lead evolved mechanism off track. Betzig is looking into the origin of socially imposed monogamy, and Turke is researching the reasons for modern fertility reduction (Turke 1989).

NEPOTISM

A very basic prediction of evolutionary theory is that human beings should be nepotistic (Alexander 1974), that is, they should be more helpful and less competitive in dealing with others to the extent that they share genes by recent common descent (or "share close genealogical ties," as anthropologists say). This is a straightforward application of "Hamilton's Rule" (Hamilton 1964) to human beings, and it has been extensively confirmed. Chagnon supplied the first dramatic confirmation of this prediction in his analysis of Yanomamo marriage and politics (Chagnon 1975, 1979a) and in his analysis with Paul E. Bugos of a particular Yanomamo fight for which very detailed data was available (Chagnon and Bugos 1979). Kristen Hawkes (1977) supplied another early test of this prediction in her analysis of assistance in gardening among the Binumarien of Highland New Guinea. Other early tests of this prediction include Susan Essock-Vitale and Michael McGuire's (1980) analysis of nepotism and reciprocity, using data gathered in thirteen different social settings.

The study of a fight in a Yanomamo village analyzed by Chagnon and Bugos has become something of a classic, and it can serve to illustrate the logic of studies of nepotism. The data in this case consisted of a filmed record of a fight, which, like most human squabbles everywhere, had a complex plot and a soap-opera-like character. The basic source of conflict was that a group of visitors from another village were overstaying their welcome. These visitors had close relatives among the village residents. Yanomamo custom says the villagers should feed the visitors out of their garden; custom also says that visitors should leave after a respectable interval. The villagers thought it was time for them to go. The visitors, however, were trying to call on their status as relatives to justify a longer stay. In the midst of these growing tensions, one of the visitors, Mohesiwa, met a woman on a trail to the village carrying a load of plantains for her family. He demanded she give him some as a guest. She refused. He beat her. She ran screaming to the village. Her half-brother Uuwa rushed to the center of the village hurling insults at Mohesiwa and threatening him with a large club. Mohesiwa came to the center of the village to respond in kind. A minor scuffle ensued, and supporters of each man gathered at their respective sides. Mohesiwa's mother and sister flung especially colorful insults at Uuwa while the two groups of men engaged in a glaring contest while holding their menacing weapons ready. Finally, each group of men retired to their respective houses (consisting of lean-tos) on the edge of the village circle.

The fight appeared to be over, but at this point the husband of the beaten woman and his brother rushed across the village brandishing a machete and an ax. A confusing struggle ensued, and a large number of men came rushing to aid one side or the other. Now they came with axes and machetes and exchanged a number of crushing blows with the blunt sides of these weapons. The fighting subsided with a young man knocked unconscious on the ground and his mother stroking his arms and crying. Meanwhile, the two groups of men glared at each other some more while everyone wondered if the young man was dead. He regained consciousness and was helped to his hammock. Eventually the men returned to their houses to cool their tempers, while the women of each group hurled more colorful insults at each other. The next day, some of the visitors went home. Any reader should be able to recognize the underlying dynamics of a typical category of fight among individuals who have many complaints about one another. (Despite the exotic context and ways of expression of disagreement, the underlying struggle is remarkably like that of a barroom fight or a verbal squabble in a department of anthropology.)

The filmmaker, Timothy Asch, who was accompanying Chagnon to make ethnographic films, recorded the entire sequence of events, and Chagnon had already collected a complete record of all the remembered genealogical and marriage ties among the participants. Clearly there were data here to test the general proposition that people are nepotistic. The costs in terms of risk and injury would be roughly comparable for all participants. The benefit in terms of protecting an ally and enhanced reputation would also be roughly comparable. But some individuals were more closely related genetically to one antagonist than to the other. Did this difference in relatedness make a difference? The answer that emerged from the data was that genetic closeness made a definite difference. Those who rushed to Mohesiwa's aid were more closely related to him, and the same was true of Uuwa's supporters. Marriage ties also made a difference. Individuals also had a tendency to support those to whom they were allied by marriage (and to whom their children were therefore closely related).

To many, these results will seem mere common sense. We know from personal experience that people support their kin in our own society and find it unsurprising when members of an exotic society do the same. Anthropological thinking at the time, however, had moved away from common sense. To anthropologists, expecting Yanomamo to act according to our commonsense expectations was a form of Western ethnocentrism. Yanomamo feelings about social distance could be expected to follow a very different set of ideas about who is close and distant. Much of this feeling was butressed by the knowledge that groups like the Yanomamo label their kin very differently. A man among the Yanomamo has many "fathers" and "mothers." A father's brother among the Yanomamo is not an uncle labeled in a way that indicates he is more distant than a father. Rather, he is labeled the same way as another "father." In a similar fashion, many of the father's cousins, including ones we would consider distant kin, are also labeled "father." Likewise, a Yanomamo has many "mothers," "brothers," and "sisters." Some of these "mothers," "brothers," and "sisters" are genealogically close; others are quite distant.

In fact none of the basic kin terms in Yanomamo distinguish genealogically close from distant kin. To Sahlins (1976), these classifications of kin are real plans for social action and they have nothing to do with genealogical distance or portions of genes shared. In a category such as "father," there would be one's biological father sharing half of one's genes, but also very distant kin sharing only a small fraction of one's genes, and even possibly a few individuals to whom one was not tied by known genealogy at all. Hence, the real plan for social action implied that our commonsense expectations about social distance and Yanomamo expectations would be very different. Most anthropologists at that time agreed with Sahlins. Thus, the results Chagnon got were more surprising to anthropologists than the layperson might expect.

It is true that the way Yanomamo label kin has nothing to do with coefficients of relatedness as understood by evolutionary biologists. Rather, they have to do almost exclusively with who can and cannot marry whom, and who can arrange whose marriage. But when it comes to a fight, the real plan for social action, and social action itself, go in a quite different direction. Even though kin terms do not label genealogical distance, people do know their genealogies, and these provide a large part of their plan for social action when it's time to take sides in a fight. The result is that an evolved propensity to be nepotistic in the sociobiological sense played a much bigger role in the events described above than Sahlins (1976) would lead one to believe. The spur to do the anlaysis in the first place came from evolutionary theory, and, in my estimation, it served as a valuable corrective to the anthropological thinking of the time.

As with the issue of cultural and reproductive success discussed above, the inference in favor of evolutionary theory does not rest on a single study. Chagnon did a number of other analyses of data on a large body of Yanomamo data. For example, he was able to show that Yanomamo villages in which the average portion of genes shared among residents is low are very likely to split into smaller, often hostile groups, and that those who stay together when the split occurs are those who are more closely related (Chagnon 1975). The result is that the new, smaller villages have a higher average relatedness (portion of genes shared by recent common descent) and much less internal conflict. Also, a large number of studies in other societies have uncovered the same tendency to be nepotistic (see Borgerhoff Mulder, in press; Gray 1985; Cronk in press b; and Irons, in press, for discussion of these other studies). In my opinion, this tendency to be nepotistic regardless of cultural background is extremely well-documented; so much so that it can be considered a fact rather than a theory.

Philip Kitcher (1985) and others have offered the criticism that studies such as the above prove nothing that commonsense does not already tell us. Blood is thicker that water, as everybody knows. However, there is a problem with Kitcher's criticism. The commonsense belief that blood is thicker than water is not reflected in the wisdom of social scientists. Over several years, I have made a habit of checking anthropology textbooks and have yet to find in any of them any mentions of a widespread human tendency to be nepotistic. The same is true of psychology and sociology textbooks. I might also note that in the late 1970s, when the controversy about sociobiology was at its noisiest, I was often invited to debate the issue in one context or another. A frequent challenge from social scientists in those debates was that well-known "facts" about homicide did not fit the expectations of kin selection theory. It was well known that people are more frequently murdered by family members than by strangers. Did not that show that people were not nepotists? Where was the commonsense knowledge that blood is thicker than water when those challenges were made? Interestingly enough, Martin Daly and Margo Wilson have now shown in their book *Homicide* (1988) that the frequencies with which people kill kin and non-kin *do* fit the expectations of evolutionary theory. I invite the reader to have a look at their interpretation.

PARENTAL AND MATING STRATEGIES

Closely connected to the issue of nepotism in general is the issue of *parenting*, and the related issue of *mating*. After all, the most widespread form of kin altruism, or nepotism, among humans consists of the large amount of effort that people put into child rearing. Evolutionary theory makes a number of predictions about parenting. It predicts (1) that individuals will evolve to invest in their own and not others' offspring, (2) that they will invest more in those offspring that can be predicted to be more successful reproductively, and (3) that parents will terminate investments in particular offspring when the probable success of the offspring is sufficiently low to outweigh the costs of child rearing. Evolutionary theory also makes predictions about mate choice that have to do with the choosers' prospects for reproduction. For example, it predicts (according to Darwin's theory of sexual selection) that males may choose to mate promiscuously, in hopes of having the largest possible number of offspring, while females may mate "discriminately" in hopes of rearing a few high-quality offspring. In other words, parental strategies and mating strategies are closely interwoven in sociobiological research. This may be noted below in the discussions of paternity confidence and bridewealth.

Paternity Confidence. One of the sociobiological studies of particular significance for anthropology has been that of the effect of paternity doubts on parenting efforts. In his seminal 1974 article, Richard Alexander suggested that in societies where extramarital sex and divorce are widespread, men will react to the lowered probability that their wives' children are their own by investing less effort in rearing their wives' children and more in rearing their sisters' children. This will occur because, if paternity misassignment is common enough, men will on average be more related to their sisters' children than to children borne by their wives. This prediction has been tested empirically and confirmed by Steven Gaulin and Alice Schlegel (1980) and by Mark Flinn (1981). This issue is especially interesting because it suggests that a variation in individual reproductive strategies may underlie the cultural difference between what anthropologists have labeled "matrilineal" and "patrilineal" societies.

This again was a case where research opened up questions as well as answered them. Much of the above discussion is based on the assumption that when only a fraction of a wife's children are her husband's, a man will prefer aiding his sister's children because they are, on average, genetically closer to him. However, this is true only when approximately three out of four of a wife's children are not her husband's (Alexander 1974). It would not seem that a society-wide average of misassignment of paternity would often be that high. Why then did Gaulin and Schlegel (1980) and Flinn (1981) get the results they did? Hartung (1985) provided a good answer. He pointed out that the aid in question for the most part is inheritance of property. Where a man's property goes when he dies is rarely something he decides himself. Rather such things are decided by society-wide rules. These rules are negotiated over time by many people and are likely to reflect the interests of many people. If even a minimal number of a man's wife's children are not his own, then his mother, brothers, and sisters are more related to his sisters' children than to his wife's. Thus, formal rules saying that sisters' children, rather than wife's children, should inherit wealth reflect the interests of these people rather than the interests of the man himself. Hartung (1985) found support for this interpretation in more refined analyses of data from the Human Relations Area Files.

Adoption. The issue of adoption has received less attention but is nevertheless relevant as a special topic related to parenting. As noted above, Sahlins in his 1976 book, *The Use and Abuse of Biology,* suggested that the widespread practice of adoption in Polynesia constituted a *prima facie* discon-firmation of the prediction that people are nepotistic. Joan Silk (1980, 1990) took a closer look at adoption in Polynesia and pointed out that this argument is not persuasive. She found, among other things, that in Polynesia children are usually adopted by close relatives (uncles, aunts, and grandparents). They do not, as a result, sever ties with their biological parents and in fact usually continue to reside with their parents. Adopted children usually leave their biological parents to live with their adoptive parents only when their natural parents have many children and few resources and their adoptive parents have few children and many resources. Other than Silk's 1980 and a more general study (Silk 1990), there has been little empirical work on adoption from an evolutionary point of view. (See chapter 6, "Primatology," this volume, for discussion on adoption among monkeys and apes.)

Bridewealth. Another issue that has been investigated is bridewealth. Borgerhoff Mulder (1987, 1988a, 1988b) has shown that, among the Kipsigis of Kenya, bridewealth can be seen as a reproductive strategy in the sense that higher bridewealth is paid for brides who can be predicted to have a higher reproductive success—namely, brides who are fatter than average and who mature earlier than average. In contrast, brides who have already produced children out of wedlock before marriage fetch lower bridewealth, since such brides offer their husbands lower reproductive opportunities. Borgerhoff Mulder has also been able to show that changes in bridewealth practices over time reflect changes in the circumstances affecting competition for brides. Recently, scarcities of land among the Kipsigis have limited opportunities for polygyny, and younger Kipsigis men are more often faced with the prospect of monogamy or at least limited polygyny. Given this, competition for the more desirable brides has increased as men have decided to—or been forced to—emphasize quality rather than quantity. The result has been an inflation in the bride-wealth paid for the most desirable brides, and an increse in the variance in bridewealth (Borgerhoff Mulder 1988b).

Additional Research. In addition to the topics discussed above, a number of other aspects of mating and parenting have been studied: birth spacing, incest, the effect of polygyny on women's reproduction, the effect of polygyny on inheritances rules. Reviews of these can be found in Borgerhoff Mulder (in press) and Cronk (in press b). Evolutionary anthropologists have also studied foraging strategies among hunters and gatherers, aggression, and culture change. I must emphasize that evolutionary anthropology is a changing and growing thing. In addition to doing more and more empirical studies of the sort above, evolutionary anthropologists also argue among themselves and with other evolutionary social scientists about the future direction of research. One suggestion that is much discussed at the moment is that future research should pay more detailed attention to *proximate* psychological mechanisms (Cosmides and Tooby 1989). Another possible new direction for future work will probably consist of attempts to evaluate "dual inheritance" models of the sort developed by Robert Boyd and Peter Richerson (1985). These are also known as gene–culture models (see chapter 12, "Socioecology of Religion," this volume).

ACCOMPLISHMENTS OF
SOCIOBIOLOGICAL ANTHROPOLOGY

The empirical work cited above supports a number of novel statements about human behavior. Some examples are the following: (1) Striving for culturally defined goals is a means of enhancing reproduction, (2) people are everywhere nepo-tistic, (3) lowered paternity confidence encourages the development of social rules favoring relatives through female links such as matrilateral inheritance of property, and (4) many social institutions—such as inheritance rules, dowry, and bridewealth—are, in effect, instruments for enhancing inclusive fitness. These statements are all sufficiently novel that they have not yet found their way into standard textbooks in anthropology, psychology, or other human sciences.

Sahlins's statement, that human sociobiology was likely to disappear soon after the initial excitement generated by Wilson's 1975 book, has not turned out to be correct. Instead, as we have seen, a number of anthropologists have taken up the task of evaluating the use of evolutionary theory to illuminate anthropological issues. The literature they have produced as a result of their efforts contains a large number of empirical studies. Despite this empirical thrust, however, the "image" of human sociobiology is (or at least until recently was) that it is speculative. See, for example, the third edition of Nelson and Jurmain's *Introduction to Physical Anthropology*, (1985, 305, 548) for a statement to the effect that sociobiology is largely a matter of speculation.

In my estimation, the research summarized above carries us beyond the realm of speculation and, judging by the methodological standards applied to other types of anthropological research, evolutionary anthropology has a very solid empirical basis. This is not to say that the issues have been resolved definitively or that the quality of evolutionary research could not be enhanced. There are many open questions, and there is much room for improvement. Nevertheless, something important has been accomplished.

5

Economics

Robert H. Frank

═══════════════════════════════════════

Economics is the study of choice under scarcity. "Economic behavior" is predicted by economists on the basis of theories about human motivation and human nature. In the early days of the science of economics, in the eighteenth century, it was customary to offer theoretical explanations about people's regard for others in economic transactions. Adam Smith, for example, wrote *A Theory of the Moral Sentiments* in 1759 (though he is better known for his later idea of the "invisible hand of the marketplace"). In this earlier work he argued that the central motivating force was each person's desire to please an "impartial spectator." In the twentieth century, however, *rational self-interest* has come to be accepted by economists as the leading, or even the sole, explanation for economic behavior and individual decision making.

Economists nowadays like to think of themselves as the most hardheaded of social scientists. Richard Posner, for example, the author of a major reference work, *Economic Analysis of Law* (1972), speaks only of costs and benefits. He and his followers are skeptical of any nonmaterial motives in human economic behavior. Motives that actually *conflict* with the quest for material gain are viewed with particular suspicion. Posner speaks, for example, with thinly veiled contempt about woolly legal notions like "fairness" and "justice," which he calls "terms which have no content" (Barrett, 1986, 1).

I believe that the Posnerians are indeed "hardheaded"— but not in the sense they mean! On issues such as fairness they are merely stubborn, for they refuse to acknowledge compelling evidence that *fairness is an extremely powerful source of human motivation.* In this chapter, I present some of that evidence and offer my own explanation for it. I outline a "commitment model" as opposed to the "self-interest model," as a predictor of economic behavior. This could be done without reference to sociobiological theory—using, for instance, game theory. However, I believe that when the commitment model is explained in terms of the evolution of certain emotions, it gains extra credibility.

The reader may note that there is a paradox here. The caricature of the sociobiological view of the individual (animal or human) has been that the individual is doggedly self-interested. But a closer look at sociobiology reveals that there is room for other interpretations, including the interpretation that some human behavior is genuinely noble. In this chapter, I first describe "fair transactions" and analyze why people take fairness so seriously. Second, I show how certain emotions give people an unexpected advantage in economic and other transactions. Last, I describe statistical movements in populations, in which the proportion of cooperators and cheaters (or "defectors") changes—and show how this can, apparently, bring *honesty* into being.

WHAT IS A FAIR TRANSACTION?

Fairness almost always refers to the terms of a transaction (not necessarily an economic one) that occurs between people. Some of the economist's terminology is as follows. A *transaction* occurs when two parties exchange something. A gives B a dollar, B gives A a pineapple. When a transaction takes place voluntarily, it is assumed that both parties benefit. We infer that the pineapple is worth more than a dollar to A (else he would not have bought it), less than a dollar to B (else he would not have sold it).

In any transaction, there is a *reservation price* for both the buyer and seller. For the buyer, it is the most she would have paid. Had she been charged more, she would have walked away from the transaction. The seller's reservation price is the smallest amount he would have accepted. The *surplus* from any transaction is the difference between the buyer's and seller's reservation prices. In the pineapple example, if these reservation prices are, say, $1.20 and $0.80 respectively, the resulting surplus is forty cents.

The traditional economic model says that exchange will occur if, and only if, there is a positive surplus—that is, if and only if the buyer's reservation price exceeds the seller's. Whenever an exchange does occur, the total surplus is divided between the buyer and seller. For the particular values assumed in the pineapple illustration, the surplus was allocated equally, both parties receiving twenty cents, or 50 percent of the total.

In the self-interest model of economic behavior, the reservation price for one party to a transaction is defined independently of the circumstances of the other. It makes no difference to the seller whether the buyer is rich or poor; nor does the buyer care how much the seller might have paid for the thing he is now trying to sell. This theory seems to think of people as though they were conducting all of their business with vending or purchasing machines. Each transactor is viewed in isolation, facing a take-it-or-leave-it decision that depends only on what the product itself is worth to him.

I believe, by contrast, that people are interested in the fairness of the transactions. A fair transaction could be defined as one in which the surplus is divided approximately equally. In the pineapple example I said that the pineapple is *worth* $1.20 to the buyer—that is his reservation price. The decision as to how "badly" he wants the pineapple, however, may include not only such things as his state of hunger or the limitations of his shopping time, but may incorporate his feelings about the fairness of the price. If he thinks the seller is acting unfairly—that the seller is getting the lion's share of the surplus—he may give up the chance to buy the desired pineapple. Indeed, people often *do* reject such transactions even though the price at which the product is offered is equal to, or even less than, their hypothetical reservation price. (Note that in the self-interest model this can never happen.)

People's concern with the fairness of transactions can be studied in various ways. Thaler administered the following question to two groups of businessmen:

> You are lying on the beach on a hot day. . . . For the past hour
> you have been thinking about how much you would enjoy a
> nice cold bottle of your favorite brand of beer. A companion
> gets up to make a phone call and offers to bring back a beer
> from the only nearby place where beer is sold [either a fancy
> resort hotel or a run-down grocery store]. He asks how much
> you would be willing to pay for the beer [and says] if it costs
> more than the price you state he will not buy it. (Thaler 1985,
> 206)

For half of his subjects, Thaler inserted the word "fancy resort
hotel" and for the other half "run-down grocery store."

The self-interest model states unequivocally that the price
offered should not depend on who is selling the beer. Yet the
median response for the resort hotel group ($2.65) was over a
dollar more than for the grocery store group ($1.50). Drinking
the beer, apparently, is "worth" $2.65 to the former, yet the latter
would refuse to pay even $2.00 for it—even though both are
equally thirsty. It appears that the resort hotel, having higher
operating costs than the grocery store, has a correspondingly
higher reservation price for its beer. Thus even though it
charges a higher price, it does not command a larger share
of the surplus. The "fair price" at the resort hotel is higher than
at the grocery, in the eyes of the buyer. This, I believe, is the
likely explanation for the different answers that Thaler
received.

"ULTIMATUM BARGAINING" EXPERIMENTS

Reservation prices are often difficult to determine in practice,
but it is possible to design experiments that remove all
uncertainty about them. German economists Werner Guth,
Rolf Schmittberger, and Bernd Schwarze (1982) have followed
this strategy in a series of provocative studies. One of their
experiments, the so-called "ultimatum bargaining game,"
provides an elegant test of the self-interest model.

The game is played a single time by pairs of subjects who
do not know one another. Player 1 in each pair is given a sum
of money and asked to divide it between himself and Player
2. He must propose an allocation, which Player 2 must then
either accept or refuse. If he accepts, they divide the money

as proposed. If he refuses, however, neither player gets any money at all. Thus, for example, if Player 1 proposes to divide ten dollars by allocating three dollars to Player 2 and the remaining seven dollars to himself, Player 2 can either accept, in which case Player 1 gets seven dollars and he gets three dollars, or he can refuse, in which case each gets nothing. Player 1's proposal is an ultimatum, hence the name of the game.

All of the relevant reservation prices and surpluses are transparently clear in the ultimatum bargaining game. The total surplus is simply the amount of money the two players have to divide. Player 2's reservation price, as reckoned by the traditional self-interest model, is the smallest possible positive amount, namely one cent. Since this is obvious to both players, the "rational" strategy for Player 1 is also clear: he should offer Player 2 a penny and keep the rest for himself. It is similarly rational for Player 2 to accept—he knows they will not be playing this game repeatedly, so there is no point refusing the offer in hopes of establishing a tough reputaion. The experimenters have neatly contrived a pure one-shot bargaining problem with which to test the rational theory of bargaining.

The findings from one version of this experiment (in which the game was played fifty-one times) are as follows. Just over a quarter of Player 1s (25.5%)—a very large share—proposed a fifty-fifty split. The *average* Player 1 proposed to keep two-thirds of the money for himself. In short, Player 1 rarely employed the rational strategy. That is, he almost never proposed an extremely one-sided division. In only six of the fifty-one cases (that is 11.8%) did Player 1 demand more than 90% of the total.

The response of the Player 2s was equally interesting. More than one-fifth of the time (21.5%) they turned down the offer—which means they got nothing where they could at least have got something. They responded not as Posnerian rationalists but in the manner predicted by the fairness model. In fully five out of six of the cases in which Player 1 claimed an egregiously large share for himself (more than nine dollars), Player 2 refused to take his "pittance."

The Punishment Motive

In a somewhat different experiment, Kahneman, Knetsch, and Thaler (1986) explored the motivation for making fair offers. Player 1 was asked to divide twenty dollars between himself and an anonymous Player 2. He was limited to these two choices: (1) ten dollars for each; or (2) eighteen dollars for himself, two dollars for Player 2. This time, Player 2 did not have the option of rejecting Player 1's proposal. Player 2 got either two or ten dollars, depending solely on Player 1's choice. Assurance was given that Player 2s would not learn the identities of Player 1s.

Out of 161 subjects, 122, or 76 percent, proposed the even split. Since the design of the experiment completely eliminated both fear of rejection and any threat of retaliation, Kahneman et al. conclude that an intrinsic concern about fairness was the primary motive for these allocations.

Some uncertainty surrounds Player 2's motives for rejecting a onesided offer. An obvious possibility is that he wishes to punish Player 1 for being greedy. Or perhaps he just wants to avoid participating in an unfair transaction. To find out more about what drives Player 2, Kahneman et al. conducted a second stage to the preceding experiment. In the follow-up stage, subjects selected from the first stage were placed in groups of three. Each group contained at least one subject of each type from the first stage—that is, one who picked the even split (E) and another who chose the uneven split (U).

The third member of each group was then given the following choice: he could either divide twelve dollars evenly with U, or else divide ten dollars evenly with E. Most of the subjects (74%) chose to split ten dollars with E. Most people, in other words, were willing to incur a cost of one dollar in order to punish U and reward E. Of the subjects who had themselves chosen the ten-ten split in the first stage, an even larger percentage (88%) chose this more costly option in the second stage. Kahneman et al. conclude that the motive for rejecting unfair offers must be at least in part to punish those who make them.

IT PAYS TO BE IRRATIONAL

So now let us try to explain *why* people are concerned with fairness. It could of course be due to cultural conditioning:

children are raised with the ideal of fairness. But it is at least worth considering that the predisposition to fairness is innate.

Let me first discuss the word *irrational*. I mean it as the opposite of *rational* in the sense in which one is said to do the rational thing by calculating his self-interest. Some of the Player 2s mentioned above acted irrationally—they refused to garner the ten cents, or one dollar, or whatever happened to be the "unfair" amount proffered. We might say they acted emotionally, passionately, or irrationally—based on some sense of anger, envy, or disgust toward Player 1. If in fact this is a correct assessment—that they are acting emotionally—how is it that such "harmful" emotions (harmful in the sense of causing one to act against one's rational interest) could have evolved?

I believe it is easy to see that the having of irrational behaviors can be beneficial overall, as long as one is *known* to have them. Consider the following three types of behaviors— vengeful, envious, and guilt-ridden. Possession of these traits— and advertisement of them—can help a person fare better in his dealings with others.

Vengeance. First, consider a person who threatens to retaliate against anyone who harms him. For his threat to deter, others must believe he will carry it out. But if others know that the costs of retaliation are prohibitive, they will realize the threat is empty. Unless, of course, they believe they are dealing with someone who simply *likes* to retaliate. Such a person may strike back even when it is not in his material interest to do so. Furthermore, if he is known in advance to have that preference, he is not likely to be tested by aggression in the first place.

Envy. Second, a person who is known to "dislike" an unfair bargain can credibly threaten to walk away from one, even when it is in her narrow interest to accept it. By virtue of being known to have this preference, she becomes a more effective negotiator. (Her irrationality could be based either on envy of the other party, or on a sense of offended justice.)

Guilt. Third, consider the person who "feels bad" when he cheats. These feelings can accomplish for him what a rational assessment of self-interest cannot—namely, they can cause him to behave honestly even when he *knows* he could get away with cheating. If *others* realize he feels this way, they will seek him as a partner in ventures that require trust, whereas they will steer clear of known cheaters.

In sum, being known to experience certain emotions enables us to make *commitments* that would otherwise not be credible. The clear irony here is that this ability, which springs from a *failure* to pursue self-interest, confers genuine advantages. Granted, following through on these commitments will involve avoidable losses—not cheating when there is a chance to, retaliating at great cost even after the damage is done, and so on. The problem, however, is that being unable to make credible commitments will often be even *more* costly.

I will return later to the important point that *being known* to have tendencies *not* to follow self-interst can in fact confer genuine advantages. Economists have long noted the paradox that in many situations, *the conscious pursuit of self-interest is incompatible with its attainment.* (In part, I build on an idea from Thomas Schelling's 1960 book, *The Strategy of Conflict*.) My thesis is that specific emotions act as "commitment devices" to help us solve certain dilemmas that cannot be solved by rational action.

For the remainder of this chapter I show (1) how emotions act as primary incentives or "proximate causes", (2) the importance of emotions as cues to people's behavioral predispositions, and (3) the circumstances under which unopportunistic behavior can come to prevail in a population.

EMOTIONS AS PRIMARY INCENTIVES

I use the term *commitment model* as shorthand for the notion that seemingly irrational economic behavior is sometimes explained by emotional predispositions that help solve commitment problems. Material incentives at any given moment may prompt people to behave in ways *contradictory* to their ultimate material interests. One way to solve this is to alter the relevant material interests, but this is often impractical. Fortunately, though, there is an alternative approach. Material incentives are by no means the only force that governs behavior—in fact they play no *direct* role in motivation anyway. Rather, behavior is directly guided by a complex psychological reward mechanism.

The system that governs food intake provides a clear illustration of this mechanism. Man or beast, an individual does not eat in response to a rational calculation about food intake. Instead, a complex of biological forces causes it to "feel hungry" when its stomach contents, blood sugar level, and other nutritional indexes fall below various threshold values. To "feel hungry" is to experience a subjective sensation of displeasure in the central nervous system. Experience, and perhaps even inborn neural circuits, tell us that food intake will relieve this sensation.

In a proximate sense, this is *why* we eat. There is a material payoff to eating, to be sure. Any organism that did not eat obviously would not be favored by natural selection. The important point is that the relevant material payoffs are more likely to be realized if eating is motivated directly through the reward mechanism. Intense feelings of hunger, apparently, are more expedient than rational reflections about caloric intake for motivating a starving individual to focus on the most important threat to its survival.

The fit between the behaviors favored by the reward mechanism and those favored by rational calculation is at best imperfect. The reward mechanism provides rules of thumb that work well much of the time but not in all cases. Indeed, when environmental conditions differ substantially from the ones under which the reward mechanism evolved, important conflicts often arise. Again, the reward system governing food intake provides a convenient illustration. It is now believed that food shortages were a common occurrence during most of evolutionary history. Under such conditions, it paid to have a reward mechanism that favored heavy food intake whenever abundant food was available. People thus motivated would be more likely to fatten up as a hedge against periods of famine. In modern industrial societies, however, people are much more likely to die of heart attacks than of starvation. A rational calculation of self-interest currently dictates that we stay slim. This calculation, needless to say, is at war, often on the losing side, with the reward mechanism.

In short, feelings and emotions are apparently the proximate causes of most behaviors. The biochemical workings of some of them—hunger, anger, fear, and mating urges, for example—are sufficiently well understood that they can be induced by electrical stimulation of specific brain sites. Others are less well mapped. Certain of the emotions—anger, contempt, disgust, envy, greed, shame, and guilt—were described by Adam Smith as moral sentiments. The reward theory of behavior tells us that these sentiments, like feelings of hunger, can and do compete with the feelings that spring from rational calculations about material payoffs. My thesis is that, for exactly this reason, they can help people solve the commitment problem.

It is clear, at any rate, that these sentiments can alter people's incentives in the desired ways. Consider, for example, a person capable of strong guilt feelings. This person will not cheat even when it is in her material interests to do so. The reason is not that she fears getting caught, but that she simply does not *want* to cheat. Her aversion to feelings of guilt effectively alters the payoffs she faces. It is not necessary to monitor such a person to prevent her from cheating (which thus avoids the problem that it may be impractical or impossible to monitor her anyway!). By the same token, someone who becomes enraged when dealt with unjustly does not need a formal contract to commit him to seek revenge. He will seek revenge because he *wants* to, even when, in purely material terms, it does not pay. His feelings of anger will offset his material incentives.

Commitment problems in close personal relationships, too, are likewise better solved by moral sentiments than by awkward formal contracts. The best insurance against a change in future material incentives is a strong bond of love. If ten years from now one partner falls victim to a lasting illness, the other's material incentives will be to find a new partner. But a deep bond of affection will render this change in incentives irrelevant. This security opens the door for current investments in the relationship that might otherwise be too risky.

EMOTIONS AS CUES TO BEHAVIORAL PREDISPOSITIONS

If we are to show that the emotions underwriting the commitment model evolved by natural selection, then we must show

how they work to the individual's advantage. The potential gain from being honest, as alluded to earlier, is to be able to cooperate with others who are also honest. In order for the noncheater to benefit in material terms, others must thus be able to recognize her as such, and she, in turn, must be able to recognize other noncheaters. The impulse to seek revenge is likewise counterproductive unless others have some way of anticipating that one has it. The person in whom this sentiment resides unrecognized will fail to deter potential predators. For similar reasons, a sense of justice and the capacity to love will not yield material payoffs unless they can be somehow communicated clearly to others.

But how do people know that a person's feelings commit him to behave honestly in the face of a golden opportunity to cheat? Or that he will seek revenge, even when it is too late to undo the injury he has suffered? Or that he really will walk away from an unfair bargain, even when he would do better by accepting it? It is insufficient merely to *declare* one's emotional predispositions ("I am honest. Trust me."), but subtle clues of facial expression, voice, and gesture often reveal them very clearly. This fact plays a central role in the workings of the commitment model.

A burgeoning literature describes how we draw inferences about people's feelings from subtle behavioral clues. Posture, the rate of respiration, the pitch and timbre of the voice, perspiration, facial muscle tone and expression, movement of the eyes, and a host of other signals guide us in this task. We quickly surmise, for example, that someone with clenched jaws and a purple face is enraged, even when we do not know what, exactly, may have triggered his anger. And we apparently know, even if we cannot articulate, how a forced smile differs from one that is heartfelt. At least partly on the basis of such clues, we form judgments about the emotional makeup of the people with whom we deal. Some people we feel we can trust, but of others we remain ever wary. Some we feel can be taken advantage of, others we know instinctively not to provoke.

Even a Dog Can Tell

One day over twenty years ago I attended a large and high-spirited political rally at Sproul Plaza on the Berkeley campus.

One young man, apparently lost to drugs, sat as still as a stone on the steps of the plaza, his face and eyes empty of expression. Presently a large Irish Setter appeared, sniffing his way through the crowd. He moved directly to the young man sitting on the steps and circled him once. He paused, lifted his leg, and, with no apparent malice, soaked the young man's back. He then set off again into the crowd. The boy barely stirred. This dog had apparently found it easy to locate the one person in that crowd who would not retaliate for being used as a fire hydrant. Facial expressions and other aspects of demeanor apparently provide clues to behavior that even dogs can interpret. None of us was really surprised when the boy did nothing. Before anything even happened, it was somehow *obvious* that he was just going to go right on sitting there.

It could be said that the boy's reaction was "rational." After all, once his shirt was soaked, it was already too late to undo the damage. And since he was unlikely ever to encounter that particular dog again, there was little point in trying to teach the dog a lesson. On the contrary, any attempt to do so would have courted the risk of being bitten. Our young man's problem was not that he failed to respond angrily, but that he failed to communicate to the dog that he was *predisposed* to do so. The vacant expression on his face was somehow all the dog needed to know he was a safe target. Merely by wearing "normal" expressions, the rest of us were spared.

HOW CAN UNOPPORTUNISTIC BEHAVIOR EVOLVE?

We have not yet considered how the emotional predispositions characteristic of the commitment model could have come about. Above, I argued that these predispositions are often beneficial. Those who are adept at *reading* the relevant signals (about honesty, for example) will be more successful than others, because they will know whom to trust. There is a payoff, also, to those who are able to *send* effective signals about their honesty: they will be trusted. Yet it is not so easy to say how these emotions could have got started. Let me show now how the behavior of cooperating could come eventually to prevail over the behavior of defecting. (By "defecting" I mean cheating, or abandoning an agreement.)

We may begin with a classical "Prisoner's Dilemma" example. Smith and Jones are each given an option to cooperate or defect, but neither of them can know what the other will choose (because each is sequestered in a prison cell). In the original Prisoner's Dilemma the choices had to do with accusing the other party of a crime or defending his innocence, but here I use a simple monetary payoff to illustrate the "dilemma." The four possible payoffs are shown in table 1. Both men are aware of how the game works and what the payoffs are.

		Smith	
		Defect	Cooperate
Jones	Defect	2 for each	0 for Smith 6 for Jones
	Cooperate	6 for Smith 0 for Jones	4 for each

Table 1. Monetary Payoffs in a Joint Venture

If Smith cooperates, and Jones does too, they each get 4 units. If Jones cooperates and Smith defects, Jones gets 0 and Smith gets 6. If they both defect they each get 2 units. Each is guided by the belief that the other will behave in a self-interested way. Jones must know that Smith would be reluctant to risk cooperation, because it *could* mean 0 units for him. So, he assumes Smith will take the safer option and defect—thus he (Jones) also opts to defect. The result is that they each get only a 2-unit payoff. The frustration is that both could easily have done better. If they had been able to predict cooperation in each other, they could each have gotten a 4-unit payoff.

Now suppose we have not just Smith and Jones but a large population. Pairs of people again form joint ventures, and the relationship between behavior and payoffs for the members of each pair is again as given in Table 1. Suppose further that everyone in the population is of one of two types—cooperator or defector. In this model, cooperators always refrain from cheating—even when there is no possibility of being detected. Viewed in the narrow context of the choice at hand, such behavior is clearly contrary to their material interests. Defectors, by contrast, are pure opportunists. They always make whatever choice will maximize their personal payoff. Our task, again, is to determine what will happen when people from these two groups are thrown into a survival struggle against one another. The key to the survival of cooperators, we will see, is for them to devise some means of identifying one another, thereby to interact selectively and avoid exploitation with defectors. But the first step in the argument is to investigate what happens when voluntary, selective interaction is not possible.

Population Movements when Cooperators and Defectors Look Alike

Suppose, for argument's sake, that cooperators and defectors look exactly alike. Naturally, cooperators (and defectors, for that matter) would like nothing better than to pair with cooperators, but they have no way of choosing. Because everyone looks the same, they must take their chances. The expected payoffs to both defectors and cooperators therefore depend on the likelihood of pairing with a cooperator, which in turn *depends on the proportion of cooperators in the population.*

Suppose, for example, the population consists almost entirely of cooperators. A cooperator is then virtually certain to have a cooperator for a partner, and so expects a payoff of nearly 4 units. The rare defector in this population is similarly almost certain to get a cooperator for a partner, and can expect a payoff of nearly 6 units. (The defector's unlucky partner, of course, gets a payoff of zero, but his occasional misfortune does not significantly affect the average payoff for cooperators as a group.)

Alternatively, suppose the population consists of half cooperators, half defectors. Each person is then just as likely to pair with a defector as with a cooperator. Cooperators thus have equal chances of receiving either zero or 4 units, which gives them an average payoff of 2 units. Defectors, in turn, have equal chances of receiving 2 or 6 units, so their average payoff will be 4 units. In general, *the average payoffs for each type will rise with the proportion of cooperators in the population*— the cooperator's because he is less likely to be exploited by a defector, the defector's because he is more likely to find a cooperator he can exploit. The exact relationships for the particular payoffs assumed in this illustration are shown in figure 1.

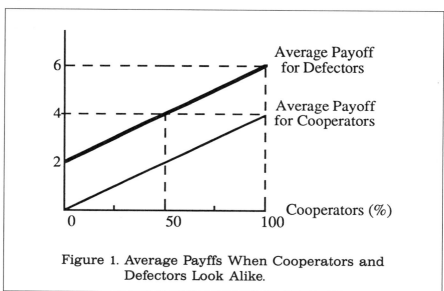

Figure 1. Average Payffs When Cooperators and
Defectors Look Alike.

When cooperators and defectors look exactly the same, how will the population evolve over time? In *evolutionary* models, each individual reproduces in proportion to its average payoff: those with larger material payoffs have the resources necessary to raise larger numbers of offspring. Since defectors always receive a higher average payoff here, their share of the population will grow over time. Cooperators, even if they make up almost the entire population to begin with, are thus destined for extinction. When cooperators and defectors look like, genuine cooperation *cannot* emerge.

Population Movements when Cooperators Are Easily Identified

Now suppose everything is just as before except that cooperators and defectors are perfectly distinguishable from each other. Imagine that cooperators are born with a red *C* on their foreheads, defectors with a red *D*. Suddenly the tables are completely turned. Cooperators can now interact selectively with one another and be assured of a payoff of 4 units. No cooperator need ever interact with a defector. Defectors are left to interact with one another, for which they get a payoff of only 2 units. Since all element of choice has been removed, payoffs are no longer related to the proportion of cooperators in the population (see figure 2). Cooperators always get 4, defectors always get 2.

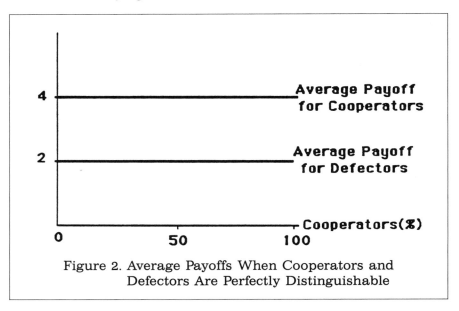

Figure 2. Average Payoffs When Cooperators and Defectors Are Perfectly Distinguishable

This time the cooperators' larger payoffs enable *them* to raise larger families, which means they will make up an ever-growing share of the population. When cooperators can be easily identified, it is the defectors who face extinction.

Mimicry without Cost or Delay

The defectors need not go quietly into the night, however. Suppose there arises a mutant strain of defectors, one that behaves exactly like other defectors, but in which each individual has not a red *D* on his forehead but a red *C*. Since this particular strain of defectors looks exactly the same as cooperators, it is impossible for cooperators to discriminate against them. Each imposter is therefore just as likely to interact with a cooperator as a genuine cooperator is. This, in turn, means that the mutant defectors will have a higher expected payoff than the cooperators.

The nonmutant defectors—those who continue to bear the red *D*—will have a lower payoff than both of these groups and, as before, are destined for extinction. But unless the cooperators adapt in some way, they too face the same fate. When defectors can perfectly mimic the distinguishing feature of cooperators with neither cost nor delay, the feature loses all power to distinguish. Cooperators and the surviving defectors again look exactly alike, which again spells doom for the cooperators.

Imperfect Mimicry and the Costs of Scrutiny

Defectors, of course, have no monopoly on the power to adapt. If random mutations alter the cooperators' distinguishing characteristic, the defectors will be faced with a moving target. Imagine that the red *C* by which cooperators originally managed to distinguish themselves has evolved over time into a generally ruddy complexion—a blush of sorts—and that some defectors have a ruddy complexion as well. But because cooperators actually experience the emotions that motivate cooperation, they have a more intense blush, on the average.

In general, we might expect a continuum of intensity of blushes for both groups. For the sake of simplicity, however, suppose that complexions take one of only two discrete types: (1) heavy blush and (2) light blush. Those with heavy blushes are cooperators, those with light blushes, defectors. If the two types could be distinguished at a glance, defectors would again be doomed. But suppose it requires effort to inspect the intensity of a person's blush. For concreteness, suppose inspection costs 1 unit. For people who pay this cost, the veil is lifted: cooperators and defectors can be distinguished with 100% accuracy. For those who don't pay the 1-unit cost of scrutiny, the two types are perfectly indistinguishable.

To see what happens this time, suppose the payoffs are again as given in table 1, and consider the decision facing a cooperator who is trying to decide whether to pay the cost of scrutiny. If he pays it, he can be assured of interacting with another cooperator, and will thus get a payoff of 4 − 1 = 3 units. If he does not, his payoff is uncertain. Cooperators and defectors will look exactly alike to him, and he must take his chances. If he happens to interact with another cooperator, he will get 4 units. But if he interacts with a defector, he will get zero. Whether it makes sense to pay the 1-unit cost of scrutiny thus depends on the *likelihood* of those respective outcomes.

Suppose the population share of cooperators is 90%. By not paying the cost of scrutiny, a cooperator will interact with another cooperator 90% of the time, and with a defector only 10%. His payoff will thus have an average value of (.9 × 4) + (.1 × 0) = 3.6. Since this is higher than the 3-unit net payoff he would get if he paid the cost of scrutiny, it is clearly better not to pay it.

Now suppose the population share of cooperators is not 90% but 50%. If our cooperator does not pay the cost of scrutiny, he will now have only a fifty-fifty chance of interacting with a cooperator. His average payoff will thus be only 2 units, or 1 unit less than if he had paid the cost. On these odds, it would clearly be better to pay it.

The numbers in this example imply a "break-even point" when the population share of cooperators is 75%. At that share, a cooperator who does not pay the cost has a 75% chance at a payoff of 4 units, and a 25% chance of getting zero. His average payoff is thus 3 units, the same as if he had paid the cost. When the population share of cooperators is below 75%, it will always be better for him to pay the cost of scrutiny.

With this rule in mind, we can now say something about how the population will evolve over time. When the population share of cooperators is below 75%, cooperators will all pay the cost of scrutiny and get a payoff of 3 units by cooperating with one another. It will not be in the interests of defectors to bear this cost, because the keen-eyed cooperators would not interact with them anyway. The defectors are left to interact with one another, and get a payoff of only 2 units. Thus, if we start with a population share of cooperators less than 75%, the cooperators will get a higher average payoff, which means that their share of the population will grow.

In populations that consist of more than 75% cooperators, the tables are turned. Now it no longer makes sense to pay the cost of scrutiny. Cooperators and defectors will thus interact at random, which means that defectors will have a higher average payoff. This difference in payoffs, in turn, will cause the population share of cooperators to shrink.

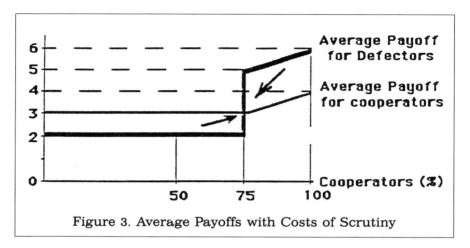

Figure 3. Average Payoffs with Costs of Scrutiny

For the values assumed in this example, the average payoff schedules for the two groups are plotted in figure 3. As noted, the cooperators' schedule lies above the defectors' for shares smaller than 75%, but below it for larger shares. The sharp discontinuity in the defectors' schedule reflects the fact that, to the left of 75%, all cooperators pay to scrutinize, while to the right of 75% none of them do. Once the population share of cooperators passes 75%, defectors suddenly gain access to their victims. The evolutionary rule, once again, is that *higher relative payoffs result in a growing population share.* This rule makes it clear that the population in this example will stabilize at 75% cooperators.

Now, there is obviously nothing magic about this 75% figure. Had the cost of scrutiny been higher than 1 unit, for example, the population share of cooperators would have been smaller. A reduction in the payoff when cooperators pair with one another would have a similar effect on the equilibrium population shares. The point of the example is that when there are costs of scrutiny, there will be pressures that pull the population toward some stable mix of cooperators and defectors. Once the population settles at this mix, members of both groups have the same average payoff and are therefore equally likely to survive. There is an ecological niche, in other words, for both groups. This result stands in stark contrast to the traditional evolutionary idea that only opportunism can survive.

Conclusion

I cannot develop all the particulars of the argument here as I have in my book *Passions within Reason* (Frank 1988). The important point is that opportunistic behavior is not *inevitable*. There is also room for unopportunistic behavior to evolve. The honest individual in the commitment model is someone who values trustworthiness for its own sake. That he might receive a material payoff for such behavior is completely beyond his concern (and it is precisely because he has this attitude—and is known to have it—that he can be trusted). Of course, the fact that trustworthy persons *do* receive a material payoff is what sustains the trait in evolution.

It will be obvious that I find the commitment model more satisfactory than the self-interest model in terms of explaining actual behavior. Moreover, the effects of the self-interest model, so prominent in our day, have been pernicious. That model tells us that to behave morally is to invite others to take advantage of us. By encouraging us to expect the worst in others, it brings out the worst in us. Dreading the role of the chump, we are often loath to heed our noble instincts. By contrast, the commitment model encourages people to cooperate in a way that, as in the Prisoner's Dilemma, could work to the benefit of all parties concerned.

6

Primatology

Biruté M. F. Galdikas and Paul Vasey

Primatology is the study of primates—monkeys, apes, and prosimians. It takes place in the laboratory, in "natural enclosures," and in the wild. There are many long-term studies of primates in the wild, the oldest being the study of the Takasakiyama troop of macaques in Japan. Our orangutan research station in Borneo is a center both for observation of this species and for the "rehabilitation" of orangutans that have been in captivity to prepare them for a return to the wild.

Orangutans are the world's largest arboreal animal. They are unique among higher primates in their semisolitary nature (MacKinnon 1974; Galdikas 1979). Their social life, or lack of it, appears to be dictated by their diet. Orangutans are fruit-eaters, and the distribution of fruit in the tropical rain forest is such that competition among the females for food (for themselves and offspring) requires that they disperse. Since they lack many of the social interchanges of great interest to sociobiology, orangutans will not feature prominently in this chapter.

The main question for this chapter is: has sociobiology had an impact on primatology? The answer is an emphatic yes. Sociobiology has altered the face of primatology. It has shifted the discipline of primatology, at least that aspect dealing with behavior, away from anthropology and toward biology. Sociobiology has provided a much needed paradigm that permitted primatologists (and ethologists in general) to elucidate a common functional pattern underlying the behavior of widely divergent species. A quick survey of the journal *Primates* shows that in the 1970s, nine papers in *Primates* directly used sociobiological theory to interpret their results, and in the 1980s, forty-four articles did so. Thanks to sociobiological theory, primatologists are now able to make broad predictions about how behaviors may be patterned, before actually setting foot in the field.

In this chapter we shall consider four topics: kin altruism among primates, parent–offspring conflict, adoption and allo-mothering, and infanticide. In each case we shall be interested to see how well sociobiological theories holds up, and in some cases we shall find that the theory may be cast into doubt, while in other cases its tenets hold. We make no claim that our survey of sociobiology in primatology is exhaustive. The reader may refer to A. F. Richard and S. R. Schulman's article "Sociobiology: Primate Field Studies" (1982), M. P. Ghiglieri's "Sociobiology of the Great Apes and the Hominid Ancestor" (1987), and J. Patrick Gray's book-length bibliography, *Primate Sociobiology* (1985).

KIN ALTRUISM

Long before the dissemination of Hamilton's 1964 theory of kin selection (which occurred mainly through the publication of Wilson's *Sociobiology* in 1975), primatologists were aware of the effect that *kinship* had on structuring behavioral inter-actions within groups. The early studies of macaques, conducted in Japan and at Cayo Santiago Island, Puerto Rico, as well as Goodall's study of chimpanzees, laid the foundation for other researchers of kinship to build upon. Japanese researchers emphasized genealogical descent from a common grandmother (or earlier ancestor), known as the primogenetrix. Based on this concept of common descent within the female line, primatologists have studied both the *matrifocal unit,* consisting of a mother and her immediate offspring, and the *matriline,* which traces several generations back, through the females, to the primogenetrix. Using this approach, most monkey social groups were found to consist of immigrant males whose tenure with the group is variable, and of several matrilines that form the core of the group. Some species exceptions to this pattern are the gorilla, chimpanzee, and red colobus monkey, in which the females emigrate from their natal group.

Hamilton's theory of kin altruism, or kin selection, holds that individuals share a percentage of their genes with their relatives. Therefore some of an individual's genetic material can be passed on to future generations through relatives who are reproductively active. The significance of this theory was that it provided a means for animal researchers to explain why an individual would exhibit altruism toward another when such energy could be put to more personal use in the "struggle for existence."

Consider the common primate behavior of *grooming*. This is altruistic because the groomer expends energy that it could put to other uses, it exposes itself to ectoparasites as it grooms, and it runs the risk of ingesting hair balls that may block the intestine (for example, see Kurland 1977; for an alternative interpretation, see Altmann and Walters 1978). Many studies do show that primates appear to discriminate in favor of kin as grooming partners. (For this behavior in bonnet macaques, see Silk, Samuels, and Rodman 1981; for yellow baboons, see Walters 1981, for patas monkeys, see Rowell and Olsen 1983.) Yet many other studies find an appreciable amount of grooming among unrelated individuals as well. (For gelada baboons, see Dunbar 1983; for Japanese macaques, see Takahata 1982; for olive baboons, see Smuts 1983.)

Another altruistic behavior is that of *alliance-formation.* Again, the data indicate, as kin selection theory would predict, that primates often seek alliances with kin. They do so in pigtailed macaques, chacma baboons, and several other species. Moreover, evidence indicates that in some species individuals aid close kin rather than distantly related kin in defending against aggressors (see, for example, Silk, Samuels, and Rodman 1981). Yet non-kin also form alliances, especially against an agonistic third party.

So it seems that Hamilton's kin altruism theory is not adequate to explain all expressions of this behavior. A sister theory—the theory of reciprocal altruism—is often evoked to explain grooming or alliance formation by non-kin. Critics of sociobiology say that this very substitution of one theory for another renders sociobiology untestable and unfalsifiable (Allen et al. 1976).

This adult female orangutan is one of the individuals being studied at the Orangutan Research and Conservation Project in Indonesian Borneo, in the hopes of elucidating the life histories of orangutans. (Photo: Jane Fitschen).

A more interesting criticism of kin selection theory arises from the fact that, in primate studies where paternity is known, paternal halfsiblings (rather than maternal half-siblings) tend not to receive altruistic favors. As mentioned above, primatologists study kinship by concentrating on matrifocal units and matrilines. The paternity of individuals is often not known to the researchers (and, we assume, is not known to the offspring). Genetic paternity investigation is possible, but costly, and so far has not been used much. If at some point, field studies can show that in fact individuals do not perform altruism toward individuals related through their father, then this will call Hamilton's premise into question. His premise is that all kin (maternal and paternal) should be the recipients of the same degree of altruism, when they have the same degree of relatedness.

This brings up the question of what mechanism animals use to discriminate kin from non-kin. According to Sherman (1980) there may be four kinds of mechanisms: (1) spatial proximity, (2) familiarity through association, (3) phenotypic matching, and (4) allele recognition. Thus far, discussion of the last two mechanisms has been mainly in the theoretical realm. The most important mechanism of kin recognition seems to be association during development (Gouzoules 1984). Can non-human primate fathers recognize their offspring based on Sherman's first two mechanisms? Among wild savanna baboons, there is evidence that adult males recognize classes of infants as potential offspring according to when they entered the group, but do not make finer differentiations (Packer 1979). However, it has been demonstrated that wild adult male olive baboons, that develop a close bond with infants, do so based on their prior relationship with the mother. This relationship need not be a sexual one and hence, proximity and friendly relations with the infant may not be based on paternity (Smuts 1985).

Another possible refutation of Hamilton's theory comes from evidence about aggressive encounters between groups that share kin. Members of neighboring groups often contain emigrated kin, yet, during territorial interactions, it is the members within a group, both kin and not kin, that bond together to show aggression toward, and drive off, other such invading groups. Here, an individual may unknowingly aid non-kin in attacking kin! The fact that familiarity is, apparently, the best mechanism a primate has for deciding whom to help may, of course, mean that there will be such occasional breakdown of "accurate" choice, yet the system may work well enough, on average.

In short, the primatological evidence does not conclusively prove or disprove, the theory of kin selection. Let us turn to Trivers's (1974) theory of parent–offspring conflict, where the evidence is much more conclusive.

PARENT–OFFSPRING CONFLICT

The parent–offspring relationship has traditionally generated many studies in primatology. The dynamics of the primate mother–offspring bond were initially examined from a psychodynamic/developmental framework, and much emphasis was placed on discerning which individual in the dyad—mother or offspring—was responsible for sustaining this most primary of social bonds. Strong behavioral parallels of the mother-offspring bond cut across virtually all species of the primate order and generated hope among primatologists that this research could provide models for human behavior.

With the publication of Trivers's 1974 essay on parent-offspring conflict, interest in the psychodynamic/developmental aspect of the mother–offspring bond waned, in favor of analyzing the cost and benefits accrued by both individuals in the dyad. Prior to the publication of Trivers's (1974) parent-offspring conflict theory, primatologists were aware of the conflict that developed during the weaning process, but Trivers's contribution allowed them to frame this relationship within an evolutionary perspective.

According to Trivers (1974), conflict between the parental caregiver (usually the mother) and the offspring arises over disagreement as to how much investment in the form of time and energy the offspring should receive. The parental caregiver invests time and energy into the current offspring in order to increase the offspring's chances of survival, but this investment simultaneously involves decreasing the parent's ability to invest in other offspring at that time. Parents, said Trivers, will allocate investment in their offspring in such a way as to maximize their own "lifetime reproductive success." Thus, the amount of investment the parent is willing to put into any one infant should be negatively correlated with that infant's level of self-sufficiency. The parent must ensure that investment has been sufficient so that offspring survival is not in jeopardy (or else risk the offspring's death and suffer a decrease in fitness). The offspring, on the other hand, will be motivated to encourage the parent to donate more than the investment level optimal for the parent, so it can increase its individual fitness.

These conflicting motivations of parent and offspring can be thought of as remaining negotiable throughout the offspring's maturation period. The resolution usually, but not always, results in offspring independence. Those parent-offspring conflicts that are not resolved may prove fatal to both members of the dyad, as witnessed by Jane Goodall's (1971) famous observations on the chimpanzee mother–offspring dyad of Flo and her son Flint. Flint's continual resistance of Flo's attempts to encourage his independence eventually led to his demise. Following his mother's death (which was probably hastened by Flint's demands), he had acquired none of the skills necessary for survival that normal chimpanzees learn during maturation; not long after, he died himself. This scenario underlines that the "rejection behavior" that accompanies weaning and encouragement of independence is performed not only in the interest of the mother, but in the interest of her offspring as well.

Parent–Offspring Conflict (weaning): Rhesus monkey mother tries to prevent infant from reaching her nipple. Infant rounds its mouth to give a soft coo—a distress signal. (Photo: Barbara Smuts/ Anthropophoto)

While assessing the exact costs and benefits to each member of the mother/offspring dyad proves difficult, such costs and benefits can be examined in a broad sense. Lactation is a metabolically costly process that increases the primate female's energy needs 20-50%, and imposes an added nutritional requirement of one thousand kilocalories per day (Buss and Voss 1971). Access to this rich food source by the infant, requiring no energy or time allocated to foraging on his part, is obviously to his benefit. Obviously, too, it is in the mother's best interest to wean her infant as soon as it is capable of surviving without this food source.

Various factors may complicate a mother's attempts to wean. For example, Hiraiwa (1981) reports that the cold weather in the northern extremes of the Japanese macaques' range results in prolonged dependence on mothers for warmth, and Chalmers (1972) suggests that arboreal primates may require longer periods of dependency in order to learn how to locomote among the the branches and keep up with group movement. While the duration and intensity of weaning vary markedly among species of the primate order based on brain/body ratios, maturation period, and habitat, a general pattern of behavior during weaning conflict emerges. As the nonhuman primate infant matures, time at the nipple decreases gradually, as opposed to abrupt refusal on the part of the mother to suckle (Goodall 1968, Hiraiwa 1981, Nicolson 1986). Abrupt rejection of the infant's attempts to suckle may in fact lead to greater rather than lesser dependence on the mother, as the infant may be inhibited to break off contact (Nicolson and Demment 1982).

Because of the underlying motivational conflict between the mother and infant at this time, refusal to allow the infant to suckle is often followed by aggression on the immature's part toward the mother in the form of slapping, pushing, or hair pulling, accompanied by screaming and tantrums. At times such as these the mother–offspring conflict is most clearly evident. Indeed, Struhsaker (1971) found that aggression between mother vervets and their offspring peaked during the most intense periods of weaning. In comparison to humans, nonhuman primate mothers are usually extremely tolerant of their infants' persistent attempts, and thus aggression during weaning is rare. Commonly mothers will simply block access to their nipples by moving away or lying down on their chests. Offspring learn to manipulate their mothers more adeptly as they are increasingly rejected from the nipple. Some researchers have reported that older infants participate in fewer suckling bouts, but the time per bout increases (Nicolson 1986, Hiraiwa 1981).

In summary, the data gathered on nonhuman primates supports the existence of a parent–offspring conflict involving how much energy the parent should invest in the offspring. Most evidence for this comes from studies of weaning, but transportation and carrying costs incurred by mothers are also of importance and deserve attention in the future. More life-history research also needs to be carried out to determine the extent to which early weaning actually improves the mother's lifetime reproductiveness. Obviously, patterns concerning this will vary across species, and particularly it seems reasonable to suggest that among seasonally reproducing species, parent-offspring conflict will take a form different from that in species that breed year round. Seasonally breeding mothers may be more motivated to wean offspring faster, so as not to miss reproductive opportunities the following season and be forced to wait an extra year to become pregnant. Hence, parent-offspring conflict may appear more intense in such species where time is of the essence, in contrast to species such as the Great Apes in which more time and a more gradual weaning process are possible without the loss of breeding opportunities due to seasonality in breeding.

ADOPTION AND ALLOMOTHERING

Now let us look at instances in which primates may raise or care for individuals other than their own offspring. Raising a dependent other than one's own is termed *adoption,* while caring for a dependent than one's own is termed *allomothering* or *alloparenting.* These phenomena can be used to either support or refute the sociobiological theory of kin altruism.

Infant adoption and allomothering among nonhuman primates is of special interest to the primatologist because the relationship between the caregiver and the receiver can have considerable effect on the fitness of both. Critics of sociobiology sometimes cite adoptions and allomothering among animals as evidence of altruism that has no underlying selfish motive. Such critics argue that kin selection theory cannot account for adoptions and allomothering by nonkin—nor can the theory of reciprocal altruism, because the acts of caregiving and rearing are not returned in kind or in degree. Does the primate literature support the stance that adoption and allomothering represent pure forms of altruism?

Early reports on nonhuman primate orphans observed in the wild indicated that adoption was contingent on whether the orphan had any siblings (Goodall 1967, 1968; Sade 1965). Following an accumulation of data from other studies including their own, Hasegawa and Hiraiwa (1980) categorized adopters into four different groups. In order of most commonly to least commonly observed, these are: (1) older siblings, (2) close relatives other than a sibling, (3) adult males who may be the fathers, and (4) non-related adult females. Their data on adoption among Japanese macaques can be interpreted, using kin selection theory, in those cases where orphans were adopted by a relative. It could be argued that the caretakers are attempting to increase their inclusive fitness by aiding in the survival of a close relative with whom they share a relatively large percentage of genes.

However, adoption by the non-related adult females, while rare, complicates the issue, since kin selection theory cannot account for such behavior and full reciprocity by the orphan appears unlikely (although, in theory, such a scenario could no doubt be constructed). Allomothering, or temporary caregiving by a female other than the mother, is often interpreted as engaged in by the allomother so as to perfect her caretaking skills to enhance the likelihood of survival of her own future offspring at the expense of her present charge (Hrdy 1976, Quiatt 1979). Quiatt (1979) states that "the benefits of allomaternal behavior to those who practice it outweigh those to any other individual (except of course their direct descendants)" (316). Therefore, adoption by these non-kin Japanese female macaques could be interpreted as classical individual selection: the caregiver is merely helping *herself.* The only neglectful behavior the Japanese macaque foster mothers were seen to exhibit was not protecting adoptees from attacks, although the adoptees were groomed and held (Hasegawa and Hiraiwa 1980). In all, observation on non-kin Japanese macaque foster mothers provides cautious evidence in support of the theory that non-kin adoption is a rare event and non-kin adoptees *are* treated differently from kin.

Evidence from hamadryas baboons shows that young males sometimes adopt and raise young females in order to mate with them in latter life (Kummer 1968). Hence, such adoptions appear to be a reproductive strategy on the part of the male.

In a study of adoption among chacma baboons, Hamilton et al. (1982) found that prereproductive males and females between the ages of four and five were the age group that adopted orphans. Because both parties were still in their natal troop and most individuals born in the natal troop are related, the authors suggest that these caregivers were probably relatives of the orphans. Hamilton, Busse, and Smith (1982) note that four of the female caregivers had adjacent social rank to their charges' mothers. Because daughters rank closely to their mothers in baboon society, it is likely that the female caregivers and their charges were related. These results, like those of Hasegawa and Hiraiwa (1980), support the predictions of kin selection theory.

While the line of argument followed herein was that the orphan is unlikely to reciprocate in kind or degree the caregiving act, the reader would do well to remember that the reciprocity of an altruistic act can be in ways so subtle as to elude the most astute primate watcher. For example, Hasegawa and Hiraiwa (1980) speculate that adoption by an adult male Japanese macaque may be a strategy to maintain residence in the troop for a longer than normal period of time and thereby enhance the male's overall reproductive success by avoiding group transfer. In a more recent study of care and lactation by ringtailed lemurs for unrelated infants, Pereira and Izard (1989) suggest that lactation and caregiving by the allomother was a manifestation of reciprocal altruism in exchange for not being expulsed from the group by the mother who was dominant. Once again, the problem is that if the act of reciprocity is so subtle, how can it be recognized as such, let alone measured?

So, is adoption and allomothering among nonhuman primates adequate to negate the predictions of kin selection and reciprocal altruism theories? Do these behaviors represent altruism that lacks any underlying selfish motive? Because the primate data on adoptions is scant and information on genetic relatedness is lacking, interpretation of this data must be cautious. The data do indicate that the overwhelming numbers of adoptions among nonhuman primates are by kin and that the kin that are adopting are suffering the least cost to their fitness, all of which would be expected by kin selection theory.

Allomothering in most instances is most beneficial to the caregiver and can thus be viewed as having underlying selfish motives aimed at refining the maternal skills of the caregiver at the expense of the charge.

Adoption by non-kin, however, represents a unique case where the potential for "pure" altruism appears high, but much more data on genetic relatedness, and many more observations of adoptions in nature and the relationship between the adopter and adoptee are needed. Also, a good methodology for measuring the cost and benefits of behaviors will be necessary before a definite answer can be advanced as to whether adoption represents a behavior that neither reciprocal altruism or kin selection theory can explain.

We might note here the unusual adoption statistics among the ex-captive orangutans in our field station in Tanjung Puting National Park. Some free-ranging ex-captive females and the occasional subadult male have adopted newly arrived infants rescued from captivity—presumably nonrelatives. Interestingly, of the five currently most dominant ex-captive females in the vicinity of the camp, four have adopted non-kin infants. In another case, a lactating female adopted two female infants sequentially while continuing to nurse her juvenile son. A second biological offspring, a robust male infant born between the two adoptions, mysteriously disappeared soon after birth, possibly taken by a predator. Analysis of data on adoptions by orangutans at Tanjung Puting is not yet complete.

PRIMATE INFANTICIDE

Now, we turn to the subject of infanticide. Sugiyama (1965) was the first to report infant-killing behavior among nonhuman primates in nature, and since that time infanticide has been one of the most controversial areas of inquiry within the discipline of primatology. Polarity exists on a very fundamental level regarding whether infanticide is an adaptation or a pathological behavior induced by abnormal environmental conditions. The disagreement over interpretation also runs deeper as researchers dispute its function, its cause, and how widespread it is in occurrence (see Curtin and Dolhinow 1978, Hrdy 1974, Boggess 1980, Hausfater and Vogel 1982).

Following Hrdy's (1974) supposition that infanticide could be interpreted in an evolutionary context, many primatologists misinterpreted this to imply that infanticide was invariant across all populations of a species and exhibited by all males in such species. Observational data, in all but a few cases, is lacking in completeness; nevertheless, an obsession of sorts concerning the entire issue was witnessed throughout much of the late 1970s and early 1980s, and the literature of this periods contains numerous references. This history has only hindered our understanding and served to fuel disputes, when in reality infanticide in any primate species is a rare event (Hrdy 1979, Hausfater and Vogel 1982).

Many nonhuman primates have been observed to exhibit infanticidal behavior, including chimpanzees, gorillas, Hanuman langurs, douc langurs, chacma baboons, hamadryas baboons, gelada baboons, rhesus, barbary and crab-eating macaques, red tailed guenons, guerezas, Mentawei Island leaf-monkeys, purple-faced langurs, and a single species of New World monkey, the howler monkey (see Hrdy 1979 and Angst and Thommen 1977 for reviews of this data). It becomes obvious that infanticide, regardless of how frequently it is observed, is taxonomically widespread in its appearance across the primate order. In many of these species, infanticide has only been observed once, while in others it appears to occur more often. Certainly, there are species that have been the subject of long-term studies that have not exhibited this behavior, such as the orangutan (Galdikas 1979).

Studies of nonhuman primates that exhibit infanticide have revealed that both adult and immature males and females of some species commit infanticide, but the most common pattern observed involves infant killing by alpha males establishing themselves in a new group (Angst and Thommen 1977). The killing of offspring by nonhuman primate *parents* appears to be extremely infrequent and occurs most frequently in abnormal, captive situations (Zuckerman 1932, Carpenter 1942). Commonly, it is individuals who are strangers to the mother and her infant who commit infanticide (Angst and Thommen 1977). Fatal attacks by females on the infants of subordinates have also been observed, but reports thus far are confined to female emigrating primates such as the African apes (Goodall

1977, Fossey 1984). It is highly likely, given the implications of the local resource hypothesis (Clark 1978, Silk 1983), that non-dispersing females of other primate species may be killing the competing offspring of other adult females. It should also be said that the reason why infants are killed at proportionately higher numbers than other age classes may simply be that their vulnerability makes them easier victims than adults or immatures who possess significant mechanisms (such as sharp canines) for deterring an aggressor.

A host of hypotheses to explain the causation and function of infanticide among nonhuman primates exists. Hrdy (1979) suggest that by examining the effect of infanticide on the *fitness of the aggressor,* a clearer understanding of the behavior's function can be achieved. Effects on the fitness of the aggressor can stem from (1) exploitation of the infant as a resource, (2) elimination of resource competition by the infant, (3) parental manipulation of their own overall lifetime reproductive success, and (4) increasing reproductive opportunities by shortening the interbirth interval of females, thereby hastening their estrous (Hrdy 1979).

Exploitation of the infant as a resource can take various forms. The aggressor can cannibalize the infant, thereby gaining advantage in the immediate sense by acquiring a meal. This situation has been described as occurring among the chimpanzees at Gombe, where a mother, Passion, and her male and female offspring systematically killed and cannibalized dependent individuals (Goodall 1977). Alternatively, the aggressor can utilize the infant as a "buffer" during agonistic encounters, which may result in its fatal injury. Buffering is a behavior observed in males and has been described among barbary macaques and baboons (Deag and Crook 1971).

Infanticidal individuals can also increase their fitness by eliminating resource competition by the infant, whether in the present or what would be incurred in the future by oneself or one's kin. (Here, victims would be unrelated individuals.) Among primate species that are matrilineal, females who commit infanticide could be doing so to reduce competition with themselves or their kin. However, female infanticide— which the primatologist has interpreted as being motivated by resource competition—has thus far been observed in patrilineal societies such as chimpanzees and gorillas (Goodall 1977, Fossey 1984). This pattern has been interpreted as occurring because the low degree of relatedness among females in patrilineal groups increases the likelihood that the victim is not kin (Hrdy, 1979).

Hrdy (1979) contends that parents may kill their own offspring if the cost of raising the infant would detract from the overall lifetime reproductive success of the parent, or result in the loss of an offspring into which the parents have already invested time and energy. She feels that this situation may present itself if the birth is ill-timed due to unfavorable environmental conditions, if the infant is handicapped, or if too many infants are born so that attempting to raise all would be unsuccessful and result in the potential loss of all. Examples exist in nature where even when the cost of raising an infant is high, for example when the infant is handicapped, the parent does raise it (Fedigan and Fedigan 1977). However, in such instances where these handicapped offspring die, which they often do, a more subtle form of infanticide may occur by way of parental neglect relative to the care exhibited toward more healthy siblings. Infanticide by parents for reasons of fitness has not, to date, been an explanation invoked for primates. If it does occur, it is likely to be exceedingly rare.

The most common hypothesis invoked to explain patterns of infanticide whereby a new male establishes himself in a group and proceeds to kill unweaned infants has to do with the *reproductive advantages* gained by the infanticidal male. Killing unweaned infants often results in the interbirth interval of the victim's mother being shortened and her estrous being induced much more quickly than if the infant were weaned (Hrdy 1979). Thus, infanticide allows the killing male to fertilize females quickly, which can be important if a male's tenure in a group is limited. This hypothesis has been championed by Hrdy (1974, 1977, 1979), who invokes it to explain infanticidal patterns among Hanuman langurs at her Abu study area site in India.

Other explanations of infanticide emphasize its non-adaptive nature, thereby casting it as a pathology. It is argued that primates living at high densities suffer higher levels of stress, which causes the breakdown of normal patterns of social interactions and the occurrence of social pathologies such as infanticide (Curtin and Dolhinow 1978). It is hypothesized that primates living in areas recently disturbed by humans (such as Hrdy's Abu langurs) will suffer higher levels of pathological behavior such as infanticide. However, given that all individuals in a population should exhibit the effects of such stress, it seems likely that the age and sex classes capable of exhibiting infanticidal behavior would show no particular pattern. Doubt is cast upon the pathology argument because these patterns do exist, for as mentioned, stranger adult males establishing themselves in a new troop appear to commit infanticide relatively more than other age or sex classes (Angst and Thommen 1977). Hrdy (1979) argues that animals sometimes make "mistakes" and that adaptive strategies are probabilistic so that they only need to be adaptive on average, not necessarily in all situations.

A consideration of female reproductive strategies for circumventing infanticide as a male reproductive strategy is necessary for a fuller picture. Hrdy (1979) suggests that females may be selected for to maintain close proximity to males who will aid them in defense against others who may attack their infant. Therefore, females with infants living in patriarchal societies are unlikely to transfer out of their group with a dependent infant. Females may also be selected to evolve a physiological mechanism allowing them to abort or reabsorb (Bruce effect) their fetus when enviromental conditions are inappropriate at the time for raising an infant (Hrdy 1979); this ability, however, has not yet been documented among primates. Finally, Hrdy (1979) suggests that females could mate with as many males as possible to confuse paternity certainty, and this might also result in increased levels of parental investment by numerous males being directed at the infant. This multiple mating strategy is exhibited by a number of primate species including barbary macaques, savanna baboons, chimpanzees, and rhesus macaques.

As Hrdy (1979) has commented, infanticide *is* a rare event and one that is contingent on numerous social, phylogenetic, and ecological factors coalescing, so that the benefits of the behavior rise above its otherwise usually prohibitive costs. It is important that primatologists keep in mind the rare nature of infanticide. It is also important that the saturation of the literature concerning the adaptive functions of infanticide not cloud over the fact that a pathological expression of infanticide is possible in many "natural" situations as well. The challenge lies with developing theoretical and methodological approaches to differentiate the two.

RECIPROCAL ALTRUISM

As mentioned in the section dealing with kinship, unrelated individuals often interact in an altruistic manner. In order to account for such behavior, Trivers (1971) constructed his reciprocal altruism theory, whereby an altruistic behavior will be performed, provided (1) that it is more beneficial to the recipient than costly to the donor regardless of genetic relationship between the two, (2) that an altruistic act will be returned by the recipient to the donor, and (3) that the individuals interact repeatedly so that the potential for reciprocation by the recipient exists. Trivers believed that for this system to function, "cheaters"—those individuals who do not reciprocate acts received—would have to be remembered by altruistic donors and discriminated against in future interactions. Trivers claims that natural selection should favor individuals who direct their altruism only toward those who reciprocate, and that the temptation to cheat would be kept in check when the benefits gained through cooperation outweighed those gained by cheating. Due to a lack of kinship data and the difficulty of studying reciprocal altruism in the wild, only a handful of primatologists have examined this behavior. Here we review some of the available data.

Packer (1977) studied reciprocal altruism involving coalition formation among individual male olive baboons (Papio anubis) from three troops at Gombe National Park, Tanzania. Over a period of one year, ninety-seven solicitations resulting in coalitions were observed, twenty of which occurred against an opponent who was consorting with a female at the time. Six of these twenty resulted in disruption of the consort pair, and formation of a new consort relationship between the female and the soliciting male, while the solicited coalition partner continued to fight. Packer found that on separate occasions, unrelated and related males reciprocated in joining coalitions at each other's request, and that "favorite partners" existed who solicited support from each other more than from other potential partners. These partner preferences suggest reciprocal altruism as the mechanism mediating coalition or alliance formation (Packer 1977).

Packer was unable to determine whether the cost of joining a coalition was less than the benefit received by the soliciting male, since it was unclear whether the potential immediate benefit of gaining access to an estrous female offset the potential cost of injury to the solicited male. Moreover, if access to an estrous female was the motivation for joining the alliance, then the solicited male would in actuality be joining for direct gain, not in hopes of future reciprocation. Packer also found it difficult to determine whether cheaters were excluded from being future recipients of altruism. Hence, Packer's work represents an important step for primatologists toward testing the theory of reciprocal altruism, but lends only tentative support to Trivers's (1971) theory.

Another study by Seyfarth and Cheney (1984) examined reciprocal altruism among nonrelated vervet monkeys *(Cercopithecus aethiops)*; the altruism involved coalition formation and grooming. The authors made tape recordings of the solicitation vocalizations of various individuals who were attempting to enlist support for coalitions. Later, following a dyadic grooming interaction involving one of these individuals, they broadcast the recording and observed the reaction of the grooming partner. The authors found that grooming in the immediate past had a very strong effect on the subject's motivation to aid non-kin individuals that solicited partners for coalitions. In other words, grooming by one individual was reciprocated with coalition aid by the other. This study provides tentative support for Trivers's (1971) theory, even though the authors were unable to quantify the costs and benefits associated with these interactions. However, in another study of nonrelated vervet monkeys, Fairbanks (1980) found no evidence that motivation to form coalitions was based on any mechanisms independent of kinship, thus casting doubt on the theory of reciprocal altruism.

In a study carried out on a group of captive chimpanzees, de Waal (1982) observed various types of reciprocal interactions, which he classified as (1) coalitions, (2) nonintervention alliances (A remains neutral if B does the same), (3) sexual bargains (A tolerates B's mating, after B grooms A), and (4) reconciliation blackmail (A refuses to have contact with B unless B "greets" A). De Waal points to the interesting fact that "negative reciprocity"—wherein individuals reciprocate agonistic acts— has hardly been considered by primatologists and yet is fundamental to primate social interactions. As with all the other studies discussed, de Waal was unable to quantify the cost and benefits of such interactions as would be required by Trivers's (1971) theory.

In conclusion, we note that reciprocity among unrelated nonhuman primates may be in ways so subtle, such as information sharing (Kummer 1978), as to evade even the most astute primatologist. Also, as Fedigan (1982) argues, it is difficult to say within what time period the reciprocated act should occur and what form the reciprocation should take, thereby limiting the testability and explanatory power of this theory. Perhaps the greatest obstacle to operationalizing reciprocal altruism theory is our inability to quantify the costs and benefits of behaviors as would be required by any solid test of Trivers's (1971) theory. It seems likely that primates pattern their interactions, particularly those with non-kin, based on reciprocal interaction. Obviously, the problems encountered by primatologists to date indicate that the theory needs modification if it is to be of greater use. Primatologists who are interested in how non-kin pattern their interactions or in the origins of reciprocity and sharing among the first transitional hominids no doubt eagerly await such a modification.

7

History

Laura Betzig

═══════════════════════════════════════

> Loves and hates are thrust
> Upon me by the acrimonious dead
> The buried thesis, long since rusted knife,
> Revengeful dust.
> A stony or obstreperous head,
> Though slain so squarely, can usurp my will
> As I walk above it on the sunny hill. . . .
> Nothing can come of history but history.
> —Edwin Muir, "The Wheel"

We've been after that "buried thesis" for centuries. Charles Darwin may have read it at last a hundred years ago. It says that all life, including human life, evolved to reproduce.

How far is such a simple thesis going to get us? Darwin himself was hopeful. He wrote, "Much light will be thrown on the origin of man and his history" (Darwin 1859, 573). Historians seem to have been more doubtful. Not one, so far as I know, has tried to write human history as natural history. But others have—especially anthropologists, biologists, and psychologists. In the last twelve years or so they've published just about as many times. But what they've written has started, in my opinion, to vindicate Darwin. Topics have ranged from things close to reproduction, like sex, to things farther removed, like politics. The ground covered has ranged from China to Europe to the Americas; the time has included all of written history, from ancient to medieval to modern.

Much of that work, which I'll cover in this chapter, has turned around two main points. The first is that competition *within* either sex should be expected to increase inequality *between* them. Important effects of this can be seen in bias toward sons or daughters, whether family names descend in the male or female line, which sex gets the bulk of the family wealth, and what becomes of disinherited daughters or sons. This research has taken into account, and could be taken account of by, histories of the family like those that have proliferated in the last ten to twenty years. Works like Peter Laslett's *The World We Have Lost* (1983), David Herlihy's *Medieval Households* (1985), and Georges Duby's *The Knight, the Lady, and the Priest* (1983) would be included here.

The second point, a more obvious one, is that competition *within* either of the sexes should up inequality *within* them. The most important implication of this is that politics may follow, in part, from sexual competition. The stress here so far has been on how political inequality corresponds to "unequal access"—to borrow a phrase from Napoleon Chagnon (1979a)—to the modes of production and *r*eproduction. This line should merge with the new work being done by historians like Lawrence Friedman (1984), who studies American legal history and has begun to ask how the law evolves and *why.*

NATURAL HISTORY

If people, like every other life form from protozoans to primates, have evolved to spread their genes, how might they do it? One way would be by helping raise sisters and brothers and other collateral kin. A more obvious way would be by raising children and grandchildren of their own (see Fisher 1930, Williams 1966, and especially Hamilton 1964).

Most obviously, to make a child it takes one female and one male. But, as Darwin pointed out in *The Descent of Man and Selection in Relation to Sex* (1871), males and females are designed to solve this problem in different ways (see Parker, Baker, and Smith 1972, on the evolution of sex; see Trivers 1972, on sexual selection). Males in the vast majority of species are able to father many more progeny than females can mother. For females, including women, the key to producing children is often being able to feed them; for males, including men, the key is often being able to find— and that sometimes means to feed—mates (see Wittenberger 1979, Wrangham 1980).

The result for the vast majority of species, including the human species, should be greater reproductive inequality among males—that is, polygyny. The rare exceptions prove the rule: where females, rather than males, contribute less to each offspring and so are capable of producing more, the result is greater reproductive inequality among females—that is, a polyandrous breeding system (see Trivers 1985). The point, again, is that reproductive inequality is expected to raise social inequality—both between the sexes and within them. It is a point that could be extremely illuminating in regard to history. Here are some reasons why.

First: the logic of inequality between the sexes. To the extent that there are winners and losers in competition for mates—to the extent that polygamy is common—winners should favor *heirs of the same gender.* Why shouldn't a polygynous father leave his rank and his wealth to his daughters? The answer is that a rich, high-ranking son might father hundreds of children, while a rich, high-ranking daughter might be lucky to mother ten (Trivers and Willard 1973). If the name of the game is the proliferation of genes, the heir should clearly be male. We should expect sons to inherit, daughters to be disinherited.

Next: the logic of inequality within either sex. To the extent that there are winners and losers in mate competition—again, to the extent that polygamy is common—we should find winners and losers at politics. Why? Because while a monogamous man might provide everything that his family needs, a polygamous man—to provide each mate and child as much—must either work harder or reap the fruits of others' labors (Chagnon 1979). Reproductive inequality, in short, makes economic inequality necessary. And extra food and extra mates tend to be got by force. We should expect polygynous societies to be despotic societies; monogamous societies should be more democratic.

It seems straightforward, then, to make this prediction: men should compete for access to women. In fact, if the stakes are high enough, even women should compete for fertile women for their brothers and sons (Weatherhead and Robertson 1979). Powerful men should be polygynous men.

ANCIENT HISTORY

Nowadays, no matter where you look, there is scant evidence that they are. History, on the other hand, is replete with evidence to the contrary. The most powerful men in the world have held harems of hundreds or even thousands of women. Mildred Dickemann (1979a) was the first to put that fact in an evolutionary light. As she pointed out, a Tang Dynasty Chinese king kept ten thousand women in his harem; the Mediterranean sultans Caliph Al-Mutawakkil and Abdur Rahman III kept on the order of four to six thousand; and one nineteenth-century Indian Maharaja kept twelve hundred "wives." As Dickemann (1981) went on, pains were often taken to keep kings from becoming cuckolds. "Harem" means "forbidden." Foot-binding in China, veiling in the Middle East, cloisters, and many other restrictions kept harem women apart from other men.

Correlations like these, between power and reproduction, have since held up on more systematic samples. The one most in use in cross-cultural research is the "standard cross-cultural sample" of Murdock and White (1969). It includes 104 politically autonomous societies supposed to represent all kinds of cultures known in space and time. In almost every case, power predicts the size of a man's harem (Betzig 1986). In, for instance, Polynesian Fiji and Samoa, African Ganda and Dahomey, and the Asian Khmer kingdom, kings consistently kept hundreds or thousands of women in well-defended harems. Ordinary men, of course, often went without.

The early historical evidence is consistent. Written evidence—from stele on which Hammurabi's laws were kept, to Shang Dynasty oracle bones, to Herodotus's tales of Pharaohs, and other more conventional sources—is rich on six of the world's first "civilizations." They are Babylon, Egypt, India, China, Aztec Mexico, and Inca Peru. Kings in all six of these cultures kept huge harems (Montezuma II, who met Cortes, kept four thousand concubines); and consorts were consistently chosen for their youth, virginity, and looks (a twentieth-century Maharaja had them raised in a nursery). Ample nutrition, little exertion, and the use of wet nurses probably contributed to their fecundity (there are references to wet nurses as early as the eighteenth-century B.C. Code of Hammurabi). And copulations were restricted to those most likely to conceive (Tang Dynasty emperors had records of the last date of menstruation and the day and time of every sexual union, and the first signs of conception were meticulously kept with a red brush); emissions of sperm were reserved for the ripest of these (Yogis in India and Taoists in China advised that salvation could be reached through careful semen conservation) (Betzig 1990).

In all these ways, imperial sex lives early in history seem calculated to raise the production of emperors' children. In many other ways, emperors seem to have calculated how to pass sex lives like these along to their sons. A multitude of rules of inheritance and succession can be understood as strategies that raised the production of emperors' grandchildren. They include singling out successors through "monogamy," concubinage and divorce as contingency strategies in case the first wife failed to bear an heir, and royal inbreeding and even incest as means to concentrate wealth (see Thornhill 1990 on incest). They also include succession and inheritance in the male line (see Hartung 1982 on inheritance). Nobles in these first six civilizations predictably left titles and land to firstborn sons (Betzig 1990). Noble daughters and latter-born sons were often unable to marry; many spent their lives in nunneries or monasteries (see Dickemann 1979b, Boone 1988, and below).

Finally, each of these six early empires, and many others, were despotic empires. Emperors took their subjects' lives arbitrarily and with impunity. Inequality was built, for instance, into Hammurabi's system of "justice"; Egypt's great Pharoah, Akhenaten, is depicted with ubiquitous armed guards; in Inca Peru, commoners were killed for cursing; in Aztec Mexico, they were sacrificed under a catchall statute for "insubordination." Torture, particularly for rebellion, in India, China, and elsewhere in the Orient, was highly refined (Betzig 1990). Even very simple societies may be exploitive societies (Betzig 1986, 1988, 1991). In any case, the bigger a polygynist's harem, the more likely he is to depend on exploitation. As it turns out, polygynous societies *are* despotic societies after all. Exceptions are hard to find (Betzig 1986).

MEDIEVAL HISTORY

Less has been written about medieval history than about ancients or moderns, from an evolutionary point of view. So far, almost nothing has been done in a Darwinian vein on medieval politics (but see MacDonald 1990). Intriguing things, though, have been done on the subject of Medieval inheritance. Mildred Dickemann (1979b) began with the question: What becomes of disinherited daughters and sons? She proposed that medieval nunneries were well-stocked with well-to-do women because their polygynous brothers could better proliferate their parents' genes, via titles and lands.

Following Dickemann's lead, James Boone (1988) used the *Peditura Lusitana,* a genealogy of fifteenth- and sixteenth-century elite Portuguese, to follow the paths of disinherited daughters and sons. He divided these elites into four ranks. The highest held "primary titles," the second were the royal bureaucracy, the third were the landed aristocracy, and the last included the untitled and the military. Boone found that about 40% of the women of highest rank, but only about 30% of the women of lowest rank, became nuns. In other words, women of highest rank were most likely to stay chaste; presumably, women of lowest rank were more likely to reproduce. Was this the best of all reproductive options? Why not, as Philip Kitcher (1985) has asked, disinherit daughters but let them fend for themselves on the mating market? The answer may be that women of rank may have more luck spreading genes through their kinsmen's children than through their own children. The logic follows Hamilton's (1964). Because a sister is, on average, twice as closely related to her own children as to her brother's children, it may pay a nobleman's daughter to become a nun when the reproductive prospects of a high-ranking brother are, roughly, better than twice the reproductive prospects of her potential, low-ranking son.

Boone (1988) went on to find a corresponding trend among noblemen's sons. About 15% of the men of the highest rank, and 25% of lowest ranking men, died in war. The mortality of men of intermediate rank was in between these figures. In other words, men of lowest rank were most likely to risk death. Mortality in war coincided with birth order, too. Firstborn sons, to whom estates were left most often, were significantly less at risk of war death than second-, third-, and fourth-born sons. In both cases, the payoff for fighting may have been direct—these sons of low rank and latter-born sons might have won the status, riches, and harems they needed to reproduce. At least as likely, there might have been a payoff to kin at home—to kin whose status, riches, and harems were defended.

Last, Boone showed that both sons' risks of dying in war, and daughters' risks of becoming nuns, increased dramatically between the fourteenth and sixteenth centuries. As he explained, "The number of males [and females] who are noble by birth increases with each generation, while the number of discrete titles remains the same, or increases at a much lower rate" (Boone 1988, 212). More women and men were disinherited as a result.

MODERN HISTORY

Modern societies are different. They tend to be monogamous rather than polygynous; wealth and rank tend to be passed down equally to all children without regard to birth order or sex; and government tends to be less despotic, and more democratic, than in ancient or medieval times. As argued above, it makes evolutionary sense for three things—big harems, patrilineal bias, and despotism—to rise and fall together. The interesting question becomes: what conditions might make monogamy, bilaterality, and democracy come about?

The evidence on modern societies strongly suggests a switch toward reproductive equality. There are a few indications, for instance, that monogamy may have been on the rise even over the past two hundred years in the United States (Betzig and Weber 1990). Among average American men, as revealed by the U.S. census, marriages dissolved through death or divorce more often in the 1980s than in 1860, when the earliest reports were made. And in the last two decades, the ones for which figures have been kept, remarriage rates of average men increased too. By contrast, biographies of Washington D.C. men, including members of the executive, judicial, and legislative branches of national government, show that remarriage rates have significantly declined over the past two hundred years. In other words, remarriage rates among rich and average may have converged. Insofar as a man's ability to attract a wife is indicative of his ability to attract a mate, *mating* may be becoming monogamous in the modern U.S.

Along with mating opportunities, inheritance opportunities seem to be leveling out. A pair of studies concerning Europe in the last two centuries shows a residual tendency of the wealthy to favor sons, while of three North American studies, one shows the same persistent son bias while two show no sex bias. In Europe, Eckart Voland (1984), in his study of a Schleswig-Holstein parish from 1720 to 1869, found that though infant sons died more often than daughters in the families of poor tradesmen, farm laborers, and small landholders, infant daughters died more often than sons in the families of large landholding farmers. This suggests better treatment of rich parents' sons. Similarly, Bobbi Low (1990), who looked at Tuna parish in Sweden, found that though equal inheritance was legally mandated by Swedish law in 1844, landholding records from 1845–96 show that 104 out of 106 landowners were men! In North America, Martin Smith, Bradley Kish, and Charles Crawford (1986) looked at a thousand wills collected from the Vancouver Registry of British Columbia; they found sons still twice as likely as daughters to be heirs to the richest estates. On the other hand, Debra Judge and Sarah Blaffer Hrdy (1988) found virtually no sex difference in the heirs to Sausalito estates. And wills of the first thirty-six U.S. presidents show almost no sex bias (Betzig and Weber 1990).

Finally, big modern societies seem, much more often than big historical societies, to be democratic societies. Unlike prehistoric states in Polynesia, Africa, and Asia, and unlike the first civilizations on written record in the Middle East, the Americas, and Asia, many modern states are neither very polygynous nor very despotic. As far as we know, in modern China, modern Mexico, and other modern cultures, access to power is not clearly matched by access to women (Betzig 1986).

CHANGE

The big question remains. *Why* are ancient and medieval societies polygynous, patrilateral, and despotic, while modern

History   139

societies are monogamous, bilateral, and democratic? What determines the differences in sex and politics across space and time? Ludicrous questions become plausible, even important, questions. For example: Why didn't Richard Nixon keep a thousand women in a harem? Why did Jimmy Carter limit himself to lust "in his heart"? Why was Gary Hart effectively eliminated from serious contention for the United States presidency after spending a weekend with a Florida model? If, according to Darwinian theory, most competition boils down to mate competition, these questions raise other questions. Why isn't the Iron Lady a Red Queen? Why, unlike Idi Amin, Hsiao-Ching, and past kings and queens in her own country, is Margaret Thatcher unlikely to get away with arbitrary executions of her countrymen?

When Darwinians are forced to explain things that seem to *impede,* rather than advance, the spread of individuals' genes, they consider two lines of explanation. Both hinge on one point: understanding the environment. According to the first, novel stimuli sometimes lead to novel responses. Genes selected to solve reproductive problems in an old environment may fail in a new one. Each evolutionist has his favorite example; I have one of my own. Every spring cardinals are hurt or killed when they fly into glass. This is, almost without doubt, not an adaptive response. What brings it about? During most of the time cardinals were evolving, windows were not a regular feature on the landscape. Other birds, though, certainly were. At the sight of a bird of about the same age, size, and sex as itself, staring the cardinal unflinchingly in the face, a quick charge might have meant a genetic payoff more often than not. But when windows became common, this changed the environmental rules of the game. Cardinals have yet to catch up.

The second reason why we moderns may not seem to be spreading our genes "correctly" is even simpler. Familiar stimuli may be there, but we may be unaware of them. We may *seem* to be failing to solve reproductive problems because we don't yet understand what those problems are. Let me use another example to make this point. As Stephen J. Gould (1977) has pointed out, the huge antlers of the extinct Irish elk were thought, early in this century, to counter Darwin's theory. They must, some insisted, have gotten in the way of feeding and fleeing; they must have killed more elk than they helped survive. What the skeptics forgot was that for male elk, female elk were a crucial part of the landscape. The well-fed, well-sped Irish elk who couldn't attract a mate wouldn't have left many modestly antlered little elk behind.

The big question, then, becomes: Are modern, monogamous, democrats more like cardinals flying into glass, or like poor, misunderstood Irish elk? A lot of evolutionists are opting for the former (for example, Lumsden and Wilson 1981, Symons 1989, Tooby and Cosmides 1990). Others, perhaps more impressed by the fit between theory and fact in the past, are reluctant to give up the possibility that people in modern societies are still acting adaptively (for example, Betzig 1989, Turke 1990).

It seems to me that two conditions should be fatal to polygyny—and so to male bias and to despotic politics. The weak will lose to the strong less often when they are free to *flee* from them, and when they are able to *bargain* with them. Freedom to flee must go up in the absence of obstacles to flight. As Robert Carneiro (1970) pointed out, important obstacles to flight include geographic barriers like the Andes in Peru, ecological barriers like the dearth that surrounded the Tigris and Euphrates deltas, and population pressure. Perhaps just as importantly, I think, subjects should be able to bargain with the strong when their services become essential and irreplaceable (Betzig 1982, 1986, 1990). Such bargaining power should rise—and over the course of modernization seems to have risen—with the division of labor. My tentative hypothesis is that we are more monogamous, less sex biased, and more democratic now than we once were simply because we *need* each other more than we did.

Whether or not that's so—whether we're Irish elk after all or cardinals flying against glass—a Darwinian approach should help us explain why we do what we do, in terms of *what we have done*. For historians, this is a common theme—we might understand the present by understanding our written past. Darwinians add this variation—we might understand the written past by understanding our evolutionary past. Edwin Muir (1952) began with the question, How can I turn this wheel that turns my life? The answer must be, by knowing where it was meant to go.

8

Political Science

Roger D. Masters

═══════════════════════════════════════

BIOPOLITICS: A HISTORY OF THE SUBFIELD

Political philosophers have traditionally been concerned with the impact of "human nature" on politics. Theorists from Plato and Aristotle to Rousseau and Marx were thoroughly familiar with the life sciences of their own times and considered it essential to relate their own ideas to biological facts and theories. Modern academic students of political theory have, however, typically showed little interest in the kind of scientific study of human nature that once was central to philosophical reflection.

The same aversion to, or distance from, biology also characterizes the *empirical* studies of politics. The twentieth-century profession of political science early on adopted a resolutely "environmentalist" view of social behavior. Biology became equated with social Darwinism (and viewed as a politically motivated defense of capitalism) or, later, with simplistic genetic determinism (and thus associated with the horrors perpetrated by Nazi Germany). As a result, by the 1960s there were virtually no political scientists trained in biology or interested in its relevance for their research.

This situation has begun to change as an increasing number of scholars show interest in the biological aspects of politics. The word *biopolitics* was coined by Lynton K. Caldwell in 1964 to describe public policy issues, such as those concerning the ecological degradation associated with modern industry, that require technical understanding of research in the life sciences. Others have followed Caldwell in using the word to refer to such policy issues. *Biopolitics* has, however, taken on a second meaning, related to evolutionary theory, with which I shall be primarily concerned in this chapter.

In 1968, Albert Somit published an influential article, entitled "Toward a More Biologically Oriented Political Science," in the *Midwest Political Science Review*. Two years later, Thomas Thorson gave the title *Biopolitics* to a book in which he argued that contemporary evolutionary biology should become the framework for political theory. In the same year, 1970, a number of papers on empirical political research in biopolitics were presented at the International Political Science Association meeting in Munich, reflecting the emerging awareness that ethology, neurochemistry, and other approaches in the life sciences are relevant to political analysis. In 1979, John Wahlke's presidential address to the American Political Science Association was a call for a more ethological or "biobehavioral" perspective in the profession, based on his critical evaluation of the disappointing results of environmentalist and behaviorist research in political science.

By the late 1970s, scholars active in biopolitics—including Albert Somit, Glendon Schubert, Thomas Wiegele, Elliott White, Meredith Watts, Fred Kort, Jean Laponce, and myself—formed the Association for Politics and the Life Sciences. This organization, which has since become an organized section of the American Political Science Association, began publishing *Politics and the Life Sciences* under Wiegele's editorship, in order to provide a journal presenting new research and multiple peer reviews in biopolitics. Paralleled by a section on biopolitics in the International Political Science Association (led by Somit) and other groups with similar interests—including the Gruter Institute for Law and Behavioral Research (applying evolutionary theory by law) and the Hastings Center (focusing primarily on medical ethics)—this convergence of activity led to many conferences and workshops as the new subfield of biopolitics took form.

Along with these organizational developments, publication of biopolitical research began to proliferate. In addition to articles in various professional journals, much of this research has appeared in edited volumes focused on specific topic areas or issues. After Somit's pioneering *Biology and Politics* in 1976, subsequent edited works have included Elliott White's *Sociobiology and Human Politics* (1981), Meredith Watts's *Biopolitics: Ethological and Physiological Approaches* (1981), Thomas Weigele's *Biology and the Social Sciences* (1982), Margaret Gruter and Paul Bohannan's *Law, Biology and Culture* (1983), Meredith Watts's *Biopolitics and Gender* (1984), Elliott White and Joseph Losco's *Biology and Bureaucracy* (1986), Margaret Gruter and Roger Masters' *Ostracism: a Social and Biological Phenomenon* (1986), and, most recently, Glendon Schubert and Roger Masters' *Primate Politics* (1990). In Germany, Heiner Flohr and Wolfgang Tönnesmann edited a parallel volume, *Politik und Biologie,* in 1983. As might be expected, integrative studies in which a single author brings the entire field together have been slower to appear: after Wiegele's *Biopolitics* in 1979, a decade passed before the publication of Glendon Schubert's *Evolutionary Politics* (1989) and my own *The Nature of Politics* (Masters 1989).

THE SCOPE OF BIOPOLITICS

Although others have divided the area slightly differently, I think it is convenient to distinguish five areas of interest within the subfield of biopolitics. These are (1) human nature and political theory, (2) sociobiology and the evolution of politics, (3) ethology and political behavior, (4) somatic correlates of political behavior (ranging from neurochemistry or psychophysiology to overall states of health), and (5) public policy implications of the biological sciences. A brief outline of these five areas follows.

HUMAN NATURE AND POLITICAL THEORY

As noted above, political philosophers traditionally based their theories of politics on an assessment of human nature. Hobbes (1962) argued in the *Leviathan* that humans are naturally competitive, describing the "natural condition of mankind" as a "war of all against all" in which the "life of man [is] solitary, poor, nasty, brutish and short" (100). By contrast, Rousseau

(1964) asserts in the *Second Discourse* that humans are naturally peaceful and isolated animals, "wandering in the forests, without speech, without domicile, without war, and without liaisons" (137). Which of these theories is correct? Or was Aristotle right in his insistence, in the *Politics,* that we are the *zoon politikon* or "political animal"? And what about Marx's claim in his *1844 Manuscripts* that humans naturally cooperate freely in the production of goods and services because, like any other animal, "the whole character of a species—its species character—is contained in the character of its life activity"? (Marx 1964, 113).

It has been customary to study the works of these great political philosophers with the tools of textual analysis and intellectual history. One considers the writer's intellectual coherence or historical context rather than subjecting his theory to currently available scientific evidence. As Moors (1984) put it, "each major work of political philosophy provides a unique unity of form (manner of portrayal), substance (material considered), and method (how one investigates...)" (140). The conventional approach of most scholars to the history of ideas has thus been suspicious of, if not openly hostile to, the establishment of falsifiable hypotheses like those of the natural sciences.

In political theory, biopolitics challenges this conventional approach (Hartigan 1989). Human nature is one of the fundamental questions in all political thinking, and the theories put forth by political philosophers *can* be evaluated more or less objectively. As it happens, the issues posed when contemporary biologists study the origins of social behavior in other species turn out to be identical to those defined by secular political philosophers in the Western tradition. For example, sociobiologists often discuss the sources of "selfishness" and "altruism" in terms of the individual animal's costs and benefits. The existence of group interests as distinct from the advantages of potentially competing individuals has been vigorously debated by evolutionary biologists over the last two decades. In political philosophy, the questions—and often even the terms—are identical (Somit 1976, White 1981, Masters 1982, 1989a).

Plato, Aristotle, Hobbes, Rousseau, and Marx could be said to have elaborated, in archetypical form, the various ways of understanding social behavior. Each of their perspectives contains an element of truth, articulating a model or understanding of human nature that is consistent with some aspect of the evolutionary view of human social life. For instance, Plato and Aristotle were right to insist that humans were naturally sociable animals. Hobbes was correct to assert that, over most of human existence, the centralized State was inconsistent with the balance of individual costs and benefits. Rousseau properly objected to the Hobbesian definition of the "state of nature" as a misleading image of hominid evolution. Marx intelligently pointed to differences in modes of resource acquisition as essential to the explanation of differences between one human society and another.

Today it looks as though Plato and Aristotle had insight into the ethological foundations of human social behavior, Hobbes saw that cost–benefit models (like the Prisoner's Dilemma or inclusive fitness theory) can explain social cooperation among small groups of kin or reciprocating neighbors but not the existence of centralized governments with coercive powers. Rousseau focused on the need for an adequate evolutionary account of the emergence of human rationality and complex social organization. And Marx anticipated the application of behavioral ecology to the analysis of cultural and historical differences in human economic and political structures.

Yet if each of these major positions in Western political philosophy has an element of validity, none is entirely consistent with evolutionary knowledge. Each great theorist's concepts and explanations properly apply to only a limited domain, and they need to be restated in the light of contemporary scientific findings and theories (Ruse 1986, Masters 1982). As a result, we are witnessing a return to naturalism in political philosophy (Hartigan 1989). Much of my own research—notably *The Nature of Politics* (Masters 1989a)—has focused on this aspect of biopolitics.

SOCIOBIOLOGY AND THE EVOLUTION OF POLITICS

The second of the five research areas of biopolitics is closely related to the one just described. In 1975, Edward O. Wilson used the term *sociobiology* to describe the natural selection of animal social behavior. The human applications of this term have stirred a great deal of controversy, yet the underlying conception of a cost–benefit theory explaining differences in social behavior has had a long tradition both in economics (and game theory) and in political philosophy. Some political scientists now see that *theoretical models* of animal social behavior based on the cost–benefit approach of evolutionary theory and behavioral ecology are directly relevant to questions of *human cooperation and competition* that are basic to human politics.

This level of analysis concerns "ultimate causes"—as seen from the perspective of the theorist or scientist—as distinct from the "proximate causes" that operate at the level of the organism. When one says that natural selection favors bodily structures or behaviors that have net benefits for transmitting genes to future generations (reproductive success), one is not saying that organisms knowingly calculate their "inclusive fitness" when responding to different ecological circumstances. As we shall see, this perspective—which I prefer to describe as "behavioral ecology" in order to emphasize the varied adaptive responses to the social and physical environment— is quite unlike the genetic determinism implied in the simplistic presentations used to popularize sociobiological theory.

Among the key works in this area, several emphasize human political and social behavior. Robert Axelrod and William D. Hamilton's "The Evolution of Cooperation" (1981) and Axelrod's *The Evolution of Cooperation* (1984) show how the Prisoner's Dilemma can be used to explore the TIT-for-TAT strategy as an explanation of cooperation, formalizing Trivers's insightful conception of "reciprocal altruism" (Trivers 1971). In *Economic Behaviour in Adversity* (1987) and several articles, the economist Jack Hirshleifer integrates the basic models of cooperation in economics and evolutionary theory, showing the parallel between Wilson's approach to sociobiology and standard cost-benefit calculus of utility theory. Howard Margolis, in his *Selfishness, Altruism, and Rationality* (1984), developed an elegant model of the duality of preferences for individual and collective "goods." Supplementing the prevailing emphasis on natural selection at the individual level, Margolis indicated how collective goods can evolve; his model could account for Richard Alexander's extension of reciprocal altruism to indirect reciprocity and the emergence of largescale societies and states (Alexander 1979).

To be sure, critics—notably Richard Lewontin, Steven Rose, and Leonard Kamin, in their *Not in Our Genes* (1984)—have emphasized the ideological dangers of sociobiology. Even more important, Philip Kitcher's *Vaulting Ambition* (1985) stresses the methodological hazards of inferences based on presumed adaptiveness. He believes models of natural selection should not be treated as explanations of observed phenotypes and behavior unless they are treated as falsifiable hypotheses that have been confirmed by experimental or observational data. Nevertheless, as Alexander Rosenberg noted in his *Sociobiology and the Preemption of Social Science* (1980), the perspective of evolutionary theory seems destined to become the central paradigm of social and political science.

It is worth mentioning here that many scholars in other disciplines have recently used evolutionary theory to analyze issues that have direct implications for the study of politics. For example, Lionel Tiger's *The Manufacture of Evil* (1987) discusses modern industrial society in the light of our species' evolved behavioral repertoire, and thereby explains many of the tensions underlying contemporary politics. Robin Fox's *The Search for Society* (1989) attacks the predominant relativism underlying theories in cultural anthropology—and most of political science. From a different perspective, Stephen Jay Gould's *Wonderful Life* (1989) shows how fossil evidence from the Burgess Shale of the late Cambrian can explain the process of history; Gould demonstrates the ideological nature of the progressive view of history shared by nineteenth-century social Darwinists, twentieth-century Marxists, and conventional liberal reformers.

ETHOLOGY AND POLITICAL BEHAVIOR

Stimulated by best-selling popularizations of ethology by Robert Ardrey and Konrad Lorenz, the application of ethology to human political behavior has been the focus of widespread interest. While the ecological approach has methodological implications for political science as a whole (Watts 1981, Schubert 1989), it has been particularly valuable as a way of illuminating specific phenomena. Let me mention a few examples.

Political Socialization. The behaviors of dominance, submission, and authority in groups of preschool children were among the first areas in biopolitical research (for example, Barner-Barry and Strayer, in Watts 1981, White, in White 1981). These studies show that patterns of behavior with political implications develop as thchild matures. Here, empirical observation informed by ethology shows that the nature and ontogeny of social interaction and status formation is similar in nonhuman primates and the learning process of child development.

Political Decision Making. The ethological techniques used to study nonhuman primates and children have also proved valuable in observational studies of political decision making. Particularly notable have been explorations of the roles of age and nonverbal cues. See, for example, James Schuberts' "Ethological Methods of Observing Small Group Political Decision-Making" (1983) and work by Schubert, Wiegele, and Hines (1986) on age and political behavior in collective decision making.

War and International Relations. Because the early popularization of ethology by Lorenz and Ardrey focused on aggression, it is hardly surprising that some scholars have looked at "the biology of war and peace." In addition to Eibl-Eibesfeldt's 1979 work of that name, recent studies include Vernon Reynolds, Ian Vine, and Vincent Falger's collected volume, *The Sociobiology of Ethnocentrism* (1987) and R. Paul Shaw and Yuwa Wong's *Genetic Seeds of Warfare* (1989), and Mary Maxwell's *Morality among Nations* (1990).

Gender and Politics. Reconsideration of the politically relevant differences between male and female behavior, stimulated by Lionel Tiger's *Men in Groups* (1969), has been explored by numerous scholars (for example, Watts 1984). Work has varied from Schubert's emphasis on the unique methodological and theoretical contributions of women (Schubert 1989,

Schubert and Masters 1990) to studies of cultural differences in gender roles from an evolutionary perspective (Dickemann 1979a, Masters 1984) and gender differences in political information processing (Masters 1989b).

Nonverbal Cues and Popular Attitudes. An ethological perspective has also illuminated the way human leaders establish and maintain their positions. Stimulated by Ray Larsen's insight that the phenomenon of charisma would be illuminated by ethology, and Michael R. A. Chance's observation that among primates status is associated with patterns of attention, political scientists have begun to reconsider the dynamics of leadership. Below I describe in detail some current work on facial displays of political leaders.

In short, ethology in general—and primatology in particular—has much to offer on many specific issues in political science. Because an evolutionary approach cuts across conventional boundaries within political science, it is hardly surprising that this research can contribute to deepening methodological sophistication and exploring issues in political philosophy as well as to empirical discoveries concerning contemporary politics. *Primate Politics,* a volume edited by Glendon Schubert and myself (1990), illustrates this integrative role of biopolitics. It contains essays touching on most of the themes mentioned above.

SOMATIC CORRELATES OF POLITICAL BEHAVIOR

For some specialists in biopolitics, direct studies of the physical substrates of political behavior are valuable complements to more traditional techniques. Early studies concerned such things as the effect of depressants (such as alcohol) on political behavior, the effect of stress on leaders during international crises, and psychophysiological arousal as a predictor of student protest. A more recent example is the work of Michael McGuire and his colleagues. They use vervet monkeys, rather than humans, to study the role of the neurotransmitter serotonin in dominance and submissive behavior (see McGuire and Raleigh in Gruter and Masters 1986). Douglas Madson (1985) has shown how this biochemical property may be related to power seeking in humans.

Such research has both theoretical and practical implications, as was evident in a conference at Dartmouth College
organized by the Gruter Institute for Law and Behavior Research
and the Rockefeller Center for the Social Sciences. At this
meeting, scholars from a number of disciplines discussed the
legal and social implications of behaviors associated with
serotonergic functioning, which has been implicated in some
forms of violent crime, suicide, depression, and seasonal affective
disorder (McGuire and Masters, in preparation).

PUBLIC POLICY

Since the term *biopolitics* was first used with reference to
ecological issues in public policy, it is fitting that considerable
work continues to focus on these problems. Numerous articles
now appear in mainstream political science journals on such
policy matters as pollution, biomedical technologies, genetic
engineering, and food aid. Implicit in many of these endeavors
has been the desire to call attention to the issue of species
survival for consideration by political elites and policymakers
(see Corning in Somit 1976).

There is also a broader range of biopolitical writings that
conjure up the prospect that public policymakers need first to
be better informed about biology. Consider, for example, Lionel
Tigers's *The Manufacture of Evil* (1987) or Robin Fox's *The Search
for Society* (1989). They question the very viability of
contemporary industrial society from a naturalistic perspective.
For example, they ask whether excessive stress is placed on our
species' evolved behavioral propensities in a densely populated
and polluted world, where the resource surplus (to which
Westerners are accustomed) may be impossible to maintain. The
evolutionary approach to politics and policy seeks standards of
analysis and judgment capable of accounting for the continually
changing relationships among social institutions, environmental
circumstances, and human behavior.

THE ETHOLOGY OF POLITICS IN THE TELEVISION AGE

The foregoing, rather sweeping, survey of biopolitics may or
may not persuade the reader that a biological approach can

make a difference to the study of politics. In this section, I elaborate on one of the five types of research mentioned above—that of ethology—and describe in some detail the work done by my colleagues and myself on facial expressions. The work consisted of experiments carried out from 1982 through 1989, a period that included two American presidential campaigns. Our interest was in finding out how the nonverbal cues, in the facial displays and voice of political leaders, and especially of candidates in the 1984 and 1988 elections, affected onlookers.

We started from the not-particularly-sociobiological premise that the nonverbal behavior of two rivals for power might be a relevant cue in the formation of public attitudes toward them. Western literature provides ample evidence that leaders have traditionally attended to such behavior as a crucial element in establishing and maintaining status and power (for example, see Gloucester's speech in Shakespeare's *Henry VI*, act 3, scene 3, lines 168–95; or Milton's *Paradise Lost*, II, 302–9.) Indeed, in the study of rhetoric, training in nonverbal behavior—and especially in the appropriate facial displays of emotion—was once considered a necessary element in social and political success.

We also started with insights from Darwin, as well as modern ethologists, about the specific roles that facial expression can play in guiding behavior. See, for example, R. A. Hinde's *Ethology* (1982); M. R. A. Chance's *Social Fabrics of the Mind* (1989); and Kevin MacDonald's *Social and Personality Development* (1988). Much work had already been done on human responses to the facial expressions of others, and some work had been done on primates showing how facial gestures can help an individual establish and maintain social dominance (Van Hooff 1969, Chance 1976, de Waal 1982). It was known, for example, that responses to facial displays can be influenced by other nonverbal or verbal cues, by the social context or setting, and by the prior experience or status of the interacting individuals.

Among both human and nonhuman primates, there are three types of facial display that are particularly important in interactions between leaders and followers: anger or threat, fear or evasiveness, and happiness or social reassurance. It should be noted that each can be an indicator of the individual's actual state, *or* it can be a message being sent to others. The two are not always the same: for instance, one can fake anger in order to intimidate a child. The smiling face is often used as a signal of reassurance. Eibl-Eibesfeldt (1979) has observed that the human "greeting display" includes elements of surprise (head tilted back and eyebrows raised, as well as the smiling mouth) and that taken together these indicate "pleasant surprise" at seeing a friend. Apes use a similar greeting display when they see strangers or associates who have been away for a long time. It may be presumed that the display indicates an absence of hostile intent and thus lowers the probability of an aggressive encounter.

In our study we could hardly investigate every aspect of leader-follower nonverbal signals. We limited ourselves to reactions of viewers when President Reagan and other presidential candidates are shown on television with different facial expressions. In the first study, we collected videotapes from President Reagan's appearances on TV, selecting short excerpts that contained particularly good examples of the three major social emotions: anger/threat, fear/evasion, and happiness/reassurance. (See table 1 for the components of the three relevant facial expressions.) To insure that our results were not limited to a single leader, subsequent experiments showed either comparable excerpts of three French leaders (Masters and Sullivan 1989) or happy/reassuring and neutral excerpts of all candidates in the 1984 and 1988 presidential campaigns (Sullivan and Masters 1988, 1990b).

In the first type of experiment (Masters et al. 1986, Lanzetta et al. 1985, Masters and Sullivan 1989), three examples of each type of display— or nine excerpts in all—were shown with different modes of presentation to different groups of viewers: some saw the excerpts with sound plus image, some saw image only (no sound), others saw sound only (no image). Later studies focused on the contrast between seeing video images of a number of candidates with and without the sound (Sullivan and Masters 1988, 1990b). To control for the effect of showing isolated excerpts of leaders, an additional study inserted silent images of President Reagan's displays in the background of standard TV news stories (Sullivan and Masters 1990a).

CRITERIA FOR CLASSIFYING FACIAL DISPLAYS			
	Anger/ threat	Fear/ evasion	Happiness/ reassurance
Eyelids:	Opened wide	Upper raised, lower tightened	Wide, normal, or slightly closed
Eyebrows:	Lowered	Lowered and furrowed	Raised
Eye orientation:	Staring	Averted	Focused then cut off
Mouth corners:	Forward or lowered	Retracted, normal	Retracted and/or raised
Teeth showing:	Lower or none	Variable	Upper or both
Head motion:			
Lateral	None	Side-to-side	Side-to-side
Vertical	Up	Down	Up-down
Head orientation:			
To body	Forward from trunk	Turned from vertical	Normal to trunk
Angle to vertical	Down	Down	Up

Table 1. Adapted from Lanzetta et al., 1985 (reproduced by permission of Sage Publications, Inc.) Although earlier versions of this table do not indicate vertical head motion for anger/threat or fear/evasion, recent work of other scholars (such as Eibl-Eibesfeldt, 1989) and careful observation of videotapes indicate these cues may also be present.

In our experiments, subjects were merely told that we were interested in the effects of the media on politics; they generally did not suspect that our interest was in nonverbal behavior. After answering a standard questionnaire, indicating political opinions and attitudes, they were shown the close-up videos. After the viewing they were asked to describe the leaders' behavior (using 0–6 scales to provide measure of perceived display intensity). Then they were asked to report their own emotional feelings during the viewings. At the end of most of our studies we measured changes in attitude in order to see whether the excerpts had changed the viewers' opinions of the leaders.

In this series of experiments, we tried to find out several things: (1) Did the audience correctly interpret the displays (that is, were their descriptions of the leader's behavior consistent with the objective criteria used to choose the excerpts)? (2) Did they accurately report their own reactions? (This was investigated by comparing their states of physiological arousal, such as heart rate and blood pressure, to their written reports). (3) Did they have different reactions when the picture or sound was off? (4) Did they react differently from one another, according to their previous loyalty to a particular candidate? (5) Did their opinions of the leaders change as a result of the leader's facial expressions on the videotape?

The answer to the first question was a resounding yes: viewers easily recognized and described the leader's behavior in ways consistent with the objective definition of their nonverbal displays. Secondly, the viewers' own emotional reactions differed depending on the kind of display they saw— and these reactions were validated by physiological measurements. Third, there was a difference in emotional response depending on the channel of communication, since image-only presentations elicited stronger responses to happiness/reassurance videos than did presentations accompanied by sound (Masters et al. 1986, Masters and Sullivan 1990).

The results regarding questions 4 and 5 above were especially important. Not only did viewers' reactions to a leader's display differ depending on their previous attitudes to him, but some changes in viewers' attitudes were often discovered. On the one hand, differences in a leaders' display behavior had a bigger emotional effect on viewers who already supported him than on neutral or critical viewers (Masters et al. 1986); on the other hand, the experience of seeing nonverbal displays had the largest lasting effects on the attitudes of neutral viewers (Sullivan and Masters 1990a).

Happiness/reassurance displays elicited stronger emotion from supporters, and had the effect of neutralizing the negative feelings of critics. Fear/evasion elicited negative feelings from supporters and critics alike. The responses to anger/threat were more complex, depending on attitude, nationality, and channel of communication (Lanzetta et al. 1985, Sullivan and Masters 1990a, 1990b, Masters and Sullivan 1989, 1990).

Of the numerous other findings, a few will indicate the complex effects of nonverbal behavior.

Context of rivalry. When rivals are both shown during the experiment, particularly at election time, descriptions of the leaders' emotions have a higher correlation with the viewers' established political attitudes (Masters and Sullivan 1990).

Performance style of the leader. Displays perceived as mixtures of distinct cues elicit weaker emotions, are less likely to activate prior opinions favorable to the leader, and produce less favorable attitude change (Sullivan and Masters 1988, 1990b, Masters and Sullivan 1989, 1990).

Intensity of display. Higher intensity happiness/reassurance displays elicit stronger psychophysiological responses, and the greater the perceived difference between a leader's neutral and happy/reassuring display, the more that happy/reassuring excerpt enhances viewers' emotional responses (Masters and Sullivan 1990).

Culture. In a cross-cultural comparison we have completed, descriptive ratings and emotions showed a similar structure in France and the United States, but French viewers were more likely to respond with positive emotion to an anger/threat display, and their prior attitudes were more likely to influence descriptions and emotional responses (Masters and Sullivan 1989).

Status of leader. The more favorable the public opinion toward a leader, the stronger the effects of the same displays (Masters and Sullivan 1990).

Without going further into the system of response and its neurological substrate (see Masters and Sullivan 1990, Appendix 1), suffice it to say that these studies show that biopolitical research is far from reductionist or simplistic. Our experiments permit a more realistic assessment of the way episodic memories are formed under the influence of perceptions and emotional memories at the moment of watching a leader. Given the importance of nominating conventions, major speeches, or press conferences, and—more generally—the emergence of television as the medium by which leaders communicate with the public, such effects are critical if we are to understand the contemporary political process.

Conclusion

The foregoing examples should indicate the variety and interest of recent studies in biopolitics. Research inspired by evolutionary biology can improve our understanding of politics and illuminate issues in public policy. Not only do the latest evolutionary or ethological approaches to the study of human politics avoid the genetic reductionism or determinism originally associated with sociobiology and ethology, but the consequences may be quite different from those imagined by early critics.

In matters of public policy, the proposals of our leaders and the rules of our governmental agencies frequently rest on highly oversimplified conceptions of human nature and an outmoded understanding of the life sciences and biomedical technology. Equally important, however, may be the contribution of biopolitics in improving our understanding of the political process itself. How do emotions interact with judgments in forming political attitudes (cf. Frank, Kenrick and Hogan, and Crawford, this volume)? Why do males and females often differ in their responses to the same events (cf. Betzig, and Kenrick and Hogan, this volume; Masters 1984, 1989b)? What are the circumstances in which centralized states emerge and collapse—and why do democratic regimes differ from despotic ones (cf. Betzig, this volume; Masters 1989a)?

At a more theoretical level, an evolutionary perspective suggests that human nature may establish limits to the social experiments consistent with what could properly be called justice and the good society (Masters 1989a, Hartigan 1989). Reflection on such issues is in keeping with a long tradition of moral and political philosophy that can best be called naturalism (cf. Chandler, Ruse, and Lumsden, this volume). From my perspective, biopolitics can enhance our ability to engage in scientifically informed dialogue concerning the nature of a healthy and decent human community.

9

Ethical Philosophy

John Chandler

Ethics is that branch of philosophy that inquires into human morality. Some of the topics that have been considered philosophically over the centuries are: Why are people moral? Which acts are good? How can we know which acts are good?

Can evolutionary biology deepen our understanding of human moral behavior and the basis of moral codes? Sociobiologists claim that it can. E. O. Wilson, in his *Sociobiology: the New Synthesis* (1975), which was the first manifesto for this approach, goes so far as to claim that natural selection "must explain ethics and ethical philosophers at all levels" (3). In this chapter I shall assess Wilson's claim from several points of view.

As the philosopher Philip Kitcher points out in his book *Vaulting Ambition* (1985), there are a number of ways in which empirical biological theories could be relevant to the understanding of ethics (417). First, evolutionary considerations may help to causally explain why people make the moral judgments they do, why they behave morally, and why moral codes exist. Second, sociobiology may reveal facts about human nature that are of significance in the light of moral principles we already accept; most dramatically, many writers have argued that evolutionary theory shows that altruism as ordinarily understood is a myth. Third, sociobiology may have metaethical implications about the logical status of moral judgments. For example, if sociobiology can show that ethical "intuitions" are the outcome of biological causes, it may undermine confidence in their objectivity.

Each of these possibilities will be scrutinized in this chapter. Before proceeding to that task, however, let me first grant that morality is apparently universal. While there is much variation in their content, moral codes, in the broad sense of sets of principles specifying right and wrong conduct, are possessed by every human society. Along with these moral codes go dispositions in individuals to approve and disapprove of behaviors, to experience moral emotions such as sympathy, indignation, and a sense of obligation, and dispositions to cooperate with others. The apparent universality of moral phenomena has suggested to many that their origins are to be found in biologically derived human nature rather than, or in addition to, culture and reflection.

HOW SOCIOBIOLOGY EXPLAINS BEHAVIOR

Sociobiologists take evolution to be a competition for survival among genes. Natural selection does not operate at the level of species or (usually) of social groups; selection pressures operate directly upon individuals and their genes. With this recognition has come a change in the notion of fitness from *individual* fitness to *inclusive* fitness. Inclusive fitness is a measure not of an individual's own chances of survival (no individual does survive indefinitely) but of the chances of that individual's gene set being replicated in future generations.

This very notion makes it possible to see how so-called altruism could have been produced by natural selection. At first sight, *selfish* behavior would seem to be more fitness enhancing than altruism. As Peter Singer says, "If evolution is a struggle for existence, why hasn't it ruthlessly eliminated altruists, who seem to increase another's prospects of survival at the cost of their own?" (Singer 1981, 5). Sociobiologists answer this by declaring that evolution is really a competition among genes rather than among individuals. (*Gene,* here, refers to a gene type, the gene for a particular characteristic, loosely speaking, rather than to particular pieces of DNA). Genes that increase the chances of their carriers reproducing will tend to be more prevalent in successive generations, and will gradually supplant rival genes.

There are two mechanisms by which altruistic traits could proliferate. One has to do with kin altruism (already discussed in previous chapters), in which Ego's traits are passed down through his or her direct or collateral descendants (Hamilton 1964). The other is reciprocal altruism (Trivers 1972, 1985), in which favors can be exchanged even among genetic strangers, so long as there is a likelihood of long-term benefit to the altruist (that is, that the altruist will get more in return than she or he originally gave to others).

DO THESE IDEAS HELP TO EXPLAIN
THE EXISTENCE OF MORALITY?

Human behavior is immensely varied, and there is considerable variation in moral codes and moral behavior, too. This diversity is probably the result of environmental factors such as cultural and economic differences. Biology merely implants broad propensities toward cooperation with, and altruism toward, one's own kin and one's partners; these propensities are modified by environmental factors and can be resisted by the individual.

Yet the types of morality we observe seem relatively "fixed"; and they cohere well with sociobiological theory. Reciprocity, for example, is recognized as a moral requirement pretty universally. The Golden Rule, "Do unto others as you would have them do unto you," bears a resemblance to the policy of reciprocal altruism, "Do unto others a you *expect* them to do unto you." Kinship, likewise, is a central component of social obligation networks, even in modern industrial societies. The morality most people practice is *not* one of "universal benevolence," as promoted by the utilitarian school of ethics. Rather, the strongest obligations are those to family and kin, then to friends who have benefited oneself, then, in diminishing order of urgency, to one's group, tribe, neighborhood, nation— and only lastly to humans in general.

I believe that without innate dispositions toward cooperation, sympathy for others, and care for one's kin and members of one's group, there could be no society, no culture, and no developed moral codes. We cannot explain morality in purely cultural terms, because human culture, and with it morality, could only have developed in a species that was cooperative by nature. Social contract and rational choice theories—two theories widely discussed by philosophers—face the problem of how cooperative social institutions could have originated, and why they survive, given the public nature of many of the "goods" they provide. They also face the problem of the rationality of free-riding and cheating: namely, why don't all people try to duck out of their moral obligations? Sociobiologists William Hamilton and Robert Axelrod (Axelrod and Hamilton 1981, Axelrod 1984), show how cooperative and tit-for-tat strategies could have arisen through natural selection. This approach appears very promising.

In sum, in regard to the first item in Kitcher's list, I believe that evolutionary theory *does* help explain why people make the moral judgments they do, and why moral codes exist. Before leaving this point, though, I should say that I think some philosophers may *too* readily accept the idea that moral phenomena conform to sociobiological predictions. The philosopher Michael Ruse, for example, argues that John Rawls's contractarian account of justice is very much the sort of substantive code "the evolutionist would expect biology to have put in place" (Ruse 1988, 38). Ruse also thinks that the utilitarians' principle of "the greatest happiness for the greatest number" fits readily into evolutionary expectations. Yet these two philosophies are hardly compatible. Rawls himself (author of *A Theory of Justice,* 1971) is a deontological critic of utilitarianism. Deontological ethical theories hold that actions can be right or wrong intrinsically, that is, independently of their consequences, while utilitarians judge entirely by consequences.

Moreover, I note that both these theories criticize *partiality* toward kin and close associates, which is most people's operative morality—and which, *prima facie,* seems more likely to enhance inclusive fitness than universal altruism. The *variety* of moral theories and moral behaviors that Ruse considers to be in line with sociobiological predictions (and thereby confirming the theory) suggests that the implications of that theory are rather imprecise. As a rule, the more possibilities a theory is compatible with, the less explanatory power it possesses and the harder it is to test. These are undesirable attributes in a scientific hypothesis.

IS ALTRUISM A MYTH?

The second of Kitcher's observations that I will take up here is that sociobiology could reveal facts about human nature that are of significance to well-accepted moral principles—especially by showing that altruism is a myth. Sociobiologists do seem to have claimed that there is no such thing as altruism in the sense in which lay people and moralists refer to it. Is this so?

Altruism, in this traditional sense, refers to that which benefits others and is motivated by the desire to benefit others *for their own sake.* Sociobiologists counter that all human action—like all animal action—is really motivated by self-interest. Richard Dawkins (1976) claims that people are "born selfish" (3); Wilson (1978) sees himself as exposing the selfish nature of most forms of altruism (154); and Richard Alexander (1987) maintains that, what philosophers refer to as altruistic or utilitarian behavior is in fact biologically self-interested (88).

I think they are mistaken. Alexander, for instance, in his book *The Biology of Moral Systems* (1987), attacks philosophical ideals of morality that uphold indiscriminate or self-sacrificing beneficence. He claims that instead, "Moral systems are systems of indirect reciprocity" (77)—that is, that one can account completely for the evolution of moral systems in genetically selfish terms. Moral philosophers, Alexander says, erroneously think that morality involves sacrifice, because they have noticed only *direct* altruism. They think the donor does not reap any reward, but in fact his or her descendants—or the donor at a later date—do get rewarded. (In an apparently unguarded moment, however, Alexander lets slip that "I do not doubt that occasional individuals lead lives that are truly altruistic and self-sacrificing" [191]). Thus Alexander appears to deny that genuinely altruistic *motives* are of significance. But let us pay close attention to his level of analysis. Once his distinction between proximate and ultimate mechanisms is noticed, the impression changes.

Proximate mechanisms or causes are the immediate explanations of behavior; they include hormones, muscles, and other physiological causes, and also drives and desires. Alexander is concerned not with these, but with the search for ultimate causes, in the sense of evolutionary explanations for the most general and basic human goals and motivations (14). For example, why is it (or was it during our evolution) adaptive for humans to be *nepotistic*? The ultimate-cause answer to this question is given in terms of nepotism's contribution to inclusive fitness. Now it can be seen that Alexander is *not* denying the existence of altruism in the lay sense. Rather, he is giving the occurrence of altruistic motives an evolutionary explanation!

This yields a sounder position. Once one distinguishes between the "interests" of genes and those of the real human beings whose behavior they influence, it becomes clear that the attribution of "selfishness" to genes in the sociobiological sense of the term is perfectly compatible with genuine altruism on the part of the individual and, indeed, explains it. It is not in the mother's interest *as an individual* to sacrifice herself for her offspring (even if doing so may increase her inclusive fitness and if her sacrifice thus would be in her "genetic interest.") Hence her actions may be genuinely altruistic.

On this interpretation, sociobiology suggests evolutionary explanations for the sorts of motives we already ascribe to people, such as altruism, *rather than discovering hitherto unsuspected impulses toward fitness maximization.* It may be true that proximate causes evolved because of ultimate causes, and therefore may be expected to serve them in most cases, as Alexander claims. It does not follow that proximate causes are not what they seem to philosophers to be. Alexander's hope is that placing our motivation and behavior in an evolutionary context will deepen our understanding of them. It seems to me that this will happen, though not, as Wilson suggests, in ways that "subvert ethics and ethical philosophers." Rather, as Alexander himself has developed at length (Alexander 1987), it lends support to some moral theories (contractarian and Humean) as against others (utilitarian and Kantian).

Finally, a further difference between evolutionary altruism and lay altruism needs notice. This is that the benefits the ordinary altruistic wishes to bestow need not be *reproductive* benefits, and the benefits altruism confers on the altruist likewise need not enhance his or her genetic success. Out of kindness I may distribute Christmas gifts to the unemployed of my neighborhood. This may make them happier, and me happier, but it is unlikely to enhance either their evolutionary fitness or my own.

Rival Explanations of Morality

I hope I have conveyed the idea that the biological research on altruism poses no fundamental threat to the enterprise of ethical philosophy. It is worth adding here that there are, in any case, explanations that rival the theory of the evolution of altruism. Some writers hold that morality has not been directly selected for but is a spin-off from the acquisition of other characteristics that *were* directly selected for. This option has been canvassed by, among others, Peter Singer and Francisco Ayala. Singer's book *The Expanding Circle* (1981), was the first major appraisal of sociobiology by a philosopher. He suggests that the thing that may have been selected for may not have been altruism itself, but other characteristics such as the ability to reason and to calculate the consequences of actions. These abilities—plus preference for kin—may have evolved because of their evolutionary advantages. But once in place, he says, they can lead to new ways of thinking and behaving which are not themselves products of evolution, and not always fitness enhancing.

Singer suggests that human beings' intelligence, which evolved as a general competence, led them to to recognize—over time—that there is no *rational* basis for counting the interests of non-kin as mattering less than the interests of kin. That recognition would lead to the concept of morality as enjoining impartial consideration of the interests of *all* human beings, indeed of all sentient beings. (Hence the title of his book, *The Expanding Circle.*) This is a less deterministic, less reductionist account of the origins of morality than that of Wilson and Alexander, but equally consistent with the Darwinian approach.

The reader will note that the existence of a *rival* explanatory theory that satisfies the same background conditions and appears capable of accounting for the phenomena, implies that it is insufficient to argue for the sociobiological (direct) account of morality merely by arguing that the phenomena are what that theory would lead one to expect. It must be shown to be a better theory than its rival.

Ayala's article "The Biological Roots of Morality" (1987) appeared in the journal *Biology and Philosophy*. Ayala claims that ethical behavior evolved not because it was *itself* adaptive for early hominids but rather because it was the indirect outcome of other abilities and propensities that were selected for. These include the ability to anticipate the consequences of one's actions, to make value judgments, and to choose between alternative courses of action. Specific moral norms, he says, are the result of culture and reflection, not of biology. Moral altruism could not be the product of biological altruism, since their underlying causations are completely disparate: namely, the ensuing genetic benefits in (biological) altruism and regard for others in (moral) altruism (249).

Ayala grants that our biology may predispose us to accept certain moral norms, but that it does not constrain us to do so: we remain free to override our natural inclinations, and we may have the moral duty to do so if we judge them to be bad, even if this reduces our fitness. In fact some moral norms forbid fitness-maximizing behavior, such as impregnating as many women as possible. Behavior that promotes social cooperation is often contrary to an individual's inclusive fitness; but morality customarily enjoins the former nonetheless (250).

In sum, then, in regard to the second item in Kitcher's list, I do not agree that sociobiology reveals anything about human nature that must change our acceptance of the moral principle of altruism. Sociobiology helps to explain our motives to be altruistic, but does not prove that genuine altruism is a myth. Moreover, its particular evolutionary explanation of altruism may be incomplete—we may choose to be altruistic because of other human characteristics, such as intelligence and forward planning.

METAETHICAL IMPLICATIONS

Finally, we come to the third item in Kitcher's list, concerning metaethics. Thus far in this chapter I have been discussing the *biological explanations of morality*, but another topic to be considered is whether biology can offer anything as to the justification and validity of ethics. Most philosophers have denied that it can. Even if our moral sense has an evolutionary cause, the question of the validity of its deliverances remains unaffected, just as the fact that our senses are the products of evolution provides no reason for doubting their deliverances (rather the contrary).

In our everyday life, we assume that moral judgments can be true or false. For instance, we think that someone who believes slavery can be justifiable is plain mistaken, and that what obligations we have, we have regardless of whether we want to have them or whether they are in our interests. Morality appears to stand above and outside nature. Thus, it is often thought that the existence of human moral codes and moral behavior is a response to our recognition of morality's binding injunctions, not a result of strategies of fitness maximization.

Ruse and Wilson, in a joint article published in *Philosophy* in 1988, deny that our morality is a response to *objective* morality. They argue that there is no need to invoke a realm of queer objective values for moral judgments to be true descriptions of, or to account for, our sense of its unconditional demands. Our biological past (and present) is enough to account for morality. For the remainder of this chapter, let me briefly introduce the concepts of justification, intuitionism, subjectivism, and rationality—as they are used by moral philosophers—in order to deal with Ruse and Wilson's joint (and separate) claims.

Moral argument typically involves the invocation of moral principles. Disputed principles are defended by being shown to follow from more general, more basic principles. This process must halt after relatively few steps. The *justification* of ultimate moral principles comes to a terminus with moral convictions for which no further argument is possible, or felt to be needed, convictions that one merely "sees" to be right. These are termed "intuitions." Intuition as a way of knowing ethical truths, however, has been thought by philosophers to be deeply problematic. If two people's basic intuitions conflict, intuition cannot decide who is correct. So although intuitionism is an objectivist metaethic, that is, it asserts that moral beliefs are capable of objective truth and falsity like other beliefs, it appears to have no defense against subjectivists and skeptics who maintain that so-called intuitions are nothing more than the result of early conditioning. In reality, they express personal preferences, and none has any more validity than any other.

For Wilson, what we take as intuitions of moral truth—or *revelations* of objective values—are emotional responses produced in the limbic system by our evolutionary history. When I judge that killing is wrong, for example, I am merely expressing an emotional preference that has a biological cause. Wilson says:

> Like everyone else, philosophers measure their personal emotional responses to various alternatives as though consulting a hidden oracle. . . . Human emotional responses and the more general ethical practices based on them have been programmed to a substantial degree by natural selection over thousands of generations. (Wilson 1975, 6)

So there is no reason to suppose that our intuitions put us in touch with moral values if they are the result of our evolutionary history.

Michael Ruse develops Wilson's case. Morality has a purpose, that of enabling us to cooperate with others for mutual benefit. It serves this purpose only if we believe it is objectively and categorically binding. There *are* nothing but feelings; but unless we believed that morality transcended our feelings and desires, it would not lead us to put aside our selfish desires and cooperate with others so as to keep society going. "In a sense then, morality is a collective illusion foisted upon us by our genes" (Ruse 1986, 253).

This position (without the genetic hypothesis) is basically that of David Hume. Hume first argues against morality being based upon reason, then locates moral judgement in emotional responses to situations. Finally, he argues, we unwittingly project our approvals and disapprovals onto external objects. Hume, however, sees morality as a humanly created artifice rather than a biological phenomenon, which aligns his position with that of Singer and Ayala rather than that of Ruse. I myself fail to see why any illusion is needed for us to act morally. Why suppose we can set self-interest aside only if we believe there is an objective requirement on us to do so? Could not our genes simply have given us propensities to be altruistic or to cooperate for mutual benefit (to remain with sociological explanations) without filling our heads with moral illusions?

The sociobiologist's case against objective values employs a causal argument. It is not necessary, they say, to postulate the existence of values "out there" in order to explain why people have the moral intuitions and beliefs that they do, since their existence is sufficiently explained without invoking objective values. As a matter of fact, the case against objective values is quite strong independently of evolutionary considerations, for instance, "intuitions" can be the result of the internalization of social norms. But the case against objectivism does not mean that the case for ethical *subjectivism* or skepticism is thereby established.

Rationality

The *rationality* of morality does not depend, as Ruse appears to assume, on there existing objective or absolute values. There are alternatives to both subjectivism and the sort of ethical objectivism he and Wilson reject. Wilson makes the case for subjectivism seem stronger by attending only to Intuitionism and religious bases for ethics and ignoring more plausible theories. Many philosophers argue that moral statements can still be rationally justified even if they are not taken to describe a hidden realm of moral facts—indeed, that even if there were such a realm it would be irrelevant to answering practical questions. Morality is practical; moral codes regulate conduct. What matters therefore is finding *reasons* for acting in moral ways.

The standard notion of rationality, for example the one employed in Rational Choice Theory, defines a rational action as one likely to maximize the satisfaction of the agent's desires, whatever these happen to be, provided they are consistent. Thus one has good reason for acting in a certain way if it will achieve more of what you want than anything else you could do. The problem of showing that each of us has good reason to be moral (given this account of "good reasons"), is to show that being moral *is* always the best way of attaining what we most want. Notice that whether a justification of morality along these lines is successful does not depend on the existence of objective moral facts. On this account, what determines the rationality of an action is its relation to what the agent most wants, not necessarily whether the action is in their interests (even less, in the interests of their genes).

This point has considerable importance. As Ruse shows, morality makes it possible for people to cooperate with others for mutual benefit. It is in everyone's interests to live in a moral society. But it is sometimes even more advantageous for a member of a moral society to cheat, when there's no risk of detection. He'll get the benefits of cheating, and the actions of one cheat won't destroy the cooperation on which his, and everyone's well-being depends, so he'll still get the benefits of this. Then, since each individual can reason in the same way, the system of cooperation which benefits them all is endangered. What is individually rational becomes collectively irrational. But *if human beings have altruistic desires* as well as self-interested ones, it will still be rational for them to be moral when it is not in their interests. They will still be achieving what they most want. Altruistic motivation can indeed be seen as natural selection's answer to the cheat, or as it is sometimes called, the "Free-rider problem." (Cf. chapter 5, "Economics," this volume.)

Many of the most popular defenses of the rationality of morality today are Kantian in spirit. John Rawls, for example, portrays the principles of morality as those principles that would be freely adopted by rational agents placed in an ideal position of equal power. Ruse correctly challenges Kant's belief that morality must be the same for all rational beings of whatever species. The point of morality derives from *contingent* facts about human beings such as their limited sympathies, as Hume maintained. Ruse does grant that "in order to go on interacting socially, we must obey the same formal constraints" (1988, 64). But isn't this sufficient to establish the rationality of those constraints? If moral constraints make social cooperation possible, and if social cooperation is necessary for ourselves, our families and other members of our society to achieve their best interests, (whether genetic or phenotypic), and we desire all this, we have excellent reason for doing our bit to ensure that morality flourishes. Here is one basis for a moral theory that is neither objectivist nor subjectivist.

There are others, for example that of Peter Singer (1981) already mentioned. Whether any of these positions is adequate cannot be settled here. The point is that Wilson does not consider them, and that Ruse dismisses them too brusquely. One many wonder why the objectivity of morality should concern sociobiologists at all. As a scientific theory, it is only concerned to explain behavior, not to intervene in philosophical disputes. Ruse's interest in the matter is, I believe, explained by his ambition to develop a naturalistic world view based on Darwinian ideas, to pit against religious and metaphysical world views in every area of thought (Ruse 1986, xii). Moral objectivism is an obstacle to a global Darwinian metaphysic—not to sociobiology as a Darwinian science.

Conclusion

In this chapter I have tried to do three things. First, I showed that sociobiology *does* yield a plausible explanation for the existence of moral codes and moral motivations. Second, I argued that this account does *not* require a denial of the existence of altruism; and that alternative explanations in which human reason plays a larger role are compatible with evolutionary theory and with the observed phenomena. Third, I maintained sociobiology does nothing to undermine the rationality of morality. Overall, I judge that far-reaching claims for the "biologicization of ethics" cannot be sustained.

Sociobiology is a young science and undoubtedly has much of its development ahead of it. Its application to humans is likely to remain controversial since different views of human nature underlie most disagreement between radicals, conservatives, and liberals. Sociobiology, it seems, can neither be dismissed as merely an ideological successor to social Darwinism, nor hailed as the master science of human nature. But it does throw light on the evolutionary origins of human morality. This is no negligible achievement.

10

Cognitive Psychology

Douglas Kenrick and Robert Hogan

Nothing is commoner than the remark that Man differs from lower creatures by the almost total absence of instincts, and the assumption of their work in him by "reason"....On the contrary, there is no material antagonism between instinct and reason.
—William James, *The Principles of Psychology*

The notion that there is an antagonism between "instinct" and "reason" has persisted throughout most of this century, despite William James's (1890) arguments to the contrary. Indeed, psychologists interested in the cognitive processes underlying human reason often compare the brain to an unprogrammed (and instinct-barren) computer. The recent interest in what William James called "evolutionary psychology," however, has increased the general recognition that there is no necessary antagonism between instinct and reason. The evolutionary perspective shows us that if the brain is a computer, it is one that is prewired, preprogrammed, and committed to a strict hierarchy of priorities for receiving and processing information. Human cognitive processes can best be understood only by understanding what those "instinctive" priorities are.

This chapter discusses five ways in which the evolutionary or sociobiological approach can alter the outlook of cognitive psychology. First, the evolutionary approach shows that the

171

study of cognitive *processes* is, by itself, meaningless. To understand cognition, it is essential to consider the *content* as well as the structure of thought. Second, it shows that cognition should not be studied independently of *emotion*. The reasoning computer in the cortex is ultimately the servant of the passions of the limbic system.

Third, an evolutionary or sociobiological approach suggests that the reproductive strategies of males and females are different. Although all humans share extensive common features in the way they think, one should expect to find certain *gender differences* in cognition. Fourth, the evolutionary approach shows that social cognition may be *domain specific;* that is, there may be special programs of the brain devoted to dealing with certain kinds of social interactions. Fifth, an evolutionary perspective allows psychologists to interpret short-term cognitive processing in the light of *long-term* evolutionary factors, and to thereby understand their ultimate significance.

THE CONTENT OF THOUGHT

Piaget, Levi-Strauss, Chomsky, Kohlberg, Vygotsky, Luria, and other writers associated with the "cognitive revolution" in North American psychology argued that in trying to understand human thought, its specific content is essentially irrelevant (cf. Kohlberg 1971). The content of thought, they proposed, is a text to be interpreted. Their goal has been to identify the invariant linguistic or judgmental structures (for example, Chomsky's language acquisition device, Piaget's circular reflexes, Kohlberg's stages of moral development) that underlie the highly changeable surface content of cognition, because these structures generate the overt content of thought.

The search for regularity beneath the diversity of surface phenomena is, of course, the historic mission of science, and in searching for the elementary structures of thought, cognitive psychologists are doing what good scientists have always done. But the content/structure distinction in cognitive psychology is problematic for at least three reasons. First, from a methodological point of view, it has proven very difficult to separate the two; the presence of certain structures is often denoted by certain kinds of content (Levine 1979). For instance, endorsing the Koran signifies Level 4 moral reasoning.

Second, we believe these earlier writers were searching for the wrong kind of structure. The real structure underlying cognition is likely to be neurological; contained in the wiring of the central nervous system. More importantly, prewired "feature detectors" are always triggered by the specific content of events in the environment. Sometimes the triggering is erroneous, as when a cat pounces on leaves rippled by the wind, but in the absence of specific content, particular neurological structures of thought will not be activated. So, once again, we believe that the traditional structure/content distinction of cognitive psychology cannot be rigorously maintained.

Third, and perhaps most important, we note that the structures that cognitive psychologists have postulated to underlie thought have an arbitrary quality—they seem to have little to do with biological reality. Our cognitive/ intellectual architecture, as shaped by the pressures of evolution, must be designed to solve certain kinds of problems. We suspect that the "real" structure of cognition will reflect these different, concrete, problem-solving capacities. Thus, humans are likely to reason differently when they are thinking about how to attract a mate than when they are thinking about how to hunt a lion, and both of these tasks may overlap little with the way people think when they are deciding whether a penguin is a bird or not.

In support of this general idea of reasoning, Sherry and Schacter (1987) review extensive evidence that suggests that animals have qualitatively different memory systems to deal with different types of information. For instance, a bird learns to sing the songs of its species during an early sensitive period, often before it is capable of performing the song adequately, and later practice may only serve to improve the fidelity of performance. By contrast, memory for food stores is frequently erased and remains flexible throughout life. Yet memory for sickening foods provides a completely different pattern, in which the animal may learn an aversion on one trial and store its memory permanently with little or no input from experience.

In humans, the assumption that the brain is an unpro-grammed general-purpose computer has been challenged by recent work on "brain modules" (see Gazzaniga 1985, Gardner 1983.) It has been found, for example, that particular types of brain damage may hinder a person's ability to remember human faces even though other types of complex memory remain intact. Still other types of brain damage may destroy the ability to act in a socially appropriate manner, without destroying other problem-solving abilities. These and other findings from physiological psychology suggest that different areas of the brain are more specialized and differentiated than psychologists previously believed.

Thus, the "structure of thought" is not something that can be discovered apart from content.

COGNITION AND EMOTION

Researchers studying social cognition often distinguish between "cold" and "hot" cognition (for example, Markus and Zajonc 1985). Hot cognition is thought that occurs under conditions of aroused motivation or emotion; cold cognition is more like the "information processing" done by a computer. Some models of cognition reduce even motivational and emotional states to cold cognition, and treat them as nothing more than additional bits of information for the cortical computer. For instance, Wyer and Srull (1986) assign emotional states the same status as any other informational tags or labels used to store and retrieve linguistically coded memories. From this viewpoint, emotional information is distinctive only in that it is stored along with representations of the person's internal subjective reactions.

An evolutionary perspective on social cognition differs in two important respects from this traditional approach. First, from such a perspective, cognitive processes are assumed never to be truly cold; cognition always serves the motivational goals of the limbic system. Second, cognitive processes associated with one emotional state should be qualitatively different from those associated with other emotional states. We think differently when we are afraid than when we are in love.

Over a century ago, William James (1890), was concerned with the relation between cognition and emotion. It was James who suggested that people's intuitions about emotion might be completely wrong, and that a person does not run from a bear because he is afraid, but instead surmises that he is afraid because he observes himself running.

James's successor at Harvard, William McDougall, provided a more definitive conceptual analysis of the problem. McDougall, in his 1908 book *Social Psychology,* argued that human social behavior is organized around twelve instincts. Contrary to later caricatures of this position, neither McDougall nor James believed that human instincts were rigid or unchanging; rather they described instinct in much the way that we would discuss "drives" today—although they differed from later drive theorists in two important ways. First, they believed that motivation is the product not of one undifferentiated state of physiological arousal, but of several different states. For McDougall, the main emotional states included fear, disgust, wonder, anger, shame, elation, tenderness (toward children), and sexual arousal. Second, these early functionalists believed that each arousal state was part of a system comprised of not only an internal state, but also of a particular pattern of attention, cognition, and behavior:

> We may, then, define an instinct as an inherited or innate psychophysical disposition which determines its possessor to perceive, and to pay attention to, objects of a certain class, to experience an emotional excitement of a particular quality upon perceiving such an object, and to act in regard to it in a particular manner, or at least to experience an impulse to such action. (McDougall 1913, 29)

Although early researchers had difficulty finding physiologically differentiated emotional states, more recent research indicates that the notion of a single generalized emotional state (for example, Schacter and Singer 1962) was wrong, and that James and McDougall were right. There are physiologically distinguishable emotional states that involve different patterns of brain activity and different accompanying patterns of hormonal activation (Panskepp 1982). R. Plutchik's view of the link between emotion and cognition exemplifies the modern evolutionary view. Based upon extensive factor-analytic studies, Plutchik (1980) identifies eight general emotional states: fear, anger, joy, sadness, acceptance, disgust, anticipation, and surprise. He argues that each emotion helps us respond to a particular set of survival demands. His scheme of the relationship between cognition and feeling looks like this:

Stimulus Event → Cognition → Feeling → Behavior → Effect
(a dog)   (danger)   (fear)   (run)   (protection)

Plutchik conceptualizes each emotional state as part of a system involving (1) particular survival-relevant stimulus events (like the sight of a growling dog), (2) cognitive interpretations of those events (like the distinction between my dog growling at my neighbor, and my neighbor's dog growling at me), (3) particular feeling states linked to those interpreted events (like fear), (4) particular behaviors (like running away) naturally designed to produce (5) particular effects (like self-protection).

Other research on the relationship between cognition and affect concerns the importance of facial expressions. Some recent research suggests that there may be "preperceptual" attention mechanisms that allow us to be especially sensitive to emotional displays on others' faces (Hansen and Hansen 1988). In particular, people are especially good at picking out an angry face from a tachistoscopically presented "crowd." Subjects performed this task under time constraints that made separate verbal encoding of each face very unlikely. Increasing the number of neutral faces made it more difficult to detect a happy face, but that increase had little influence on subjects' ability to detect angry faces. Hansen and Hansen (1988) argue that an angry facial expression "jumps out" from the perceptual background, and that such preperceptual sensitivity is based on an evolved adaptive mechanism. This research supports the view that, even at the simplest levels of information processing, the brain is specially constructed to respond to emotion-linked stimuli. (See Chapter 9, "Political Science," this volume, for experiments on facial expression.)

GENDER DIFFERENCES IN COGNITION

Do men and women think alike? Evolutionary theory suggests that if there are sex differences in requirements for survival and reproduction, different mental processes will evolve in relation to these. Let us mention some recent research on sex differences in cognition.

Kenrick and Dengelegi (1988) asked students to browse through college yearbooks with the ostensible goal of forming an impression of the modal type of personality at each school. Subjects were later asked to spontaneously recall any of the students in the yearbook and to find their photographs. When the spontaneously recalled photographs were compared to randomly selected faces of the same sex on the same page, they were found to be significantly more physically attractive. There was a tendency for the spontaneously recalled pictures to be of members of the opposite sex (from the subject), and this tendency was pronounced among males. Approximately three out of four males recalled an attractive member of the opposite sex, while only about half the females did so.

In other research, Kenrick, Gutierres, and Goldberg (1989) asked males to look at centerfolds from magazines like *Playboy* and *Penthouse* (as part of a study that ostensibly dealt with "aesthetic judgments" of controversial artistic materials). These men later rated themselves as less attracted to their wives or live-in girlfriends than did a control sample. Females exposed to similar nude photographs of attractive males also found the men in the photos attractive and arousing, but this did not subsequently lower their evaluations of their own male partners. This research suggests that being exposed to attractive members of the opposite sex decreases men's, but not women's, attraction to their mates.

A recent study replicates this sex difference with nonerotic stimuli (Kenrick, Neuberg, Krones, and Zierk 1989). Subjects in this study were asked to judge their existing relationships after being exposed to attractive or unattractive opposite-sex participants in a dating service. Exposure to highly attractive opposite-sex others lowered men's commitments to their current relationships, but did not affect women's judgments of their relationships. These findings and the finding regarding selective memory of yearbook photos suggest that males and females differ in their attentional and perceptual processes regarding attraction to members of the opposite sex.

Why should this be so? Here it might be fruitful to employ the "ultimate cause" reasoning characteristic of sociobiology. Males and females have different requirements when they search for mates, and these differences are often explained in terms of sexual selection (Darwin 1871) and parental investment (Trivers 1971). Females usually make a larger investment in their offspring than do males. Whereas a male may contribute only a sperm, a female contributes an egg plus her own bodily resources throughout the gestation and nursing period. Hence, it costs a male little to mate unselectively, but it costs a female greatly. So, in choosing mates, females are expected to behave like discriminating shoppers and males to behave like zealous salesmen. In their 1983 book *Sex, Evolution, and Behavior,* Martin Daly and Margo Wilson report that this finding among animals is borne out in human behavior as well. Males, for example, are opportunistic about mating, engaging more often than females in casual liaisons (see also Kenrick and Trost 1989).

Unlike most other mammals, human males contribute considerable resources to their offspring—consequently, both males *and* females should be selective about their mates. Indeed there are abundant findings to support such an assumption (Daly and Wilson 1983, Kenrick and Trost 1989). Nevertheless, human males and females still differ. With regard to information processing, the evolutionary perspective suggests that males should be attentive to features related to a female's reproductive potential, whereas females should be attentive to information regarding a man's potential to generate resources. This could explain our findings, mentioned above, that males are more likely to recall physically attractive females, and that males' commitments to their current partners are more easily undermined than females' by exposure to attractive available members of the opposite sex.

Other researchers have also found gender differences in cognition. Foa and his colleagues (1984) found that men and women categorize words related to love and sex differently. Whereas women are likely to put words related to love into the same category with words related to sex, men separate them. Numerous findings in the social cognition literature suggest that subjects use gender as a primary and primitive category even when they are simply asked to memorize gender-neutral lists of personality adjectives (Hastes and Park 1986). In short, given the importance of sex differences in reproduction, an evolutionary model would have difficulty with the notion that anyone could be "aschematic" with regard to gender.

SOCIAL COGNITION AS DOMAIN-SPECIFIC

Thus far we have covered three areas in which evolutionary theory gives rise to new ideas in cognitive psychology. These were: the idea that to understand cognition we must look at the content as well as the structure of thought; the idea that cognition and emotion are related; and the idea that we should expect to find gender differences in cognition. Now we turn to our fourth idea, which is that much cognition is *social* cognition, and that this may be domain-specific.

Research on social cognition has often assumed that reasoning about other people is, for the most part, simply an extension of more general cognitive processes. Markus and Zajonc (1985) note:

> In attempts to examine the workings of internal cognitive structures, social psychologists have relied quite heavily on the computer metaphor. In the course of analyzing information storage and retrieval, we have very often ignored much of what is unique and special about the social stimulus. (174)

Despite this warning, Markus and Zajonc themselves go on to say this:

> The fact that cognitive processes as they are studied by experimental psychologists differ in a number of ways from those that are of interest to social psychologists should not be construed to infer that there are two "kinds" of cognition— social and nonsocial. The features... that characterize social cognition are also true largely of cognition in general. (210)

In contrast to this view, recent evolutionary approaches to cognition assume that social cognition *is* inherently different from other cognitive processes.

Leda Cosmides and John Tooby (1989) have argued that

> the human psyche cannot, *even in principle*, be comprised
> only of a general-purpose learning mechanism. . . . Instead,
> the human psyche appears to consist of a large number of
> *mechanisms*, many or most of which are special purpose and
> *domain specific*. (29, emphasis added)

Their idea is that various environmental circumstances,
especially social ones, call forth a sort of "package" of
cognition. This, they say, is because the brain *evolved* that
way—to cope with particular events that affected the survival
of the individual. Cosmides (1988) developed the idea that

> in order to successfully engage in social exchange—
> cooperation between two or more individuals for mutual
> benefit—humans must be able to solve a number of complex
> computational problems, and do so with special efficiency. (1)

One domain-specific mechanism of the brain is postulated
by Tooby and Cosmides (1989) to detect cheating in social
groups. In support of this argument, Cosmides and Tooby (1989)
review a series of studies indicating that people can solve
otherwise difficult logical problems easily when the problems
are phrased in terms of a broken social rule. For instance,
subjects attempting to solve the "Wason" task might be asked
to turn over as few cards as necessary to prove whether it is
true that "all Lithuanians wear earrings." They would then be
given four cards, each of which has a person's nationality on
one side and his earring status on the other. Card A shows
Lithuanian, card B shows *earrings,* card C shows *Frenchman,*
and Card D shows *no earrings.* Subjects often turn over cards
B and C though they are irrelevant to the task (for this problem,
it matters not whether any person of another nationality wears
earrings, or whether a particular Lithuanian *is* wearing
earrings: only a Lithuanian wearing no earrings could disprove
the rule.) However, if the problem were phrased such that all
Lithuanians are *required by law* to wear earrings, the evidence
suggests that subjects *would almost* always get the problem
correct, and not examine the Frenchman or the man already
wearing earrings. Cosmides and Tooby argue that people solve
this type of problem better when it is phrased in terms of a

rule violation because our prehistoric ancestors needed to be especially sensitive to violations of reciprocity in the groups in which they lived.

The "look for cheaters" heuristic does not always result in more logical thinking. In other types of problems, in fact, it causes subjects to make more mistakes than they would have otherwise. The jury is still out on whether an evolutionary mechanism is needed to explain people's success at "looking for cheaters" on Wason-type tasks. Whether or not one agrees that an evolutionary perspective is necessary to explain Cosmides and Tooby's data, however, it illustrates one point. People seem to reason very differently about logical problems when those problems involve certain types of social situations.

There is cross-cultural evidence that humans the world over use similar constructs to think about their fellows. That is, the structure of "social reputation" seems to be a cultural universal. From data gathered in a study of North Americans, Wiggins and Broughton (1985) argue that interpersonal personality descriptors can be arranged into a two-dimensional circumplex. As shown in figure 1, the circumplex can be described by two axes. The vertical axis refers to "dominant vs. submissive," and the horizontal axis refers to "agreeable vs. quarrelsome."

Another researcher, Geoffrey White (1980), independently used a multidimensional scaling procedure to analyze interpersonal trait terms from several Asian and Pacific cultures. For each of these cultures, White found that a two-dimensional circumplex produced the most satisfactory classification of the trait terminology used by those people. He also found that virtually the same two dimensions defined the axes of the trait circumplex for each of the cultures he studied, despite their having quite separate languages. White called the second dimension "solidarity vs. conflict," which is interchangeable with Wiggins and Broughton's "agreeable vs. quarrelsome" dimension. For the first dimension, White used almost the same label as Wiggins and Broughton. This suggests that when people around the world think about the other people in their lives, two questions come to the fore: Is this person dominant or submissive? and Is this person an agreeable person with whom to associate?

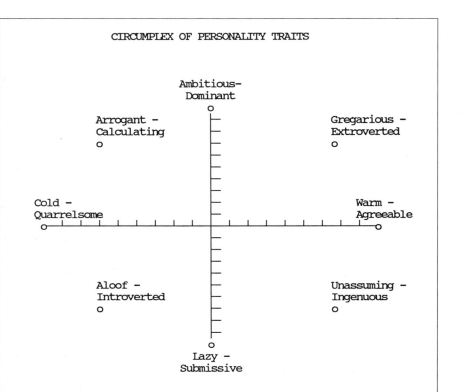

Figure 1. Circumplex arrangement of personality traits (Wiggins & Broughton, 1985). This shows the relationship of social traits to one another. Ambitious-dominant characteristics are opposite to lazy-submissive traits. However, they are independent of the cold-to-warm dimension. That is, it would be possible to be either ambitious and cold or ambitious and warm. Gregarious/extroverted characteristics tend to be associated with both ambitiousness and warmth, so they are placed in the upper right corner of the circumplex, whereas, for example, arrogant/calculating characteristics appear in the upper left because they are associated with both ambitiousness and coldness.

In a review of the existing literature on social cognition, Markus and Zajonc (1985) argued that certain categories of social stimuli have intrinsic salience, and that "these include age, sex, race, and physical attractiveness" (167). These authors did not explain why these particular classes of stimuli are intrinsically salient. Yet as we suggested above, each of the categories they discuss fits with an evolutionary perspective. Just as research on neural bases of perception has revealed "bug detectors" in frogs, and other highly specialized detectors in mammals (Hubel and Wiesel 1968), we would expect to find specialized neural systems for encoding features that are relevant to a person's survival and reproductive fitness (such as the gender and physical attractiveness of others). In general we believe that "content specialization" should apply not only to complex thought processes, but to simple processes of sensation, perception, attention, encoding, and retrieval as well. Therefore, rather than simply studying the "general processes" that underlie these phenomenon, it is worthwhile for cognitive psychologists to ask: What is salient for attention? What is encoded? and What is retrieved?

In sum, evolutionary theorists generally assume that different parts of the brain are used for different types of cognitive processing, and, in particular, that extensive portions of the human brain are primarily dedicated to thinking about people.

THE CONTINUUM FROM EVOLUTIONARY HISTORY TO MOMENTARY COGNITION

For the most part, human cognitive processes have been studied with laboratory experiments. A subject in a typical experiment might be asked to categorize rapidly presented words or symbols in order to test the lower limits of his or her capacity to process the particular type of information in question. Or the subject might be given a few minutes to solve a problem such as the Wason task described above ("What is the minimum number of cards to prove the rule that all Lithuanians wear earrings"). Laboratory experiments have been a useful way to examine cognitive processes, but they have an important limitation. They may lead cognitive psychologists to overemphasize *ahistorical* theoretical approaches.

In reading classical cognitive psychology one often gets the impression that the half-hour duration of a typical experiment is the only time frame with which psychologists need be concerned. Experiments on social cognition, for instance, have focused extensively on "priming" (for example, Srull and Wyer 1979, 1980). In a typical priming experiment, a subject might be asked to make a judgment about the foolhardiness of skydiving. The subject who had previously been asked to memorize a list containing words like *reckless,* will judge skydiving as more foolhardy than subjects who had previously been exposed to words like *adventurous.* Priming experiments thus focus on changes in judgment that occur over short periods of time.

Although most cognitive processing does happen within a short time frame, it is important not to lose sight of the historical context of those momentary processes. How a person interprets a stimulus presented in a laboratory experiment depends upon what has happened in the preceding few minutes, but it also depends on what has happened to that person throughout her or his life. People whose friends are skydivers will make different judgments than those who have only read an occasional news report of a skydiving accident. And a person who is chronically anxious will remember a story about a skydiving adventure very differently than will someone who is chronically underaroused. In short, momentary experience needs to be considered within a larger time frame. Figure 2 presents one way to think about how cognitive events in the present moment are connected to more historically distant processes.

We all learned in high school that the first World War was "caused," in one sense, by the assassination of Archduke Ferdinand. But the assassination of Archduke Ferdinand would have been just one of the millions of murders committed this century if not for a set of longer range "causes" (like militarism, nationalism, and multinational alliances) that completely changed the implications of that event. A psychologist who focuses only on the cognitive processes that occur during a laboratory experiment would be like a historian who only focuses on daily events (like Ferdinand's assassination). He or she would be able to make a number of accurate causal statements about particular events, but would have no idea about why certain events were more significant than others.

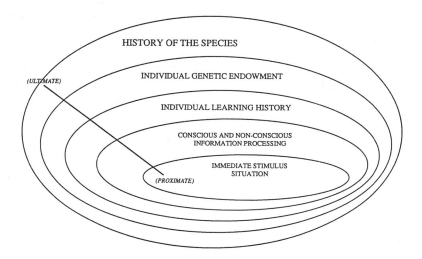

Figure 2. Proximate/ultimate continuum. Evolutionary explanations of behavior adopt a historically distant frame of reference. Evolutionary history constrains the individual differences in genetic endowment within a species, which in turn constrain learning history and cognitive processes.

Conclusion

The lesson of modern sociobiology for cognitive psychology is not that all psychologists need to work in the field with chimpanzees before they can make meaningful statements about how people think. It is instead that all psychologists need to be aware of the larger context of what their subjects are thinking about during an experiment. In this chapter, we have argued that humans are naturally inclined to think in ways that would, on average, have helped our ancestors survive and reproduce. Knowing about the ultimate evolutionary context of our species helps us make sense of immediate psychological processes. Modern psychology is often divided into subdisciplines that study physiology, sensation, perception, cognition, learning, development, motivation, personality, and social psychology. By viewing behavior from the distance of the ultimate context of human behavior, the evolutionary perspective allows psychologists to see the unity within the field.

A little over a century ago, William James wrote the definitive textbook in American psychology. James himself was trained in biology and philosophy. He believed that psychology could link the study of mind, the traditional province of philosophers, with the developments that had been revolutionizing biology. Consistently, James believed that "the mind has a native structure" (James 1890, 676). The recent developments in cognitive science, in concert with the recent developments in evolutionary biology, have put us in a position to glimpse that structure.

11

Epistemology

Michael Ruse

What, we are then compelled to ask, made the hypothalamus and limbic system? They evolved by natural selection. That simple biological statement must be pursued to explain ethics and ethical philosophers, if not epistemology and epistemologists, at all depths.

—E. O. Wilson, *Sociobiology*

Epistemology is one of the major fields of philosophy, along with ethics, metaphysics, and logic. It is concerned with the origin and nature of knowledge. Epistemology inquires how we know things, for example, whether by observation or by intuition, and it also considers the problem of truth. Some of the great contributors to epistemology are Descartes, Berkeley, Locke, Kant, and Hume. A related field is that of the philosophy of mind, many of whose concerns—such as memory, reason, and perception— have been taken over by the science of psychology.

The philosophy of science is another related field and is one that I shall particularly consider in this chapter. An important debate in the philosophy of science concerns whether science is based on observation of evidence (the classical view), or whether scientists more or less force their ideas, their theories, or their cultural views onto the facts. (See Kuhn 1962; Popper 1959, 1962, 1972.)

How does sociobiology relate to epistemology and the philosophy of science? First, since Darwin's publication of *On the Origin of Species* in 1859, there has existed an "evolutionary epistemology," consisting of the general proposition that our various mental processes evolved as adaptations to the environment. Since evolution has no preordained direction, the brain is not "meant" to discover "truth" but is simply a device that helps its owner to survive. (One philosophical implication of this is that the truths that the brain discovers may or may not be objective truths.) The sociobiologist E. O. Wilson updated this idea in his book *On Human Nature* (1978), showing that the ultimate units of evolution are the genes and that "the brain exists because it promotes the survival and multiplication of the genes that direct its assembly" (2).

Second, as a continuation of this idea, scientific knowledge seems itself to have adaptive value. The person or the society that has a grasp of the principles of, say, mechanics, will probably be better able to exploit the environment than one that does not. Yet evolutionary biology gives little clue to the actual content and nature of science. No one claims the explorer lost in the jungle will be better off for knowing that $E = mc^2$. Nor is the person with a better scientific theory particularly destined to have reproductive success. After all, Copernicus, Descartes, and Newton—to name three of the giants of the Scientific Revolution—died childless!

Third, there are the more specific writings of E. O. Wilson concerning epigenetic rules (Wilson 1978), and the major work by Charles J. Lumsden and E. O. Wilson, *Genes, Mind and, Culture* (1981), describing "culturgens." These go to the heart of the matter concerning the philosophy of science debate. Wilson portrays an "epigenetic rule" as a sort of intermediate item in between genetically fixed knowledge (which both animals and humans have to a varying extent) and culturally learned knowledge (which a few animals have, in small doses, and which humans have to a great extent).

EPIGENETIC RULES AND CULTURGENS

The new notion of "culturgen" arose from Lumsden and Wilson's theory that the human mind and culture coevolved. The culturgen is a basic unit of culture, and can be one of a number of things: an artifact, a specified item of behavior, a concept (a "mentifact"), or any element one would identify as being part of a person's or society's general cultural dimension. Lumsden and Wilson do not pick out science for particular attention, but I shall assume for our purposes here that a scientific theory is comprised of culturgens, thus any particular scientific theory can be compared with and distinguished from any other in terms of its viability as a culturgen.

The problem Lumsden and Wilson face is how the culturgens get learned, organized, altered, and passed from one generation to the next, and how these processes relate back to the genes. They explain such processes and connections through the concept of an "epigenetic rule." These are biological constraints on development and on our consequent capacities for learning. Lumsden and Wilson divide the epigenetic rules into two sets. First, there are those that affect and organize the reception of the basic items of information about the world and ourselves. Included here are color sensations, sounds and smells, and the like. Second, there are those rules that organize this basic information, enabling us to act in various ways upon it. In their words:

> Existing information on cognition is most efficiently organized with reference to gene-culture theory by classifying the epigenetic rules into two classes that occur sequentially within the nervous system. *Primary epigenetic rules* are the more automatic processes that lead from sensory filtering to perception. Their consequences are the least subject to variation due to learning and other higher cortical processes. [These explain why all people perceive four basic colors, for example.] The *secondary epigenetic rules* act on color and all other information displayed in the perceptual fields. They include the evaluation of perception through the processes of memory, emotional response, and decision making through which individuals are predisposed to use certain culturgens in preference to others. (Lumsden and Wilson 1981, 36)

How might this all work in the case of science? Lumsden and Wilson do not delve into this area, but it is easy to project their thinking. On the one hand, science is empirical: it is based on the evidence of the senses. (It is nothing if not that!) So, presumably, we get scientific information as filtered through the primary rules. On the other hand, science isn't just a random collection of empirical notions. It is a highly formalized enterprise with a definite methodology, and with canons dictating what is acceptable and what is nonacceptable. Here the secondary rules come into play. What sorts of things would be produced through the influence of the secondary rules? Most obvious would be basic mathematics and logic. For instance, science accepts that if a pressure is five pounds per square inch, it can't simultaneously be ten pounds per square inch.

In regard to the methodology of science, a much-debated topic is that of exactly how crucial *laws* are to the scientific enterprise. Some think all explanation demands reference to laws. Others are not so sure (see, for example, Hempel 1966, Goudge 1961). However, all agree that thinking in terms of laws is central to science. Even more central is thought in terms of *causal* laws. Forces *cause* bodies to fall. Continental drift causes changes in the geographical distributions of organisms. It is most likely, then, that there is an innate epigenetic rule (or set of such rules) that directs us to think causally. Given the same initial conditions, we expect the same consequences— and if we don't get them, we don't throw out our causal thinking, but rather we persist until we find some way of bringing our experience in line with our expectations. (The strange path of a boomerang, for instance, doesn't make us give up Newton's Law.)

Along with the drive for causal laws, within science we find a push toward simplicity and unification. The best science aims to show how different ideas and areas all bind together into one unified whole. If one accepts that continents move, one has an explanation of earthquakes, volcanoes, continental shapes, organic distributions, deep-sea rifts, and so on. Everything fits simply together, in what the nineteenth-century philosopher William Whewell termed a "consilience of inductions" (Whewell 1840, Kitcher 1981, Ruse 1982).

Why do we value consilience? Because, as with logic and mathematics, our epigenetic rules make us think that the best science is consilient. Now we can grasp the outlines of a *sociobiological analysis of science*. It does not claim that every last item in a scientific theory has direct biological value. It does not even claim that a theory judged better by scientists will confer superior biological power on its supporters. But it does claim that the mathematics of science, the logic of science, the methodology of science, emerge as *products of the secondary epigenetic rules,* and these rules have supposedly been forged in the evolutionary struggle for survival and reproduction. Thus—I claim—biology informs and dictates the very skeleton of science!

This means, of course, that choice between scientific theories is governed by biology. Hence, in the long run one expects to see superior science prove to be of reproductive value to its holders. Why does a scientist prize predictive capacity in a scientific theory? Why is it a merit of a scientific theory that we can draw checkable inferences from it? Why is it, for example, that a great merit of continental drift theory was its ability to predict great geological similarities in Africa and South America? Why should one care whether a theory can so predict, and why should this be a major factor in one's choice of one theory over another?

The answer simply is that those protohumans who took predictive capacity seriously tended to outsurvive and outreproduce those that did not. The Australopithecine who, say, took note of changing leaf color and who then predicted coming climatic changes (and took appropriate action) tended to get through the winter a lot better than a rival who blithely frittered away the autumn. Again, take the notion of a consilience. The prehuman who refused to take coincidences at face value, but who looked for underlying connecting causes, was at an adaptive advantage over the credulous. Sounds in the jungle, marks at the water hole, traces of blood, add up to tigers—even though they may be unseen. Beware!

Today, in our science, this kind of inference is all very much sanitized. The average physicist is about as far from a caveman as it is possible to imagine. (In fact, refusal to accept unseen entities may lose you the Nobel Prize, rather than make you an animal's dinner.) But caveman and physicist are linked by the same epigenetic rules. Sophisticated modern science is simply jungle lore writ large. The reasons why we accept one modern scientific theory rather than another—and why indeed we create and accept science at all—is firmly rooted in our biology. Moreover, even now adaptive advantage is not totally divorced from the success of science. As modern science has gotten more sophisticated, scientific-minded cultures and societies have outstripped the reproductive efforts of previous societies. The methods of science, applied in technology, and medicine, are superb adaptations for the struggle for reproduction.

In short, today, as always, the genes hold culture on a leash (Wilson 1978, 167).

THE NATURE OF SCIENCE

Here I'd like to apply this sociobiological evaluation of science to the settlement of a raging debate. Philosophers divide over the ultimate nature of science and the reasons for acceptance of one theory rather than another. Until recently, orthodox opinion had it that it is the empirical evidence that is decisive. Does a particular theory "fit the facts"? If it does, then this is good reason to accept the theory. If it does not, then we must go on looking. One well-known version of this viewpoint is that of Sir Karl Popper (1959). A genuine scientific theory must be falsifiable, he says, and it is this measure that is absolutely decisive. However attractive a theory may seem, if it goes against the facts it must be rejected.

In the past two decades, thanks particularly to the work of such thinkers as Thomas Kuhn (1962), many have started to emphasize strongly the inadequacy of any such straightforward appeal to "the facts." One has to (and does in fact) invoke other criteria in theory choice—criteria like simplicity and elegance. Indeed, some thinkers, primarily sociologists and historians, have been so impressed by these nonevidential criteria, that they have downgraded the empirical side of science to little more than a shadow! Ideology and like factors, they say, are virtually everything!

Wilson's analysis helps one to tread a careful middle-line through this debate—a middle line that has the virtue of staying true to the way in which scientists actually behave. On the one hand, the Wilsonian agrees that the "facts" are absolutely basic determinants in the nature and progress of science. However, he or she would say that for the evolving human, grappling with the world of experience is what counts, and *if this means molding it somewhat,* then so be it. Indeed, the Wilsonian would take factors like simplicity so seriously, that she or he may even expect scientists to go against the facts at times, if necessary. Einstein's commitment to relativity, on aesthetic grounds, whatever the evidence, makes sense. If certain epigenetic rules have served well in the past, there's good cause to stay with them—even when they push you beyond or against the evidence.

Suppose we grant the essential truth of the picture of science being sketched here. Suppose we agree that *scientific knowledge is regulated according to certain principles or norms that have their foundation in our evolutionary heritage.* At once a pressing question intrudes. It is obvious that even in those societies that have pushed science to its highest peaks, many people refuse to take science as seriously as a Wilsonian analysis would seem to merit. Astrology flourishes. Varieties of psuedomedicine abound. And as the recent controversy over creationism well attests, the crudest forms of religious belief soak up enthusiasts and sympathizers. How to account for this?

A more conventional analysis of science—one that supposes that there is an objective reality and that science attempts to map or capture it— explains such alternatives to science in terms of simple error. People confuse the true nature of causal understanding (or some such thing), and that is all there is to it. However, the kind of position we are considering cannot dismiss superstitious ways of thinking quite so readily. Science is supposed to be based on rules that confer survival value. How then can so many people ignore or modify the rules and still survive? What possible survival value could there be in the vagaries of causal thinking implicit in astrology or creationism?

In fact, what may seem at first to be a refutation of our neo-Darwinian evolutionary epistemology turns out to be strong support. To the sociobiologist such scientific alternatives are virtually to be expected. *Being human requires compromises.* We are not simply calculating machines, trying only to understand and master nature. We are also social beings, with some needs, for instance, to get on with our neighbors. This requires ethics, and if (as it happens) religion can help to reinforce and maintain ethics, then this is a good selective reason why people should have a biological disposition toward religious (and like) beliefs, even if they may clash with science.

For another major reason why people embrace notions of supernatural beings, able to break at will with the regular course of nature, one need look no further than the Old Testament story of Job. People need supports like religion to help them to get through life—to give meaning to their daily existence and to help comfort in times of stress. Why didn't Job curse God, which certainly would have been the rational thing to do? Because it's precisely when things go wrong that you need something to help you to get through. And if that something is belief in an entity (or system) that can break or soften the harsh realities, and that can give meaning and purpose, then so be it.

But now let me return to the debate about which view of science is correct. What is being argued is that our knowledge of the external world is not something just "read off," as it were, from experience, as crude empiricists are supposed to claim. Rather, such knowledge is *a product of the mind actively interfering with and interpreting the data of the senses.* Our epigenetic rules filter and structure experience. Claims like this immediately call to mind one of the greatest of all modern philosophers, Immanuel Kant. He, too, argued that empirical knowledge is not simply received by the mind, but rather is something made and structured by the mind acting on the evidence of the senses. In other words, our empirical "synthetic" knowledge is infused by elements that do not come from the external world, and that are thus *"a priori."*

PHILOSOPHICAL PREDECESSORS: KANT?

Let me now consider two possible philosophical predecessors for E. O. Wilson: Kant and Hume. The case regarding Wilson as thinking in a neo-Kantian fashion is given strength when one starts to consider some of the specific claims of their respective positions. Thus, for instance, Kant argues that claims of mathematics like 5 + 7 = 12 are claims *based on experience, but interpreted by the mind.* They are "synthetic *a priori*" claims. Similarly, Kant argues that causal claims like "the lead ball falling on the cushion caused the depression" are mind-structured. "We can extract clear concepts of them [that is, causes] from experience, only because we have put them into experience, and because experience is thus itself brought about only by their means" (Kant 1929, 223).

We have seen that both mathematics and other areas requiring *causal understanding* are subjects where Wilsonian epigenetic rules would pay crucial roles. The human who thought that 5 + 7 = 12 rather than 5 + 7 = 13 would be fitter than one who thought otherwise. The human who realized that falling lead balls are liable to cause depressions—in cushions, heads, or whatever—would likewise be fitter than one who thought otherwise. Thus, in both cases, the human mind has been fashioned by evolution to see the world in the manner suggested by Kant.

But even if we agree on the mind-given element, there is more to mathematics and causality than this. And here, I begin to wonder just how deeply Wilson is entrenched in a Kantian framework. The point about mathematics and causality (and like claims) is that we don't simply believe them, but that we believe them to be *necessary*. We think that 5 + 7 must equal 12, and that, given the falling ball striking the cushion, there must be a depression. Now, both Kant and Wilson acknowledge this necessity, but for different reasons.

For Wilson, the necessities of knowledge are all very much contingent, psychological matters. If you shove your hand in the fire, you damage it. Thus there was adaptive advantage in pain sensations, a belief that fire "causes" pain, and a corresponding fear. But if the world had been different, no such necessary connections would have been drawn. Similarly in mathematics and other subjects. Necessity really is in the eye of the beholder and is a quirk of accident and selection. If there had been some other, more efficient, way for selection to do the job, we might not have had any sense of necessity at all.

For Kant, things are different. There is nothing accidental about his necessity. Even if it starts in the mind, the necessity of the synthetic *a priori* comes as a condition of the possibility of any rational thought whatsoever. Having allowed the importance of sensation, Kant asks rhetorically:

> The question now arises whether *a priori* concepts [like causality] do not also serve as antecedent conditions under

which alone anything can be, if not intuited, yet thought as object in general. In that case all empirical knowledge of objects would necessarily conform to such concepts, because only as thus presupposing them is anything possible as *object of experience*. (Kant 1929, 126, his italics)

And Kant's answer, resoundingly, is that such necessary conformation is a feature of empirical knowledge.

In short, although Wilson's approach is Kantian in that he invokes a mind-structuring element in knowledge, in spirit it seems very different. For Kant, the *a priori* has a hold on knowledge that seems lacking from the form that Wilson's epigenetic rules impose on knowledge. For the evolutionist, in a very real sense, had things been otherwise, one could imagine different rules and thus differently structured knowledge.

PHILOSOPHICAL PREDECESSORS: HUME?

The other possible predecessor of E. O. Wilson is the empiricist David Hume. Kant himself was responding to problems set by Hume, so it could well be that Wilson's *prima facie* similiarity to Kant is a function of a similar response to the same issues. Also, there are historical reasons to look toward Hume, since Wilson is working directly in the Darwinian tradition, and Darwin in turn was much influenced by British empiricism. Moreover, unlike Kant, Hume always stressed the *links between human thought and animal thought.* He wrote: "No truth appears to me more evident, than that beasts are endow'd with thought and reason as well as men" (Hume 1978, 176).

When one looks especially at Hume's *Treatise on Human Nature,* Wilsonian epistemology can readily be seen as progress down the path first trodden by the great Scottish philosopher. Consider Hume's central discussion, on which so much of his theory depends, his deservedly celebrated analysis of causal connection. Hume argues that we do not see any necessity in nature. We see only that one event is being followed by another. Nevertheless, we *impute* a sense of necessity to nature. We pick out phenomena that we identify as "causes," and we believe that they *must* be followed by phenomena we identify as "effects." We say that the fire causes pain and burning, and that the effect (pain and burning) necessarily follows on the cause (fire). Moreover, we distinguish such connections from merely accidental successions. No one thinks there is any necessity between (say) a rainstorm and the new moon then arising.

Hume argues that the mind, as it were, reads necessity into nature. What happens is that we see that those things that we call "causes" are constantly followed by those things that we call "effects," and so this sets up a notion of necessity in the mind, which then puts it into nature, as though it were an external power. " 'Tis the constant conjunction of objects, along with the determination of the mind, which constitutes a physical necessity" (Hume 1978, 171). But why do we think necessity itself is objective? Hume says, " 'Tis a common observation, that the mind has a great propensity to spread itself on external objects, and to conjoin with them any internal impressions, which they occasion, and which always make their appearance at the same time that these objects discover themselves to the senses" (Hume 1978, 167).

Let's spell out what's going on here. Events follow each other with regularity in nature. People notice these successions, which trigger in the mind expectations and feelings of necessity. Why is there such a triggering? Because of the way the mind is made. It has a propensity to see necessity in successions—and this propensity is activated by the successions themselves. Then, finally, the mind (unbeknownst to itself) reads necessity into nature, thinking nevertheless that it has found it as an objective facet of nature (Wolff 1960).

This is Wilson's position almost literally. The only thing missing is the terminology of epigenetic rules. These are Hume's "propensities."

Commonsense Realism

Hume was, notoriously, a skeptic. Because of his analysis of causal connection and his related discussion of the nature and existence of material objects, he was led at times to doubt the reality of just about everything—at least, he was led to doubt the certainty of any claims he might want to make.

> 'Tis impossible upon any system to defend either our under-standing or our senses; and we but expose them farther when

we endeavour to justify them in that manner. As the skeptical doubt arises naturally from a profound and intense reflection on those subjects, it always increases, the farther we carry our reflections, whether in opposition or conformity to it (Hume 1978, 218).

Does this mean then that Wilsonian epistemology is likewise infected with skepticism, and is this not therefore good reason to look to refute it? Let me make a number of points in response to this important question.

First, even if Wilsonian epistemology does end up in skepticism, one should not think this any philosophical criticism of it. The key starting point of Wilsonian (and Humean) epistemology is that there are no guarantees about knowledge and truth. Wilson claims that we have abilities evolved through natural selection, not a God-given hotline to ultimate reality. He does not say that, when our reason is stretched to the limit, in the artificialities of philosophical discourse, it will remain strong and adequate. Rather, we should almost expects it to fail (Wilson 1978, 2). (Ability to manage the jungle has little to do with metaphysics!)

Second, following on the first point, any failure in philosophy to avoid skepticism doesn't matter at all, when it comes to the things that really count! What we really need to do is to live and to survive and to reproduce. Epigenetic rules not only let us do these things, but help us to do them. The burnt child fears the fire and avoids it the next time. The human mind is such that, even if abstract philosophy leads to skepticism, unreasoned optimism keeps us afloat. As human beings we all believe in the reality of causality and the external world and so forth, whatever philosophy might prove. And here we have another reason for linking Wilson with Hume. Hume saw that the skepticism toward which his philosophy points doesn't really have much effect at all. Wilson's contribution is to pick up on Hume's astute psychological observations and show just why skepticism fails to conquer. We are animals and have adaptations to protect us from the worries of our reason. If we got too depressed about the conclusions of our thinking, we'd simply stop functioning properly.

Finally, I might mention that according to the evolutionists, we even get a sharing of thought patterns across species. Some organisms like insects have completely different senses from us. They use chemicals (pheromones) for sensing. Obviously, therefore, the information of the insect is not the information of the human. But there is a stability and correspondence in how the information is used, which supports the evolutionist in his or her belief in an objective world shared by all living things. We don't find insects flying through objects like trees, things that human regard as solid and thus impenetrable. To the contrary, all organisms seem as if they are adapted to the same objective world as we. Thus, Wilson's epistemology supports a "shared reality" that organisms react to in various ways. Moreover, as best as we can tell, there's a shared logic (or, inasmuch as animals use reasoning, it is a rudimentary version of our own). It is modified in understandable ways to cope with the peculiarities of the situation in which the organism finds itself. (For more on this point see Ruse 1984.)

In short, at a commonsense level, Wilson is no more of a skeptic than is Hume. He is a commonsense realist.

THE ULTIMATE FOUNDATIONS

There remains yet another question, the most crucial question of them all. What about the circularity that haunts every discussion of the kind we have just been having? The findings of evolutionary theory have been taken as basic. From these, we have argued to a neo-Humean epistemology, claiming that our understanding of such things as casuality is very much dependent upon human nature. But can't we—shouldn't we—turn the argument back on itself? Are not the very claims about evolution *themselves* infected with the same relativity? Consider the position of someone who says that everything is relative or subjective. Why should we take this general claim seriously, since it, too, must be subjective? Analogously, if our understanding of the world is a function of our evolution, have we any answer to the person who refuses to take us seriously? What can one say to the person who insists that in order to command attention we must find some extra-evolutionary "objective" claims to serve as our initial premises?

Two things can be said at once to such a critic. First, as we have seen, whatever relativity there may be in Wilsonian epistemology, it is certainly not a crude individual relativism. We're all in the struggle for existence together! We have the same rationality across the species, if not indeed (thanks to our common past) across all living things here on earth. So, no one that we know of has been given license to go around denying the law of excluded middle or causal connections, or whatever.

Second, in line with a point made previously, we must not assume that an answer can be found to this circularity problem, or that failure to answer implies that the whole Wilsonian position must be rejected. Such an assumption is predicated on the very worldview we have challenged, namely that there is an objective truth out there and we humans have the powers to find it. It cannot be overemphasized that we are using faculties to probe into areas for which we were neither designed nor selected. And we might come up less than satisfied. After all, it wouldn't be the first time in life's history that adaptations have not done all their possessors might have wished.

But these caveats are certainly not causes for despair or for giving up. Having come this far, we must push our analysis to its outer limits. We cannot simply ignore the circularity problem. Could it be, given our evolutionarily evolved natures, that any claims about evolution are themselves necessarily fallible, and thus that ultimate intellectual bedrock must be sought elsewhere? (Note that this is a philosophical query. We're assuming that claims about evolution, including Wilson's extensions, are well confirmed in the normal sense of the term.)

How would one go about challenging claims about natural selection (which, I take it, depend in turn on claims about the reliability of observation, of causal processes, and the like)? Perhaps the most obvious critical argument would go something like this: We know that natural selection can "deceive" organisms for their own good. The human belief in the existence of an almighty God is a paradigmatic case. The notion of a necessary being, who is all-powerful and all-loving, and who yet allows evil, is a hopelessly incoherent notion; and yet, for good biological reasons, people go on believing in its existence. Perhaps, therefore, humans are deceived for their own good, about the methods of science, even to the very basic principles on which natural selection rests! (See Trivers 1976 for just such an argument.)

If one's claim is simply that the world is "really" other than we think it is, then the claim is meaningless, unless one posits knowing subjects (other than us). We've seen already that *existence without perception and thought just doesn't make sense.* ("The oak is really an elm, but no one could ever know it.") But what would it mean to posit such knowing subjects, who are not beings living at the same level of existence as we? The most obvious suggestion seems to be something akin to Berkeley's or Descartes' Evil Demon: a being who is responsible for the world as it appears to us, but who "knows" that truly things are not as they seem to be. The world marches to a different drummer when we're not around. Perhaps even the appearance of evolution is all a sham. Perhaps, thanks to God or the Demon, creationist Philip Gosse was right when he said that fossils are not the remains of dead organisms, but God's artifacts put in the rocks to test our faith!

Other Intelligences

Now let me speak for a moment about "other intelligences" in the universe. I am hesitant to say that *any* successful advanced life-form must think in the way that we do. Why do I hesitate? Consider for a moment what we know about life's history. The world started some 4 1/2 billion years ago; life some 3 1/2 billion years ago; an explosion of higher forms just over 1/2 billion years ago; the mammals 60 million years ago (the mammals have been around for 200 million years, but their real development came only with the extinction of the dinosaurs); and humankind some 1/2 million years ago (Ruse 1982). All of this looks incredibly progressive—at least it's been taken to be so, for as long as the fossil record has been known (Rudwick 1972, Bowler 1976). From low to high; from simple to complex; from amoeba to man. This has been the interpretation by Christian students of paleontology before Darwin, and more than a few evolutionists after Darwin have continued the tradition. And with such a reading of the past, it is natural to see a kind of inevitability in the history of life— a teleological inevitability that leads inexorably toward life's unique, highest form. It ends with *Homo sapiens:* a conscious, rational being, with insight into the necessary laws of thought.

Clearly, if this is all there is to be said, then Kant was probably right. But appearances are deceptive, at least they are if you take Darwinism seriously (Mayr 1982). To the Darwinian, there is randomness built into the evolutionary process. There was no inevitable climb up to humans—they evolved purely by chance, given a certain earth-history, available mutations, conducive environmental conditions, and so forth. If, for instance, the dinosaurs had not died out, then it's highly improbable that the mammals would have taken over the world. Nor is there any reason to think that the dinosaurs would have developed their own superintelligent, conscious species. The world might still be inhabited by beings with very low intelligence.

What I'm suggesting, therefore, is the possibility (actually elsewhere in the universe?) of life forms totally unlike anything we know. These are forms that are highly successful in the struggle for existence, and that would simply not think (or "think") in a way recognizable by us. I don't mean that they would think that 2 + 2 = 5, because that's our way of thinking, but wrong. Rather, mathematics and science, as we know it, just wouldn't be part of their thought. Their "thought" would be quite alien to us, and yet of great help to them in life's struggles.

You might object that we do see some parallel evolution here on Earth—whales and sharks "solve" hydrodynamical problems in the same way (Lewontin 1978). Hence, perhaps all intelligence is (and must be) the same—whether here on earth or elsewhere in the universe. But countering this hope is the fact that all terrestrial beings (at least, all whales and sharks) share some common ancestry here on earth, together with having had similar materials to draw on. Moreover, the fact that one organism comes up with an answer to a problem puts pressure on others to take that problem seriously (with possibly similar answers). And in any case, there are lots of instances where organisms took drastically different paths. Parallel evolution is not inevitable.

What I argue, therefore, is that if we drop the notion of progression, we simply can't assume that any intelligent successful organism will have a consciousness and intelligence like ours. You may deny that such a being would really think or be conscious; but that is to win your case by definition. In some other world, with other materials and other processes, other modes of thought might have evolved, but they—quite literally—would have a different way of looking at things. (For a start, they wouldn't be Darwinians. But they wouldn't be creationists either!)

My conclusion (my very hesitant conclusion) is that if what I have suggested is plausible, then perhaps at bottom, evolutionary epistemology is Humean after all. If you are going to think in a human way, then you must think causally. But perhaps you don't have to think in a human way. Thus, ultimately, our patterns of thought and our claims for truth have no validity beyond our own contingent human existence.

Other Writings on Evolutionary Epistemology

Have I demonstrated that sociobiology has some relevance for epistemology? I hope so. Now let me mention a few related matters. There is a small publishing industry today centered on something called "evolutionary epistemology" that I have neglected—deliberately—to cover in this chapter. In general, advocates of such an evolutionary epistemology have grasped at what they believe to be a firm analogy between the evolution of organisms and the growth of human *knowledge* itself, particularly scientific knowledge. They argue that the probable (and only) reason for the success of knowledge lies in some mechanism *analogous* to natural selection. They claim that just as organisms must prove their worth in the ongoing struggle for existence, so also ideas must prove their worth against other ideas in an intellectual struggle for existence.

I believe that the main place where such traditional evolutionary epistemology comes unstuck is in the appearance of new, putative elements of knowledge. It is a crucial premise of Darwinian theory that the "raw stuff" of evolution—that which natural selection selects or rejects— appears without reference to the needs of organisms. New variations are not created to order. They are "random." But this is rarely the case with human knowledge, particularly with scientific knowledge. New ideas, approaches, theories, come as the result of hard thought, in turn provoked by needs. One has some problem to solve, and new ideas are produced as tentative answers. In short, the raw stuff of knowledge is anything but random. Nevertheless, irrespective of my objections, readers may wish to pursue this matter further. H. C. Plotkin's 1982 volume *Learning, Development, and Culture: Essays in Evolutionary Epistemology* is a useful introduction to this subject; James Fetzer's 1986 collection of essays, *Sociobiology and Epistemology,* is a more advanced and critical piece.

Readers who are interested in a *philosopher of science's* approach to sociobiology itself may peruse Elliott Sober's 1984 book, *The Nature of Selection,* and will find some pertinent points in my 1986 book, *Taking Darwin Seriously.* Dedicated epistemology fanciers may wish to look at Hilary Putnam's 1981 book, *Reason, Truth, and History,* which denies the coherence of the notion of ultimate external reality. There is no such thing, he says, as "the metaphysical objectivity of the God's Eye View" (55).

This essay was written during a time of support by the John Simon Guggenheim Memorial Foundation.

12

Socioecology of Religion

Vernon Reynolds

Ecology is the study of interrelationship between living organisms and their environment.[1] The environment includes both the physical setting—the terrain, the resources, the climate—and other creatures, particularly conspecifics and those that have a prey or predator relationship with the species under consideration. In Darwin's theory of evolution, the two important elements are the *inheritance of traits* and the *pressures of the environment.* Certain traits—or the genes for those traits—will proliferate if they are adaptive to the environment.

Sociobiology has, among other things, been concerned with the genetic side of evolution, especially on the theoretical level. (Sociobiologists don't spend any time at all looking for real genes in the DNA.) Their discussions may revolve, for example, around the way kin or reciprocal altruism may underlie cooperative behaviors such as grooming. They are also concerned with showing how genetic processes—and the dynamics of inclusive fitness—underlie certain mating strategies in humans. Nevertheless, it should be remembered that the *environment* also contributes to evolutionary forms. Mating strategies in animals can often be directly related to food supply. For example, it has been shown that in dunnocks it is the availability and distribution of food that determines whether the mating system will be monogamous, polygamous, or polyandrous (Davies and Lundberg 1984). Likewise, it has been argued that patterns of food distribution explain forms of sociality in primates (Wrangham 1987).

This chapter will have two parts. Part 1 is a socioecological study of religion. It asks whether specific cultural ideas, namely religious ideas, are related to environmental circumstances. Are religions adaptive? Do they help their members survive by promoting behaviors that are suitable in a particular environment? And if they do this, what is the mechanism by which such adaptive religious ideas come into being? Religious leaders do not emphasize the ways in which their teachings are ecologically appropriate; they claim, rather, that these ideas come from purely religious inspirations. We shall look beyond their claims to see if any significant correlations indicate a degree of ecological influence. Part 1 consists mainly of a comparative, ecologically based study of two religions— Christianity and Islam. (The justification for this excursus into ecology in a book entitled *The Sociobiological Imagination* is that it forms the backdrop for a discussion of gene–culture coevolution.) Part 2 surveys some ideas that have been put forward concerning the relationship between genes and culture, and discusses the relationship of these to ecological anthropology.

PART 1: A COMPARATIVE, ECOLOGICALLY-BASED STUDY OF RELIGION

In 1983, R. Tanner and I published *The Biology of Religion*. When we began the study, we had a hunch that religions were interested in the processes of reproduction, and by the end of writing that book we realized that religions were more than just interested, they mapped out for people a complete set of attitudes and beliefs about sex and reproduction that saw them through adolescence and parenthood. In all parts of the world, religions take a great interest in the reproductive process. They establish the right and wrong conditions for conception to take place, the rights and wrongs of abortion and infanticide; they control adolescent sexuality; they regulate marriage, divorce, remarriage, and widowhood.

Our book concentrated on the major world religions: Christianity, Judaism, Islam, Buddhism, and Hinduism. We looked at each one for its precepts concerning sex, marriage, and reproduction. We found that it was possible to sort the

A Japanese Buddhist–Shinto belief holds that girls born in the Year of the Horse will be difficult to marry off. Early neonatal mortality in 1906 and 1966, which were such years, was significantly higher for girls.

THE ƆEAR OF THE HORƧE

different religions' positions on various items (such as celibacy, or approval of divorce) into two categories: *pronatalist—* favoring reproduction and population growth, and *antinatalist—*not favoring these things.

PRO-NATALIST AND ANTI-NATALIST RELIGIOUS PRECEPTS		
Area of Concern	Pro-natalist	Anti-natalist
Conception	Many better	Few better
Infanticide and abortion	Disapproved of	Approved of
Birth and childhood	Many births, less care	Few births, more care
Adolescence	Early reproduction	Delayed reproduction
Marriage	Early marriage	Late marriage
Celibacy	Disapproved of	Approved of
Divorce and widowhood	Remarriage encouraged	Remarriage discouraged
Middle and old age	Reproduction continues	Reproduction ceases

Table 1. After Reynolds and Tanner (1983), Table 1.2.

Table 1 shows these categories. No major religion conforms precisely to pro-natalism or anti-natalism, yet in comparison with one another they show interesting patterns, as will be discussed below. Let us look at just two items, contraception and abortion, to see the differing precepts of various religions.

Contraception. None of the major religions explicitly upholds contraception or birth control. Hinduism widely emphasizes the need to beget and rear a son to ensure salvation of the father; this will lead people to resist contraception until several children have been born and at least one son has prospered. Buddhism is inexplicit, but it is in general opposed to taking life; further it has been argued within Buddhism that contraception is interference with rebirth, the working out of a person's destiny. Traditional Islam has emphasized the positive value of a large family and thus tacitly opposes mechanical contraception (about which the Koran is silent, though *coitus interruptus* is said by some authorities to be condoned). Westernized Muslims in some countries support family planning actively, but not all Muslim countries are demonstrating the decline in birthrates that elsewhere so often accompanies an increased spread of wealth (Nagi 1983). Modern Protestant Christianity in general is tolerant of contraception; although it emphasizes the family, it lays unusual stress on the husband-wife relationship, and marriage is considered acceptable even if there are no children.

Abortion. Just as religions have rules relating to conception and contraception, so, too, they concern themselves with survival during pregnancy and after birth. Abortion raises interesting questions about when life begins, or when the spirit enters the body. The teachings of the Gautama Buddha state that "rebirth takes place when a father and a mother come together, and the one to be born is present" (Suryabongse 1954). A study in Sri Lanka (Ryan 1952) quotes a Buddhist as saying: "If a dead soul wishes to be born into your family, it would be a terrible sin to prevent its birth." Judaism, Christianity, and Islam all oppose abortion unless it is necessary to save the mother's life. Islamic scholars have divided pregnancy into two stages, before and after the instillation of life, which normally occurs at four months. In Islamic law, abortion is an offense against the husband, who at marriage "buys" the future contents of his wife's womb. Willful abortion is thus punishable by compensation, the amount depending on the age of the fetus (Hathout 1972). In Christianity, abortion became punishable in the fourth century A.D.; St. Augustine made a distinction between a formed and an unformed fetus that is widely held today.

In our study, Tanner and I hoped to find a theory that would account for the fact that some religions have precepts that fall mainly into the pronatalist or antinatalist category. We thought of the biological theory of K selection and r selection (MacArthur and Wilson 1967). Natural selection appears to act differently on species in two ways according to ecological conditions. Where resources are consistently "tight" throughout the year (as in the seasonless tropics), species often produce relatively few young but use a lot of parental care to assure the survival of the few who are born. This is known as K selection. By contrast, where resources are plentiful at one time of the year, but scarce at another, evolution often results in species that produce a superabundance of young at the good time, and these get thinned out later. Parental investment by the male is usually less here: his activities are geared to moving from one mate to another. This is called r selection.

In this scene at a Buddhist fertility shrine in Bangkok, a woman is praying that she will conceive. In front of her are a number of small spirit shrines and red tin penises.

We considered the possibility that an antinatalist religion would develop in areas of environmental security and/or predictability, while a pronatalist religion would more likely develop in conditions of insecurity and unpredictability of resources. Here I shall mention certain aspects of Christianity and Islam to see how they may fit into this hypothesis.

Christianity. Christianity has a predominantly negative attitude to premarital and extramarital conceptions. There is an illegitimacy stigma, a concept of sex for its own sake as sin, and a strong feeling that the sex urge should be controlled, especially in adolescence when it is at its most urgent. Celibacy is seen as close to godliness, divorce and remarriage after divorce are disapproved of, especially in the Catholic sector. Children, once they have arrived, are, however, most attentively cared for; such life as exists is sacred, and there is much emphasis on hygiene and good health care. Christianity thus has a negative attitude to many aspects of sex, but within marriage it can be either very proreproductive indeed, as among the Protestant Amish and Hutterites of North America, or quite antinatalist as in contemporary Western Europe or mainstream United States.

Islam. Middle Eastern Muslims take more pride in large families than do today's European Christians. The father has high status, his religion permits polygyny, and he may be head of a very large household, up to four wives being allowed, the actual number being very much determined by wealth. Marital sex is encouraged (Koran 2:183), and erotic instruction is available in religiously sanctioned sex manuals such as *The Perfumed Garden.* Betrothal is early, as is marriage; but premarital sex is not allowed, nor is adultery. Celibacy is not encouraged for men and is unthinkable for women. On balance, Islam is in many ways more pro-natalist than Christianity.

Now let us consider the physical environment of Islam in Asia and compare it with that of Christianity in Europe. Asia has been blighted by food shortages far more often than Europe has, including many severe famines (Jones 1981, 28-31). Besides famines, fatal diseases, especially the infectious ones, have been endemic (and still are) in hot countries, which provide a more favorable breeding ground for bacterial agents than wintry northwestern Europe. Wars, too, have historically been more destructive in Asia and the Middle East than in Europe. Certainly Europe has experienced severe fluctuations of population and has had to endure epidemics and pandemics during the last millennium (see, for example, Russell and Russell 1983 for an excellent summary). But as Russell and Russell (1983), Jones (1981), and others have shown, it is a characteristic peculiar to northwestern Europe to have an exceptionally resilient soil cover and a benign climatic pattern, which together have enabled its physical environment to survive population crashes and social disintegration.

The point of interest now is to ask whether religions follow any ecological pattern in regard to *r* and *K* selection. One would predict that a religion will exhort individuals *to have large families in areas where diseases have been endemic, wars and famines common, and mortality rates consequently high.* E. L. Jones commented along this vein in his 1981 book *The European Miracle:*

> Income per capita was higher in Europe than Asia partly because natural disasters were fewer. There was less of the compulsion that Asians felt to breed as many sons as possible in order to ensure family labour for the phases of recovery. Voluntary control of fertility in Europe was a safer option, the means being delayed marriage and a lower marital participation rate. The slightly smaller families produced by late marriage made possible a greater investment in the individual: that is in the quality of human capital" (226–27).

In 1983, Tanner and I presented figures for GNP and energy consumption showing that energy resources and available wealth per head are great in the Protestant world, low in the world of Islam. (Reynolds and Tanner, 1983). Our object in using these figures was to show how much more secure of its food supply and other scarce resources the (by and large) affluent Protestant world is today compared with the (by and large) poor Muslim one. This is not a new situation but a very old one predating Protestantism to medieval times at least, as has been well documented by economic historians. What have changed are the relative *levels* of affluence: these have steadily progressed further in Europe than in Asia, where historically

the short flowerings of affluence have always been confined
to elites, the masses being perpetually poor.

The major religion of Europe, Christianity, in deemphasizing
fertility, may thus be reflecting the relative security its inhabitants
have felt with regard to famine, war, and disease, the converse
being true in the Muslim world. Table 2 gives fertility and
mortality figures for some countries in the areas concerned,
together with figures for per-head GNP in these countries.

DEMOGRAPHIC CHARACTERISTICS OF
SELECTED PROTESTANT AND MUSLIM COUNTRIES

Protestant	CBR	IMR	TFR	LEB	GNP
United Kingdom	13	10.1	1.8	73	9050
Norway	12	7.8	1.7	76	13820
Sweden	11	7.0	1.6	76	12400
Finland	14	6.0	1.7	74	10440
Denmark	10	8.2	1.4	74	11490
Netherlands	12	8.4	1.5	76	9910
North Germany	10	10.1	1.3	74	11420
Switzerland	11	7.7	1.6	76	16370
Iceland	19	7.1	2.2	77	10270
Muslim					
Syria	47	57.0	7.3	64	1680
Jordan	46	63.0	7.4	64	1710
Saudi Arabia	42	103.0	7.2	56	12180
Turkey	35	110.0	5.1	63	1230
North Yemen	48	154.0	6.8	44	510
Algeria	45	109.0	7.0	60	2400
Libya	46	92.0	7.2	58	7500
Morocco	41	99.0	5.9	58	750
Tunisia	33	85.0	4.9	61	1290

Key: CBR = Crude Birth Rate (per 1000 members of population)
      IMR = Infant Mortality Rate (per 1000 live births)
      TFR = Total Fertility Rate (average number of offspring
            per woman)
      LEB = Life Expectancy at Birth
      GNP = Gross National Product per capita (US$)

Table 2. Source: World Population Data Sheet

Comparison of the Protestant and Muslim data in table 2 shows that the Muslim group is characterized at the present time by a higher birthrate, a higher fertility rate, a higher death rate, a higher infant mortality rate, and a lower per-head GNP than the Protestant group. These are, of course, modern data relating to the present time. Among the early Christians, mortality and birthrates were high. This does not affect the present hypothesis, which aims to show correlations and posit connections between religious teachings and demographic regimes, rather than to claim unalterable differences between religious rules. On the contrary, religious rules appear to change with changes in the environment, though there is an extreme dearth of studies bearing on this important point.

The data presented here are thus compatible with the idea that people in the Protestant world today are affluent, secure, and confident about their children's survival. This in turn supports the hypothesis that family size, and its associated religious rules, beliefs, and attitudes, is at least in part determined by ecological factors. According to our hypothesis, ecological differences give rise to different levels of confidence in the ability to survive, rear children, and solve the family's needs for food and other basic resources. Ecological conditions give rise to different *perceptions*. It is the *perceived* level of unpredictability of the environment that determines family size, that is, how many children they *think* they are going to be likely to lose through death and disaster. Such perceptions are based on the real, objectively obtaining situation, but exactly how close the match is must depend on recent history as much as anything, and this is a fascinating area for further study. From the data given above, it appears that in the Muslim world the level of perceived environmental unpredictability is high while in the Protestant world it is low.

Two important points regarding table 2 must, however, be mentioned. First, the sample is not random. The countries in table 2 were deliberately chosen to represent the ends of the reproductivity spectrum. Thus, countries with a strong Protestant following rather than countries that are mostly Roman Catholic have been selected to represent the antinatalist end. Nonaffluent European Catholic countries such as Portugal do not appear here, nor, of course, do the very poor Catholic countries outside of Europe, such as in Latin America. On the Muslim side, some of the newly wealthy oil states in the Gulf are not listed. They have both high fertility and wealth; this does not agree with the correlation we have sketched, unless we allow for the recency of the affluence and the possibility of cultural lags. Nor, as already mentioned, does table 2 take into account changes over time. As is well known, birth control is rapidly moving into areas where it was previously forbidden. J. Chamie (1981) showed that there was a fertility decline in pre–civil war Lebanon, but even there the more affluent Druze Muslims both wanted and had fewer children than the less affluent Sunni Muslims.

The ideas of r and K selection have been outlined above to give the reader a handle on to where a socioecological analysis might begin. In our own study, Tanner and I abandoned the r and K model. Originally, that model was developed for the comparison of reproductive strategies of different *species* in different or changing environments. As such it is concerned with the biological evolution of reproductive systems, including their associated anatomy and physiology. Our study was concerned with the evolution of social forms (the cultural, religious rules governing reproduction) in relation to the environment. Despite this major difference, we should still have been happy to use the terms r and K selection, but there was another far more pressing reason to question them. This was the fact that humans, almost alone in the animal world, change, manipulate, and increase (and sometimes decrease) their own food supply, from year to year and from generation to generation. This makes any idea of environmental determinism very problematical indeed. It does not make it impossible, because humans are still very subject to environmental features such as drought, flood, earthquake, and in particular social conflicts. But they can and do in many parts of the world consciously change and manipulate their food supply, whereas an important part of the r and K selection model is that the distribution of food for any species is an objectively measurable and reasonably predictable entity down the generations.

The above discussion raises the central issue: how do biological and cultural evolution interact with each another?

PART 2: THEORIES OF THE RELATIONSHIP
BETWEEN GENES AND CULTURE

This area is so complex that it is difficult even to sketch it. Let me start by mentioning an historical idea of environmental determinism and cultural determinism. Heraclitus in the fifth century B.C. wrote in his *Influences of Atmosphere, Water, and Situation*:

> The countries which have the greatest and the most frequent seasonal variations of climate...also have the wildest landscape...and if the variation is great, the differentiation of (human) bodily type is increased proportionally...and their possessors have headstrong self-willed characters and temperaments, with a tendency towards ferocity instead of tameness. (quoted by Toynbee 1935, 1:251–52)

Arnold Toynbee noted that theories of environmental determinism are inadequate, insofar as certain environments have produced great flowerings of culture while similar environments elsewhere have failed to do so (Toynbee 1935, 1:249ff.). Environmental challenges may spur events along, but—for Toynbee—the most important element shaping the evolution of each culture is its inner, spiritual force, its *Geist*.

Culture as Autonomous

The idea that a culture is a more or less autonomous thing has been expressed by some twentieth-century social anthropologists. They hold that most of culture is not "functional" (in Bronislaw Malinowski's sense of serving the bodily needs of individuals) nor "adaptive" (in Marvin Harris's sense, which will be described below). Rather, culture has a life of its own, and rules unto itself that were first brought into existence by the imaginations of our ancestors and have ever since been subject to interpretation and modification by other people down the ages. Emile Durkheim (1915) and later Lesley White (1949) gave this idea its clearest expression.

Another school I might mention here, but only to exclude it from our study, is that of the early environmentalists such as Franz Boas and his student Margaret Mead. They assisted the swing away from biological explanations to purely psychological and sociological explanations of human behavior. Their environmental determinism, however, concerned the influence of culture on the *individual's* behavior: culture shapes the individual.

Ecological Anthropology

In this review I am more concerned with the shaping of the culture itself. Here, the newer school of *ecological anthropology,* including the works of Roy Rappaport, Andrew Vayda, and Marvin Harris, is of interest. This school tries to explain cultural forms as adaptations to the environment. Harris' work on the Hindu sacred cow is an example. He attacks the notion that the Hindu prohibition against eating cattle is a disadvantageous, maladaptive rule resulting from an outdated religious ideology. He disputes that the ideology should be taken as a "prime mover" when in fact more mundane, practical considerations are far more likely to be the ultimate determinants of action, and the ideas of sanctity serve to perpetuate these.

In particular he lays stress on the positive uses of the cattle by Hindus for traction power, milk, dung, beef, hide production, and so on, when considered against the costs of ecologically viable alternatives.

In general, the exploitation of cattle resources proceeds in such a way as not to impair the survival and economic well-being of the human population. The relationship between the human and bovine population is symbiotic rather than competitive; more traction animals than are presently available are needed for carrying out essential agricultural tasks (Harris 1966, 59). In other words, a culture may contain sacred rules about behaviors whose primary purpose is ecological.

Throughout Hindu India cows, because of their religious significance, roam freely in both town and countryside and are not prevented from eating human food exposed for sale in shops.

Cultural Selection and "Selective Retention"

That notion brings us to the question, again, of how such religious rules get invented and spread. It is possible that they are "random mutations" (analogous to the changes that bring about new genetic traits) that get "selected for" if the culture they help design is in competition with other cultures. Picture, for example, two cultures that need cattle for their survival. If one culture happens to invent religious rules to protect the cow, and the other allows profligate slaughter of cows, the first culture may prevail over the second: "cultural selection" will have occurred. Cultural selection may occur very quickly (much more quickly than natural selection acting on individuals, over many generations, to shape some new biological trait). Furthermore cultural ideas are exportable: they are not tied to those individuals who possess certain genes—they may be copied widely by others.

But what are the supposed selection mechanisms by which culture passes from generation to generation? A productive idea in regard to cultural selection is that of the anthropologist William Durham (1979) and the psychologist Donald Campbell (1975), who, meaning much the same process, both refer to "selective retention." Selective retention implies that culture, far from being monolithic and homogeneous, consists of a variety of choices, and according to the choices made by people down the generations it remains either more or less static, or undergoes directional change. This gives rise to two questions. First, *What is the criterion of a successful choice?*—that is, what is it that determines whether Choice A or Choice B, once made, goes on down the generations or fizzles out? Second, *At what level are these choices made?*—individual, group, or wider level, such as the nation? As we shall see, these two questions are closely related to each other.

Both Durham and Campbell have been concerned with the relationship between human cultural evolution and Darwinian, organic evolution. It is today more or less universally accepted that Darwinian selection occurs principally at the genetic or the individual level. As George C. Williams (1966) and Richard Dawkins (1976) have stressed, only those genes that "win out" in one generation can be transmitted to the next, and they are transmitted according to the relative success of their carriers in the reproductive "rat-race." Is the same true of aspects of culture? This question raises the basic issue of the relation between natural and cultural selection. Are they quite different and separate processes, or similar by analogy, or truly interactive? All shades of answer occur in the current literature.

For Dawkins (1976) they were considered as rather separate. Dawkins coined the term *memes* for the learned ideas transmitted by cultures, and differentiated sharply between their transmission mechanism from generation to generation, and the genetic one. Memes had the advantage that, being able to spread very much faster than genes, they enabled individuals to adapt faster; hence the whole evolutionary process in humans was somewhat removed from the animal one. The idea of memes was useful in that it laid emphasis on the unique properties of human cultures and their unique method of evolution. Unfortunately, though, it was based on a rather close analogy with "genes" and tended to deflect attention away from interactionist theories that see cultural ideas and practices interacting with genes in some way or other.

Gene–Culture Coevolution

This brings us back to the idea of selective retention. In this view, the criterion of success for aspects of culture is not directly measured in terms of how far they succeed in perpetuating *themselves,* for that degree of success is itself a part of the wider process of natural selection. The cultural items are successful *if they enhance the inclusive reproductive fitness of their bearers.* The result is a coevolution of the cultural and physical aspects of human life (Durham 1978).

Some such idea as that of coevolution is becoming quite widespread, particularly among evolutionary-minded anthropologists. They fall into roughly two camps. On the one hand we have a "hard-nosed" group who wish to retain a genetic perspective, and on the other a "softer" group who feel this is unnecessary or at least do not discuss it explicitly. The former group holds to a view that makes certain demands, which have been very well expressed by Richard Alexander as follows: "One might suggest that there are *genetic instructions* which somehow result in our engaging in [say] arbitrariness in symbolic behavior in whatever *environments* it is genetically reproductive to do so" (Alexander 1979, 77, his italics).

William Durham (1978) and more recently Lumsden and Wilson (1981) have gone to some trouble to produce a brain-based model of coevolution. In this model the process of natural selection, acting on individuals via their success in reproducing themselves, has led to the emergence of brain structures that create biases in human behavioral tendencies. Such biases produce "ease of learning" of adaptive actions (that is, actions that have in the past been adaptive), but these can be overridden (by ontogenetic processes) if the culture is changing or the individual is for any reason unable or unwilling to follow them.

A not dissimilar brain-based, genetic theory was produced by Hamilton (1975) to explain the in-group-amity, out-group-enmity found in the relationships between human groups. Hamilton had the idea of a "template" in the brains of individuals, by reference to which human relationships would be organized. Lumsden and Wilson (1981) posit not a brain template but a series of neural pathways along which learning occurs easily. Durham (1978) suggests three kinds of "biases": adaptive learning, feelings of satisfaction, and canalized learning (23).

Clearly this hard-nosed group has been struggling to find a down-to-earth mechanism whereby the outcome of following *the cultural rules that happen to prevail* at any one time in any one place *can be reflected, via the genetic process, in the next generation.* This inclusion of the genetic process in the system can link up with natural selection theory and integrate human action into animal behavior and general biological theory.

Nevertheless we need not accept such a theory, for it makes an unnecessary demand, namely that the transmission of culture should have any genetic basis at all. This brings us to the soft view referred to above, and with it the end of our survey. We noted that the soft view deemphasizes genes, tending to emphasize reproductive success as such. In brief, following, changing, choosing among, or rejecting cultural rules will lead to people having more or fewer children. Thus, people's ideas of what to do and how to do it will be perpetuated, by parent–child interaction and other processes, in proportion to their reproductive success. (For example, people who chose to follow the sacred cow rule would survive—and reproduce—more than others.)

A religion may encourage a practice that is contrary to survival, as seen in the mass suicide by members of the Christian Assembly of God at Jonestown, Guyana, in 1978.

Maximizing Reproductive Success

The anthropologists Chagnon and Irons (1979) have emphasized reproductive success in this general way, as has Durham (1979), together with a number of anthropologists, notably Les Hiatt (1980) and Monique Borgerhoff Mulder (1985). They show that aspects of cultures such as marriage strategies or parental strategies appear to be very much concerned with maximizing, or in some cases optimizing, reproductive success. Irons (1979a), for instance, writes as follows: "Human beings 'track' their environments and behave in ways which, given the specific environment in which they find themselves, maximize inclusive fitness; what is observed as culture and social structure is the outcome of this process" (258). His statement arises from his field studies of the Turkmen people. Dickemann's (1979b) argument concerning the occurrence of female infanticide in the Indian caste system—relating this to the prevailing levels of relevant resources and the amounts of parental energy needed to utilize these to maximize inclusive fitness—is of the same general type. Betzig's (1986) work similarly falls into the soft view, that is, the view that does not postulate any particular genetic mechanism for the control of culture.

Such arguments are complex, and justice cannot be done to them by brief references; the reader is referred to the original papers for a fuller appreciation. An excellent summary of many of the arguments bearing on this debate, and a dismissal of some of the confusions, is to be found in Borgerhoff Mulder (1985). Perhaps the most comprehensive treatment of biological–cultural evolution is that of Boyd and Richerson (1985), which includes some important models for the transmission of cultural rules in general and some specific rules.

The ideas of Hiatt (1981) are also of interest, as they go beyond the analysis of strategies to include consideration of an underlying stratum of "emotions." Cultural responses to this are "free" in that they can go along with, or oppose, the underlying tendencies. Hiatt's nongenetic parental investment idea implies that individuals learn or are explicitly taught during their lives the appropriate ways of behaving in their particular culture, taking account of their social positions, gender, and possible future happenings based on a knowledge of the past. There is no need for gene-based "node-link structures" channeling action toward certain goals rather than others (Lumsden and Wilson 1981). All we need to posit is a process whereby children are differentially produced by members of the community, and that processes exist whereby they discover the cultural know-how to reproduce successfully in their turn and to transmit the know-how down the generations.

Conclusion.

The world is full of cultures with different rules; some of these are encoded in religions and have religious backing. Among them are many that affect the extent of childrearing regarded as appropriate as discussed earlier in the pronatalist and antinatalist model. Such rules and emphases might be entirely arbitrary ("culture by whimsey," as Blurton Jones (1976) has memorably called it). In fact, however, we have not found this to be the case. In company with others who have emphasized the ecological circumstances of cultural forms, we have found evidence of rules within cultures that would tend to enhance the survival and reproductive success of individuals in the prevailing, and in light of the past, environmental conditions. Some of these rules are encoded in religious systems, which (contrary to first expectations) seem to be very much concerned with *this* life and its practical goings-on.

NOTE

1. Grateful acknowledgment is made to the following colleagues who have given thought and time to criticisms of earlier drafts of this paper: A. Anderson, D. Coleman, W. Hamilton, G. A. Harrison, A. Hinde, E. L. Jones, J. Odling-Smee, D. Sieff, P. Stewart, R. Tanner. Responsibility for the paper's remaining deficiencies rests with the author.

13

Studies of Conflict

Johan M. G. van der Dennen

The Concept of Conflict

Polemos pantoon pater.—Heraclitus

Controversy, having an argument, fights, duels, fisticuffs, debates, lawsuits, rivalry, fierce competition, wars, riots, purges, imbroglios. . . these are some of the manifestations of what is generally called "conflict": the incompatibility of interests, values, needs, preferences, behavioral tendencies, goals, ideas, ideologies, and so on—in short, the clash of incompatible forces or qualities. The science of conflict (conflictology) and the more recent science of war (polemology) are interdisciplinary fields of research. Conflicts are studied by sociologists, anthropologists, psychologists, historians, economists, and ethologists, and, now, by sociobiologists.

One contribution sociobiology makes to the study of conflict is simply its explanation of why conflict exists. Sociobiological reasoning predicts a conflict potential in every area where there is a relative difference in coefficients of relatedness, and where the reproductive interests of two parties are not absolutely identical: parent–offspring conflict, sibling rivalry, conflict between the sexes (the "battle" of the sexes), ingroup–outgroup differentiation, and intergroup conflict along ethnic, tribal, and other cleavages.

If this chapter were meant to emphasize interindividual conflicts, I would outline various sociobiological ideas about competition and aggression. I would also discuss game-theory approach. For example, in their important theory of Evolutionary Stable Strategy (ESS), John Maynard Smith and G. R. Price (1973) envisioned ways in which certain strategies could have evolved, by measuring the costs and benefits, to the individual, of hawk-like or dove-like behavior. However, this chapter must concentrate on intergroup, rather than interindividual, conflict. I thus shall limit myself to a two-part discussion: Part 1 concerns human warfare; Part 2 concerns the quite recent findings about chimpanzee "warfare," which may or may not shed light on human warfare.

PART 1: HUMAN WARFARE

How did warfare originate? What is the best explanation for why humans engage in war? When, in the 1970s, I developed an interest in the origin of human warfare, there was not much to go by. There existed a clear consensus: war was ("only") a cultural invention (this was the Mead school of anthropology clearly predominating: the creed had a progressive, environmentalist outlook, and it implied, of course, that war could also be "de-invented" and abolished). War, thus, had a history but no evolution.

At that time there were a few "giants" in the field of "primitive" war, the authoritative sources you should have read and properly digested: H. H. Turney-High, the strategist, interested more in the how of tribal warfare than in the why (though his enumeration of what we now would call the "proximate causes" of tribal warfare is still impressive and perceptive); Quincy Wright, the categorist and compiler of the "Summa summarum" of the academic wisdom of that age, modestly entitled *A Study of War,* and including a chapter on primitive war among more than 650 primitive peoples; M. R. Davie, who asserted that scarcity of resources led to competition, and that war was just a quick and dirty way to get rid of the competition; and S. Andreski, who invented the word *ophelemities* to refer to everything people want, such as sex, power, glory, and prosperity, and said that the human craving for these ophelemities was the natural cause of war.

There were also some minor deities, two Dutchmen who hardly reached the Anglosaxon world because they wrote in

German and Dutch. S. R. Steinmetz proclaimed that man was an aggressive, predatory, and cruel creature from the dawn of his evolution, and that primitive warfare was a logical outcome of this human nature. The other Dutchman, T. S. Van der Bij—characteristically perhaps—reached the opposite conclusion: the more "primitive" the people, the less warlike; war, he said, grew with cultural development and civilization.

Later, when I had the opportunity to study the sources on which these twentieth-century authorities based their theories, I discovered that the basic tenets and controversies were already alive and kicking in the era of social Darwinism (or perhaps better: not-so-social Spencerism). So—before we get to the sociobiological theories—I invite you to a very brief "tour d'horizon" of this remarkable period in which Man, the "Crown of Creation," was downgraded to "Homo destructor," the nasty, sanguinary, and apish brute.

SOCIAL DARWINISM

In the middle of the nineteenth century a new phenomenon occurred: the purely racial interpretation of history. The most influential were the racial theories of Gobineau, Gumplowicz, and Chamberlain. Gobineau's (1853) thesis was that "inequality of races is sufficient to explain the entire enchainment of the destinies of peoples" (viii). There are the inferior and the superior races, and only the latter are able to attain true civilization. Chamberlain (1911) added little, except by trying to show that the most superior race is the white, particularly the Aryan "race." Gumplowicz (1883) hypothesized an inherent and deadly hatred and animosity in the relationship of one racial group to another, resulting in an inevitable and deadly struggle ("Rassenkampf") between the groups. The victorious group, having conquered its victim, pitilessly exploits it, turning it into slaves or subjects.

Note that this racialist intellectual input to the movement or period called "social Darwinism" has very little to do with Darwin. The Zeitgeist was apparently such, however, that it could easily be incorporated into mainstream social Darwinism.

The idea of conflict and struggle comes into its own with Spencer, Darwin, Wallace, and Huxley. Of course, conflict and struggle had long been declared a fundamental law of life, and indeed the source of all change and progress. Even the theory of the survival of the fittest was outlined not later than the fifth century B.C. by Empedocles and Heraclitus, and may also be found in the Zend-Avesta. Darwin took his idea of a struggle for existence from Malthus. The Malthusian idea is that population tends to increase faster than the means of subsistence and that this increase is checked by wars, epidemics, and famines. Malthus (1978) regarded warfare in the earlier ages of the world as "the great business of mankind"; and considered it as one of the most powerful impulses of war.

WARFARE AND GROUP SELECTION

The idea of group selection started with Darwin (1871), when he considered the possibility of group selection in relation to war in human evolution. He could not find any other mechanism to explain sociality, altruism, morality, human brain development, and other peculiar features of humankind. Thus, he envisaged that group selection would favor tribes of brave and self-sacrificing individuals over the selfish and cowardly. Spencer, who coined the term *survival of the fittest,* was even more outspoken on this subject. In his *The Study of Sociology* (1873), he states the group selection thesis as follows:

> Warfare among men, like warfare among animals, has had a large share in raising their organizations to a higher stage. The following are some of the various ways in which it has worked. In the first place, it has had the effect of continually extirpating races which, for some reason or other, were least fitted to cope with the conditions of existence they were subject to. The killing-off of relatively feeble tribes, or tribes relatively wanting in endurance, or courage, or sagacity, or power of co-operation, must have tended ever to maintain, and occasionally to increase, the amounts of life-preserving powers possessed by men. (192)

Bagehot (1884) believed that warlike competition among societies in early times would select for those with the best leadership and most obedient populace. Hence his much-quoted adage: the tamest are the strongest. (In this regard he anticipated Robert Bigelow—see below.) For the American sociologist W. G. Sumner (1911), the foundation of human society was the man/land ratio. Conflict over the means of subsistence is the underlying fact that shapes the nature of human society. When population presses upon the land supply, earth hunger arises, races of men move across the face of the world, militarism and imperialism flourish, and conflict rages.

This is but a small collection of quotes about human militancy and violence. It will be obvious that in the public's mind, by the turn of the century, Darwin's word *fitness* had already lost its biological meaning of reproductive success and gradually came to imply physical strength and individual—or group—survival. This may have been aided by the popularity of "instinctivism" in psychology. William James in 1910, was one of the first to postulate an "instinct of pugnacity": "modern man inherits all the innate pugnacity and all love of glory of his ancestors" (James 1964, 22). Numerous other scholars "explained" war by appealing to "human nature," and a rich variety of other quasi-instinctive drives and motives—from herd instinct to the need for adventure. I believe it is fair to say that prejudices of various sorts have greatly influenced the theorizing about the causes of war.

THE CONTEMPORARY THEORIES

Now we come to the contemporary theories of the origin and evolution of primitive war including the sociobiological ones. The question is: Have we progressed since Spencer? Did anything change between Darwin and Alexander? The answer is a firm and emphatic maybe. Here I shall briefly look at four current explanations of the origin of human warfare. Three of them use either ethology or sociobiology as their starting point: they concern *hunting, balances of power,* and *ethnocentrism.* The fourth is the cultural anthropologists' theory of *materialism* as the cause of war. Following this, I shall look at Napoleon Chagnon's study of war among the Yanomamo.

The Hunting Hypothesis

Sherwood Washburn and his associates postulate a special learning disposition in the human animal for hunting and killing, with its own intrinsic source of satisfaction, pleasure, and lust—the so-called carnivorous psychology of man. In this view, the hunting and killing of prey animals facilitated the move to the hunting and killing of conspecifics—and even torture and the (vicarious) enjoyment of cruelty. These authors also point to the popularity of war even in recent times (Washburn and Lancaster 1968). In a similar vein, John Pfeiffer (1972) writes: "War, the cruelest and most elaborate and most human form of hunting, became one of the most appealing ways of expressing aggression" (150).

Raymond Dart (1953), one of the first finders of hominid fossils, had earlier concluded from the condition of some of the skulls that "man's predecessors differed from living apes in being confirmed killers," and that "the loathsome cruelty of mankind to man. . .is explicable only in terms of his cannibalistic origins" (quoted in Wilson 1975, 255). This is, as Wilson (1975) aptly remarked, "very dubious anthropology, ethology, and genetics." Dart's views inspired *African Genesis* (1961), the first of Robert Ardrey's series of popular books. Ardrey opined that contemporary humans are descendants of a race of "terrestrial, flesh-eating killer apes," and that this fact, *an sich,* explains the aggressiveness and warlikeness of modern humans. The hunting hypothesis has lost considerable ground in recent years. Keep it in mind, however, for our later discussion on chimpanzee warfare.

Balances of Power

Why did our hominid forebears gain so rapidly in brain size? What environmental pressure caused *keen intelligence* to be selected for? Darwin was first to suggest that warfare, or intergroup competition, may have aided the evolution of human intelligence. This theme was later developed by Arthur Keith (1947), Robert Bigelow (1969), Richard Alexander and Donald Tinkle (1968), Alexander (1979), and Roger Pitt (1978). Pitt notes that during the Pleistocene, hominid populations must have reached critical densities at fairly frequent intervals. Several scenarios can be pictured: (1) peaceful coexistence of the groups; (2) peaceful competition between groups with the losers starving; (3) violent conflict between individuals; (4) scrambling competition; and (5) violent group conflict, that is, warfare.

Assuming that different groups tended toward one or another of these strategies, in varying degrees, it is easy to see that the warmongers would be the most sucessful, and could indeed overrun any group attempting to practice one of the other strategies (Pitt 1978).

Alexander has called attention to the little-considered fact that there is no automatic or universal benefit from *group living*. To explain primate and hominid groups, only the causative factor of predation will do, he says. And once predation from other species relaxed, early man became his own predator: "When man developed his weapons, culture, and population sizes to levels that essentially erased the significance of predators of other species, he simultaneously created a new predator: groups and coalitions within his own species" (Alexander 1974, 335). In subsequent publications, Alexander (1979, 1987) proposed the so-called Balance-of-Power Hypothesis. He contends that at some early point in our history the actual function of human groups (that is, their significance for their individual members) was protection from the predatory effects of other human groups. The premise is that war—or at least intergroup competition—is the necessary and sufficient force to explain the maintenance of every group beyond the level of the nuclear family. "Balance of power" means that one group enlarges (and strengthens) itself to equal a neighboring, threatening group.

The interplay between the need for balances of power and the further development of human intelligence, particularly conscious self-control, has been elaborated by Robert Bigelow in his popular 1969 book, *The Dawn Warriors*. He shows, surprisingly, that skill at *avoiding* warfare can be just as adaptive as warlikeness. Alexander (1974) shows, too, that weapons invented by one side call forth the ingenuity of developing better weapons by the other side.

More recently, McEachron and Baer (1982) have shown that the development of weapons increases the costs of being attacked. Thus there was a selective pressure for the evolution of preemptive strike behavior— that is, to attack before being attacked. Earlier, Peter Meyer (1981) proposed that "fear itself," that is, fear of the other potentially hostile group—leading to perceptions of threat and preemptive strike—may be the universal motive behind primitive war.

Ethnocentrism

E. O. Wilson stated in his book *On Human Nature* (1978):

> The force behind most warlike policies is ethnocentrism, the irrationally exaggerated allegiance of individuals to their kin and fellow tribesmen. The practice of war is a straightforward example of a hypertrophied biological predisposition. Primitive men cleaved their universe into friends and enemies and responded with quick, deep emotion to even the mildest threat emanating from outside the arbitrary boundary. . . .The evolution of warfare was an autocatalytic reaction that could not be halted by any people, because to attempt to reverse the process unilaterally was to fall victim. A new mode of natural selection was operating at the level of entire societies.

In his 1981 book, *The Ethnic Phenomenon,* Pierre van den Berghe argued in detail (using case studies from much of human history) that one of the best explanations for warfare is ethnocentrism. Ethnocentrism, in turn, is a result of kin selection. Paul Shaw and Yuwa Wong have developed this idea in their book, *Genetic Seeds of Warfare* (1988). They build on Alexander's balance-of-power hypothesis, and on McEachron and Baer's hypothesis on the evolution of weapons. They propose that inclusive fitness considerations have combined with competition over scarce resources, intergroup conflict, and weapon development, to (1) reinforce humanity's propensity to band together in groups of genetically related individuals, (2) predispose group members to act in concert for their own well-being, and (3) promote xenophobia, fear, and antagonism among genetically related individuals toward strangers (Shaw and Wong 1988).

Materialism

Lately, theorists of ecological, ethological, sociobiological, and Marxist perspectives and/or signature have found themselves happily united, "bien etonnés de se trouver ensemble," in a common emphasis on primitive war as a strategy to secure scarce and vital or strategic resources, such as land, protein, or women. Simply "cherchez la ressource" and you will find the basic cause of that war. (Vulgar materialists apply this contemporaneously to mineral deposits, oil, etc.)

The basic tenets of materialism have recently been well described by R. B. Ferguson in his 1984 book, *Warfare, Culture and Environment*. Materialism, he says, contrasts with theories that explain war as generated by certain values, social structures, and so forth, in the absence of any material rationale. Such factors do affect the conduct of war and thresholds of violence. But they are secondary and not regularly capable of generating and sustaining war patterns in themselves. Ferguson does admit that "the focus on land and game has created an oversimplified picture of ecological explanations. . . .War is never a simple function of the natural environment" (32).

There is a neo-evolutionist school of cultural anthropology that emphasizes ecological aspect of materialist motivations. Marvin Harris, one of its main exponents, holds that "high-energy societies replace low-energy societies" and thus "long-range trends toward higher levels of productivity are related to intergroup hostility" (Harris 1975,224). Harris's explanation of primitive warfare is that it "arose as part of a complex system that prevented human populations from exceeding the carrying capacity of their habitats" (Harris 1972, 18). Or to use Vayda's terminology, war functions to adjust the man/land ratio (Vayda 1968).

Multilevel Explanations

Before leaving this survey of the contemporary theories, I must note that the fact of having multiple explanations for the origin of war (hunting, balances of power, ethnocentrism, and materialism) is pretty unsatisfactory to the polemologist. Of course, these explanations are not necessarily mutually exclusive. Ethnocentric traits can help strengthen the hostility of groups in regard to material resources, the need for balances of power can sharpen ethnocentric feelings, and so forth. Still, it would be more useful if the theories sorted out the various factors *and* expressed them in the context of actual cultural events.

Peter Meyer (1987, 1990) and I (van der Dennen 1990) are working on a two-stage model of the role of ethnocentrism and warfare in human evolution. In the first stage, there is low-level feuding based on fear and xenophobia, and the revenge motive figures prominently (see discussion of Chagnon below). In the second, much later stage, war has become transformed into an instrument to obtain material resources and/or political supremacy. This *instrumentalization* of warfare probably developed in "warrior societies" and accompanied cultural inventions in technology and the logistics of battle.

HYPOTHESIS TESTING AND
THE YANOMAMO CASE STUDY

Thus far, the sociobiological theories have mentioned a host of ways in which warfare could plausibly be an evolutionary phenomenon. But none have strictly defined the level of selection involved. Is it cultural selection, individual selection, or group selection? William Durham (1976b) points out that ideally, the adaptiveness of primitive warfare would be ascertained by a rigorous test of three competing hypotheses: (1) Cultural traditions of warfare in primitive societies evolved *independently* of the ability of human beings to survive and reproduce; (2) Cultural traditions of primitive warfare evolved by the *selective retention* of traits that enhance the inclusive fitness of *individual* human beings; and (3) Cultural traditions of primitive warfare evolved by some process of *group selection* that commonly favored the *altruistic* tendencies of some warriors.

One reason why it is difficult to test these hypotheses empirically is, of course, that the historical record usually does not contain enough detail for us to work with, in terms of investigating primitive wars of the past. Even as far as contemporary primitive societies are concerned, as Napoleon Chagnon complains, there is often little recording of the statistics, such as number of deaths and the relationships among the killers and the killed. His own long-term study of the Yanomamo people of Venezuela and Brazil *has* yielded the prerequisite statistics, however. Among the statistics for this society, known as "the fierce people" during the past twenty-three years, 44% of males estimated to be age twenty-five or older, have participated in the killing of someone, approximately 30% of adult male deaths are due to violence, and nearly 70% of persons over forty have lost a close genetic relative due to violence.

Yanomamo raiders, just prior to departure.
(Photo: Napoleon Chagnon)

Chagnon has conducted very complex statistical analysis to determine whether or not participation in wars (actually, village raids) enhances the fitness of individual warriors or their families. It seems that both gain in fitness. *Unokais* (men who have killed) have a higher rate of marital success than non-unokais. As of 1987 in one group of villages, 88% of the 137 unokais were married compared to 51% of the 243 non-unokais (Chagnon 1988, 989). Chagnon observes that "the higher reproductive success of unokais is mainly due to their greater success in finding mates, either by appropriating them forcibly from others, or by customary marriage alliance arrangements in which they seem to be more attractive as mates than non-unokais" (989).

There is more to it than individual fitness, however. The main motive for raiding is revenge, often for the killing of a kinsperson. Villages with an impressive reputation for fierce revenge do succeed in deterring attacks against themselves. This may look like group selection—the whole village benefits from their protection. However "in most villages, well over 80% of the members are related to more than 75% of [their fellow villagers]" (988). There are other complications, too, insofar as the leaders within a village, who decide when and where to raid, are always from the largest families, that is, these leaders have a high rate of relatedness to fellow villagers. Chagnon concludes "If, as Clausewitz suggested, (modern) warfare is the conduct of politics by other means, in the tribal world warfare is *ipso facto* the extension of kinship obligations by violence, because the political system is organized by kinship" (988). I refer the reader to this study for more details, and for Chagnon's interesting observation that the men do not necessarily enjoy going to war and may even feel trapped by the unending cycle of revenge.

PART 2: CHIMPANZEE "WARFARE"

In general, field observations of a great number of species have confirmed sociobiological predictions about infanticide, siblicide, homicide, and rape. These gory forms of "conflict resolution" are much more widespread than was ever envisaged by the first generation of ethologists, who thought that animals had innate inhibitions against killing conspecifics, and that man was a biological freak because he apparently lacked those inhibitions. A particularly surprising discovery in the 1970s was made by Jane Goodall, concerning chimpanzees. She found that at Gombe, some chimps had developed a taste for cannibalism, some hunted young monkeys and shared the food, some patrolled the borders of their home range, eagerly seeking members of the rival group in order to brutally kill them—in all respects resembling a human primitive raid.

For the remainder of this chapter I shall look at chimp warfare, and consider how it came about (with an eye to seeing if it illuminates human warfare). I shall first outline Goodall's own explanation, and then consider other possibilities, including the theme of "deinstinctivation." Finally, I shall show once again the problematic relationship between the evolution of hunting behavior and the evolution of intergroup aggression.

GOODALL'S EXPLANATION:
TERRITORIALITY AND COOPERATIVE GROUPS

Goodall explains chimpanzee proto-warfare in terms of the idiosyncratic pattern of chimp territoriality and other "preadaptations." In four important ways, she says, chimpanzee behavior does not comply with classical territoriality: (1) Both at Gombe and Mahale it is the relative size and composition of the two neighboring parties that determine the outcome of an encounter, rather than the geographic location. (2) Chimpanzees have a large home range with considerable overlap between neighboring communities. (3) It is perhaps in the *violence* of their hostility toward neighbors that chimpanzees, like hyenas and lions, differ most from the traditional territory owners of the animal kingdom. Their victims are not simply chased out of the owners' territory if they are found trespassing; they are assaulted and left, perhaps to die. (4) Moreover, chimpanzees not only attack trespassers, but may make aggressive *raids* into the very heart of the core area of neighboring groups.

> In the chimpanzee, territoriality functions not only to repel intruders from the home range, but sometimes to injure or eliminate them; not only to defend the existing home range and its resources, but to enlarge it opportunistically at the expense of weaker neighbors; not only to protect the female resources of a community, but to actively and aggressively recruit new sexual partners from neighboring social groups. (Goodall 1986,528)

In a subchapter entitled "The Precursors of Warfare," Goodall highlights the common preadaptations of chimp and human warfare. She grants that destructive warfare in its typical human form (organized, armed conflict between groups) is a cultural development, nevertheless it required *preadaptations* to permit its emergence in the first place. The most crucial of these probably were *cooperative group living, group territoriality, cooperative hunting skills, weapon use,* and the *intellectual ability to make cooperative plans.* Another basic preadaptation would have been an inherent *fear of,* or aversion to, *strangers,* as is expressed in these aggressive attacks.

Early hominid groups possessing these behavioral characteristics would theoretically have been capable of the kind of organized intergroup conflict that could have led to destructive warfare. Chimpanzees not only possess, to a greater or lesser extent, the above preadaptations, but they show other inherent characteristics that would have been helpful to the "dawn warriors" in their primitive battles. If the early hominid males were *inherently* disposed to find aggression attractive, particularly aggression directed against neighbors (as chimps appear to do), this trait would have provided a biological basis for the cultural training of warriors. In humans, cultural evolution permits *pseudospeciation* (this has been described by Erikson 1966). In its extreme form, pseudospeciation leads to the "dehumanizing" of other groups, so that they may be regarded almost as members of a different species. This process, along with the ability to use weapons for hurting or killing *at a distance,* frees group members from the inhibitions and social sanctions that operate within the group and enables acts that would not be tolerated within the group. Thus, Goodall finds that it is of considerable interest that the chimpanzees show behaviors that may be precursors to pseudospeciation in humans.

Three male chimpanzees startle while on patrol. (Photo: Jane Goodall, 1986, with permission of Harvard University Press)

First, the chimpanzees' sense of group identity is strong; they clearly differentiate between individuals who "belong" and those who do not. This sense of group identity is far more sophisticated than mere xenophobia. The members of the Kahame community had, before the split, enjoyed close and friendly relations with their aggressors. By separating themselves, it is as though they forfeited their "right" to be treated as groups members—instead they were treated as strangers. Second, not only may nongroup members be violently attacked, but the patterns of attack may actually differ from those utilized in typical intracommunity aggression. The victims are treated more as though they were prey animals; they are "dechimpized."

COGNITIVE AND AFFECTIVE FACTORS— AND DEINSTINCTIVATION

Data on nonhuman intergroup agonistic behavior seem "grosso modo" to confirm the observation by Itani (1982) that the more advanced the species is, phylogenetically, the more frequent and varied is its intraspecific killing. This is, in my opinion, only a more specific instance of the more generic proposition that the higher the species phylogenetically, the less *festgelegt* is individual behavior. There is no instinct, in other words, to account for all the agonistic acts. But if there is no instinct or similar mechanism operating here, there must be something else: it may be a combination of "male bonding" that is sort of a synergistic effect bringing about a strong demarcation against anybody outside (a kind of proto-ethnocentrism), and a more elaborate cognitive makeup.

I hypothesize that advanced species have extra-strong group delimitations, the strength of which must be somehow related to the species' affective systems. Maybe chimps, like our own species, have very strong imaginations of *we* and *they,* which stress discreteness just like our symbols do. This discrimination may well be the price for deinstinctivation in both humans and chimps. But deinstinctivation is a very valuable asset: the individual is much less dependent on immediate external stimulus configurations. He or she "knows" symbolically about relevant phenomena in the external cosmos. This may be less so in chimps, but to a certain extent there must be something similar at work here.

In a similar vein, John Tooby and Leda Cosmides (1988) reason that

> It may be that the distribution of war in the animal kingdom is limited by the same factor that limits the emergence of the multi-individual cooperation on which war depends: the cognitive prerequisites necessary to exclude cheaters from benefiting from joint action as much as, or more than, genuine cooperators. We suggest that, for example, elephant seals and langurs, despite the reproductive pay-offs implicit in their ecological situations, did not have the cognitive preadaptations necessary for the emergence even of enduring dyadic coalitions, which, for example, baboons [Packer 1977] are capable of orchestrating. (4)

They agree that both chimpanzees and humans appear to have the cognitive mechanisms it takes to observe, assess, and to regulate the appropriate pattern of response towards several different males structured into a coalition (as observed, for example, by Frans de Waal in 1982). They therefore propose that humans and a few other cognitively preadapted species have evolved specialized "Darwinian algorithms" (cognitive programs) that govern coalitional behavior and constitute a distinctive coalitional psychology. "These cognitive mechanisms regulating reciprocation and social exchange cannot simply be either culturally 'learned' or be the product of 'general intelligence', but must be adaptively designed information processing systems specialized for these functions" (4).

THE PROBLEM OF THE EVOLUTION
OF GROUP HUNTING

There is another fact that sets the chimpanzee apart from most, if not all, of the other primates, namely, the fact that they are capable of coordinated cooperation on a hunt. Van Hooff (1990) writes:

> From the Gombe study area, in Tanzania, came the first observations that chimpanzees regularly hunt baboons, colobus monkeys, and a number of smaller animals. Only the

males did this. They surrounded their victim by keeping a close watch on each other, and shutting off they prey's possible escape routes from the trees (Teleki, 1973; McGrew, 1979). Over the last few years similar behavior has been observed in other chimpanzee populations. In a West-African population, intensively studied by Boesch and Boesch (1989), the males go hunting together everyday, systematically looking for groups of colobus monkeys. Such hunting forays are almost always successful, after varying lengths of time. Afterwards, and this is remarkable, the booty is shared. (45)

Let us return now to the human being's alleged carnivorous psychology, that is, the hypothesis that hunting somehow facilitated the transition to human warfare. Here it is of great interest to ask whether, in chimps, the development of cooperative hunting techniques has also promoted *cooperation* in intergroup conflicts and made warlike behavior possible, or vice versa. Van Hooff believes that the ability of chimps *to band with each other for hostile action* began in relation to a type of territorial possession in which males guarded a group of females to whom they had exclusive mating access. In his opinion, cooperation in tribal warfare *subsequently* set the scene for cooperative hunting.

Here we see that it is a complex business to understand evolution! The ultimate ecological causes must be separated from the more readily observable tie-ins between psychological predispositions (for instance, the urge to attack a stranger) and the development of a behavior (such as warfare or the group hunt). Let us review the socioecological theorizing of van Schaik and van Hooff (1983) and van Hooff (1988, 1990) on the ultimate causes of primate sociality. In their model, ecological factors, such as distribution properties of preferred foods, largely determine the nature of social organization and structure of a primate species with respect to social hierarchies, coalition systems such as female kin bonds, and migration patterns. In chimps the females disperse (female exogamy), while the males remain in their natal groups. This state of affairs has a profound impact on the proximate mechanisms of chimp social structure. It facilitates, for instance, the development of male bonding and coalition formation. In order to maximize their mating opportunities, male coalitions do attempt to monopolize females not directly, but indirectly through the monopolization and "conquest" of territory.

A positive feed-back loop of escalating intensity may then be established between successful conquest of territory, elimination of competitor groups by means of intimidation or violence, and the development of the male "gangs" into true "warrior coalitions." In this model, the amazing cognitive and affectional makeup of the chimp is a spin-off of this ongoing evolution. By contrast, in baboons and other primate species, the males monopolize females in harems or engage in scramble promiscuity. Such mating strategies do not give rise to male bonding.

Let me conclude Part 2 by noting that it still remains for sociobiologists, primatologists, behavioral ecologists, and others to reconstruct plausibly the order of events in the evolution of chimp warfare, before it can be of use—if indeed it ever can be of any use—in explaining human warfare.

Conclusion

It is my mission in contributing to this volume, to say something about the influence, to date, of sociobiology on my field, polemology. This is easy to record: there has been no influence whatsoever. One has only to browse through the volumes of the *Journal of Conflict Resolution* and the *Journal of Peace Research* to acknowledge this fact. Whether this is due to the ignorance or downright rejection of the sociobiological paradigm by peace and war researchers, or the irrelevance of sociobiological conflict concepts for the contemporary state system, is a question yet to be answered.

I myself am skeptical, and I have been aware of the problems that *misinformation* can cause. To the public mind, for example, knowledge of sociobiology probably includes "knowledge" of the fact—which is no fact at all—that the innate human trait of "aggressiveness" leads to warfare. Also, in the early part of this chapter I alluded to the carryover of social Darwinist ideas, particularly the notion (quite unjustified) that war is positively functional, universal, and an "agent of progress." So, I am not gung-ho on incorporating sociobiological ideas into polemology just now. But I do expect to see some cross-fertilization in the future with regard to the study of the evolution of war in preindustrial societies.

As for my own guess about the genetic determinism of human warfare, it is summed up in the words of the turn-of-the-century polemologist, J. Novikow (1896): "No grim fatality obliges us to massacre one another eternally like wild beasts" (102).

14

Marxist Thought

Regina Karpinskaya

The invitation to take part in the present work, which is meant to provide full support for sociobiology as a scientific discipline, both flattered and perplexed me. With all my respect for sociobiology, I regard it as only one of the possible models of coevolution and one not without serious shortcomings. I think that the problem of coevolution, and consequently the assessment of the contribution of sociobiology to this problem, is strictly speaking no longer a scientific problem that can be solved exclusively by scientific means.

The underlying ideas and the scientist's world outlook are so important in this case that we must recognize that the problems of coevolution are not only interdisciplinary. They are related to all spheres of material and intellectual human life and, therefore, are connected equally with knowledge, on the one hand, and convictions, beliefs, modes of thinking, and cultural traditions, on the other.

If this is the case, we must separate the level of empirical research and its results from theoretical generalizations, which include the scientist's philosophical position. I support the idea of the Canadian paleobotanist R. Sattler that "biological assertions are based on philosophical premises which are already there in our mind even before we enter the laboratory." All the more so when the biologist is thinking about the meaning of life and evolution, about human beings and their role in the world.[1]

The complicated relations between the empirical and theoretical levels of research make an important problem in gnosiology and the philosophy of science. One can ignore this problem only if one considers the research premises used as the only true ones. But such a position makes the conception vulnerable to criticism. The numerous opponents of socio-biology (I mean honest critics who do not ascribe to sociobiologists nonscientific ideological objectives) are not satisfied with the declarative nature of many initial postulates of the conception. They are unwilling to understand that the current debate in evolutionary biology demands serious consideration of the universalizability of Darwinian principles, which is the essence of sociobiology.[2] In both Western and Soviet literature there have been many criticisms of socio-biology in relation to its insufficient development of this and other postulates.[3]

Yet I would like to begin with those things that unite the supporters and opponents of sociobiology. To clarify these common points would be to see a certain general trend in the study of the human being, which would be promising not only for science, but also for the intellectual atmosphere of society and its philosophical climate.

SOCIOBIOLOGY AND THE BIOSOCIAL APPROACH

Though the notion "sociobiology" is probably recurring most frequently in this book, it needs some clarification. It is not enough to identify sociobiology, for convenience, with "the sociobiology of the human being," brushing aside other aspects of sociobiology. I think that it is more important to demonstrate that the term *sociobiology* is sometimes used to describe both a particular scientific discipline started by E. Wilson's book *Sociobiology: The New Synthesis* (1975), and a great number of other empirical and theoretical studies of the role of natural and biological foundations of human behavior as a whole. One does not have to be enthusiastic about sociobiology as a scientific discipline. Yet one can usefully develop the ideas discussed in sociobiology. This balance of approach is typical of research in the Soviet Union.

The initial reaction in our country to sociobiology as a scientific discipline was strictly negative. It could not have been otherwise in a society whose ideology was based on false sociological schemes of the human being. The one-dimensional social image of the human being in the USSR is akin to this country's hostility toward genetics, and reminds us of the tragic caricature of biology in the form of Lysenkoism. The Soviet bureaucracy is deeply interested in the idea of a natural homogeneity of the human material that can be used, without any scruple or second thought to "troublesome genes," to mold a personality that will be pliable and easy to control. The support of the state and of the party ideology for this concept of the human being, as a social functionary and mere cog in the state machinery, greatly blocked research into the natural and biological foundations of human behavior.

I want to give only one example, leaving aside many others, to prove that such research has a very long tradition in our country. In 1971, our literary and sociopolitical magazine *Novii Mir* (New World) published an article by V. P. Efroimson, "The Genealogy of Altruism." The commentary on this article was written by Academician B. L. Astaurov, one of the most broad-minded theoretical biologists not only of his own time, but probably in the whole history of Soviet biology. He thought that Efroimson's evolutionary approach to the moral foundations of human activities could be promising in that the analysis of the biological basis of behavior, and the understanding of altruism as an important evolutionary factor, created new opportunities for the study of evolution. Being an enthusiastic scientist, V. P. Efroimson—Astaurov said—sometimes presented unsolved problems as facts, but the very idea of an evolutionary foundation for the norms of human behavior, including moral norms, was extremely interesting for both scientists and the general public.

It should be noted that this interest reflected a general trend in the development of world science. In 1975, four years after Efroimson's article, E. Wilson published his book *Sociobiology: The New Synthesis,* which started a new discipline to investigate the biological foundations of human behavior. Instead of a serious and persistent research of this subject, we in the Soviet Union yet again conceded our priority [that is, that Efroimson got there first—Ed.], got frightened by the new, and preferred to keep to the artificial sociological explanation of human behavior, which by definition had no need of any biological knowledge. Paradoxically, the decisive role in closing down further research into the problem was played by the famous Soviet geneticist Academician N. P. Dubinin. He came down upon V. P. Efroimson for "biologizing" and for incompatibility with Marxism.

A lot of dubious ideas have been pronounced in our country on behalf of Marxism, and it will take us years to sort them out. What, then, is a true Marxist position on any specific issue? Only when we answer this question will Marxism reveal both its outdated characteristics and its potential for productive ideas. One of these is "the dual qualitative determination" of human nature, that is, the existence of the human being as both "the natural subject" and "the social subject." Let me quote Marx: "the being of people is the result of the past process of organic life."[4] Certainly, Marxism insists on the asymmetry of the biological/social opposition, stressing that the social aspect makes the substance of human life. But this does not necessarily mean that the human being is a tabula rasa, as it is often interpreted to be in Western literature. Sociobiologists also criticize Marxism for exaggerating the role of culture. But this criticism can be explained only by the lack of information.

In fact, current literature in the USSR on human problems makes a wide use of notions such as "the biosocial nature of the human being," "the biosocial evolution of the human being," and "the biosocial approach." It is from consideration of the biosocial approach that I have published a detailed critical analysis of sociobiology,[5] disagreeing in principle with those Soviet authors who are trying to make sociobiological discussions purely ideological.

The biosocial approach reflects the conviction that it is absolutely impossible to study the human being on the basis of either only biological or only sociohumanitarian knowledge. But the declaration of the need of a synthesis of these two aspects can serve only as a broad intellectual premise or a general orientation. It in no way prescribes the forms of the synthesis. Such forms are to be developed by concrete sciences. I shall give only two examples. Studying human ecology, Academician V. P. Kaznacheyev deals with a big number of factors in the life activities of human populations and makes use of biological, medicobiological, geographical, psychological, economic, and sociological knowledge to achieve the main goal of his conception—to serve the good of the people and perfect their physical and psychological abilities.[6] One of the central notions of his conception—population health—is investigated on the basis of his understanding of the human population as an integrated dynamic system having a socionatural, or biosocial, nature.

The other example, on the contrary, deals with individual human beings. Advancing his version of the biological theory of human individuality, Doctor of Biological Sciences V. M. Rusalov is investigating the so-called formal, observable characteristics of individual behavior.[7] Following socio-biologists, as he points out, we understand by the biological factors of individual psychological differences not only the bodily, morphofunctional organization of the human being, but also the whole complex of inborn, including social-group, behavioral programs that have developed during the evolution of the animal world and people.

At the same time, Rusalov recognizes that there is a certain hierarchy of psychological levels, with the higher levels (intellect, character) forming in somewhat different ways than the lower levels (temperament). As the author writes, the principal difference of our approach from the sociobiological one is that the evolutionary biological (inborn) behavioral programs, according to his theory, determine only the temperamental (that is, lower) traits. The discrimination between at least two levels of potentialities (relating to temperament and more complex psychological formations, such as intellect and character) does not mean any under-estimation of biological factors, because personality development is viewed as an integrated systemic interaction between the biological and the social. This interaction (interdependence, complementarity), discussed in most general terms, makes a special topic in coevolutionary conceptions.

THE HUMAN BEING AS A PREREQUISITE AND A RESULT OF COEVOLUTION

The sociobiological conception of gene–culture coevolution demonstrates the wish of sociobiologists to create a new human science. This gives the name to the closing section, "Toward a New Human Science," of Lumsden and Wilson's book *Promethean Fire* (1983).[8] The relations between genes and culture are discussed in accordance with the thesis that "cultural determinism can be as much of a straitjacket as genetic determinism" (page 174). Particularly unacceptable for sociobiologists is the idea of the dominant role of culture in the evolution of the human mind. "It is often said," write the authors of *Promethean Fire*, "that nothing makes sense except in the light of history, meaning cultural change over a few centuries. More accurately, nothing makes sense except in the light of organic evolution, which encompasses a tightly linked form of cultural and genetic change and spans hundreds of thousands of years" (page 170).

This means that the historical approach to the human being should be changed for the evolutionary biological one. This makes the core of "a new human science" for sociobiologists. It is appropriate to recall H. Spencer's words here that "we shall have to study the Human Being as a product of Evolution; Society as a product of Evolution; and Morality as a product of Evolution."[9] It is these premises, far from being new, that sociobiologists are trying to materialize. But the only consequence could be the biologization of human and societal problems. The transformation of the evolutionary biological approach into the main methodological principle of the new human science is accompanied by the exaggerated role of the genetic foundations of human activities. In the conception of gene–culture coevolution, culture has no "language" or definitions of its own that could breed new hypotheses. How, then, are the characteristics of culture translated into genes?

When Lumsden and Wilson (1981) stress the variety of the definitions of culture and discuss "the culture unit," all manifestations of civilization happen to be reduced to the semantic memory of the individual. Using the classification of memory units from cognitive psychology, the authors specify the notion of "culturgen," proposed by them earlier, as the culture unit. In earlier works, the culturgen was defined very vaguely as a certain culture trait (forms of behavior, long-lived mental constructions, scientific or religious conceptions, etc.). Within the context of the problems of semantic memory, the culturgen is equated with "nodes" (the semantic memory level including constructors, proposiums, and schemata). Culture turns out to be a result of cognitive operations with multiple culturgens, which in turn are based on nodes. And the evolution of culture, in the final run, is determined by physiological processes, since all the events with culturgens and nodes are controlled by epigenetic rules in-built in the human brain.[10] This understanding of culture leaves no room for its splendid colorful features or its variety at different times and in different peoples. One of the many aspects of human activities, connected with human cognition, is made so absolute that it becomes the only one.

However highly I could estimate the sociobiologists' breakthrough into the new area of theoretical thinking, I cannot get rid of the feeling of an extremely rationalized world produced by the theory of gene–culture coevolution.[11] By contrast, one feels much better and more natural in the world of E. Wilson's ideas as presented in his book *Biophilia*.[12] There we can find living nature with all its mysteries and attractions. There we find living human beings experiencing contacts with nature and trying to understand it and solve the riddles of their unbreakable ties with nature. The moral beginnings of the human being happen to blend with these generic relations with nature, which are indestructible in spite of our industrial civilization. But these relations take on the form of a real historical process, renewed in each generation and always changed by time! Can we "land" this process on a gene structure and expect an answer to the problem of coevolution from natural sciences?

When we speak of human relations as being central in the life of an individual, when we place this life above all ideological and political goals of society, let us be consistent. We do not need in this case a material substrate like genes or any substrate characteristics like culturgens, but *theoretical* notions expressing relations. If human relations have always been the central issue of human existence, if the brightest minds, starting with the first authors of the Bible, have always been concerned with the workings of truly human relations, it means that the central problem of coevolution is to be found in the evolution of social relations.

It is this aspect that seems most valuable in socio-biology—the wish to trace the development of the social in the relations among living organisms. The study of invariant behavioral characteristics that promote social organization is to my mind a fruitful way of bridging the gap between natural and social sciences. Unfortunately, the theme of invariants is often reduced to genetics, while naturalistic, biological thinking is leaving the stage under the pressure of physicalistic ideals and norms.

In the modern world any intellectual efforts aimed at studying the human being cannot ignore the being of people, their life processes, and the value of human life itself. At a time when we face the problem of the survival of mankind, and not only of an individual, this global emphasis on the general atmosphere of the existence of civilization makes it necessary to revise the traditions of the sciences. The life characteristics of human beings, and not only the characteristics of their minds, come within the philosophical focus.

And conversely, biologists are ever more attracted by human life activities as a whole, by human behavior, by forms of human interaction, and not only by the natural biological foundations of being. The growing proximity of these two positions is made possible by the increasing popularity of humanitarian ideas and the use of these ideas in assessing scientific knowledge and prospects for its development. The value-based orientation in the investigation of the world and human life is acquiring ever clearer and ever simpler forms—it is imperative that science should help the survival and prosperity of humankind and help to fight hunger, diseases, and poverty.[13]

In other words, the human and humanitarian aspect of coevolutionary problems is at the top of the list and determines the purpose of their investigation. In studying the biosphere, one cannot be isolated from the purpose-oriented nature of human activities and from human creative abilities. In turn, it is impossible to understand the meaning and role of the purpose-oriented activities only on the basis of natural sciences or such general scientific approaches as systemic, informational, or thermodynamic. The laws of self-organization, when formulated, will considerably promote our explanations of the transition from chaos to order and from one structural level to the next one. But orientation in development does not necessarily imply purpose orientation, while the evolution of the biosphere takes place in the unity of the natural orientation of processes and the purpose orientation of human life activities and interactions. Hence the important role of social and humanitarian disciplines and the importance of the philosophy of history.

Philosophy can make a valuable contribution to the study of the human being–nature–society system, not only by correcting the methodology of interactions among sciences. Its main contribution is in its participation in the formation of the humanitarian content of the purpose of such interactions and in molding their philosophical foundations. The novelty of the problem of coevolution is that it takes to a higher level the interrelations between specific scientific knowledge and philosophical knowledge and sets new tasks for establishing more meaningful contacts between these types of knowledge.

NOTES AND REFERENCES

1. Sattler, R. Biophilosophia. Toronto. 1986.

2. The philosophical grounds for such universalization are given in the book by Ruse M. Taking Darwin Seriously. A Naturalistic Approach to Philosophy. Oxford: Blackwell. 1986.

3. Levontin, R.C. Sociobiology as an adaptationist program. Behavioral Science (Louisville). 1979. Vol.24. N.1; Gould, S.J. Sociobiology and the theory on natural selection. - Sociobiology: Beyond Nature - Nurture? Ed. by G.W.Barlow. Boulder (Col.). 1980; Stent, G. Glass Bead Game: A Review of Alexander Rosenberg. The Structure of Biological Science.-Biology and Philosophy. 1986. Vol.1. N.2; Панов Е.Н. Современное состояние и перспективы развития эволюционной социобиологии.-Зоологический журнал. 1982. Т.LXL, вып.7; Карпинская Р.С., Никольский С.А. Критический анализ социобиологии. Москва. 1987.

4. Маркс К., Энгельс Ф. Соч. 2-е изд., т.26, ч.3, с.516.

5. Карпинская Р.С., Никольский С.А. Критический анализ социобиологии. Москва. 1987.

6. Казначеев В.П. Очерки теории и практики экологии человека. Москва. 1983.

7. Русалов В.М. Вклад биологической теории индивидуальности в решение проблемы социального и биологического в человеке.-Биология в познании человека. Москва. 1989.

8. Lumsden, Ch. Wilson, E. Promethean Fire: Reflections on the Origin of Mind. Cambridge. 1983.

9. Спенсер Г. Основные начала. Санкт-Петербург. 1897. С.330-331.

10. Lumsden,Ch. Wilson,E. The relation between biological and cultural evolution. J.Social Biol.Struct. 1985. N.8, pp.343-385.

11. Lumsden,Ch. Wilson,E. Genes, Mind and Culture. Cambridge (Mass.). 1981.

12. Wilson E. Biophilia. Harvard Univ. Press. Cambridge et al. 1984.

13. Фролов И.Т. Перспективы человека. Москва. 1983.

15

Aesthetics

Charles J. Lumsden

Aesthetics seeks to understand the conditions, origin, meaning, and value of beauty, especially as it is experienced in works of art. As distinct from the history, psychology, and sociology of art, which are concerned with the way human beings make and relate to art, aesthetics is a normative enterprise. It addresses questions about value, not fact—in particular the significance and value art has in the life of rational beings (us, supposedly; for introductions and reviews see Danto 1981, Scruton 1983). As such, aesthetics joins ethics in demarcating that part of our experience that conventional science can hope to inform but can never touch.

Thus it would seem that sociobiology and the socio-biological imagination are irrelevant to aesthetics. So far they have been. But I believe there is much lurking here to tempt the sociobiologist, particularly the gene–culture theorist. Indeed, aesthetics could be in the 1990s what ethics was for sociobiology in the 1980s: a principal new source of ideas that test the fact–value distinction and that make a science out of matters now considered strictly part of philosophical discourse.

In this chapter I shall outline two issues that are poised immediately to stimulate this new dialogue between socio-biology and aesthetics. Let me refer to them as (1) resolving "aesthetics fights" and (2) breaking the "tyranny of function." In discussing the first I shall be able to bring in the concepts of *epigenesis* and *epigenetic rules,* which best explain the interaction between nature and nurture. In the second I shall give an example of how gene–culture coevolution works, in regard to art.

Before beginning, however, I must furnish some definitions. Francis Sparshott (1982) has recently laid out terminology in a way that gives meaning to scientific as well as philosophical approaches to art and aesthetics; I will use his terms here. So, to *contemplate* something is to attend to and dwell on its appearance, rather than on what it is—or on what we can do with it. An *aesthetic object* is anything whatsoever, so long as it is taken to be well-suited as an object for contemplation. We *appreciate* something when we recognize the value it has in any respect we take to be the relevant one. A *design* is all the aspects of any performance that constitute it as a single aesthetic object. A *work of art* (or what I shall call an *artwork*) is a performance considered strictly with respect to its design. (By contrast, an *art object* is anything one intends to be *received* as an artwork, or that within a community is generally so received.)

I will not argue here for the virtues of this specific terminology, or for its historical rationale. That is done at great length elsewhere (Sparshott 1982). Its value, or the value of something like it, to any real meeting of sociobiology and aesthetics is evident: absolutely nothing interesting can happen unless common terms are clear enough to sustain rigorous (and vigorous) disagreement.

AESTHETIC FIGHTS

Suppose I come to you extolling the merits of a painting I've just seen (fig. 1.) How beautiful it is! Your own evaluation, however, differs. Even in extended, face-to-face encounter with the artwork you find little engaging—just a meandering assortment of pigmented blots and smears. Ugly. We have a disagreement about the attribution of aesthetic value and may rightly wonder whether there is a systematic, reasonable way our difference might be resolved. Should one of us be prepared to acknowledge an error in judgment, even though we both admit our attributions of value arise not from the object itself, but from our beholding it?

The eighteenth-century philosopher David Hume believed it possible to settle disputes like this. All we need do is know—

and, as logical animals, methodically apply—certain precisely statable, universally valid rules of aesthetic judgement (Hume 1965). His contemporary, Immanuel Kant, rejected this view. While not denying the possible universality of judgments about beauty, Kant could find no place for rules in matters of aesthetic evaluation. *Shared similarity in our mental constitutions,* he thought, might provide a basis for raising our individual claims about beauty above the articulation of merely private experience and make them relevant to everyone. Yet divergent evaluation cannot seek recourse to universal logic and "rules of art" to settle the matter (Kant 1952).

Figure 1. Beautiful, don't you think?

Contra Hume, there is no universal assent waiting at the end of aesthetic disputes, because there is no proof anyone can use to prove finally one thing beautiful and another not. Instead, to convince you I must literally recreate in you, a creature of similar evolutionary pedigree, the brain state I have in response to contemplative absorption in the object of our disagreement. Still, you might reject this state or prove refractory to it or fail to see its point, and, unlike Humean rule-followers, we are left with a potentially insoluble residue of individual diversity in aesthetic judgments. (On Hume's aesthetic, see Sverdlik 1986; on Kant's, see Haskins 1989.)

Of utmost importance in this standing confrontation over aesthetic rationality are ideas about how the mind works when it comes to judge or create works of art. In this respect one must immediately remark how many problems from Hume's time, about how the mind works, have become postphilosophical rather than continuing as issues for metaphysical dispute. With an amazing burst of intellectual energy, the new empirical sciences of mind have withdrawn such questions from philosophy. Today, questions about the nature of perception, evaluation, and judgment are matters that cognitive psychology pursues. This is true whether the stimuli be art objects or toothbrushes. The psychology of art (Gardner 1982, Dissanayake 1988) shows, for example, that we are born with a tendency to give most of our attention to patterns of intermediate (and, as we age, increasing) complexity (fig. 2). We are able to parse fields

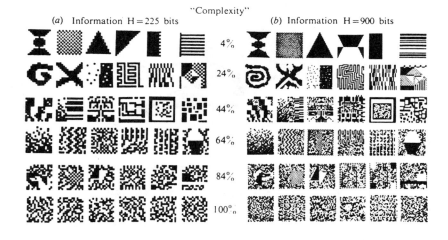

Figure 2. Maximum arousal produced by visual patterns of intermediate complexity. The complexity of a pattern is measured here by the per cent redundancy in two visual series that differ in the number of binary elements they contain (one series has 225 bits of information-theoretic uncertainty per pattern, the other 900). The arousal measure is the time the alpha wave of the electroencephalogram was blocked (desynchronized) following presentation of each pattern to human viewers. For both the 225-bit and 900-bit patterns, arousal peaked around patterns of 20 per cent complexity. Reproduced with permission from Lumsden and Wilson (1981).

of chromatic, aural, and gestural stimuli into clusters and categories—some of which we prefer over others (Rosch 1973, Bornstein 1984).

These initial capacities for automatic engagement become *defined pathways of interpretive growth,* whereby from art we take progressively less ego-centered experiences of meaning and value (Parsons 1987). Moreover, our *evaluative* bent shares brain space with impressive capacities for *creative* performance. Despite essential differences in the symbol systems used (the arts are dense, the sciences notational), the human imagination probably works in much the same way whether the artifacts be sonnets or supernova simulations. That is, it draws ultimately on shifting connections among memory's encoded representations (see Goodman 1975, Findlay and Lumsden 1988).

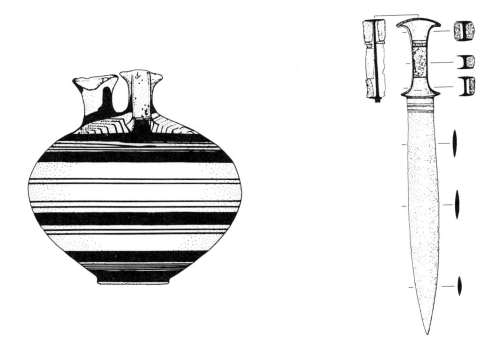

Figure 3. *Left,* stirrup jar KW 305 from the Late Bronze Age shipwreck at Ulu Burun, Turkey. Tentative date 14th century B.C. Reproduction ratio 1:2. *Right,* bronze sword KW 275 from the same site. Reproduction ratio 1:5. Reproduced with permission from Pulak (1988).

I must also remark here that the making of art objects and the valuing of art objects (to judge in the first case from their ubiquity, and in the second from their association with the graves of the well-to-do) are neither recent nor geographically restricted in our species. All cultures surveyed have objects valued for their beauty, and words that describe beauty and the esteem we give it. The sheer aesthetic potency of common pots and implements (fig. 3), made and discarded all along the way between horticultural times and now, finds them a ready new home in today's museums and galleries. And as anyone lucky enough to have hefted an Acheulean handaxe knows, for millions of years the production of stone implements evinced a commitment to impeccable standards of form and balance (fig. 4).

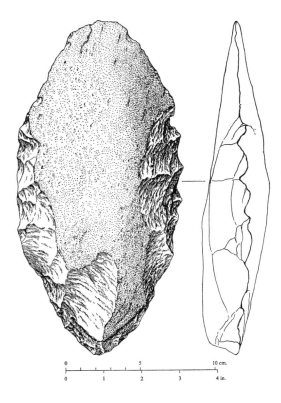

Figure 4. Lava biface with a denticulate edge. From site EF-HR, Upper Middle Bed II, Olduvai Gorge. Reproduced with permission from Leakey (1971).

All this counts toward understanding in scientific terms the making and beholding of art. But we are left considerably short of a position squarely backing either Hume or Kant on the objectivity of aesthetic judgment and decidability of aesthetic dispute. This is to be expected, given the present state of the sciences of mind. Scientific versions of their philosophical outlooks must state as testable hypothesis the role that contemplation plays in judgment. To the cognitive scientist, however, human "judgment" has until now meant something much more rigid and deterministic than *contemplating* something—usually the deductive application of discursively expressed rules, not a mental process based on feelings! The sciences of mind have trouble with feelings. Feelings do not fit nicely into the tidy logical niches made up when reason is modeled, as it has been for three decades, as the lockstep activity of a central automaton—the computer in the head, running programs written in a neat, clear "language of thought."

Thus, until cognitive science abandons the clockwork-in-the-head tack and begins to rejoin, as it were, deduction with passion, a truly profound understanding of aesthetic judgment (and the fights it causes) simply must wait. (The wait may not be too long. Novel ideas about microcognition and parallel distributed processing, about thought as lived metaphor, and about the passions as astute guides to judgment are breaking deductive logic's stranglehold on mind theory. Now there is room for a "calculus of felt distinctions" that makes possible a newly resynthesized science of mind in which feeling, understanding, appreciating, and contemplating are all of one piece—as are we. (See McClelland, et al. 1988; Johnson 1987; de Sousa 1987).

While the ruling on *Hume v. Kant* pends, a moment's sociobiological reflection suggests the likely decision. It will favor Hume while accommodating Kant. What neither philosopher could appreciate was epigenesis and its significance to understanding mind. *Epigenesis* is a term referring to the total content, and results, of the interaction between genome and environment during development (Lumsden and Wilson 1981, 1983). For human mental development, the principal environment is culture, of course; my primary research focus has been on the question, *What happens when genomic and cultural information are jointly expressed in the brain?* So far every aspect of mental development that has been looked at empirically shows strong evidence of *rule-governed* genomic shaping along with cultural influences. Wilson and I call these "epigenetic rules." A partial list of epigenetic rules, covering attributes of mind prominent in the psychology of art, includes the innate discrimination of four basic categories of color: red, yellow, green, blue; infant preference for visual patterns of intermediate complexity and ratios of order to disorder (fig. 2); the basis of abstract thought in metaphors of the body's lived sensations (Johnson 1987); the development of linguistic knowledge (Piatelli-Palmarini 1989); mental imagery (Kosslyn 1980); and the temporal syntax of rhythm, tonality, and musical understanding (Lerdahl and Jackendoff 1983).

Evidence of a genetic basis for these patterns and regularities in mental development comes from numerous kinds of studies, such as pedigree analysis and comparison of fraternal and identical twins, behavioral genetics, and the analysis of developmental timing and its cross-cultural universality. Another approach has been to compare *the complexity of the finished knowledge structure* or mental process (such as linguistic competence and musical understanding) with the (generally scant and tattered) *array of developmental clues and information accessible to the child.* (See Findlay and Lumsden 1988.)

I think that the only hypothesis warranted by this wide range of data is that most—and possibly all—aspects of the human mind are shaped and sustained by rule-like genome activity *that makes specific directions and outcomes in growth of reasoning, memory, judgment, etc., more likely than others.* It would of course be silly to read this hypothesis as one sociobiologist's proclamation that our aesthetic understanding (along with everything else uniquely human) is "genetically determined." The mind makes itself. But it does so within a context of shared meanings and significances that are neither arbitrary nor entirely shifting from culture to culture. Genome activity, in this view, makes us discriminating about what socialization pushes at us, rather than passive receptacles waiting to be filled by it.

Not all conceivable configurations of knowledge, nor all conceivable ways of working with knowledge and values, are, then, likely or even possible. Genetic information in our chromosomes makes this so. But if epigenetic rules are behind it all, the mind's genomic basis is the very opposite of genetic determinism's crass fatalism. Here is a point that has been little appreciated. Genetic determinism is a world of the dictatorial *thou shalt*—where the mind goes is spelled out by DNA. By contrast, genome activity in the epigenetic linkage of DNA and culture speaks mainly in *thou-shalt-nots.* (For example, "Avoid these strategies of thought and architectures of mind.") All the rest falls to the one genetically determined capacity so much in evidence throughout our species: that for choice and decision (Lumsden and Wilson 1983). *(Thou shalt judge, because thou must choose, because thou must act.)*

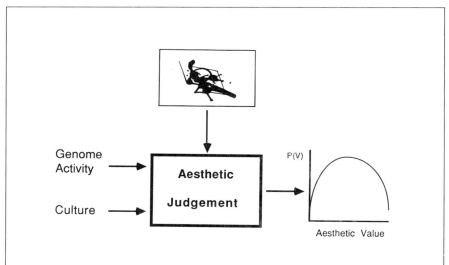

Figure 5. Gene–culture model of where objectivity resides in aesthetic debates. Minimally, observers can agree on the mathematical function that, given the viewer's genotype and enculturation, specifies the likelihood P(V) any given artwork has of being assigned aesthetic value *V.*

Beyond Hume and Kant, then, is the mind as understood by modern human sociobiology (fig. 5). Evolved patterns in genome activity (the epigenetic rules) make epigenesis less likely to pursue some outcomes rather than others. Given epigenetic rules and a sensible specification of a person's enculturation experience (say, her or his understanding and making of fine art), there results a *distribution of likelihood* that the person (or, at a higher level of statistical smoothing, the species) will value a given aesthetic object in a given way. This *distribution* is what Kant and Hume should be arguing about. Its very objectivity, as realized in the action of epigenetic rules, makes it the standard Hume sought. Its essentially statistical nature gives pride of place to the nondeductive relationship between person and artwork Kant sought to preserve. When we analyze the simplest cases of judgment— so informative because they are simple and thus analyzable— we can actually work out these distributions of likely value (review of methods in Lumsden and Wilson 1981, Findlay and Lumsden 1988). Applied to design acts, such distributions would specify the activity of culture and genome in individual aesthetic development—as well as the behavioral strategies for coping with the beautiful, as evolved in our species during its three-million-year immersion in culture.

THE TYRRANY OF FUNCTION

Art objects are not the only things in our world occasionally possessed by beauty, nor is the aesthetic experience involved only with products of artistic activity. The eye finds many comfortable resting places (fig. 6). There can be contemplative absorption in any thing's (or person's) appearance. But art objects, as both creations and artifacts, are special in this regard: among the products of our labor, they seem the only ones whose essential value is exhausted in the looking (hearing, touching,...) *per se.* While our aesthetic experience of them *may* have practical significance, it is within the experience itself that art, *qua* art, lives.

Thus, where psychology speaks in terms of the beholder's contemplative absorption, aesthetics speaks of *disinterest.* "Disinterest" here means the abrogation of self-interest and self-absorption—a condition of selflessness in which the significance of the object may be considered irrespective of its use. Outside the confines of disinterest we might be aware of beauty—perhaps intensely so—and find consequences aplenty following from this awareness. Yet, however complex or potent,

Figure 6. *Bodybuilder.* Phil Cantor/Hot Shots.

this awareness is not the aesthetic experience. According to the view now prominent in aesthetics (for example, Danto 1981, Sparshott 1982), art and our relations to it constitute an autonomous domain. They are not mere tributary results of utilitarian concerns.

Aestheticians, therefore, are not pleased by the "functionalist" explanations for our appreciation of beauty. Here I might note that explanation by appeal to function is a hallmark of evolutionary biology generally. Confronted by a behavior or hunk of anatomy, and equipped with faith in the winnowing power of natural selection, the biologist asks how this behavior or bodily structure functions to assist copies of genes into succeeding generations. The resulting conjectures are the "just-so stories" Darwinism's critics love to hate. Just-so stories elicit this negative critical response because, traditionally, they are irritatingly malleable and hard to test; with minor changes or reinterpretations they tend to slither around the obstacles empirical science would put in their way.

Figuring out how to eliminate this slipperiness was a prominent task of sociobiology, ethology, and evolutionary ecology in the 1980s. Not easy, but the decade did close with solid advances in the design of natural-selection hypotheses that can stand the scrutiny of statistical analysis (for example, Hölldobler and Lindauer 1988, Clutton-Brock 1988). It has also been noted that these stories, when accumulated *en masse,* too easily degenerate into an off-putting rhetoric that reduces the essence of everything biological to nothing more than genetic programming. This makes productive dialogue with the humanities, which deal with the most complex and complexity-integrated expressions of our behavior, almost impossible (Lumsden 1989a, 1989b).

Aesthetic disinterest comes in for some functional explanation by biologists. To paraphrase Ellen Dissanyake's wonderful question "What is art for??" (1988), they ask, "What is aesthetic disinterest *for*??" Evolutionists, including myself, have tried again and again to put the aesthetic experience at the disposal of the fittest, suggesting by turns that it allows us to judge commodious environments in which to camp and hunt; that it is an efficient and effective means of impressing values and ideas upon the uninformed (or unconvinced); that it is a means of using culture to gain the edge in competing for valuable resources; that it is a repository for myth, ritual, and symbol essential to our societies; that in the creative making, appreciating, and exercise of the imagination we gain competence for decision and action in the "real world"; that form follows function, and the aesthetic experience began as our guide to judging the match; that it guides us to the best mates; and so on (Marschack 1979, Pfeiffer 1982, Maxwell 1985, Davis 1986, Halverson 1987, Alland 1989).

Functional speculations about service to genetic fitness are as a lot charming, and may sound more than a little plausible to an ear accustomed to Darwinian refrains. Yet, as a lot, they are all bottom-heavy, directing our attention to what serves genes, and genome activity, as we search for understandings about art. So they miss entirely the basic evolutionary point of our species; we are as we are, *what* we are, not because we are genetic creatures but *because we are bred of both genomic and cultural activity*: biocultural organisms. When genes and culture come together, who's on the bottom (the Marxian base in sociobiological form) is up for grabs. A possibly endless tug-of-war ensues between two lines of descent (the Mendelian and the Boasian), with mind and behavior the mediators as well as the vehicles.

Richard Dawkins (1976) initiated serious thinking about what happens when bits of culture information with their *own* replicative interests begin evolving alongside equally selfish genes. But rigorous attempts to express this problem as a matter of *coevolution* rather than simply *conjoint* evolution of two parallel streams of information (and to work the analysis through the mathematics of population genetics) did not begin until early in the 1980s. The results have been eyeopening. When genes and culture interact as they do in human development, and coevolve as they have done over human history, the evolutionary outcomes can be very different from what happens in purely genetic evolution—and usually cannot be inferred from an understanding of genetic evolution alone (Lumsden and Wilson 1981; Findlay, Hansell, and Lumsden 1989).

One can see why: each of us has a genetic fecundity and a spectrum of cultural fecundities. The latter is measured by *the number of people our ideas influence and the number of copies of things we produce that persist into generations to come.* Since mental development is epigenetic, these "reproductive" proclivities of genes and culture become entangled, with complex results. For example, evolutionary diversity generally is higher than when genes alone have the say. Mixed polymorphisms—sometimes static and unvarying over the generations, sometimes chaotic and widely fluctuating in their evolutionary results—are common. They open a population to genomically shaped modes of thought and behavior that, considered on a conventionally Darwinian basis, wouldn't stand a chance.

Findings like these put evolved strategies such as the aesthetic understanding and judgment in a whole new light. For us biocultural organisms, sociobiology is wrong to reduce mind to survival functions of genes. In fact, in view of what is now known about the patterns of gene–culture coevolution in comparison to purely genetic evolution, this is an ill-advised explanatory tack and likely to give inaccurate or misleading results.

With this new information in mind, let us consider the claims of aesthetic disinterest once more. An absorption in appearance and form *for their own sake*—true disinterest seemingly nonsensical relative to the evolutionary demands of Darwinian gene machines—begins to sound like a reasonable, even likely outcome of genome and culture evolving together (gene–culture coevolution). For if aesthetics' central claim is accurate, it is from the disinterested stance that contemplative absorption and aesthetic understanding develop. However, it is also *within* this aesthetic understanding that the effects of the *art creator's* intentions are transferred to the beholder. Expressed in the art object, significance and meaning complete a circuit that begins in the artist's mind and ends in ours. Beauty, arresting our attention and stilling self-directed thought, *powers the circuit and the transfer of influence!* Bits of culture are able to replicate, to move from agent to agent within the population—thanks to the aesthetic experience.

Disinterest, attachment to the object for its own sake, has immediate practical significance, to be sure. These roles cannot be denied art, or its making, or its appreciation. But the assignment of practical significance is not a reductive act, or a claim of epiphenomenality for the thing in itself. Quite the opposite. For while *the replicative interests of culture* benefit from the encounter between art and viewer, these interests may be served best only if their linkage to the act of transfer is indirect and we are opened maximally to the work on its own terms. Within the conditions of that intimate relationship, the significance of the value to be had is realized and exhausted. It need go no further. The consequences do, though, and so from a biocultural mode of thinking we begin to recover the outlines of a sociobiology of art for which the aesthetic experience is more or less as we know it.

PROSPECTS

Ultimately, good aesthetics is good philosophy, and good philosophy, surely, is good (= hard to refute), normative argument about the human potential. A decidedly unbeautiful century ends with two basic questions intact: what is beauty to us, and what should it be? The first, too long monopolized by philosophical speculation, is now a matter for scientific theory and experiment, drawing together the clues that lie scattered from the gene-sequencing lab to the artist's studio. I have argued here that a sociobiology based on gene–culture thinking has much to give this descriptive enterprise.

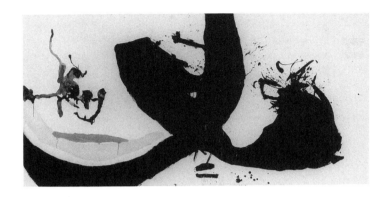

Figure 7. Sociobiologists: use your theories to deduce *a.*, the meaning of this contemporary masterwork; *b.*, its aesthetic value for someone of your genotype and cultural inheritance; *c.*, the significance and value it *should* have for any rational being. Robert Motherwell, *Black on White*, 1950. Oil on canvas, 78″ x 163 3/16″. The Museum of Fine Arts, Houston, Texas.

The second question seeks to find what significance art, beauty, and creative expression for their own sake should have in the life of rational (or, to be less demanding, reasonable) beings. This normative task in aesthetics, central to the human experience, remains untouched by sociobiology. It is the philosophers' business, and we can only wish them luck in their efforts. At the frontier cutting between fact and value, the sciences we know—descriptive activities all—stop. So far there are no crossings, despite claims to the contrary (try fig. 7). Science in a form to come may help us write down the great *shoulds* about beauty and about evil, but what shape this new science will take, and how it may begin, remain hidden in the future; perhaps sociobiology is its beginning. Such possibilities will, if we are lucky, trouble sociobiology much in the years ahead. Now, ironically, at the boundary of greatest significance for humanity sociobiology pauses, and can offer no help.

Yet.

16

Sociology

Pierre L. van den Berghe

═══════════════════════════════════════

WHY MOST SOCIOLOGISTS DON'T
(AND WON'T) THINK EVOLUTIONARILY

A century and a quarter after it was formulated, and over half a century after it was refined into the "neo-Darwinian synthesis," the theory of evolution by natural selection continues to encounter much concerted opposition. Much of it is religiously or ideologically motivated. Those sources of opposition will not concern me here, because, while interesting in their own right, they are impervious to rational argument. Here I shall address the much narrower question of why most sociologists, who for the most part claim to be scientists, continue to reject or ignore the relevance of evolutionary theory to the study of human behavior and sociality.

Most sociologists share their combination of hostility to, and ignorance of, behavioral ecology and sociobiology with many other social scientists, but perhaps in a slightly more acute form. Anthropologists, for instance, know much more about human evolution than sociologists, understand the adaptation of humans to their habitat, and seldom reject altogether the relevance of biology to behavior. American graduate students in anthropology learn the basics of human paleontology and physical anthropology, know something of other primates, understand the symbiosis of humans with other species, and tend to view culture as a complex adaptation to a complex environment.

Sociologists, on the other hand, have succeeded in purging biology even from the two specialties where its relevance would seem most glaringly obvious: demography and ecology. Demographers have disembodied the biological events of birth, death, ageing, and fertility through statistical abstraction and aggregation, and manage to ply their trade with virtually no training in human biology. As for those sociologists who claim to be ecologists, they have reduced this specialty to a pedestrian kind of social geography: they largely plot social characteristics of people on maps.

Even the most sophisticated macrosociological ecologists like the Lenskis (Lenski and Lenski 1987) espouse a brand of evolution that is overwhelmingly *technologically* rather than biologically based. They are, thus, in the tradition of looking at cultural evolution as clearly distinct from, and only tangentially related to, biological evolution. Their rather perfunctory attempt at linking the two is confined to a few pages of their first chapter, and is, to be sure, better than most competing attempts in sociobiology textbooks, but it still remains a paean to human uniqueness. Another recent statement, by Namboodiri (1988), seeks to make "ecological demography" central to sociology. Despite its ambitious program and broad definition of the field (by sociological standards, that is), Namboodiri mentions "bioecology" only in passing (629–30), and then fails to see it as the *same* discipline. Instead, he draws highly dubious analogies between species and organizations, thereby falling into a form of Spencerian organicism. My point is simply that even the best and the broadest statements from demography and "human ecology" in sociology still largely ignore evolutionary biology, and certainly fail to see themselves as a specialty within it.

SPECIES-WIDE ANTHROPOCENTRISM

Why don't sociologists think evolutionarily? The answer has, I believe, two main components, one general, the other specific. The general component might be labeled "species-wide anthropocentrism," while the specific component is traceable to the *trained* mental incapacities of social scientists. At the general level, evolutionary thinking does not come naturally to people.

The human mind is, I think, predisposed to find evolutionary theory counterintuitive and divorced from our life experiences. This is true in many different ways, a few of which might be interesting briefly to examine.

First, evolutionary theory deals with a *time scale* that boggles the human mind and transcends the human experience. With a lifespan of a few decades, our historical horizon is essentially bounded by our own lifetime and by the oral tradition of our parents and grandparents. Writing has somewhat expanded the time window of a few literati to a few thousand years, but that scarcely affects the consciousness of most people, and even so, the *longue durée* of historians is still a far cry from the millions of years of evolutionary biologists. Experientially, most of us can project ourselves back into the world of our grandparents and forward into that of our grandchildren, which is to say, some 150 to 200 years. Even that takes a degree of intellectual effort beyond the capacity of many who live in an experiential present lasting perhaps a decade or two. With our myopic temporocentricity, we tend systematically to exaggerate the importance of the superficial changes that occur fast enough to be noticeable, and to deny the significance or even the existence of changes too slow to be perceptible. Evolution is simply not on the human time scale. We listen to much faster-ticking clocks.

Second, there is the problem of *teleology*. As a partly self-conscious organism, we act purposefully, at least some of the time. Therefore, we naturally tend to project purpose onto the world around us. What more satisfying view of the world than that Almighty God created plants and animals to serve us, and us to serve Him? Why would cows have tits if not to give us milk? Why would birds sing and roses smell if not to delight us? Note that this kind of teleology has the appeal not only of simplicity but also of putting us at the center of our world. This is all very tidy and gratifying. Now consider biological theory, which tells us that evolution has no purpose and that life forms came into being through blind forces of natural selection "acting" on random mutations. We are simply one animal among millions, a totally improbable accident living on a speck of dust in a universe so vast that we do not even know whether it is finite. Clearly, at the level of gut appeal, there is no contest between creationism and evolution.

So deeply ingrained is the mental habit of teleology, the difficulty of conceiving of anything as random and purposeless, that even biologists often carelessly lapse into teleological vocabulary when speaking of "Evolution," "Nature," or "Natural Selection." Sometimes they are being taken to task for using sloppy metaphors. More often, they are listened to, to the extent that they are *misunderstood* and seem to offer a new kind of scientific teleology. Properly understood, evolutionary theory is intellectually repugnant to most of us. It is not easy to accept that evolution is a meaningless tale told by an idiot, when everything about the natural world *seems* so well and intelligently designed for a wondrous purpose: the glory of God and our endless delight.

Third, there is the *vanity* factor. Since Copernicus, science gradually displaced man and his planet from the comfortable center of the universe. The myopia of anthropocentrism is generic to our species, but doubly acute among social scientists who base their livelihood on claims of human uniqueness. It was difficult enough to accept that humans were animals and thus evolved by natural selection, but a last line of exceptionalism was erected to save the human ego. Sure, man was an animal, but a very special and unique kind of animal, an animal with a soul, a psyche, a mind (instead of a mere brain), a culture. Human *behavior,* at least, transcended the scope of biology, even if human anatomy and physiology did not.

Human sociobiology, of course, attacks this last redoubt of anthropocentric conceit. It readily concedes that *Homo sapiens* is indeed unique in a number of species-specific characteristics, but it puts that uniqueness in an evolutionary context where all species are unique in some ways, otherwise they would not be separate species. We are unique, but we are not unique in being unique. This ultimate knocking of *Homo* from his self-constructed pedestal is not only a blow to a sociologist's human ego, but a positive threat to his or her claims to scientific expertise. Sociobiology adds professional injury to general insult. Little wonder that it meets opposition.

Fourth, the evolutionary perspective on behavior is profoundly *demystifying.* It regards behavior as either self-serving or misguided; it explains away apparent altruism as sophisticated selfishness based on either nepotism or reciprocity; it relegates religion and ideology to deceit and delusion; it presents, in short, a thoroughly cynical view of human action. Such a view is, of course, a frontal attack on all believers, religious and secular, since it reduces belief systems to conscious or unconscious rationalizations for self-interest. Even nonbelievers are threatened, as they would rather not have the self-interested nature of their behavior exposed. As for intimate relations of friendship, kinship, or love, they typically cannot stand the strain of exposure to sociobiological analysis. Few people, I suggest, could bear the strain of running their personal lives as self-conscious sociobiologists. Evolutionary biology applied to human behavior is, thus, profoundly threatening to individual interests and mental comfort. It peels off the layers of mystification that we invent to live with ourselves and with others. It is too good a model of behavior to be bearable.

TRAINED AVERSION

All of the above biases against the application of evolutionary theory to human behavior, sociologists share with most other human beings. There are, however, a number of additional intellectual stumbling blocks that sociologists have erected in the path to human self-understanding. Sociological resistance to biological thinking is in large part *trained* incompetence, not simply garden-variety anthropocentrism. Many sociologists are not merely oblivious about biology; they are militantly and proudly ignorant. They *know* biology to be irrelevant to their interests, so they are determined not to make the effort to learn about it. Blessed be the biologically ignorant for they shall see the Kingdom of Sociology.

Interestingly, the sorry state of contemporary ignorance of, and indifference or hostility to, evolutionary biology among social scientists is relatively recent. It is perhaps a little over half a century old. Most of our discipline's founders in the late nineteenth and early twentieth centuries, notably those who wrote in English, were indeed very much evolutionists and admirers of Darwin. One only needs to think of Spencer, Tylor, Rivers, Morgan, Marx, Engels, Westermarck, and Sumner, to name but a few. As this brief list indicates, evolutionary thinking at the turn of the century covered the entire ideological spectrum, from the extreme left (Marx and Engels) to the extreme right (Sumner and Spencer).

To be sure, many of the early evolutionists in social science had fatally flawed ideas, many based on misunderstandings of Darwin and on prevailing prejudices of their day. The class and racial prejudices of Spencer and Sumner, for instance, are glaring. Most also adhered to questionable notions of group selection and to misleading and fallacious organismic analogies, but others, notably Westermarck (1891), were remarkably modern in their thinking. By and large, the early social-science evolutionists were no better than the biology of their day, nor could they have been expected to be. But they had the intelligence not to set themselves up *against* biology.

Early social-science evolutionists also labored under another serious limitation: they had to rely on what was still an extremely sketchy and unreliable ethnographic data base. Indeed, they shared with their contemporaries in biology most of the failings for which their successors attacked them. It was only in the last quarter-century, for example, that evolutionary biology moved away from group selection and became resolutely reductionist as to the level of selection.

It is well beyond the scope of this chapter to tell the story of how the social sciences turned their backs to biology and evolution, and how the new orthodoxy of sociocultural environmentalism emerged. Such a task would include a review of all the main currents in Western social thought: the Durkheimian school in France and its Radcliffe-Brownian offshoots in British social anthropology; Watson and the behaviorists in American psychology; Boas and his students Mead and Benedict in American anthropology; Weber, Toennies, and Simmel in German sociology; Parsons, Merton, and the American functionalists; nearly all of the self-styled neo-Marxists, the semioticians, the symbolic interactionists, and other sundry idealists. Suffice it to say that these diverse and competing schools, while singularly unable to converge on a true scientific paradigm for an explanation of human behavior, shared a common denominator of ignoring biology and evolution. We shall now turn to a brief review of some of the implicit or explicit premises that led many sociologists (and other social scientists) to igore or deny the relevance of biology to human behavior. In short, let us try to pinpoint the sources of their *trained* aversion, as distinct from their untrained naiveté.

First, there is the dogma of *environmentalism.* There is, of course, nothing wrong in believing that a multitude of environmental factors affect phenotypes, including behavior. All biologists believe that a phenotype is the product of interaction between a genotype and an environment. Likewise, human sociobiologists will readily accept that, for humans, the man-made part of the environment—human society and culture—is an essential determinant of human action. Environmentalism only becomes an untenable and obsolete dogma when it is counterpoised to a "hereditarian" position (which hardly any biologist espouses) and is held to be the overwhelmingly important determinant of behavior to the *exclusion* of biology.

Sociologists still largely think in terms of heredity *versus* environment, nature *versus* nurture, instinct *versus* learning. Biologists (and increasingly psychologists) have long recognized that these false dichotomies are a liability to understanding, as indeed are most dichotomies so dear to the human mind. The universe is one, and the scientific mode of thinking is monistic, not dualistic. Yet the human mind has a universal propensity to think in binary oppositions. Sociologists are no exceptions, and, unfortunately, they have applied their Manichean dualism to false antinomies between culture and nature, between genes and environment, between humans and other animals.

Not content with setting the environment *against* the genes, instead of in interaction with them, many sociologists proceed to demonize what they call the "hereditarian" position. They falsely assume it to be that of human sociobiologists, and they stigmatize it with every epithet in their ideological lexicon: racism, sexism, classism, conservatism, fascism, and so on. As Bishop Wilberforce's wife said of Darwin's theory of evolution, they know that sociobiology is wrong, but should it be correct, then they hope it will not become generally known.

Second, and related to the sociological notion of environmentalism, is the concept of *determinism.* In the lexicon

of most sociologists, "determinism" means "exclusive determinism." Since the environment and culture clearly determine
human behavior, in the thinking of many sociologists, it follows
that genes cannot.

Unfortunately, the nonsense does not stop here. Cultural
determinism is a comfortable ideological position to hold. Since
culture is both human-made and determining, many sociologists conclude that we are firmly in charge of our own destiny.
There is, of course, a Durkheimian school of social determinism
that holds the *individual* to be captive of societal forces, but
since society is a "collective representation," Man is still
ultimately in control. This man-in-charge-of-himself position
usually rests on two further nonsequiturs. The first is that an
ability to bring about change implies control. Any good
sociologist should know that there is a huge gulf between
changing things and changing them in a desired direction. The
road to hell, many astute observers of human affairs have
noted, is paved with good intentions.

The second nonsequitur is that since cultural determinism
implies control over one's destiny, "genetic determinism" does
not. (This nonsequitur is, of course, in the logic of binary
opposition: culture is the antigene, therefore all the properties
of one term are absent in the opposite.) Those who dare not
think that genes control behavior because then we would be
powerless to change our destiny are, however, often prepared
to take another intellectual somersault when told that we
already possess a considerable cultural ability to change our
genes. Basically, the "humanistic" stance in sociology consists
in believing that culture is determining, that genes are
unchangeable (or change too slowly for our needs and desires),
but that, even if we could change our genes, we should not.
Eugenics, to sociological humanists, raises the specter of
Nazism and Mengele's concentration camp experiments.
Perhaps it should be countered that Stalin murdered some
thirty million Soviet citizens in an intellectual climate of benign
environmentalism represented by Lysenko.

Third, there is the issue of *reductionism*. Basically, most
sociologists have no clear perception of what reductionism
means, but they are firmly against it. This combination of
ignorance and dogma is especially incapacitating when it

comes to understanding science, for the entire trend and strategy of scientific theory construction in the last five hundred years has been powerfully reductionist. In sociology, however, reductionism has been an epithet, first popularized by Durkheim, who kept insisting that social phenomena were *not* reducible to individual motivations or actions. The reductionism of science, however, is not a dogma (as the antireductionism of sociology *is*), but a *method.* It says basically: try to explain as much of a phenomenon as you can by making the fewest and the simplest assumptions possible, at the lowest possible level of organization of matter. Try to explain as much chemistry as possible through physics, as much biology through chemistry, as much psychology through biology, and so on. Then, if you are left with an unexplained residual, invoke, if you must, the emergent properties of the next level of complexity in the organization of matter.

Applied to the social sciences, reductionism calls for a *strategy* of trying *first* to explain social behavior by individual action, and individual behavior in reference to its evolutionary biology. This reductionism does not deny a priori that human language and culture, for example, have some emergent properties that are not entirely reducible to the social behavior of other animals, but it assumes that there is an area of commonality in all animal behavior that must be explored first before one invokes as a dogma the irreducibility and incomparability of human behavior with that of any other animal.

The latter dogma is unfortunately a position still widely held in the social sciences in general, and in sociology in particular. There is, of course, no possible argument against dogma, which is as many sociologists would have it. Precluding dialogue is a sure way of having the last word. The interesting question, however, is why antireductionism should be such a cornerstone of the ramshackle mental edifice of sociology. The answer is not far to seek. Antireductionism is a territorial display of sociologists, especially against their nearest intellectual rivals, the psychologists.

By asserting that *Homo sapiens* is absolutely unique and positively radiating emergent properties, social scientists can claim a turf permanently beyond the purview of biology. By further claiming that society and culture are realities that transcend the individual, sociology and anthropology have respectively created their special impregnable turf vis-à-vis psychology. The artificial distinction between sociology and anthropology also had to be rationalized better than by admitting that sociology was the study of "civilized" white folks and anthropology that of dark, "primitive" colonials. Society was declared irreducibly different from culture; sociologists took the former, anthropologists the latter. Evolutionary biology extended to human behavior constitutes the most serious challenge to their intellectual turf that sociologists have had to face since behaviorism. No wonder they raise their anti-reductionist hackles.

Fourth, evolutionary theory is *materialist*. It holds that the cultural superstructure grows out of the process of individual interaction, that is, out of the social structure, and that the latter, in turn, evolved genetically from a biological infrastructure. While there are materialists in sociology and the other social sciences, the idealist tradition had held sway in many quarters. Many sociologists believe that the key to understanding why people behave as they do is to ask them. They think that people's beliefs, values, and norms determine their actions. Human sociobiologists, on the other hand, also talk to people, but don't necessarily believe what they are told. Scratch a value, sociobiologists suggest, and watch an interest bleed. This cynicism about human motivation and behavior does not sit well with many sociologists, especially those (and they are legion) who specialize in asking people's opinions in an attempt to predict their behavior.

In its materialism, sociobiology shares much in common with classical Marxism as well as with a prominent school of cultural ecology in anthropology represented by Marvin Harris (1979). It is, therefore, particularly interesting that most of these self-styled materialists have also been hostile to human sociobiology. Most Western neo-Marxists claim to have rediscovered the voluntaristic humanism of the "younger Marx," and repudiate what they see as the "vulgar" materialism of the older Marx under the influence of Engels. What many self-styled neo-Marxists have developed, in fact, is an abstruse idealism that would be better labeled "neo-Hegelian."

Fifth, there is a *methodological chasm* between sociology and behavioral ecology. Few sociologists, in the course of their professional activities, deal with human behavior. On the face of it, this seems an extraordinary statement, but it is, alas, a true one. Very few sociologists do fieldwork and actually observe interaction. Sociobiology, which grew in part out of the ethological tradition, is based in large part on the observations of animal behavior "in the wild," and is thus methodologically closer to anthropology than to sociology.

Sociologists, on the other hand, deal mostly with abstract categories like classes and ethnic groups; engage in statistical massage of aggregated data; do secondary analysis of public opinion surveys; speculate about the impact of religious beliefs and political ideologies; project, manipulate, and interpret statistical trends; and generally pontificate about the state of society. They don't watch people being bumped over the head; they feed the FBI's Uniform Crime Reports to their computers. They don't observe women having babies; they speculate about fluctuations in birthrates provided by the Bureau of the Census. They don't attend political conventions and follow people into polling stations; they read public opinion surveys.

In short, sociologists, for the most part, parasitize data collected by others, aggregate these data into abstracted categories, subject these aggregated data to countless statistical manipulations, and intercorrelate variables that are at least half-a-dozen steps remote from actual behavior. The average sociology department of twenty-five or thirty members at a major American university is lucky to have one or two individuals who collect their own data and do actual fieldwork. Abstracted empiricism rules supreme. Human behavior gets disembodied in the statistical shuffle. *Homo sociologicus* is an eviscerated cipher.

Thus, sociology and sociobiology not only are theoretically far apart; their methodologies are widely divergent as well. The methodology of painstaking, precise, prolonged field observation, experimentation, and measurement—the stock-in-trade of behavioral ecologists—is one in which sociologists receive virtually no training. Sociologists often denigrate it as "mere descriptive ethnography" because they lack the skill, the patience, and the discipline to engage in it. Why catch malaria in Paraguay or Malawi when you can write your dissertation from U.S. Census tapes in Madison, Ann Arbor, or Bloomington?

Sixth, evolutionary theory is very *simple,* straightforward, and parsimonious in its postulates. It elegantly explains a lot with very few assumptions. These properties are all considered virtues in scientific theory construction. Not so, alas, with many sociologists, who have a penchant for obfuscation. Intellectual pretentiousness and stylistic turgidity are characteristics of all immature, derivative disciplines that have an inferiority complex vis-à-vis the more established fields. (Fields like journalism and education are at least as bad as sociology in this respect.)

The sociological argument against simplicity and parsimony goes something as follows: human beings are uniquely complex and unpredictable because they think; therefore sociology and the other social sciences cannot possibly be as neat and straightforward as the natural sciences. Sociological models must be more complex, because so is the subject matter. Furthermore, causation in human affairs is always multiple and reciprocal. The best theory, therefore, is that which states that everything is related to everything else. The more comprehensive a theory is, the better. The more variables sociologists throw into the computer, the happier they are.

It follows from this attitude that any simple, straightforward theory is received with great suspicion. Things *cannot* be that simple, and neither can theories. Not that sociological theories (or what passes as such) are always very complex, but at least they are presented in an arcane, convoluted, and turgid way. What a theory lacks in complexity is amply made up for by opaque jargon, clumsy syntax, and faulty logic. When physicists are confronted with a simplifying, unifying concept that seems to work, they get a psychic high. They equate simplicity with beauty. For the sociologist, on the other hand, simplicity equals simple-mindedness.

WILL SOCIOLOGISTS CONTINUE TO IGNORE BIOLOGY?

Let me in conclusion ask: Can sociologists continue to ignore biology with impunity? The answer depends partly on the sociologist's specialty area and the level of problems addressed. At one end of the spectrum, methodologists can safely continue their arcane pursuits with little concern for any substantive issues, but they, too, would do well to remember that population biology was one of the main sources of modern statistics. While lately sociological statistics is largely derivative of economics, an earlier generation was beholden to Galton, R. A. Fisher, and other prominent biostatisticians. Methodologists, better than other sociologists, should be in a good position to understand the continuity between biology and sociology, if only they started thinking more substantively. Game theory, for instance, is equally applicable to biological and sociological problems.

At the "humanistic" end of the sociological spectrum, sociologists interested in the ideological superstructure, in the specific cultural content of institutions, and in the detail of cultural variation, diversity, and change are probably also safe in ignoring biology. Sociologists of knowledge, of the arts, of literature, of music, of culture, as well as all those who engage in the exegesis of their predecessors, can afford to remain comfortably ignorant of biology.

For any sociologists in the central specialties of kinship and marriage, the microsociology of small groups, social psychology, class and ethnicity, demography, ecology, deviance, political sociology, and social change, I believe that the price of sticking one's head in the biological sand is a continuing trend of sociology toward a sterile, abstracted scholasticism out of touch with human behavior, and away from the scientific mainstream. Sociology's claim to scientific status can no longer be upheld primarily through a facade of quantitative methodology. It must be anchored in a theoretical paradigm that satisfies scientific canons. Such a theoretical paradigm sociology signally failed to produce in over a century of self-conscious existence. The main reason for that failure is that sociology turned its back on the one theory that was overwhelmingly successful in explaining change and variation in life forms on this planet: evolution by natural selection. If sociology fails to join the scientific mainstream, it might survive for another century as a scholastic discipline, but it will never be taken seriously as a science.

Will sociology thus adapt to the biological challenge? Will more members of the profession modify their thinking and come to see human behavior as within the purview of evolutionary biology? For the most part I think not, although that is one prediction on which I should be delighted to be proven wrong.

17

Linguistics

James R. Hurford

===========

Linguistics is the study of human languages. A language is seen by linguists as a complex system of rules linking speech sounds to meanings. Speech sounds are patterns of differing air pressure initiated by movements of the chest, throat, mouth, and nose. These airwaves impinge on the ear and are physically measurable by phonetic instruments. At this end of linguistics, phonetics, the study of speech sounds, shares its theory with acoustic physics and physiology. Meanings, on the other hand, are not concrete events in the same clear sense. There is hope in some quarters that meanings will ultimately be specifiable in neurological terms, but semantics, the linguistic study of meaning, can so far only deal with meanings in an abstract way, and here linguistics borrows some of its theory from philosophy and logic.

Sociobiology is concerned to provide evolutionary explanations for innate properties that affect an organism's social behavior. Clearly, communication via language is social behavior, and significant aspects of the complex structure of language appear to be innate. The task facing an incipient sociobiology of language is to articulate in detail how this complex innate structure serves the purposes of communication—and to show how it evolved.

In this chapter I describe the innateness of language and the problem of explaining the language aquisition device (LAD) that all children seem to possess. Then I describe why linguistics has been slow to use sociobiological ideas, and try to map out a "sociobiology of language."

LANGUAGE AND LANGUAGES:
DIVERSITY, UNIFORMITY, AND COMPLEXITY

There are over four thousand different languages in the world, some spoken by handfuls of speakers, who will presumably be their last speakers, and others spoken by vast language communities of hundreds of millions. Languages are at once both amazingly diverse and dissimilar, and strikingly uniform.

The diversity of languages is perhaps most apparent in speech. Spoken foreign languages at first sound like gibberish, with sounds we simply cannot repeat (and all articulated amazingly fast!). The range of human speech sounds is indeed very large, but nevertheless the phonetician can circumscribe and classify the whole range in his or her phonetic theory. Even though we as adults may find foreign speech sounds quite impossible to wrap our tongues around, this difficulty is *acquired*. Obviously the foreigners manage their own sounds, and probably cannot manage ours, but if we had been born where they were, we would have grown up sounding like them. Humans are born with the *capacity to learn* to make and hear *any* sounds from the phonetic range; apparently this learning involves losing the vocal plasticity required to be able to make and hear *every* sound.

Not surprisingly, and significantly for linguistics' potential relations with sociobiology, the unifying phonetic theory that accounts for the diversity of humanly acquirable speech sounds is based on the genetically given physiology of the human vocal tract and ear, and on the constraints imposed on them by properties of the earthly environment, such as the fact that air is a nitrogen–oxygen mix, rather than, say, a helium–oxygen mix. (The speech of deep-sea divers, breathing a helium–oxygen mix, sounds squeaky to the point of unintelligibility.)

At the other "end" of languages, where we are dealing with the meanings that can be expressed in them, there is arguably substantial uniformity. When we overhear an outburst of "gibberish" on a foreign street, we can ask what it means and be told reasonably satisfactorily. That is, *translation,* despite all its acknowledged imperfections, is possible for the great bulk of meaningful expressions, from any language into any other. In some sense, then, the set of meanings that different languages tap into are the same. There is a school of thought labeled "linguistic relativity" and associated with the name of B. L. Whorf ("the Whorf hypothesis"), that holds that the range of thoughts a person can have is limited and shaped by the structure of her or his language, so that thoughts (let us tentatively identify thoughts with meanings) are *not* uniform across languages, according to this hypothesis. But it is fair to say that linguists generally reject the Whorf hypothesis in its strong form, whereby one's language is a straightjacket preventing one from sharing the meanings that are conceivable and expressible by speakers of other languages. It may sometimes require a little mental effort, and a stretching of some habits, but the range of meanings that humans can conceive and express is relatively uniform across the species. That is, unlike the case of speech sounds, where adults have lost "phonetic plasticity," people do not lose much of the "semantic plasticity" required to represent the whole range of human conceivable meanings.

Now, the uniformity of meanings across languages is, like the range of speech sounds and significantly for potential connections between linguistics and sociobiology, a joint product of the genetically given mental apparatus that represents such meanings and the earthly environment that our human meanings are largely *about*. Just how this genetically given mental apparatus is realized in physical terms (perhaps of neurons and synapses) is quite unknown, but most linguists do not doubt that meanings *are* represented in the brain, and that the apparatus that stores and processes them is a largely unique part of our biological heredity.

Put simply, there are three main things to acquire when learning a language; its vocabulary, its pronunciation, and its grammar. The linguist's picture of a language as a bridge between meanings and sounds is seen at its simplest in the lexicon, or dictionary or vocabulary list, of a language. The lexicon of a language is a store of sound–meaning pairs, that is, of words and their associated concepts, basically a list, but sometimes with the individual entries in the list being complexly structured and cross-referenced with other entries. Each entry states an arbitrary association between the sound image of a word and a chunk of meaning, or a concept. This two-sided nature of the fundamental building blocks of language was recognized by Ferdinand de Saussure, the Swiss scholar sometimes referred to as the "father of modern linguistics," in his picture of the "linguistic sign."

Figure 1. The Saussurean sign. From Saussure (1959).

We need now to look closer at what kind of system a language is, that is, how languages are typically structured, beyond Saussure's simple idea of an arbitrary sign. I cannot do full justice in this brief chapter to the enormous complexity and diversity that linguists have discovered in the world's languages. But to start with, languages are obviously not *just* collections of words that may be strung together, each doing its work in isolation from the preceding and following words. Languages have *syntax,* sets of rules for arranging words into sentences. Languages also have *morphology,* sets of rules for forming new words from old ones, or adapting words to different syntactic contexts. And languages have *phonology,* rules for arranging and modifying speech sounds in context. In all these branches of language structure, as with phonetics and semantics, the linguist finds a breathtaking combination of diversity and uniformity across the world's languages.

Let's concentrate for a bit on the diversity of languages, especially in their syntax and morphology. Some languages do the craziest things, seen from our perspective as English speakers. (Of course, English seems pretty crazy to speakers of other languages.) I'll give some examples.

Grammatical *case* will be familiar to those who have studied Latin, German, or Russian. In such languages, nouns (and in agreement with them, adjectives and other modifiers) take markers indicating how they fit into the grammatical structure of the sentence, which structure is related (not always straightforwardly) to the meaning of the whole sentence. So in Latin we have the so-called nominative, accusative, genitive, dative, and ablative cases. Roughly, the nominative case markers are the ones that indicate the subject of the sentence, accusative marks the direct object of a verb and of certain prepositions in certain of their meanings, and so on. To the schoolchild learning Latin, five grammatical cases is bad enough, but Uralic languages such as Finnish and Hungarian typically use *over a dozen* grammatical cases, and some languages of the Caucasus have *over thirty* cases! (Anderson 1985, 187). Many of these cases are for expressing intricate details of location, motion, and direction, details that are expressed by circumlocution in English, and not "grammaticalized," as in these languages.

Another initially surprising thing about grammatical case is that even a language with rather few cases may organize them in a way that cuts directly across our English way of thinking about grammatical functions like subject and object. To us, the nominative case is the case of the subject of any sentence, whether it be intransitive as in Latin *Puer venit,* "the boy came," or transitive as in *Puer lupum necavit,* "the boy killed the wolf." But a large number of so-called ergative languages don't organize matters this way. In them, the *subject* of an intransitive sentence is given the same case-marking as the *object* of a transitive sentence. This case, used for intransitive subjects and transitive objects, is usually called the "absolutive" case; the remaining case, that used for the subjects of transitive sentences, is the ergative case. Here is an example from the well-known ergative language, Dyirbal, an Australian aboriginal language now nearing extinction.

Balan dyugumbil	*bangul yarangu*	*balgan*
woman absolutive	man ergative	hit ="The man hit the woman"
Balan dyugumbil	*baninyu*	
woman absolutive	came	="The woman came"

Making matters more complicated, Dyirbal organizes its case marking on nouns along these ergative/absolutive lines, but uses a nominative/accusative pattern more like Latin with pronouns.

Another Australian language, Ngiyambaa, also regrettably nearly extinct, can be used to show what an amazing array of markers a language can attach to its verbs. To illustrate the use of some of these, *-NHa:ni-y* is a suffix that can be added to verbs of position, like those for *sit, stand,* and *lie. -NHa:ni-y* converts these verbs to verbs of motion; for example, for *sit down, stand up, lie down.* The suffix *-guwa-y* indicates that the event referred to by the verb to which it is attached is emotionally affecting (Donaldson 1980, 193-95). The nearest English equivalent would seem to be tacking a curse word onto the beginning of a word, as in "He bloody saw me," but the Ngiyambaa suffix is more specialized syntactically, being only attachable to verbs, and more generalized semantically, as it can be used to express a great range of emotions, including positive ones, such as pleasure.

As another example of a language doing something that seems very exotic to us, look at how Arabic forms some of its plurals, not by a suffix, as English does, nor by a prefix, nor even by an "infix" inserted into the middle of a singular word, but by replacing vowels and inserting others between the consonants in a quite complex pattern. Their *fingaan* is the singular for "cups," while *fanagiin* is plural, "cups"; *fustaan* is the singular for "dress," while it changes to *fasatiin* for "dresses."

Arabic uses this exotic kind of method of word-formation, or morphology, in other parts of its grammar. Here are some patterns based on verbs. Notice that the same consonants are always retained, and the vowels in between them change, and sometimes a prefix is added as well.

katab—"he wrote," *maktuub*—"written," *maktab*—"writing place, desk"
fatah—"he opened," *maftuuh*—"opened," *muftaah*—"instrument for opening, key"
darab—"he hit," *madruub*—"beaten," *mudraab*—"instrument for hitting, hammer"
daxxan—"he smoked," *tadxiin*—"smoking"
sowwar—"he made a picture," *taswiir*—"photography"

The examples above are from syntax and morphology. I'll give a final exotic example from phonology, the phenomenon of consonant mutation in the Celtic languages, whereby the initial consonant of a word changes systematically according to the word immediately preceding it. These examples are from Welsh.

cant—"hundred," *tri chant*—"three hundred," *saith gant*—"seven hundred"
tair blynedd—"three years," *dwy flynedd*—"two years," *saith mlynedd*—"seven years,"
mil—"thousand," *dwy fil*—"two thousand"

Although these examples are all of numeral words, the phenomenon of consonantal mutation pervades the whole language, not just its numeral subsystem, so that very many words change (or even lose) their initial consonant, according to context. It is as if English *pill* sometimes occurred as *Phil* and sometimes as *bill*. Mutation doesn't appear to cause Welsh speakers any confusion, even though the groups of sounds related by particular mutation processes are elsewhere mutually contrastive, that is, they can signal differences in meaning.

This is just a tiny sample of the surprising phenomena that one finds in languages. The point of giving these examples was not to present a menagerie of curiosities and monstrosities, but to illustrate one side of the empirical problem facing theoretical linguistics, namely, the initially apparent diversity of human languages. And yet it would be fundamentally wrong to conclude from such examples that in human language anything is possible. That is certainly not the case. There are a myriad imaginable crazy things that languages *don't* do. For instance, there is no language that forms a question from a statement by reversing the order of all the words, so that the question corresponding to "There was a book on the table" would be "Table the on book a was there?". Linguists, marveling at the diversity of languages, sometimes joke, "Think of a crazy rule, and I bet some language somewhere has it." But they don't really believe the joke. Of all the infinity of imaginable kinds of grammatical and phonological rules languages *could* have, languages in fact only use up a tiny fraction of the "space."

THE GENETIC BASIS OF THE LANGUAGE FACULTY

The potential "sociobiology of language" to which I shall refer later must take as its starting point the genetic basis of the language faculty. One of Noam Chomsky's major contributions to the field of linguistics has been to insist that the rich, and yet at the same time constrained, structure of human languages is in some sense innate in us. Notice that the claim is not that the structure of any one particular language, for example, English, Swahili, Chinese, is innate. Rather, it is that children are innately endowed with a version of *universal grammar,* a kind of mentally represented, complexly structured, but initially empty container, into which they slot the facts of the particular language they are exposed to. Unconsciously (of course) the child is said to go through processes like "Oh, I get it, verbs have to agree with their subjects," which presupposes that she somehow already knew the categories "verb," "agree," and "subject," even though nobody taught them to her. For all the complexity and apparent diversity of languages, children have little trouble picking up *any* language as a native language.

Linguists distinguish, then, between the grammar of a particular language (for example, English, Chinese, Swahili), seen as a partial theory of the speech behavior of speakers of that language, and a *general theory of language,* (that is, the biologically given language faculty), which is a "meta-theory" of the grammars of all languages. The general theory of language is interpreted by (generative) linguists as a *theory of what the newborn child innately knows about language in general before she begins to acquire her particular native language.* The term *native language* is something of a misnomer, as children are not born actually knowing what is to become their native language. But they do know a lot about language in general. This knowledge is completely unconscious, but it distinguishes humans from other creatures. No other creatures have what it takes to learn a human language. And computers haven't been programmed to be able to learn a human language just from experiencing samples in the way human children do. This innate preprogramming in the human mind/brain is sometimes called the "language acquisition device" (LAD). The LAD is what children have that allows them to build in their own heads a cognitive map of their language from the observations of language behavior of their parents and others around them.

The question of the *evolution of language* is properly the question of the evolution of the language acquisition device. What special properties does this device have? What is it like? And how can we tell? We can tell in several ways: (1) by observing universal regularities that occur throughout all the languages of the world (regularities that cannot obviously be attributed to immediate needs of communication), (2) by observing the actual process of language acquisition in children, and in particular seeing what generalized patterns of behavior they naturally adopt without any particular prompting from outside, (3) by noting regular tendencies in historical change in languages, and (4) by studying creolization, the process whereby new languages spring up in uprooted or drastically mixed populations.

Naturally, you can find differences of opinion within the community of linguists about just *how* easy language acquisition is for children, and whether they are explicitly taught any of it, but the consensus is that there must be a lot that is innate in humans, enabling them to acquire languages, that is simply absent from any other species. Chimpanzees, for example, can't do it. In the 1960s and 1970s, there was a flurry of experimental activity devoted to seeing how much of the structure of human language chimpanzees could master. Again, there remains disagreement about just how much chimpanzees are capable of, and whether one can call it "language." Arguments at this stage can get trivially terminological, tending to forget that qualitative differences can *emerge* from a mass of quantitative differences, and that there are often no nonarbitrary criteria by which to define the precise point of an emergent qualitative step. Whether or not you would want to call it "language" (and most linguists would not, while many animal researchers would—draw your own conclusions), what chimpanzees can manage is certainly a long way from the rich structuring of human languages.

A conceivable objection to the Chomskyan hypothesis of innate language structure is that what is involved is merely the superior intelligence of humans, in some general problem-solving sense. Learning a language is just a kind of problem solving, and we possess generalized superior problem-solving abilities, so the argument would go. But this suggestion won't work, for at least two reasons. First, it is arguable that our general, admittedly impressive, problem-solving abilities are made possible through language. We verbalize problems, which helps us to solve them. Obviously, we can't use this ability to verbalize problems to "solve" language acquisition itself, as, by definition, we don't have language when we are faced with this particular "problem." Second, if the problem of language acquisition were soluble by appeal to general intelligence, then linguistic researchers in universities should take no longer than the child in figuring out the structure of some new language, and surely *should* be able to do it in a shorter time, as they would be able to intelligently apply their knowledge of their first languages to the problem of a second. But they can't. Learning a language, especially a first language, is special, and it is not like figuring out how a clock works, or how to beat your dad at chess, or how to manipulate the stock market. The specialness of language acquisition points to rich innate structure.

THE LACK OF A SOCIOBIOLOGICAL STRAND IN CURRENT LINGUISTICS

"Rich structure" is another way of saying "complexity of design." Complexity of design is the classic phenomenon supporting the hypothesis of evolution by natural selection, a key component of sociobiology. A recent ground-breaking article by Stephen Pinker and Paul Bloom of MIT, "Natural Language and Natural Selection" (1990) in *Behavioral and Brain Sciences,* is devoted to arguing in detail that the evolutionary forces that shaped the innate human LAD are of just the same type as those that shaped the evolution of another striking instance of complex design, the vertebrate eye. It is perhaps rather surprising that this should *need* arguing, but I shall review some reasons why linguistics has been slow in taking up discussion of evolution, and even slower in forging any links with sociobiology.

The Chomskyan theory of the innate LAD is in fact a special case of the theory of epigenetic rules, as developed in the later sociobiological theory of gene–culture coevolution (see for example, Lumsden and Wilson 1981). But this obvious connection is to my knowledge never mentioned by Chomsky himself, or by any of his close or even somewhat distant followers. Chomsky states, "I do not think Wilson did [have a true understanding of the fundamentals of work in generative grammar], judging by the comments that he had in the last chapter of *Sociobiology,* which, I thought, showed really far-reaching misunderstanding" (Chomsky 1982, 7).

Sociobiology has, to date, had scarcely any influence on linguistics at all. Although I argue here that the question of the evolution of language is properly the question of the evolution of the LAD (that is, the human language faculty), linguists have been interested in characterizing this device in purely static, "synchronic," nonevolutionary terms. Linguists in general are surprisingly unconcerned with evolutionary theory, either being preoccupied with idealized formal work at the level of general linguistic theory (for example, mathematical theories of the learnability of systems of rules from data, or characterizing languages in terms of the parameters children mentally set when learning them), or being involved in the descriptive details of particular languages. Sociobiology is relatively new on the academic scene, and cross-fertilization of ideas takes time.

Chomsky, who pioneered the modern view of the study of language as a psychological system rooted in biological heredity, is generally hostile to theories attributing any properties of language to functional factors, such as play a part in natural selection theories (Chomsky 1980, 99-100; 1982, 29; 1988, 167-70). There is, however, scope for the construction of a sociobiological theory of the language faculty, by demonstrating how aspects of the language faculty could or would have given their possessors *the capacity to acquire advantageous knowledge,* that is, knowledge of complex systems of rules allowing the transmission and reception of complex messages about the world. There is no doubt that the ability to communicate via human language conferred enormous advantage on humans, allowing us to get into the (potentially disastrously) dominant position we are in today.

Chomsky's ideas on "modularity" and the autonomy of the language faculty tend to discourage people from seeking links outside the language faculty. Both Chomsky and Jerry Fodor appear to think of the evolution of the language faculty as like a single step, with massive consequences, a saltation. And Chomsky in particular is averse to ideas that selection pressures can be invoked to any significant extent to explain the form of the innate LAD. This position has now been systematically attacked, and in my view demolished, by Pinker and Bloom (1990). But it is quite significant that Pinker and Bloom make no mention at all of a connection with socio-biology, or of Lumsden and Wilson's theory of epigenetic rules. I presume that one reason for this may be a diplomatic effort not to get their views entangled (and tainted) by the continuing furor over human sociobiology.

I would like to point out that some of the rather politically motivated objections to the sociobiology program, especially as it related to such matters as altruism, aggression, and so forth, cannot be leveled at a sociobiology of language. This is because the essential property of a human language, as outlined above, is not actual behavior but rather a system of rules represented in speakers' minds. Such a system of rules defines a set of possible behaviors, that is, defines what strings of sounds are actually grammatical. It is up to each speaker to choose what use to make of his or her language. Language is ethically neutral, in a way in which altruism and aggression may not be. A language is a tool that can be used to praise, insult, amuse, annoy, congratulate, define, and so on. Broadly speaking, whatever publicly communicable messages humans want to pass around to each other, language makes available. This is not to deny that specific languages, such as English, Swahili, and Chinese, have institutionalized or convention-alized biases, which we may legitimately criticize on ethical grounds. For instance, English vocabulary has a sexist bias, with many more derogatory terms for females than for males. But here is the place to remember the distinction between particular languages and the general human language faculty. There is nothing, as far as we can see, in the Language Acquisition Device tending to push a child toward acquiring a sexist vocabulary, or a racist vocabulary, or a preference for sentences that can be interpreted as insults, jokes, or peaceful remarks.

TOWARD A SOCIOBIOLOGY OF LANGUAGE

The major innovation of sociobiology has been to apply to *social behavior* the same kind of arguments and explanations that Darwin and his followers applied to the *shape* of organisms, such as, for example, the vertebrate eye. To try to extend the general sociobiological explanatory strategy to the design of language, one needs to consider carefully the relation between language and the aspects of social behavior, such as altruism, typically handled by sociobiology.

The distinction between social behavior and nonsocial behavior, although not always easy to maintain, is important. Often, behavior that is nonsocial, such as scratching an itch, cud chewing, or lone foraging for food, can be explained in the same kind of terms as an organism's shape. In fact, in many cases it is not easy to distinguish between the shape of some organ and the behavior that the animal carries out with it. Some actions are characteristic of animals with just such body parts. What a giraffe does with its neck, for example, is largely the kind of thing that only a creature with a giraffe's neck *could* do. Likewise a mole's spadelike front claws and its digging behavior just seem to be two aspects (static and dynamic, respectively) of a single phenomenon. Given the claws' shape and musculature, and the way they are attached to the front end of the mole, the kinds of behavior that can be carried out with them are quite limited, and digging is one of the conspicuously possible behaviors that could be accomplished with such equipment. In short, there is often what seems to be a close connection between an animal's shape and its nonsocial behavior. Thus the extension of Darwinian explanations to such behavior is relatively smooth and not apparently problematic.

Does this hold for language, too? It is worth mentioning that some details of the human anatomy connected with speech are related to language activity in the same close way that a gibbon's arms are related to its swinging through the trees. A Martian observing humans would note that they talk a lot, and respond to the talk of others, though the Martian might not understand or appreciate the complexity of the language structure underlying this incessant chattering. We have a vocal tract with two resonating cavities (pharynx and mouth) particularly suited to making a wide range of acoustic distinctions, an apparatus that no other animal can match, and ears that are tuned to be receptive in this acoustic range. It is well known that all the human speech apparatus also serves other life-preserving purposes, such as eating, breathing, and tightening the chest for lifting and excreting; and the ears are obviously useful for nonspeech sounds as well. But the human physical vocal and auditory apparatuses have been *adaptively refined* to "carry" language beyond (and even to some extent against) these basic life-preserving purposes.

Yet, I believe, physical adaptedness of the vocal tract to carry language is only a rather pedestrian beginning to any putative evolutionary explanation of language itself. Work such as that of Philip Lieberman (1984) comparing the evolution of the human, Neanderthal, and chimpanzee vocal tracts in terms of their usefulness for speech, tends to distract attention from the really interesting object of inquiry, namely language. Speech is only the *vehicle* of language. What we would like to be able to explain is the innate rich mental structuring that gives humans, and humans alone, the ability to acquire such complex (phonological, syntactic, morphological, and semantic) systems as French, Arabic, and Vietnamese. To use a computer analogy, the ears and vocal tract happen to be the peripheral input/output systems mainly used for human language (remember deaf sign languages, though), but we are interested in the central software, and ultimately the central hardware, all located in the brain, that make the human language machine run in such a complex way. Speech is in a sense social behavior, but consideration of speech alone sheds little light on its essential social aspect, communication.

One could imagine a very trivial theory that might be counted as a sociobiology of communication. This theory would take as its central question, Why is there communication?—just as sociobiology asks, and gives several interesting answers to, the question that puzzled Darwin, Why is there altruism? The problem of altruism was interesting and demanded ingenious answers because it seemed at first that it should not exist, as it would appear to be maladaptive to the individual. But communication poses no such initial problem. In general it is obvious that communication benefits the parties who engage in it, by the dissemination of potentially useful information about themselves, each other, and the environment. It would be surprising if communication did *not* exist; and indeed there are many species that have evolved various communication systems (bees, vervet monkeys, and whales, to name but a few). Mere communication is such a simple and broad idea that it hardly demands a theory, sociobiological or otherwise, to explain its repeated emergence in the course of evolution. If a sociobiological approach to the phenomena that interest linguists is to be developed, it will have to relate the *human propensity for the particular complex structures of language* to selective advantage. This is a far greater task than merely relating communication, an idea of very wide scope, to selective advantage.

(I will not pursue the matter here, but it seems possible that communication *presupposes* altruism. Generally speaking, despite the existence of lying and deception, communication within species takes place in a context of collaboration and friendly social relations. Communicating is like giving. Are there any communicative species lacking in altruistic behaviors?)

Any functionally oriented linguistics faces a significant problem of explaining just *how* making certain kinds of noises actually achieves communication (and is therefore advantageous). It can't be left to common sense to explain. Once we stand back and look at language objectively, it's actually pretty miraculous that our utterances have the (frequently successful) effects they do. The miraculous nature of communication through language comes out in two main ways: the *arbitrariness* of the connection between what is said and what is meant, and the sheer *versatility* of language systems in the vast scope and great subtlety of the messages they make available. I'll take up the matter of arbitrariness first.

Much communicative behavior typically involves an ingredient of arbitrariness, such as is present in the arbitrary relation between a word and its meaning. Certain gulls communicate aggression, not by any behavior we would regard as *naturally* aggressive, such as pecking at each other, but rather by plucking grass. The human smile is a *ritualized* gesture of amicability, not closely, or intimately, connected with its "meaning." That is, there is not the same intimate connection between the shape of the lips and amicability, as there is between the shape of the lips and, say, sucking or holding food in the mouth. This arbitrariness of connection between signal and meaning is present both in ritualized (typically innate) communicative behavior, and so-called conventionalized communicative behavior (typically learned).

The arbitrariness of the sign is problematical for functional theories of the most straightforward sort, because the connection between a tool or an organ and its function is not arbitrary. Classic sociobiological theories, such as that of inclusive fitness and reciprocal altruism, do not encounter this problem of arbitrariness, because they deal directly with the *effects,* for example, altruistic versus selfish, that behaviors can have, and typically don't need to spell out why particular behaviors have these effects. It is simply, and reasonably, regarded as obvious and natural, and not arbitrary, that taking the trouble to feed the young, for instance, is altruistic.

Communication benefits from the arbitrariness of the sign, because it provides for the creation of tool-like devices for achieving purposes for which no natural device exists. There exists no natural way to plant the idea of, say, a tiger, or a tree, or honey, into someone else's mind without actually drawing their attention to an object present in the immediate situation of the conversants. A particular *word* for the idea of some type of object, say a tree, is an artificial device that allows one to do just that. By uttering the sequence of sounds /triː/ "tree" I can insert the thought of a tree into your consciousness, even if we are in the middle of the Nullarbor Desert. It is also remarkable that the functioning of the sound–concept connection is *obligatory.* If a normal English speaker attends to the *word* /triː/, there is no way she can avoid the *concept* "tree" coming to mind. (To continue the tool analogy, a word is like a spade that starts to dig automatically as soon as you pick it up.)

Convention is not the right term to describe the social unanimity we find in a community's use of words. The existence of a convention normally implies that the parties involved have come to some deliberate agreement, or that there has been deliberate inculcation of the convention by teaching. For instance, when a family moves into a new house, someone will say, "Where shall we keep the cutlery?" and agreement follows that it will be kept in such-and-such a drawer, one of several that might equally well have served the purpose. Children later growing up in that household will be told the convention about "where the cutlery goes," probably with more detail added, for example, "the knives on the left, the forks in the middle, and the spoons to the right." But on the use of language, there is remarkably little deliberate agreement or teaching of this kind. Indeed, there is a traditional philosophical problem with regarding the use of language as having come about by convention, if by "convention" we mean the product of verbal agreement. Obviously, it takes prior agreement on what words mean to be able to come to any verbal agreement. And people can't come to a verbal agreement about what the most basic words are to be used for.

We have got to the position that elements of languages, such as their words and their grammatical constructions, are *like* tools in that they can be used for a (very important) purpose, namely getting ideas of remote situations into other people's heads, but that they are *unlike* ordinary tools, such as spades and knives, because some kind of social acceptance of their use is involved (hence the problem of communicating with foreigners). And this necessary social acceptance is *like* other conventions, such as how and when to shake hands, but the case of language is *unlike* any (other) case of convention-alized social behavior, both because of its complexity and because of the instinctive way, with little or no explicit negotiation or teaching, that a language comes to be shared by all members of the community. It appears, then, that individual humans have *something in them that disposes them naturally to make the arbitrary mental connections embodied in the basic building block of language,* the Saussurean sign. To the evidently significant extent that this structure serves social purposes, it can be said that a striking example of socially functional mental structure is a part of a human's biological heredity. (For more on this see Hurford 1989).

It may come as a surprise to nonlinguists that the theorists who have most stressed the biological innateness of language structure (such as Chomsky and Fodor) have also been the ones who have tended to disparage talk of language serving social, specifically communicative, functions. An unfortunate and misleading polarization between "biological formalists" and "social functionalists" has grown up in linguistic discussion over the past few decades, a false dichotomy that has only recently begun to be eroded. Scholars who have emphasized the *communicative* function of language have tended to *attack* the view that much of language structure is innate. They have located the causal mechanism relating function to structure in *cultural,* rather than biological, evolution. On the other hand, scholars, such as Chomsky, who have emphasized the biological basis of language structure, while acknowledging that functional explanations for this structure may be possible at the level of the evolution of the species, have been deliberately reticent in following up this possibility.

Chomsky's view is that the central empirical problem for linguistics is the "embryological" problem, accounting for the apparent miracle of language acquisition, whereby a complex "mental organ" (a speaker's tacit knowledge of his or her language, the basis of all his or her performance in it) develops. He appears to see no corresponding apparent miracle in the use of language for communication, which he downgrades (see, for example, Chomsky 1975, 55–77, and 1980, 229–30), as he generally downgrades the social dimension of language (see, for example, Chomsky 1975, 137–39, and 1986, 19–31). Jerry Fodor, rather surprisingly for one who holds many positions close to Chomsky's, expresses (in his 1979 book, *The Language of Thought*) the central problem for a theory of language as being the problem of how linguistic communication is possible. But in truth Fodor's work also concentrates hard on the individual-psychological aspects of language and pays little attention to its social aspect. In *my* view, the real long-term central problem for linguistics is to put together these two "central problems," Chomsky's of the innate language acquisition device, and Fodor's of how language serves communication. By investigating the structure of the LAD, or universal grammar, as generative grammarians do, and, in parallel, investigating how this structure serves communicative purposes (no easy task, as I have said), the basis can be laid for an explanation of the evolution of the device by natural selection. Formulating the ultimate task of linguistics in this way puts that task squarely in the category of a sociobiological theory of the evolution of a particularly interesting class of epigenetic rules.

STRAWS IN THE WIND

It is certain that investigating the natural selection pressures that could have given rise to the complex innate human Language Acquisition Device is a legitimate and challenging intellectual task. A small number of articles just now being published is beginning to chart out the territory. Some of the most recent of these are Newmeyer (1990), Pinker and Bloom (1990), and Hurford (1989, 1991, and forthcoming). Only one of these explicitly mentions sociobiology. So far, no subdiscipline by the name "sociobiology of language" exists. Some may even deny that it *could* exist. The choice of label is not ultimately important. If it could exist (as I believe it could), a sociobiology of language would have its own characteristic principles, theoretical terms, and flavor, many deriving from those already established in the mother discipline, linguistics, of which it is a natural and desirable extension.

18

Psychology

Charles Crawford

Nearly all psychologists would grant that the theory of evolution is the explanation for the origin of life that should be taught in high school science classes. Moreover, many psychologists have considerable enthusiasm for using the theory of evolution to help explain psychological phenomena. To them, its state of scientific development seems sufficient to provide some confidence in its use. It provides some answers to the provocative questions, Where did we come from? and What is the purpose of life? As a formal explanatory theory, Darwinism stands midway between the tightly organized theories of the physical sciences on the one hand and the metaphorical knowledge of the humanities on the other (a position many believe is also inhabited by psychology!). Many psychologists are attracted to evolutionary theory because, even after more than a hundred years of life, it has a radical aura about it; and many psychologists like to think of their science as a young and radical discipline.

Until recently, however, the theory of evolution provided few useful *constructs* for formulating detailed explanations of human and animal behavior. As a result, its use in inspiring the imagination of psychologists and in making explicit predictions about human behavior has met with considerable resistance.

In this chapter, I argue that concepts developed within the theory of evolution during the last twenty years can be of great value to the discipline of psychology. First I explain the concept of *adaptation* and discuss the value of proximate and ultimate causal analysis for psychology. Next I show how the psychologist's *repertoire of constructs* can be enhanced by three ideas: inclusive fitness, kin recognition, and reproductive value. Finally I turn to the topic of *learning* and the new "evolutionary psychology." I believe that these ideas not only can broaden psychologists' understanding of the causes of behavior, but can help relate psychology to other social and life sciences.

ADAPTATION

An adaptation is an anatomical structure, physiological process, or behavior pattern that enabled ancestral organisms to survive and reproduce in competition with other members of their species (Williams 1966). Some aspect of the ancestral social or physical environment, such as a change in climate, the arrival of a new predator, or a shortage of living space, posed a problem for ancestral organisms. A solution, perhaps thicker fur or altruistic helping, was needed. The theory of evolution explains how adaptations were formed through the process of natural selection. The concept of *adaptation* is thus the fulcrum of evolutionary theory because it enables us to understand how natural selection shaped solutions to problems posed by the ancestral physical and social environment of a species.

We are accustomed to thinking of physical features common to all members of a species, such as the eyes of eagles or the digestive processes of cattle, as examples of adaptations. However, until recently we were not accustomed to thinking of behaviors such as the cub-killing behavior of male lions (Schaller 1972) or love in humans (Barash 1979) as adaptations shaped by the ancestral environment. One reason is that behaviors are not as fixed as anatomical features. Behavioral adaptations often involve behaviors that are *contingent* on conditions in the environment. Hence, they may not appear to be characteristic of *all* members of the species.

All scorpionfly males, for example, possess three behavioral tactics for obtaining a mating with a female: (1) the male may present the female with a dead insect as a "nuptial gift," (2) he may substitute a proteinaceous mass as the nuptial gift, or (3) he may force a copulation (Thornhill 1980). The mating strategy actually employed depends upon the level of male–male competition that the male happens to encounter. Forced copulation is not seen in environments with a low level of male–male competition because, there, all males have access to resources for nuptial gifts. Experimentally, the resources available can be altered, and the tactic used is thus manipulated. This demonstrates that, in nature, the available resources determine which mating strategy will be used.

Male scorpionflies exhibit what I have called a *concurrently* contingent strategy: it depends upon current conditions in the environment (Crawford 1989). A *developmentally* contingent strategy, by contrast, is dependent upon conditions present during development. Digger bees, for example, have two mating strategies (Thornhill and Alcock 1983). They may compete for females as members of hovering masses of males that attempt to mate with females as they emerge from the ground (Alcock 1984). Alternatively, males may attempt to dig females out of the ground before they emerge. The strategy that a male uses, as an adult, depends upon the amount of food his mother placed in the nest with male eggs when she laid them.

I could give many other examples of concurrently and developmentally contingent strategies. However, these make the two important points: (1) that behavioral adaptations often provide *alternative behaviors* that depend upon either concurrent or past environmental conditions, and (2) that the study of biological adaptation provides us with a way of understanding how deliberate environmental manipulation can be used to change behavior. I will return to these points below, with regard to human behavior.

PROXIMATE AND ULTIMATE CAUSES: THE EXAMPLE OF SENSATION SEEKING

Usually when psychologists, anthropologists, and biologists study behavior they focus on its *proximate* explanations: the immediate factors, such as the internal physiology and current environmental stimuli, that produce a particular response. In contrast, evolutionary biologists are interested in *ultimate* explanations: the conditions of the biological, social, and physical environment that, on an evolutionary time scale, render certain traits adaptive and others nonadaptive (Mayr 1961). Consider hibernation in ground squirrels. The proximate explanation of hibernation is that current climatic conditions trigger physiological mechanisms to initiate it. The ultimate explanation is that climate, predator pressure, food supply, and other such forces, over an evolutionary time scale, make physiological mechanisms mediating hibernation beneficial for squirrels.

I believe that this distinction between proximate and ultimate causes can provide a sharper focus on the causes of behavior. Let me demonstrate this belief by discussing "sensation seeking." Zuckerman, Buchsbaum, and Murphy (1980) developed the concept of sensation seeking to help explain a variety of behaviors related to risk taking. Measures of sensation seeking correlate with risk taking in a number of situations, and relate to behavior variables including sexual experience, interest in new situations, social dominance, sociability, experience with drugs, playfulness, and psychopathy. When measures of sensation seeking are taken, men are found to score higher than women, and scores decline with age after age sixteen. In addition, there are many physiological correlates of sensation seeking, such as gonadal hormone levels and monoamine oxidase activity. These physiological correlates, along with the conditions in the environment that stimulate this behavior, may be considered the proximate causes of sensation seeking.

But what about the ultimate causes of the sex and age differences in sensation seeking? I suggest that they are related to benefits that males— but not females—are able to obtain from seeking numerous matings. The extent to which males can benefit from additional matings depends upon the minimal *amount of investment* males, relative to females, contribute to reproduction. In most species, including humans, the minimal investment in reproduction required from a female is considerably greater than that required from a male. Males (because they can invest less in each reproductive episode) can therefore benefit, more than females can, by seeking additional matings. Three elements must be considered in computing parental investment: (1) the cost of constructing a gamete, that is, the sperm or the egg (females usually invest much more in each gamete), (2) any additional parental effort per offspring after conception (females usually make the larger investment, such as in nutrition for the embryo), and (3) the effort or resources expended in obtaining or performing a mating that limit that individual's opportunity to compete for additional mates (males usually invest more; Thornhill and Alcock 1983). Examples that could be included in the third category are dowries and bride-prices in humans, and the nuptial gifts provided by some male insects, as well as the energy males may have to use in fighting off other males. The amount of investment in *each* of three areas influences the extent to which males and females can benefit from prolific matings.

Let us use these three factors in constructing a model for predicting species differences in sensation seeking. In species characterized by relatively low male parental investment after conception, but relatively high costs of *obtaining* mates, males are predicted to exhibit "risky" physiology, anatomy, and behavior, and, consequentially, to suffer higher mortality than females. Psychologists might call these males "sensation seekers." This model avoids the need for knowledge of the biochemistry or physiology of the species under consideration, or even of such things as emotions, motivations, and drives. Instead, it utilizes information about the *differences between the sexes* in parental investment, and resources exchanged for a mating, in order to predict sensation-seeking behavior (in a particular species).

Value of Ultimate Explanations

While the above distinctions may be interesting to zoologists who compare different species, of what value are ultimate explanations to psychologists interested in a *single* species, such as the human species? I believe the distinctions lead to many insights. A consideration of ultimate causation may help scientists (1) identify relevant variables for the development of evolutionary models and theories, (2) determine which variables ought to be considered causes and which ought to be considered effects, and (3) gain an understanding of the environmental factors that may alter a behavior. Let us see how each of these would work in the example of sensation seeking and its associated behaviors, within one species: our own.

First, with regard to identifying variables, recall my earlier remark that members of a given species may have evolved a *repertoire* of behaviors that *vary, adaptively,* in response to environmental conditions. These behaviors may depend upon current conditions in the environment or upon the conditions that were present during the individual's development. Imagine two groups of human males. The males in the first group have difficulty attracting mates because they lack social status and resources; they can increase their matings, and hence their fitness, by taking risks to obtain those items. The males in the second group who already possess resources and social status have a good chance of forming long-term bonds with females; they may attain greater fitness by pursuing a less risky tactic involving higher parental investment. The former are risk takers, and should score high on sensation-seeking traits, whereas the latter are expected to score lower on these measures. The risk-taking males are also expected to suffer greater mortality.

Second, with regard to distinguishing between causes and effects, let us reconsider the physiological correlates of sensation seeking. Psychologists have found raised levels of hormones such as testosterone in male sensation seekers. Thus it has been supposed that these levels "cause" the behavior. But in our model, the putative adaptations underlying sensation seeking evolved to deal with environmental variations (in respect to availability of matings). Therefore, these variations are likely to be an even more direct cause of sensation seeking than are differences in hormone levels.

Third, with regard to understanding how environmental factors alter human behavior, the case of sensation seeking is instructive. *If* it is true that environmental factors, rather than, say, hormones are a more direct cause of the behavior, we would predict that therapy involving training in social and technical skills, aimed at the acquisition of resources and status, would be more effective (and less invasive) in changing behaviors related to risk taking and sensation seeking than a more proximate biological therapy (such as altering the male's hormonal status.) This analysis is based on the assumption that adaptations that evolved to help ancestral males deal with varying conditions in their environment are

are still functioning, and that an understanding of the psychological mechanisms underlying these adaptations can help us understand how to modify some current behaviors.

Undoubtedly many psychologists prefer explanations that use proximate variables (Scarr 1985). For example, the concept of sensation seeking itself was originally derived from inspecting and analyzing observed data on proximate variables. Concepts developed in this way do have an intuitive and commonsense appeal, and may perform reasonably well as predictors within a particular context. However, they *lack the generality* required for psychologists desiring theories of behavior that are not situation and population specific. Unlike the natural sciences, which can call on theories such as classical mechanics, the theory of relativity, or the theory of evolution to guide the search for explanations, psychology has lacked a framework for guiding its search for more powerful explanatory theories of behavior. Evolutionary theory, which includes a consideration of ultimate causation, may provide such a framework.

ENRICHING THE PSYCHOLOGIST'S REPERTOIRE OF EXPLANATORY CONSTRUCTS

In this section I nominate three ideas from sociobiology that can enrich the psychologist's repertoire of explanatory constructs: inclusive fitness, kin recognition, and reproductive value. Following this I conjure up a scenario in which I use these insights simultaneously to help understand some of the problems in writing a will. Lastly in this section, I discuss what I call "pseudonormal" behavior and "pseudopathologies."

Inclusive Fitness and Helping Behavior

Although sociobiology has numerous beginnings, many of them in Darwin's work, many of us associate Hamilton's (1964) words with its actual beginning:

> The social behavior of a species evolves in such a way that in each distinct behavior-evoking situation the individual will seem to value his neighbor's fitness against his own according to the coefficients of relationship appropriate to that situation. (19)

Biological altruism—self-destructive behavior performed for the benefit of individuals other than offspring—had long been a problem, not only for ethical philosophers, but also for evolutionary biologists: it seemed to conflict with the notion that the number of progeny an individual leaves shapes the evolution of adaptations. As has been discussed earlier in this book, Hamilton was first to show how altruism can evolve. Although it reduces the reproductive fitness of the donor, altruism can evolve if it aids genetic kin, some of whom must inherit the helping allele from an ancestor they have in common with the donor.

The expanded notion of fitness, known as *inclusive fitness,* that follows from Hamilton's 1964 work is one of the most powerful concepts that sociobiology can offer psychologists for understanding helping and conflict behavior. Inclusive fitness is composed of two components: (1) an individual's *direct fitness,* that is, her or his personal reproductive success, stripped of the effect of actions of genetic kin; and (2) the individual's *indirect fitness,* that is her or his influence on the reproductive success of genetic kin, with the kin weighted by the degree of genetic relationship to the individual whose inclusive fitness is being considered (Grafen 1984, Crawford 1989). It has been used to help explain a variety of animal behaviors, including sterile worker castes in social insects (Hamilton 1964), coalition formation in primates (Baker and Estep 1985), and alarm calling in ground squirrels (Sherman 1980). For humans, inclusive fitness has been used to explain village fissioning in hunter-gatherer villages (Chagnon 1979b), infanticide (Hausfater and Hrdy 1984), family violence (Daly and Wilson 1987), and bequest behavior (Smith, Kish, and Crawford 1987).

Kin Recognition—and "Ethnic Harmony"

The second construct to be considered here is kin recognition. If social organisms have evolved the ability to direct their helping behavior to individuals sharing their genes, they must possess some mechanisms for recognizing these individuals. These mechanisms provide an important point of interface between psychology and evolutionary theory, and should therefore be of interest to psychologists. Possible mechanisms for kin recognition include spatial distribution (treating individuals in a prescribed geographic area as kin), association (treating frequent associates as kin), phenotype matching (treating individuals similar to oneself or similar to those one was raised with as kin), and recognition alleles (treating individuals with a particular "genetic marker" as kin). They have received attention from biologists (Holmes 1986, Waldman 1986) and psychologists (Rushton, Russell, and Wells 1984, 1985).

If kinship was an important aspect of the social organization of ancestral humans, then the *evolution of kin recognition mechanisms* can be expected to have occurred. These mechanisms may still be influencing our behavior, and understanding them may offer insight with respect to changing human behavior through social learning. Our solution to problems of behavior that may be influenced by kin recognition will be dependent upon the particular mechanism at work.

To illustrate this point, let us consider the problem of achieving ethnic harmony. If spatial proximity is an evolved cue for recognizing others as kin, then encouraging individuals of different ethnic groups to live together in the same geographic area may contribute to ethnic harmony. However, other kin recognition mechanisms may complicate the process. If persons similar to those with whom one was raised are identified as kin, then ethnically integrating schools starting at the preschool level, rather than the high school level, is more likely to lead to ethnic harmony. If our ancestors recognized as kin those who resembled themselves, then it may be necessary to encourage different ethnic groups to adopt similar accents, manners, customs, clothing, and so forth to increase ethnic harmony. However, if innately recognized signs evolved to discriminate between kin and nonkin among our ancestors, then producing ethnic harmony may, indeed, be difficult because social learning is not involved. I do not claim to know which of these mechanisms evolved in humans—perhaps all. The construct should help generate ideas for research as well as integrate evolutionary thinking with that of social psychologists and sociologists.

Reproductive Value

Reproductive value, our third construct, is defined as the *relative number of female offspring* expected to be born in the future to a female of a given age. It was developed in order to quantify an individual's value in an evolutionary context (Fisher 1930). For example, the number of female offspring still to be born to one thousand one-day-old females is less than the number to be born to one thousand one-year-old females because some of the one-day-olds will die before reaching one year of age. Hence, the one-year-old females have greater reproductive value than the one-day-old females. Similarly, a group of fifty-year-olds have less reproductive value than a group of twenty-five-year-olds because members of the latter group can expect to produce more offspring during the remainder of their lives. Thus, reproductive value rises during the early years of life, because of infant and juvenile mortality, peaks around the age of sexual maturity, and then begins a decline.

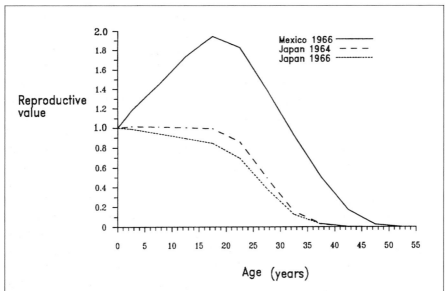

Figure 1. Reproductive value in three societies. The number of female offspring that females of various ages can be expected to produce during the remainder of their lives is plotted against maternal age. Reprinted from Crawford (1989).

The female reproductive value curves for Keyfitz and Flieger's (1971) data for two industrialized and developing nations are shown in figure 1. Note the difference between the curves for Japanese and Mexican women for the year 1966, reflecting the demographic differences between an industrialized society with a well-developed medical system, and a developing nation. Thus, depending on what group one belongs to, the same chronological age may have a different evolutionary meaning. Even within the same society, the curve may differ from year to year, as for Japan in 1964 and 1966. This seems to indicate that reproductive value curves reflect important ecological features of the populations they represent.

An essential assumption of the theory of evolution is that individuals evolve adaptations to maximize the number of their genes propagated (Barash 1982). Since reproductive value is a measure of the ability to propagate one's genes, it follows that mechanisms for *assessing and responding to the reproductive value* of oneself and others may have evolved to help individuals maximize their fitness. For example, it is not adaptive for humans to be sexually attracted to members of the opposite sex who are of low reproductive value, because mating with these individuals will not result in maximizing the number of offspring obtained.

The fact that humans respond to individual differences in physical and psychological characteristics, such as clear skin, bright eyes, vitality, and social skill, is well known. Such characteristics may be clues to reproductive value, and our emotional and cognitive reactions to them may be the products of natural selection. Therefore, considering reproductive value may contribute greatly to our understanding of human behavior. However, most psychologists appear to be unaware of its power.

Scenario: Writing Your Will

Let us consider an example to help clarify the relationships among inclusive fitness, kin recognition, and reproductive value. Suppose that you believe you have a gene for some desirable trait, such as behaving altruistically, and that you would like to do something to help its spread in the population, but that you are a childless individual who is past childbearing age. How might you choose the beneficiary of your estate in order to help propagate your gene? A consideration of your direct fitness is of no value, since you can no longer have children. However, considering your inclusive fitness, it is better for you to leave the estate to kin rather than non-kin because their offspring will have a fair chance of having your gene. By the same logic, it would serve your purpose better to leave the estate to your niece, with whom you share genes with probability 0.25, than to a cousin, with whom you share genes with probability 0.125. At the same time, however, ancestral kin-recognition mechanisms may be influencing whom you regard as kin. If spatial proximity is the kin recognition mechanism in action, you might be more likely to leave your estate to the niece who lives two blocks away from you than to the one who lives in another country. But if the mechanism is phenotype matching and the distant niece resembles you more, you may be inclined to name her as your beneficiary.

But these are not the only considerations you face. If both of your nieces are in their forties and unlikely to have any more children, it would serve your purpose better to bequeath the estate to a younger cousin, who is more likely to have children. But which cousin? If you are a citizen of a developing nation, such as Mexico, a consideration of your indirect reproductive value (which is a function of the direct reproductive values of your cousins) suggests that the estate should go to your fifteen-year-old cousin, rather than your one-week-old cousin. See figure 1 to verify this suggestion. However, if you are a citizen of a highly developed nation, such as Japan, the same considerations suggest that your estate should go to the one-week-old.

I devised this scenario to illustrate some of the factors that would have to be considered in developing an evolutionary model of bequest behavior. Similar considerations would be involved in developing models of other human behaviors, such as adoption or guardian choice. However, I leave the details of these examples to the reader's imagination.

Pseudonormal Behaviors and Pseudopathologies or Environmental Change and "Abnormal Behavior"

Evolutionary theory is concerned with understanding how various competing interests, such as those in the above hypothetical example, influenced the evolution of our cognitive and emotional systems. Our "ancestral" behaviors and their derivatives are often adequate in dealing with our current environment. There may be instances, however, when those behaviors lead us into courses of action that are not congruent with evolutionary expectations (Crawford and Anderson 1989). *Pseudonormal behaviors,* such as leaving one's estate to charity, or the adoption of unrelated children, are behaviors that are currently accepted and even encouraged, but that would have detracted from fitness among our ancestors. *Pseudopathologies,* such as extreme nepotism or male sexual harassment of women, are behaviors that would have contributed to ancestral fitness, but that, because of cultural change, have become unacceptable in our culture.

Because pseudonormal behaviors are at variance with evolved psychological mechanisms, they may be a continuing source of problems in our time. For example, it may be that a pseudonormal behavior, such as the disinheritance of close biological kin in favor of charity to unrelated individuals, will never feel comfortable or normal to most people, no matter how socially acceptable it may be. Similarly, even with extreme measures it may be difficult to completely eliminate pseudo-pathological behaviors such as nepotism or sexual harassment of women by men.

THE COSTS AND BENEFITS OF LEARNING

A final idea to be presented in this chapter has to do with evolutionary views on learning. Learning theory has been a major concern of twentieth-century psychology. The advantages of the flexibility and adaptability made possible by learning are well understood. However, less appreciated are their costs. Learning requires the development and maintenance of delicate neurological structures, which are costly in terms of the body's total energy. Moreover, animals may learn fitness-reducing information, as when a Norway rat or a human learns to avoid an edible food because on first contact it was tainted or associated with tainted food (Garcia, Hankins, and Rusiniak 1974). Some animals, including humans, may exploit learning by providing false information for others to learn (Alexander 1979). Given the costs associated with learning, the existence of completely general learning abilities in any species, including *Homo sapiens,* is unlikely.

Lumsden and Wilson (1981, 1983) argue that, because of the costs of learning, a species without genetic constraints on the learning of culture must *evolve toward having such constraints.* They note that a complex environment increases the likelihood that the individual will make fitness-reducing behavioral errors. Thus, the speed of the evolution of genetic constraints is related to the complexity of the environment. Through natural selection, they argue, the human mind has become equipped with specific *rules* and *principles* for learning about the world. Lumsden and Wilson point to a number of rules—such as brother–sister incest avoidance, the learning of color vocabularies, infant preferences for certain object shapes and arrangements, the development of facial recognition, fear of strangers, mother–infant bonding, and the acquisition of phobias—as examples of evolved constraints on learning. These epigenetic rules are the result of interactions between ancestral individuals and their social and biological environment.

Evolutionary Psychology

Evolutionary psychology is concerned with exploring the *naturally selected design features* of the mechanisms that control behavior. Cosmides and Tooby (1987) recently took up the challenge of developing a framework for it. In this framework, cognitive processes are the most essential proximate mechanisms. Cosmides (1985) developed the concept of "Darwinian algorithms," defining them as

> specialized learning mechanisms that organize experience into adaptively meaningful schemas or frames. When activated by appropriate environmental and proprioceptive information, these innately specified frame builders should focus attention, organize perception and memory, and call up specialized procedural knowledge that will lead to domain-appropriate inferences, judgments, and choices. (Cosmides and Tooby 1987, 286)

Cosmides and Tooby suggest that aggressive threat, mate choice, sexual behavior, pair bonding, parent–offspring conflict, friendship, disease avoidance, resource distribution, and social contracts are only a few of the domains of human activity regulated through Darwinian algorithms that evolved in response to ancestral problems. Note that Darwinian algorithms are not instructions on behavior; they are mental enabling mechanisms. The possible mechanisms of kin recognition I identified earlier could be examples of Darwinian algorithms.

Psychologists have tended to be leery of sociobiologists and evolutionary ecologists because of their concentration on ultimate or "why" questions at the expense of proximate or "how" questions. Cosmides and Tooby, however, are interested in the latter. Their work (1987) is ground-breaking because it establishes that use of the evolutionary approach in the study of proximate questions need not involve details of physiology and neurochemistry. Another fact is that psychologists using the theory of evolution in their work have, in the past, tended to concentrate their attention on emotion (for example, Plutchik 1980). Cosmides and Tooby (1987) have expanded the use of evolutionary theory in psychology by bringing it to bear on the fine structure of the mind. They have used it to make predictions concerning such things as social contracts.

Conclusion

Kerlinger (1966) defines a scientific theory as "a set of interrelated constructs (concepts), definitions, and propositions that presents a systematic view of phenomena by specifying relations among variables, with the purpose of explaining and predicting the phenomena" (11). Scientific theories exist in the imagination of scientists and are used to comprehend the phenomena of nature. Newton's laws of motion, Einstein's theory of relativity, and Darwin's theory of evolution by natural selection are such theories that have been developed to help explain the diversity of nature.

Social behavior is the phenomenon that sociobiologists and evolutionary psychologists wish to explain. However, by the above definition of a theory, sociobiology and evolutionary psychology are not yet so sufficiently developed that they can provide a comprehensive theory of social behavior. Kinship theory can tell us something about, for example, bequest behavior, adoption, nepotism, and infanticide—but it cannot tell us all there is to know about these things.

I believe that sociobiology can best be considered a collection of models within the field of evolutionary biology that can serve to inspire the imaginations of psychologists. The concepts of inclusive fitness and reproductive value derive from population biology. When they are integrated with the notion of kin-recognition mechanisms, as in my discussion of bequest behavior, the result is a model that psychologists can use to understand and predict a variety of social phenomena. Similar models could be developed in regard to many other behaviors. As these models grow in number, complexity, and subtlety, they will inform and stimulate our scientific imaginations and carry us toward a more comprehensive theory of behavior.

ABOUT THE CONTRIBUTORS

Editor's Note

The interdisciplinary style of this book is mirrored in the eclectic careers of many of the contributors. In order to give the reader more than the usual picture of the academics' degrees and publications, I invited each author to provide me with data about his or her interests and/or a mention of how or why he or she became involved with sociobiology.

John H. Beckstrom was a corporate lawyer in a Wall Street firm until 1966, when he became Professor of Law at Northwestern University Law School in Chicago, Illinois. He gives behavioral science seminars in both the Law School and the Anthropology Department and teaches estates and trusts at the Law School. He holds a J.D. (magna cum laude) from the University of Iowa, and an LL.M. from Harvard. He obtained an M.A. in African Studies from the University of London, where he was a Fulbright Postdoctoral Fellow. He led American and Ethiopian research teams that reported on Ethiopia's developing legal system, and directed an African Legal Studies Program at Northwestern University.

Beckstrom has coproduced and hosted five programs on the family revolution for the NBC-TV Knowledge Series. He first became aware of sociobiology by reading a *Time* magazine article about E. O. Wilson and Robert Trivers, and quickly realized that there were many implications for legal affairs. He is the author of *Sociobiology and the Law* (1985) and *Evolutionary Jurisprudence* (1989).

In 1983 he won the New Orleans Mardi Gras Marathon for men over fifty with a time of two hours and fifty-five minutes.

J. Gary Bernhard obtained a B.A. in English literature in 1967 at Brigham Young University, Utah, an M.A. from the University of California at Los Angeles, and an Ed.D. from the

University of Massachusetts in 1984. He is currently Director of the University Without Walls, a degree program for nontraditional students at the University of Massachusetts in Amherst. He has managed an on-site degree program at the General Motors Plant in Framingham, Massachusetts, and has directed an alternative school for high school dropouts. His investigation into the relationship between the "human learning adaptation" and formal education resulted in a book, *Primates in the Classroom: An Evolutionary Perspective on Children's Education.* (1988)

"As a manager," Bernhard says, "I often wondered why large, hierarchical organizations were so poorly matched to human needs, and why so many of my working adult students reported anger and anxiety about their work." He now believes that some answers can be found in evolutionary biology. He and Kalman Glantz have just completed *Staying Human in the Organization,* a book of management theory.

Laura Betzig holds a Ph.D. in anthropology from Northwestern University and is currently a member of the Department of Biology, and of the Evolution and Human Behavior Program at the University of Michigan, Ann Arbor. She is the author of *Despotism and Differential Reproduction: a Darwinian View of History* and coeditor, with Monique Burgerhoff Mulder and Paul Turke, of *Human Reproductive Behavior: a Darwinian Perspective.*

Betzig notes, "My main empirical interest is in politics. Since studying under Richard Alexander in 1974, my theoretical interest has been Darwinian." Betzig has looked at politics as reproductive competition in comparative studies of over a hundred societies, in field studies on the Western Pacific islands of Ifaluk and Yap, and in historical studies of Europe and six ancient civilizations. She is now working on a book on the rise of democracy and monogamy in the West.

Laura Betzig also writes poetry.

John Chandler was educated at the University of Melbourne and is currently Senior Lecturer in Philosophy at the University of Adelaide in South Australia. He has been Visiting Scholar at the University of Delaware. His main interests are in moral and social philosophy. He has published on metaethics, the divine command theory of morality, feminist epistemologies, and "killing and letting die."

Chandler was among the first philosophers to incorporate sociobiology into his teaching of ethics. In 1981 he established an interdisciplinary and intercollegiate course with a biologist and philosopher from neighboring Flinders University. On the University of Adelaide campus he is best known as a clarifier of ideas at that school's Friday afternoon public seminars in philosophy, and as a philosophical commentator on affirmative action.

Charles Crawford is Professor of Psychology at Simon Fraser University in Burnaby, British Columbia. He was educated at the University of Alberta and McGill University. He studied psychology, measurement, and statistics at these institutions, and devoted himself to research and teaching in multivariate analysis and human intelligence for a number of years.

During the 1970s he became weary of the traditional approach being taken by psychologists. He spent a year at the Institute of Behavior Genetics at the University of Colorado learning about the relation between heredity and environment. "During this time," he says "I discovered sociobiology and found it more exciting than behavioral genetics." His current work concerns the evolutionary significance of human psychopathology, and sex allocation in animals and humans.

Crawford is particularly interested in helping psychologists learn how they can use the theory of evolution by natural selection in their work. He is coeditor, with Martin Smith and Dennis Krebs, of *Sociobiology and Psychology: Ideas, Issues, and Applications.*

Robert H. Frank received his B.S. in mathematics from Georgia Tech in 1966, then taught math and science for two years as a Peace Corps Volunteer in rural Nepal. He received his M.A. in statistics from the University of California at Berkeley in 1971, and his Ph.D. in economics in 1972, also from Berkeley. He is currently Professor of Economics at Cornell University, where he has taught since 1972. During a leave of absence from Cornell, he served as chief economist for the Civil Aeronautics Board from 1978 to 1980. He has published on a variety of subjects, including price and wage discrimination, public utility pricing, the measurement of unemployment spell lengths, and the distributional consequences of direct foreign investment.

Frank's recent research has focused on rivalry and cooperation in economic and social behavior. His books include *Choosing the Right Pond: Human Behavior and the Quest for Status* (1985), *Passions Within Reason: the Strategic Role of the Emotions* (1988), and *Microeconomics and Behavior* (1991). He attributes his interest in behavioral biology in part to his experience of having grown up as an adopted child.

Biruté M. F. Galdikas has been studying wild orangutans at Tanjung Puting National Park in Central Indonesian Borneo for twenty years. Her research was initiated with the support and encouragement of the late Louis S. B. Leakey. She also teaches primate behavior and human evolution at Simon Fraser University in Burnaby, British Columbia, Canada, one semester per year. She is married to Pak Bohap bin Jalan and has three children, Binti, Frederick, and Filomena Jane.

Galdikas is president of the Orangutan Foundation, based in Los Angeles, California. Orangutan means "People of the Forest" in the Malay language. That species is in grave danger of extinction because its sole habitat, tropical rain forest, is being destroyed at the rate of thousands of acres per day. The Foundation was established by a small number of laypeople and scientists to support the study and understanding both of orangutans and of the rain forests of Indonesia.

Kalman Glantz, Ph.D., is a practicing psychologist at a community mental health center in Greater Boston. From 1977 to 1985 he taught social sciences at Lesley College, Cambridge. At the Hebrew University in Jerusalem he studied political science and history with J. L. Talmon, author of *The Origins of Totalitarian Democracy*. At the Sorbonne in Paris, he studied sociology and economics with Raymond Aron, and was an assistant to Aron for two years at the Ecole Nationale de Sciences Politiques and the Centre European de Sociologie.

In 1988 Glantz presented a paper, "Reciprocity in Psychotherapy," to the first Evolutionary Psychology and Psychiatry Conference and, in 1989, "Piagetian Cognition in Evolutionary Perspective" to the first meeting of the Human Behavior and Evolutionary Society. With John Pearce, M.D., he has published *Exiles from Eden: Psychotherapy from an Evolutionary Perspective* (1989). He is thus at the cutting edge of more than one application of evolutionary theory. His interest in management theory came from his academic involvement with economics, as well as from the fact that in his private practice many of his patients' problems center on the workplace. With J. Gary Bernhard, he is co-author of *Staying Human in the Organization,* soon to be published.

Robert Hogan received his Ph.D. in psychology from the University of California, Berkeley. From 1967 to 1982 he was Professor of Psychology and Social Relations at the Johns Hopkins University in Baltimore. From 1982 to 1988 he was McFarlin Professor and Chair of the Department of Psychology at the University of Tulsa, Oklahoma. He is currently Director of Research at the Tulsa Psychiatric Center and Professor of Psychology at the University of Tulsa. He was the first editor of the Personality Section of the *Journal of Personality and Social Psychology.* From the outset of his career Hogan has consistently advocated interpreting personality psychology from an evolutionary perspective, in the tradition of Freud and William McDougall. Hogan is author of *Personality Theory* (1976) and coeditor with W. H. Jones of *Perspectives in Personality* (1985).

Jim Hurford is Professor of General Linguistics at the University of Edinburgh. He received his Ph.D. in 1967, from the University of London, for a detailed phonetic study of the speech of three generations in a family of Cockneys. Since then, his academic interests have moved up through phonological theory and transformational grammar. His 1975 book, *The Linguistic Theory of Numerals,* is a generative treatment of the exotic numeral systems of a number of languages. He collaborated with an applied linguist, Ben Heasley, to write a best-selling textbook on semantics, *Semantics: a Coursebook* 1983), which has been translated into Spanish and Hebrew.

Combining his long interest in numerals with a philosophical interest in the psychological and social bases of language, Hurford published *Language and Number* in 1987. He notes, "My current work on modeling the origins and evolution of language, involving sociobiological approaches, stems from an abiding interest in the biological and social factors that interact to give human language its richly complex structure."

William Irons is Professor of Anthropology at Northwestern University, in Evanston, Illinois. He grew up in Port Huron, Michigan, on the Canadian border. After serving in the U.S. Army, he took his bachelor's and doctoral degrees at the University of Michigan. He has also studied at the London School of Economics and is a fellow of the American Association for the Advancement of Science.

Since beginning his first fieldwork in Iran in 1965, he has published many ethnographic reports of the Turkmen population and is coeditor, with Neville Dyson-Hudson, of *Perspectives on Nomadism* (1972). He is fluent in both Persian and Turkmen and hopes to go back to Iran. Among sociobiologists, Irons is known for his emphasis on hypothesis testing in the field. He and Napoleon Chagnon coedited the first volume of sociobiological anthropology in 1979, entitled *Evolutionary Biology and Human Social Behavior.*

Irons is married to Marjorie Rogasner and is the father of Julie and Marybeth Irons. He is a Sunday school teacher in the Unitarian Church and lists among his activities "gardening, clay sculpting, and reading about World War II." He mentions that he is "very attached to current canine companion, Sebastian (of unknown breed)."

Regina Karpinskaya is the head of the Department of Philosophy of Biology at the Institute of Philosophy of the USSR in Moscow. She graduated from both the Faculty of Philosophy and the Faculty of Biology at Moscow University, and holds the title Professor and Doctor of Science. She has published four books and over a hundred papers. Among her book titles are *Philosophical Aspects of Molecular Biology* and *Biology and World Outlook* (published in Russian).

Karpinskaya comments, "I am interested in sociobiology because I consider that the problems of human being are the central ones in the philosophy of biology." Among her non-academic pursuits she lists "first of all mountain skiing, and at home—cooking and knitting."

Douglas Kenrick is Professor of Environmental Psychology at Arizona State University at Tempe. He received his Ph.D. in social psychology at Arizona State in 1976, and was an assistant professor at Montana State University for four years before returning to Arizona. His interest in sociobiology began in 1975, when he read Jane Lancaster's *Primate Behavior and the Emergence of Human Culture* "as an attempt to avoid studying for doctoral exams." However, he found the topic less of a distraction than he had hoped, since the book seemed rich in potential hypotheses relevant to social psychology.

Kenrick's main research interests now focus on integrating psychological and evolutionary models to develop empirical predictions regarding personality traits and human mate preferences. He has published on these topics in the *Journal of Personality and Social Psychology*, the *Review of Personality and Social Psychology*, and the *Journal of Personality*. He has also written theoretical papers on personality that have appeared in the *American Psychologist* and *Psychological Review*.

Charles J. Lumsden, Ph.D. is Professor of Medicine at the University of Toronto, Ontario, Canada. He received all his degrees from that university, in theoretical physics. In his late twenties, when the sociobiology controversy was raging, he undertook to design a model that could link the alleged genetic control of human behavior with human thought, free will, and culture. Throughout 1979 and 1980, he and E. O. Wilson labored together, more or less around the clock, to incorporate research from psychology into a theory of gene–culture coevolution. The result was their publication of *Genes, Mind, and Culture: the Coevolutionary Process* in 1981, and *Promethean Fire* in 1983. The latter attempts to trace the evolution of human cognition.

Lumsden's main interest continues to be in the relations between biology and cultural history. He is thus concerned with mental processes and their origin, and also with the spiritual realm of art and religion. With C. Scott Findlay he coauthored *The Creative Mind* (1985), which analyzes, among other things, artistic and scientific genius. Recently, he has written about the sociobiology of other intelligences in the universe. Lumsden likes to collect reproductions of ancient pottery, particularly from the Greek classical period.

Roger D. Masters earned a B.A. (summa cum laude) at Harvard in 1955 and a Ph.D. at the University of Chicago in 1961, where he studied under Leo Strauss and Joseph Cropsey. He is currently Professor of Government at Dartmouth College in Hanover, New Hampshire. From 1961 through 1967 he taught at Yale, and from 1969 to 1971 served as U.S. Cultural Attaché to France. His works include *The Political Philosophy of Rousseau* (1968) and editions of Rousseau's *First and Second Discourses* (1964), *Social Contract* (1978), and *Dialogues* (1990).

Over the last twenty years, Masters has written widely on contemporary biology and human political life. A distillation of this work, *The Nature of Politics,* was published in 1989. He serves on the Executive Council of the Association for Politics and the Life Sciences and the Advisory Board of the Gruter Institute for Law and Behavioral Research. Since 1970 he has been Editor of the "Biology and Social Life" section of *Social Science Information,* an international journal sponsored by UNESCO.

Mary Maxwell received a B.A. in sociology from Emmanuel College, Boston, and a Master of Liberal Arts degree from the Johns Hopkins University, specializing in the history of ideas. In 1976, her psychology teacher at Hopkins, Robert Hogan, recommended that she read E. O. Wilson's newly published *Sociobiology.* "Over the next few years," she says, "I was constantly amazed at the vehement rejection of sociobiology on American campuses. In 1984 I published *Human Evolution: a Philosophical Anthropology* partly to demonstrate that the evolutionary view can support many humanistic ideas."

Maxwell earned a Ph.D. in politics at the University of Adelaide, where she was Tutor in the International Relations course and, in 1987–88, Vice-President of the Australian

Institute of International Affairs in South Australia. Since 1988 she has lived in Abu Dhabi where her husband teaches pediatrics at the University of the United Arab Emirates. She is the author of *Morality among Nations,* and *Moral Inertia: Ideas for Social Action.* She is now editing a book to be entitled *That's Politics.*

Maxwell is a regular reviewer of books, both in print and on radio; she also conducts a children's choir.

Randolph M. Nesse, M.D., is Associate Professor of Psychiatry at the University of Michigan, in Ann Arbor. He is also Division Director for Ambulatory Care and Associate Director of the Anxiety Disorders Program there. For five years he ran the Psychiatry Residency Training Program, located at University Hospital, Ann Arbor. He is a member of the University of Michigan's Evolution and Human Behavior program, which coordinates interdisciplinary studies involving sociobiology.

Nesse was a leading force in the founding of the Human Behavior and Evolution Society in 1989 and serves as its 1990–91 President. He is also Director of Psychiatry and Evolutionary Psychobiology Project, which stimulates research in this area. He also enjoys windsurfing and playing the violin.

Vernon Reynolds read anthropology at University College, London, and obtained a doctorate in that subject from London University in 1972, and an M.A. from Oxford. He is presently a Lecturer in Physical Anthropology in Oxford University's Department of Biological Anthropology, and a Fellow of Magdalen College. He teaches such courses as Human Variation and Primate Behavior. He has studied energy expenditure in daily activities of various human groups, and the effects of deforestation on villagers in North India.

Reynolds is best known for his eminently readable book *The Apes* (1967). In 1976 he published *The Biology of Human Action,* and in 1983 he coauthored *The Biology of Religion* with R. E. S. Tanner. He is the coeditor (with Vincent Falger and Ian Vine) of *The Sociobiology of Ethnocentrism* (1987). He writes, "My interest in religion goes back a long way, in fact I decided to study anthropology to find out more about religion. My swerve towards Darwinian ideas and on to sociobiology is a natural progression from an interest in religion. It is first causes— 'origins of humanity,' 'Does God exist?'—questions like that that underlie one's direction of study."

He is currently observing and conserving chimpanzees in the Budongo Forest of Uganda.

Michael Ruse obtained his Ph.D. in philosophy at the University of Bristol in 1970 with the thesis topic "The Nature of Biology." Since that time he has written extensively on many aspects of the philosophy of biology and is the founder and editor of the journal *Biology and Philosophy.* He is Professor in both the Department of Philosophy and the Department of Zoology at University of Guelph, in Ontario, Canada, and is a Fellow of the Royal Society of Canada.

Among the nine books Ruse has authored are *Taking Darwin Seriously* (1986), *Homosexuality: A Philosophical Inquiry* (1988), and *Molecules to Men* (1991). In 1981 he took part in the Arkansas Court case, which ruled that schools were not required to give "equal time" to creationism when teaching the theory of evolution. In 1986, he and E. O. Wilson jointly published the article "Morality as Applied Science" in the journal *Philosophy.* In addition to his academic assignments, Ruse is coping with fatherhood of a very young family.

Pierre L. van den Berghe is Professor of Anthropology and Sociology at the University of Washington in Seattle. He was born in Zaire (then the Belgian Congo). According to his autobiography, *Stranger in Their Midst* (1989), he developed a rebellious streak at the age of two that never left him, and which perhaps accounts for his thriving on sociobiology at a time when it was widely rejected.

Van den Berghe received a classical education in wartime Belgium and entered Stanford as an undergraduate in sociology. Further studies took place at the Sorbonne, and at Harvard where he received his Ph.D. His real education, however, has occurred largely through his immersion in a number of cultures. He and his family have resided in Nigeria, Kenya, South Africa, Mexico, Peru, Bolivia, and elsewhere.

Much of his research has been on ethnic relations within those countries, on *apartheid,* and on inequality in general.

Among van den Berghe's many books, one in particular— *The Ethnic Phenomenon* (1981)—combines his erudition in ethnography, history, race relations, Marxist economic theory, and sociobiology. His most recent work is *State Violence and Ethnicity.*

Johan M. G. van der Dennen is a researcher at the Polemological Institute of the University of Groningen, the Netherlands. He notes, "The name 'polemological' is derived from the Greek 'polemos,' which means 'struggle' or 'conflict' generally, and 'war' specifically. In the Anglo-American world this field of research is better known as 'Peace Research,' though 'War Research' would be more appropriate. It could be described as research into the causes and correlates of war and the conditions and corollaries of peace."

Van der Dennen's main interest is in the origin and evolution of human primitive warfare. He has extensively published on conflict, ethnocentrism, aggression, sexual violence, political violence, and primitive and contemporary war—and has computerized a file of over one hundred thousand titles on these subjects. His latest publications are "Primitive War in Evolutionary Perspective" in (van Hooff 1990) and several contributions in *Sociobiology and Conflict* (1990), of which he is the coeditor with Vincent Falger. He is an officer of the European Sociobiological Society, and welcomes new applications for membership.

Paul Vasey received a B.A. (Honors) degree in anthropology from the University of Alberta, Canada. Following this, he studied capuchin monkeys at Dr. Linda Fedigan's field site in Santa Rosa National Park, Costa Rica. Currently he is completing a graduate degree with specialization in primatology at Simon Fraser University under the supervision of Dr. Biruté Galdikas. His research involves a comparative analysis of the feeding ecology of two species—orangutan and gibbon. He is attempting to isolate possible variables influencing the unusual increase in brain per body weight witnessed in the pongids.

Vasey has worked in a bakery in Tunisia and is interested in film theory and criticism. He is twenty-four.

BIBLIOGRAPHY

Ainsworth, J. D., M. C. McBlehar, and E. Waters (1978) *Patterns of Attachment: A Psychological Study of the Strange Situation.* Hillsdale, N.J.: Erlbaum.

Alcock, J. (1984) *Animal Behavior: An Evolutionary Approach.* 3rd ed. Sunderland, Mass: Sinaur.

Alexander, Richard D. (1974) The Evolution of social behavior. *Annual Review Ecology and Systematics,* 5:325-383.

Alexander, Richard D. (1979) *Darwinism and Human Affairs.* Seattle: University of Washington Press.

Alexander, Richard D. (1987) *The Biology of Moral Systems.* Hawthorne, N.Y.: Aldine.

Alexander, Richard D. (1990) Epigenetic rules and Darwinian algorithms. *Ethology and Sociobiology,* 11, in press.

Alexander, Richard D., and D. W. Tinkle (1968) A comparative review. *Bioscience,* 18:245-248.

Alland, Alexander, Jr. (1989) Affect and aesthetics in human evolution. *Journal of Aesthetics and Art Criticism,* 47:1-14.

Allen, E., and members of the Sociobiology Study Group of Science for the People (1976) Sociobiology—another biological determinism. *Bioscience,* 26:182-186.

Altmann, S. A., and J. Walters (1978) Book review of "Kin selection in the Japanese monkey." *Man,* 13:324-325.

Anderson, Stephen (1985) Inflectional morphology. In Timothy Shopen, ed., *Language Typology and Syntactic Description, III: Grammatical Categories and the Lexicon,* 150-221. Cambridge: Cambridge University Press.

Andreski, S. (1954) *Military Organization and Society.* London: Routledge and Kegan Paul.

Angst, W., and D. Thommen (1977) New data and discussion of infant killing in Old World monkeys and apes. *Folia Primatologica,* 27:198-229.

Ardrey, Robert (1961) *African Genesis.* New York: Atheneum.

Argyris, C. (1964) *Integrating the Individual and the Organization.* New York: Wiley.

Argyris, C. (1968) Being human and being organized. *Transaction,* 1(1):5-14.

Argyris, C. (1985) *Strategy, Change and Defensive Routines.* Marshfield, Mass.: Pittman.

Asser, C. (1953) Handleiding Tot De Beoefening Van Het Nederlands Burgerlijk Recht. Vijfde Deel-van Bewijs. 238-44.

Axelrod, Robert R. (1984) *The Evolution of Cooperation.* New York: Basic Books.

Axelrod, Robert R., and William D. Hamilton (1981) The evolution of cooperation. *Science,* 211:1390-1396.

Ayala, Francisco J. (1987) The biological roots of morality. *Biology and Philosophy,* 2:235-252.

Badcock, C. R. (1986) *The Problem of Altruism: Freudian-Darwinian Solutions.* New York: Blackwell.

Badcock, C. R. (1990) *Oedipus in Evolution: A New Theory of Sex.* Oxford: Blackwell.

Baer, Darius, and Donald L. McEachron (1982) A review of selected sociobiological principles: Application to hominid evolution: I. The development of group social structure. *Journal of Social and Biological Structures,* 5(1):69-90.

Bagehot, William. (1884) *Physics and Politics: Thoughts on the Application of the Principles of "Natural Selection" and "Inheritance" to Political Society.* 2nd ed. 1884. New York: Appleton.

Baker, S. C., and D. Q. Estep (1985) Kinship and affiliative behavior patterns in a captive group of Celebes black apes (*Macaca nigra*). *Journal of Comparative Psychology,* 99:356-360.

Balikci, Asen (1970) *The Netsilik Eskimo.* Garden City, N.J.: Natural History Press.

Barash, D. P. (1979) *The Whisperings Within*. New York: Harper and Row.

Barash, David P., and Judith E. Lipton (1985)—Sociobiology. In H. I. Kapland and B. T. Sadock, eds., *Comprehensive Textbook of Psychiatry*. 4th ed., 70-77. Baltimore: Williams and Wilkins.

Barkow, Jerome H. (1977) Conformity to ethos and reproductive success in two Hausa communities: An empirical evaluation. *Ethos*, 5:409-425.

Barkow, Jerome (1989) Overview. *Ethology and Sociobiology*, 10:1-11.

Barnard, Chester (1968) *The Functions of the Executive*. 2nd ed. Cambridge, Mass: Harvard University Press.

Barrett, Paul (1986) Influential ideas: A movement called "Law and Economics" sways legal circles. *The Wall Street Journal*. 4 Aug.:1 and 16.

Beckstrom, John (1981) Sociobiology and interstate wealth transfers. *Northwestern University Law Review*, 76:216-270.

Beckstrom, John (1985a) *Sociobiology and the Law*. Champaign: University of Illinois Press.

Beckstrom, John (1985b) Behavioral research on aid-giving that can assist lawmakers while testing scientific theory. *Journal of Contemporary Health Law and Policy*, 25:25-37.

Beckstrom, John (1989) *Evolutionary Jurisprudence*. Champaign: University of Illinois Press.

Betzig, L., M. Borgerhoff Mulder, and P. Turke, eds., (1988) *Human Reproductive Behaviour*. Cambridge: Cambridge University Press.

Betzig, Laura (1982) Despotism and differential reproduction: A cross cultural correlation of conflict asymmetry, hierarchy, and degree of polygyny. *Ethology and Sociobiology*, 3:209-221.

Betzig, Laura (1986) *Despotism and Differential Reproduction: A Darwinian View of History*. Hawthorne, N.Y.: Aldine.

Betzig, Laura (1988) Redistribution: Equity or exploitation? In *Human reproductive behaviour*. See Betzig et al. 1988.

Betzig, Laura (1989) Rethinking human ethology: A response to some recent critiques. *Ethology and Sociobiology*, 10:315-324.

Betzig, Laura (1990) Why monogamy? *Behavioral and Brain Sciences*, in press.

Betzig, Laura (1991) Of human bonding: Cooperation or exploitation? In A. Harcourt and F. de Waal, eds., *Cooperation in Competition in Animals and Humans*. Oxford: Oxford University Press.

Betzig, Laura, and S. Weber (1990) Polygyny in American politics. *Human Nature*, 2, in press.

Bigelow, Robert (1969) *The Dawn Warriors; Man's Evolution Towards Peace*. Boston: Little Brown.

Blurton Jones, N. G. (1976) Growing points in ethology: Another link between ethology and the social sciences? In P.P.G. Bateson and R.A. Hinde, eds., *Growing Points in Ethology*. Cambridge: Cambridge University Press.

Boesch, C., and H. Boesch (1989) Hunting behavior of wild chimpanzees in the Tai National Park. *American Journal of Physical Anthropology*, 78:547-573.

Boggess, James (1980) Intermale relations and troop male membership changes in langurs *Presbytis entellus* in Nepal. *International Journal of Primatology*, 1:233-274.

Boone, James (1988) Parental investment, social subordination, and population processes among the 15th and 16th century Portuguese nobility. In *Human reproductive behaviour*. See Betzig et al. 1988.

Borgerhoff Mulder, M. (1985) Adaptation and evolutionary approaches to anthropology. *Man*, 22:25-41.

Borgerhoff Mulder, Monique (1987) On cultural and reproductive success. *American Anthropologist*, 89(3): 617-634.

Borgerhoff Mulder, Monique (1988a) Kipsigis bridewealth payments. In L. Betzig, M. Borgerhoff Mulder, and P. Turke, eds., *Human Reproductive Behavior*, 65-82. Cambridge: Cambridge University Press.

Borgerhoff Mulder, Monique (1988b) Reproductive success in three Kipsigis cohorts. In T.H. Clutton-Brock, ed., *Reproductive Success*, 419-435. Chicago: University of Chicago Press.

Borgerhoff Mulder, Monique (In press) Human behavioral ecology: studies in foraging and reproduction. In J. R. Krebs and N. B. Davies, eds., *Behavioral Ecology*. 3rd ed. London: Blackwell Scientific.

Bornstein, Marc H. (1984) Developmental psychology and the problem of artistic change. *Journal of Aesthetics and Art Criticism,* 43:131-145.

Bourne, P. (1970) Military psychiatry and the Vietnam experience. *American Journal of Psychiatry,* 127:481-488.

Bowlby, John (1969) *Attachment and Loss: Volume I, Attachment.* New York: Basic Books.

Bowler, P. J. (1976) *Fossils and Progress.* New York: Science History.

Boyd, R., and P. J. Richerson (1985) *Culture and the Evolutionary Process.* Chicago: Chicago University Press.

Brewer, M.B., and L.N. Lui (1989) The primacy of age and sex in the structure of person categories. *Social Cognition,* 7:262-274.

Buck, R., R. Parke, and M. Buck (1970) Skin conductance, heart rate, and attention to the environment in two stressful situations. *Psychonomic Science,* 18:95-96.

Buss, D. H., and W. R. Voss (1971) Evaluation of four methods for estimating the milk yield of baboons. *Journal of Nutrition,* 101:901-910.

Buss, D. M. (1984) Evolutionary biology and personality psychology: Toward a conception of human nature and individual differences. In *Sociobiology and Psychology: Ideas, Issues, and Applications.* See Crawford et al. 1987.

Buss, D. M. (1989) Sex differences in human mate preferences: Evolutionary hypotheses tested in 37 cultures. *Behavioral and Brain Sciences,* 12(1):1-49.

Busse, C., and W. J. Hamilton (1981) Infant carrying by male chacma baboons. *Science,* 212:1281-1283.

Campbell, Donald (1975) On the conflicts between biological and social evolution and between psychology and moral tradition. *American Psychologist,* 30:1103-26.

Caplan, Arthur L., ed. (1978) *The Sociobiology Debate.* New York: Harper and Row.

Carneiro, Robert L. (1970) A theory of the origin of the state. *Science,* 169:733-738.

Carpenter, C. R. (1942) Sexual behavior of free-ranging rhesus monkeys, *Macaca mulatta,* 1: Specimens, procedures, and behavioural characteristics of estrus. *Journal of Comparative Psychology,* 33:113-142.

Caton, Hiram, and Frank Salter (1988) *A Bibliography of Bio-social Science*. Brisbane, Australia: St. Albans Press.

Cavalli-Sforza, L. L., and M. W. Feldman (1978) Darwinian selection and "altruism." *Theoretical Population Biology*, 14:268-280.

Certoma, G. (1985) *The Italian Legal System*. London: Butterworths.

Chagnon, Napoleon A., and William Irons, eds. (1979) *Evolutionary Biology and Human Social Behavior: An Anthropological Perspective*. North Scituate, Mass.: Duxbury Press.

Chagnon, Napoleon A. (1975) Genealogy, solidarity, and relatedness: Limits to local group size and patterns of fissioning in an expanding population. *Yearbook of Physical Anthropology*, 19:95-110.

Chagnon, Napoleon A. (1979a) Mate competition, favoring close kin, and village fissioning among the Yanomamo Indians. In *Evolutionary Biology and Human Social Behavior*. See Chagnon and Irons 1979. North Scituate, Mass.: Duxbury Press.

Chagnon, Napoleon A. (1979b) Is reproductive success equal in egalitarian societies? In *Evolutionary Biology and Human Social Behavior*. See Chagnon and Irons 1979. North Scituate, Mass.: Duxbury Press.

Chagnon, Napoleon A. (1988) Life histories, blood revenge, and warfare in a tribal population. *Science*, 239:985-992.

Chagnon, Napoleon A., and Paul E. Bugos (1979) Kin selection and conflict: An analysis of a Yanomamo ax fight. In *Evolutionary Biology and Human Social Behavior*. See Chagnon and Irons 1979.

Chagnon, Napoleon A., Mark V. Flinn, and Thomas F. Melancon (1979) Sex ratio variation among the Yanomamo Indians. In *Evolutionary Biology and Human Social Behavior*. See Chagnon and Irons 1979.

Chalmers, N. R. (1972) Comparative aspects of early infant development in some captive cercopithecines. In F.E. Poirier, ed., *Primate Socialization*. New York: Random House.

Chamberlain, Houston S. (1911) The *Foundations of the Nineteenth Century*. (Trans. of 1899 German original.) London: Lane.

Chamie, J. (1981) *Religion and Fertility: Arab Christian Muslim Differentials*. Cambridge: Cambridge University Press.

Chance, Michael R. A. (1976) The organization of attention in groups. In M. von Cranach, ed., *Methods of Inference from Animal to Human Behavior*. The Hague: Mouton.

Chomsky, Noam (1968) *Language and Mind*. New York: Harcourt, Brace and World.

Chomsky, Noam (1975) *Reflections on Language*. Glasgow: Fontana/ Collins.

Chomsky, Noam (1980).*Rules and Representations*. Oxford: Blackwell.

Chomsky, Noam (1982) *The Generative Enterprise: A Discussion with Riny Huybregts and Henk van Riemsdijk*. Dordrecht, The Netherlands: Foris.

Chomsky, Noam (1986) *Knowledge of Language: Its Nature, Origin, and Use*. New York: Praeger.

Chomsky, Noam (1988) *Language and Problems of Knowledge: The Managuan Lectures*. Cambridge, Mass.: MIT Press.

Clark, A. B. (1978) Sex ratio and local resource competition in a prosimian primate. *Science*, 201:163-165.

Clutton-Brock, T. H., ed. (1988) *Reproductive Success: Studies in Individual Variation in Contrasting Breeding Systems*. Chicago: University of Chicago Press.

Cohen, S. (1980) Aftereffects of stress on human performance and social behavior: A review of research and theory. *Psychological Bulletin*, 88:82-108.

Corning, Peter A. (1975) An evolutionary paradigm for the study of human aggression. In: M. A. Nettleship, R. D. Givens, and A. Nettleship, ed., *War, Its Causes and Correlates*, Amsterdam: Elsevier.

Corning, Peter A. (1983) *The Synergism Hypothesis: A Theory of Progressive Evolution*. New York: McGraw-Hill.

Cosmides, Leda (1985) *Deduction or Darwinian algorithms? Explanation of the "elusive" content effect on the Wason selection task*. Doctoral dissertation, Harvard University, Cambridge, Massachusetts.

Cosmides, Leda, and John Tooby (1987) From evolution to behavior: Evolutionary psychology as the missing link. In J. Dupre, ed., *The Latest on the Best: Essays on Evolution and Optimality*, 277-306. Cambridge, Mass.: MIT Press.

Cosmides, Leda, and John Tooby (1989) Evolutionary psychology and the generation of culture, Part II: Case study: A Computational theory. *Ethology and Sociobiology*, 10:29-30.

Crawford, Charles (1989) The theory of evolution: Of what value to psychology? *Journal of Comparative Psychology*, 103:4-22.

Crawford, Charles, and Judith Anderson (1989) Sociobiology: An environmentalist discipline? *American Psychologist*, 44:1449-1459.

Crawford, Charles, Martin Smith, and Dennis Krebs, eds. (1987) *Sociobiology and Psychology: Ideas, Issues and Applications*. Hillsdale, N.J.: Erlbaum.

Cronk, Lee (1989) Low socioeconomic status and female biased parental investment: The Mukogodo example. *American Anthropologist*, 91(2):414-429.

Cronk, Lee (In Press a) Wealth, status, and reproductive success among the Mukogodo of Kenya. *American Anthropologist*.

Cronk, Lee (In Press b) Human behavioral ecology. *Annual Review of Anthropology*. 20.

Cummings, T. G., and E. S. Molloy (1977) *Improving Productivity and the Quality of Work Life*. New York: Praeger.

Curtin, R., and P. Dolhinow (1978) Primate social behavior in a changing world. *American Scientist*, 66:468-475.

Daly, Martin, and Margo Wilson (1983) *Sex, Evolution, and Behavior*. Boston: Willard Grant.

Daly, Martin, and Margo Wilson (1987) Evolutionary psychology and family violence. In *Sociobiology and Psychology*. See Crawford et al. 1987.

Daly, Martin, and Margo Wilson (1988a) *Homicide*. Hawthorne, N.Y.: Aldine.

Daly, Martin, and Margo Wilson (1988) Evolutionary social psychology and family homicide. *Science,* 242:519-524.

Danto, Arthur C. (1981) *The Transfiguration of the Commonplace*. Cambridge, Mass.: Harvard University Press.

Danto, Arthur C. (1985) Art, evolution, and the consciousness of history. *Journal of Aesthetics and Art Criticism*, 43:223-233.

Dart, Raymond A. (1953) The predatory transition from ape to man. *International Anthropological and Linguistic Review*, 1:201-219.

Darwin, Charles R. (1859) *The Origin of Species by Means of Natural Selection, or the Preservation of Favoured Races in the Struggle for Life*. London: Murray.

Darwin, Charles R. (1871) *The Descent of Man, and Selection in Relation to Sex*. London: Murray.

Darwin, Charles R. (1873) *The Expression of the Emotions in Man and Animals*. London: Murray.

Davies, N., and A. Lundberg (1984) Food distribution and variable mating system in the dunnock, *Prunella modularis*. *Journal of Animal Ecology*, 53:895-912.

Davis, Whitney (1986) The origins of image making. *Current Anthropology*, 27:193-215.

Dawe, N., and K. Dawe (1988) *The Bird Book*. New York: Workman.

Dawkins, Richard (1976, revised 1989) *The Selfish Gene*. Oxford: Oxford University Press.

Dawkins, Richard (1986) *The Blind Watchmaker*. New York: Norton.

Deag, J. M., and J. M. Crook (1971) Social behaviour and "agonistic buffering" in the wild Barbary macaque *Macaca sylvanus*. *Folia Primatolica*, 15:183-200.

De Sousa, Ronald (1987) *The Rationality of Emotion*. Cambridge, Mass.: MIT Press.

De Waal, Frans (1982) *Chimpanzee Politics: Power and Sex among Apes*. London: Cape.

Dickemann, Mildred (1979a) The ecology of mating systems in hypergynous dowry societies. *Social Science Information*, 18:163-195.

Dickemann, Mildred (1979b) Female infanticide and the reproductive strategies of stratified human societies: A preliminary model. In *Evolutionary Biology and Human Social Behavior*. See Chagnon and Irons 1979.

Dickemann, Mildred (1981) Paternal confidence and dowry competition: A biocultural analysis of purdah. In R. D. Alexander and D. W. Tinkle, *Natural Selection and Social Behavior*. New York: Chiron Press.

Dissanayake, Ellen (1988) *What is Art For??* Seattle: University of Washington Press.

Donaldson, Tamsin (1980) *Ngiyambaa: The Language of the Wangaaybuwan*. Cambridge: Cambridge University Press.

Duby, G. (1983) *The Knight, the Lady, and the Priest: The Making of Modern Marriage in Medieval France*. New York: Pantheon.

Dunbar, R. I. M. (1983) Structure of geleada baboon reproductive units. 3. The male's relationship with his female. *Animal Behavior*, 31:565-575.

Durham, William (1976a) The adaptive significance of cultural behaviour. *Human Ecology*, 4:89-121.

Durham, William (1976b) Resource competition and human aggression. Part I: A review of primitive war. *Quarterly Review of Biology*, 51:385-415.

Durham, William (1978) The co-evolution of human biology and culture. In N. Blurton Jones and V. Reynolds, eds., *Human Behaviour and Adaptation*. London: Taylor and Francis.

Durham W. H. (1979) Towards a coevolutionary theory of human biology and culture. In *Evolutionary Biology and Human Social Behavior*. See Chagnon and Irons 1979.

Durkheim, Emile (1915) *The Elementary Forms of the Religious Life*. London: Allen and Unwin.

Eibl-Eibesfeldt, I. (1979) *The Biology of War and Peace*. New York: Viking Press.

Eibl-Eibesfeldt, I. (1989) *Human Ethology*. Hawthorne, N.Y.: Aldine.

Elliot, E. (1985) The evolutionary tradition in jurisprudence. *Columbia Law Review*, 85:38-94.

Emde, R. N., and T. Gaensbauer (1981) Some emerging models of emotion in human infancy. In I. Immelmann, G.W. Barlow, L. Petrinovich, and M. Main, eds., *Behavioral Development*, 568-588. Cambridge: Cambridge University Press.

Epstein, R. (1980) A taste for privacy? Evolution and the emergence of a naturalistic ethic. *Journal of Legal Studies*, 9:665.

Erickson, Erik H. (1966) Ontogeny of ritualisation in man. *Philosophical Transactions of the Royal Society of London*, 251b:337-349.

Essock-Vitale, S. M., and L. A. Fairbanks (1979) Sociobiological theories of kin selection and their relevance for psychiatry. *Journal of Nervous and Mental Disease*, 167(1):23-28.

Essock-Vitale, Susan M., and Michael T. McGuire (1980) Predictions derived from the theories of kin selection and reciprocation assessed by anthropological data. *Ethology and Sociobiology*, 1(3):233-243.

Fairbanks, L. A. (1980) Relationships among adult females in captive vervet monkeys: Testing a model of rank-related attractiveness. *Animal Behavior*, 28:853-859.

Fantz, R. L., J. F. Fagan III, and S. B. Miranda (1975) Early visual selectivity. In L.B. Cohen and P. Salapatek, Eds., *Infant Perception: From Sensation to Cognition*, vol. 1: *Basic Visual Processes*, 249-345. New York: Academic Press.

Fedigan, L. M., and L. Fedigan (1977) The social development of a handicapped infant in a free-living troop of Japanese monkeys. In S. Chevalier-Skolnikoff and F. E. Poirier, eds., *Primate Bio-social Development: Biological, Social and Ecological Determinants*, 205-224. New York: Garland.

Fedigan, L. M. (1982) *Primate Paradigms: Sex Roles and Social Bonds.* Montreal: Eden Press.

Feierman, J. R. (1987) The ethology of psychiatric populations: An introduction. *Ethology and Sociobiology*, 8:1s-8s.

Ferguson R. B., ed. (1984) *Warfare, Culture and Environment.* New York: Academic Press.

Findlay, C. S., R. I. C. Hansell, and C. J. Lumsden (1989) Behavioral evolution and biocultural games: Oblique and horizontal cultural transmission. *Journal of Theoretical Biology*, 137:245-269.

Findlay, C. Scott, and Charles J. Lumsden (1988) *The Creative Mind.* London: Academic Press.

Fisher, Ronald A. (1930) *The Genetical Theory of Natural Selection.* Oxford: Clarendon.

Flinn, Mark V. (1981) Uterine vs. agnatic kinship variability and associated cousin marriages preferences. In R. D. Alexander and D. W. Tinkle, eds., *Natural Selection and Social Behavior*, 439-475. New York: Chiron Press.

Flinn, Mark V. (1986) Correlates of reproductive success in a Caribbean village. *Human Ecology*, 14:225-243.

Foa, U. G., B. Anderson, W. A. Urbansky, S. M. Mulhausen, and K. Y. Tornblom (1984) Gender differences in sexual preferences: Some cross-cultural evidence of evolutionary selection. Paper presented at the meeting of the Society for Experimental Social Psychology, Snowbird, Utah.

Fodor, Jerry A. (1979) *The Language of Thought*. Cambridge, Mass.: Harvard University Press.

Fossey, Dian (1984) Infanticide in mountain gorillas (*Gorilla gorilla beringei*) with comparative note on chimpanzees. In *Infanticide*. See Hausfater and Hrdy 1984.

Fox, Robin (1980) *The Red Lamp of Incest*. New York: Dutton.

Fox, Robin (1989) *The Search for Society: Quest for a Biosocial Science and Morality*. New Brunswick, N.J.: Rutgers University Press.

Frank, Robert (1988) *Passions Within Reason: The Strategic Role of the Emotions*. New York: Norton.

Freedman, Daniel (1979) *Human Sociobiology*. New York: Free Press.

Friedman, L. (1984) American legal history: Past and present. *Journal of Legal Education*, 34:563-576.

Fruin, J., ed. (1986) Burgerlijk Wetboek, Vijfde Boek, Derde Titel, Art. 1947, in De Nederlanse Wetboeken 589.

Galdikas, Biruté M. F. (1979) Orangutan adaptation at Tanjung Puting Reserve: Mating and ecology. In D. A. Hamburg and E. R. McCown, eds. *The Great Ape*. Menlo Park, Cal.: Benjamin/Cummings.

Galdikas, Biruté M. F. (1984) Orangutan female sociality at Tanjung Puting. In M. Small, ed., *Females on Females*. New York: Liss.

Garcia, J., W. G. Hankins, and K. W. Rusiniak (1974) Behavior regulation of the milieu interne in man and rat. *Science*, 185:824-831.

Gardner, R. Jr. (1982) Mechanisms in manic-depressive disorder. *Archives of General Psychiatry*, 39:1436-1441.

Gardner, Howard (1982) *Art, Mind and Brain*. New York: Basic Books.

Gardner, H. (1983) *Frames of mind: The theory of multiple intelligences*. New York: Basic Books.

Gardner, Howard (1985) *The Mind's New Science*. New York: Basic Books.

Gaulin, Steven J. C., and Alice Schlegel (1980) Paternal confidence and paternal investment: A cross-cultural test of a sociobiological hypothesis. *Ethology and Sociobiology*, 1(4):301-309.

Gazzaniga, M. S. (1985) *The Social Brain: Discovering the Networks of the Mind*. New York: Basic Books.

Ghiglieri, M. P. (1987) Sociobiology of the great apes and the hominid ancestor. *Journal of Human Evolution*, 16:319-357.

Gilbert, P. (1989) *Human Nature and Suffering*. Hillsdale, N.J.: Erlbaum.

Glantz, K., and J. K. Pearce (1989) *Exiles from Eden*, New York: Norton.

Gobineau, Arthur de (1853) *Essay sur l'Inegalite de Races Humaines*. Paris.

Goodall, J. (1967) Mother-offspring relationships in free-ranging chimpanzees. In Morris, ed., *Primate Ethology*, 287-346. London: Weidenfeld and Nicolson.

Goodall, J. (1968) The behaviour of free-living chimpanzees in the Gombe Stream Reserve. *Animal Behaviour Monographs*, 1:165-311.

Goodall, Jane (1971) *In the Shadow of Man*. London: Collins.

Goodall, J. (1977) Infant killing and cannibalism in free-living chimpanzees. *Folia Primatologica*, 28:259-282.

Goodall, Jane (1979) Life and death at Gombe. *National Geographic*, 155(5):592-621.

Goodall, Jane (1986) *The Chimpanzees of Gombe: Patterns of Behavior*. Cambridge, Mass.: Harvard University Press.

Goodall, Jane, et al. (1979) Intercommunity interactions in the chimpanzee population of the Gombe National Park. In D. A. Hamburg and E. R. McCown, eds., *The Great Apes: Perspectives on Human Evolution*. Menlo Park, Calif.: Benjamin/Cummings.

Goodman, Nelson (1975) *Languages of Art*. Hackett Publishing Company, Indianapolis: Hackett.

Goudge, T. A. (1961) *The Ascent of Life*. Toronto: University of Toronto Press.

Gould, Steven Jay (1977) *Ever since Darwin*. New York: Norton.

Gould, Stephen (1989) *Wonderful Life.* New York: Norton.

Gouzoules, S. (1984) Primate mating systems, kin associations, and cooperative behavior: Evidence for kin recognition. *Year Book of Physical Anthropology*, 27:99-134.

Grafen, A. (1984) Natural selection, kin selection, and group selection. In J. R. Krebs and N. B. Davies, eds., *Behaviourial Ecology: An Evolutionary Approach.* 2nd ed. Oxford: Blackwell Scientific.

Gray, J. Patrick (1985) *Primate Sociobiology.* New Haven, Conn.: HRAF Press.

Gruter, Margaret, and Roger D. Masters (1986) *Ostracism: A Social and Biological Phenomenon.* New York: Elsevier.

Gumplowicz, Ludmin (1883) *Der Rassenkampf.* Innsbruck: Wagner.

Gut, E. (1989) *Productive and Unproductive Depression.* New York: Basic Books.

Guth, Werner, Rolf Schmittberger, and Bernd Schwarze (1982) An experimental analysis of ultimatum bargaining. *Journal of Economic Behavior and Organization*, 3:367-388.

Halverson, John (1987) Art for art's sake in the Paleolithic. *Current Anthropology*, 28:63-89.

Hamilton, William D. (1964) The genetical evolution of social behavior, I and II. *Journal of Theoretical Biology*, 7:1-52.

Hamilton, William D. (1975) Innate social aptitudes of man: An approach from evolutionary genetics. In R. Fox, ed., *Biosocial Anthropology*, Maleby Press.

Hamilton, W. J. III, C. Busse, and K. S. Smith (1982) Adoption of infant orphan chacma baboons. *Animal Behavior*, 30:29-34.

Hansen, C. H., and R.D. Hansen (1988) Finding the face in the crowd: The anger superiority effect. *Journal of Personality and Social Psychology*, 54:917-924.

Harlow, Harry F. (1971) *Learning to Love.* San Francisco: Albion Press.

Harris, Marvin (1966) The cultural ecology of India's sacred cattle. *Current Anthropology*, 7:51-66.

Harris, Marvin (1972) Warfare old and new. *Natural History*, 81(3):18-20.

Harris, Marvin (1975) *Culture, Man, and Nature.* 2nd ed. New York: Lowell.

Harris, Marvin (1978) *Cannibals and Kings: The Origins of Cultures.* New York: Vintage Books.

Harris, Marvin (1979) *Cultural Materialism.* New York: Random House.

Hartigan, Richard (1989) *The Future Remembered.* Notre Dame, Ind.: Notre Dame University Press.

Hartung, J. (1982) Polygyny and the inheritance of wealth. *Current Anthropology*, 23:1-12.

Hartung, John (1985) Matrilineal inheritance: New theory and analysis. *Behavioral and Brain Sciences*, 8:661-688.

Hasegawa, T., and M. Hiraiwa (1980) Social interactions of orphans observed in a free-ranging troop of Japanese monkeys. *Folia Primatologica*, 33:129-158.

Haskins, C. (1989) Kant and the autonomy of art. *Journal of Aesthetics and Art Criticism*, 47:43-54.

Hastie, R., and D. E. Carlston (1980) Theoretical issues in person memory. In R. Hastie, T. M. Ostrom, E. B. Ebbesen, R. S. Wyer, Jr., D. L. Hamilton, and D. E. Carlston, eds., *Person Memory: The Cognitive Basis of Person Perception*, 1-54. Hillsdale, N.J.: Erlbaum.

Hastie, R., and B. Park (1986) The relationship between memory and judgment depends on whether the judgment task is memory based or on-line. *Psychological Review*, 93:258-268.

Hathout, H. (1972) Abortion and Islam. *Journal Medicinal Libanais*, 25:237-239.

Hausfater, G., and S. Hrdy (1984) *Infanticide: Comparative and Evolutionary Perspectives.* Hawthorne, N.Y.: Aldine.

Hausfater, G., and C. Vogel (1982) Infanticide in langur monkeys (Genus Presbytis): Recent research and a review of hypotheses. In A. B. Chiarelli and R. S. Corruccini, eds., *Advanced Views in Primate Biology.* Berlin: Springer-Verlag.

Hawkes, Kristen (1977) Co-operation in Binumarien: Evidence for Sahlins' model. *Man*, 12:459-483.

Hempel, C. G. (1966) *Philosophy of Natural Science.* Englewood Cliffs, N.J.: Prentice-Hall.

Hershenson, M., H. Munsinger, and W. Kessen (1965) Preference for shapes of intermediate variability in the newborn human. *Science*, 147:630-631.

Hiatt, Les (1980) Polyandry in Sri Lanka: A test case for parental investment theory. *Man*, 15:583-602.

Hinde, R. A. (1974) *The Biological Bases of Human Social Behavior*, New York: Mcgraw-Hill.

Hiraiwa, M. (1981) Maternal and alloparental care in a troop of free-ranging Japanese monkeys. *Primates*, 22:309-329.

Hirshleifer, Jack (1980) Privacy: Its origin, function and future. *Journal of Legal Studies*, 9:649-664.

Hirshleifer, Jack (1984) *Economic Behavior in Adversity*, Chicago: University of Chicago Press.

Hobbes, Thomas (1962) *Leviathan*, ed. M. Oakeshotte (original 1651). London: Collier.

Hogan, Robert, and W. H. Jones, eds. (1985) *Perspective in Personality*, Greenwich, Conn.: JAI Press.

Hölldobler, B., and M. Lindauer, eds. (1988) *Experimental Behavioral Ecology and Sociobiology*. Sunderland, Mass.: Sinauer.

Holmes, W. (1986) Kin recognition by phenotype matching in Belding's ground squirrels. *Animal Behavior*, 34:38-47.

Hrdy, Sara (1974) Male-male competition and infanticide among the langurs (*Presbytis entellus*) of Abu, Rajasthan. *Folia Primatologica*, 22:19-58.

Hrdy, Sara (1976) The care and exploitation of non-human primate infants by conspecifics other than the mother. In J. Rosenblatt, R. Hinde, C. Beer, and E. Shaw, eds. *Advances in the Study of Behavior*, vol. 6. New York: Academic Press.

Hrdy, Sara (1977) Infanticide as a primate reproductive strategy. *American Scientist*, 65:40-49.

Hrdy, Sara (1979) Infanticide among animals: A review, classification, and examination of the implications for the reproductive strategies of females. *Ethology and Sociobiology*, 1:13-40.

Hubel, D. M., and T. N. Wiesel (1968) Receptive fields and functional architecture of the monkey striate cortex. *Journal of Physiology*, 147:226-238.

Hume, David (1965) *"Of the Standard of Taste" and Other Essays*. ed. J. W. Lenz. Indianapolis: Bobbs-Merrill.

Hume, David (1978) *A Treatise of Human Nature*. Oxford: Clarendon.

Hurford, James R. (1989) The biological evolution of the Saussurean sign as a component of the language acquisition device, *Lingua*, 77:187-222.

Hurford, James R. (1991) An approach to the phylogeny of the language faculty. In John Hawkins and Murray Gell-Mann, eds., *The Evolution of Language*, New York: Wiley.

Hurford, James R., (Forthcoming) "The Evolution of the Critical Period for Language Acquisition," *Cognition*.

Huxley, Thomas Henry (1863) *Evidence of Man's Place in Nature*. London: Williams and Norgate.

Irons, William (1976) Emic and reproductive success. Paper read at the 75th Annual Meeting of the American Anthropological Association, Washington, D.C., Nov. 17-21.

Irons, William (1979a) Cultural and biological success. In *Evolutionary Biology and Human Social Behavior*. See Chagnon and Irons 1979.

Irons, William (1979b) Natural selection, adaptation, and human social behavior. In *Evolutionary Biology and Human Social Behavior*. See Chagnon and Irons 1979.

Irons, William (1980) Is Yomut social behavior adaptive? In G. W. Barlow and J. Silverberg, eds., *Sociobiology: Beyond Nature/ Nurture?*, 417-473. Boulder, Colo.: Westview Press.

Irons, William (1983) Human female reproductive strategies. In S. K. Wasser, ed., *Soical Behavior of Female Vertebrates*, 169-213. New York: Academic Press.

Irons, William (In press) How did morality evolve? *Zygon: Journal of Religion and Science*.

Itani, Junichiro (1982) Intraspecific killing among non-human primates. *Journal of Social and Biological Structures*, 5 (4):361-68.

James, William (1890) *The Principles of Psychology*. New York: Holt.

James, William (1964) The moral equivalent of war. Original, 1910, reprinted in L. Bramson and G. W. Goethals, eds., *War: Studies from Psychology, Sociology, Anthropology*. New York: Basic Books.

Johnson, Mark (1987) *The Body in The Mind*. Chicago: University of Chicago Press.

Jones, E. L. (1981) *The European Miracle*. Cambridge: Cambridge University Press.

Judge, D., and S. B. Hrdy (1988) Inheritance in California. Paper read at meeting of the American Anthropological Association, Phoenix, Arizona. November.

Kahneman, Daniel, Jack Knetsch, and Richard Thaler (1986) Perceptions of unfairness: Constraints on wealth-seeking. *American Economic Review*, 76:728-741.

Kant, Immanuel (1929) *Critique of Pure Reason*. Trans. N. K. Smith. London: Macmillan.

Kant, Immanuel (1965) *Critique of Judgement*. Trans. J. C. Meredith. Oxford: Clarendon Press.

Kaplan, Hillard, and Kim Hill (1985) Hunting ability and reproductive success among male Ache foragers: Preliminary results. *Current Anthropology*, 26:131-133.

Keith, A. (1947) *A New Theory of Human Evolution*. Gloucester, Mass.: Peter Smith.

Kenrick, D. T. (1987) Gender, genes, and the social environment: A biosocial interactionist perspective. In P. Shaver and C. Hendrick, eds., *Review of Personality and Social Psychology*, vol. 7, 14-43. Newbury Park, Calif.: Sage.

Kenrick, D. T. (1989) A biosocial perspective on mates and traits: Reuniting personality and social psychology. In D. M. Buss and N. Cantor, eds., *Personality Psychology: Recent Trends and Emerging Directions*. New York: Springer-Verlag.

Kenrick, D. T., and L. Dengeligi (1988) Gender differences in spontaneous recall of faces: Default processing fits a reproductive fitness model. Unpublished research.

Kenrick, D. T., S. E. Gutierres, and L. Goldberg (1989) Influence of popular erotica on judgments of strangers and mates. *Journal of Experimental Social Psychology*, 25:159-167.

Kenrick, D. T., and R. C. Keefe (1989) Time to integrate sociobiology and social psychology. *Behavioral and Brain Sciences*, 12:24-26.

Kenrick, D. T., and M. R. Trost (1989) A reproductive exchange model of heterosexual relationships: Putting proximate economics in ultimate perspective. In C. Hendrick, ed., *Review of Personality and Social Psychology*, vol 10, 92-118. Newbury Park, Calif.: Sage.

Kerlinger, Fred N. (1966) *Foundations of Behavioral Research: Educational and Psychological Enquiry*. New York: Holt, Rhinehart, and Winston.

Keyfitz, N., and W. Flieger (1971) *Population: Facts and Methods of Demography*. San Francisco: Freeman.

Kitcher, Philip (1981) Explanatory unification. *Philosophy of Science*, 48:507-531.

Kitcher, Philip (1985) *Vaulting Ambition: Sociobiology and the Quest for Human Nature*. Cambridge, Mass.: MIT Press.

Kofoed, L. (1988) Selected dimensions of personality: Psychiatry and sociobiology in collision. *Perspectives in Biology and Medicine*, 31(2):228-242.

Kohlberg, L. (1971) From is to ought. In T. Mischel, ed., *Cognitive Development and Epistemology*. New York: Academic Press.

Konner, M. (1982) *The Tangled Wing: Biological Constraints on The Human Spirit*. New York: Harper and Row.

Konner, M. (1989) Anthropology and Psychiatry. In H. I. Kaplan and B. J. Sadock, eds., *Comprehensive Textbook of Psychiatry*, vol. 1:283-289. Baltimore: Williams and Wilkins.

Kosslyn, Stephen M. (1980) *Image and Mind*. Cambridge, Mass.: Harvard University Press.

Kramer, D. A., and W. T. McKinney, Jr. (1979) The overlapping territories of psychiatry and ethology, *Journal of Nervous and Mental Disease*, 167(1):3-22.

Krebs, J. R., and N. B. Davies, eds. (1989) *Behavioral Ecology: An Evolutionary Approach*. 2nd ed. Sunderland, Mass.: Sinauer.

Kuhn, Thomas S. (1962) *The Structure of Scientific Revolutions*. Chicago: University of Chicago Press.

Kummer, Hans (1968) *Social Organization of Hamadryas Baboons: A Field Study*. Chicago: University of Chicago Press.

Kurland, J. A. (1977) Kin selection in the Japanese monkey. In *Contributions to Primatology*, vol. 12. Basel: Karger.

Lakoff, George, and Mark Johnson (1980) *Metaphors We Live By*. Chicago: University of Chicago Press.

Lane, L. W., and D. J. Juchins (1988) Evolutionary approach to psychiatry and problems of method, *Comprehensive Psychiatry* 39(6):598-603.

Lanzetta, John T., Denis G. Sullivan, Roger D. Masters, and Gregory J. McHugo (1985) Emotional and cognitive responses to televised images of political leaders. In Sidney Kraus and Richard E. Perloff, eds., *Mass Media and Political Thought*, 85-116. Beverly Hills, Calif.: Sage.

Larson, R. R. (1973) Leaders and nonleaders: Speculation on charisma. Paper presented to the Forty-Fifth Meeting of the Southern Political Science Association. Atlanta, Georgia. November.

Leak, G. K., and S. B. Christopher (1982) Freudian Psychoanalysis and Sociobiology. *American Psychologist*, 37(3):313-322.

Leakey, M. D. (1971) *Olduvai Gorge, Vol. 3. Excavations in Beds I and II, 1960-1963*. New York: Cambridge University Press.

Leibson, D. (1976-77) Recovery of damages for emotional distress caused by physical injury to another. *Journal of Family Law*, 15:163-211.

Lenski, Gerhard, and Jean Lenski (1987) *Human Societies: An Introduction to Macrosociology*. New York: McGraw-Hill.

Lerdahl, Fred, and R. Jackendoff (1983) *A Generative Theory of Tonal Music*. Cambridge, Mass.: MIT Press.

Levine, C. G. (1979) The form-content distinction in moral development research. *Human Development*, 22:225-234.

Lewontin, Richard G. (1978) Adaptation. *Scientific American*, 239(3):212-230.

Lewontin, Richard G., Steven Rose, and Leon Kamin (1984) *Not in Our Genes*. New York: Pantheon.

Lieberman, Philip (1984) *The Evolution and Biology of Language*. Cambridge, Mass.: Harvard University Press.

Likert, R. (1967) *Human Organization*. New York: McGraw-Hill.

Littlefield, C. H., and C. J. Lumsden (1987) Gene-culture coevolution and the strategies of psychiatric healing, *Ethology and Sociobiology,* 8:151s-163s.

Lloyd, L. T. (1990) Implications of an evolutionary metapsychology for clinical psychoanalysis. *Journal of the American Academy of Psychoanalysis*, 18:286-306.

Lockard, J. S. (1980) Speculations on the adaptive significance of self-deception. In J. S. Lockard, ed., *The Evolution of Human Social Behavior*. New York: Elsevier.

Low, B. (1990) Occupational status, land ownership, and reproductive behavior in 19th century Sweden: Tuna parish. *American Anthropologist*, 92:115-126.

Low, B. S., and R. M. Nesse (1989) Summary of the evolution and human behavior conferences: Ann Arbor, Michigan, April and October 1988: Dawn of a renaissance? *Ethologist and Sociobiologist*, 10(6):457-464.

Lumsden, Charles J. (1989a) The gene's tale. *Biology and Philosophy*, 4:495-502.

Lumsden, Charles J. (1989) Sociobiology, God, and understanding. *Zygon*, 24:83-108.

Lumsden, Charles J., and E. O. Wilson (1981) *Genes, Mind, and Culture: The Coevolutionary Process*. Cambridge, Mass.: Harvard University Press.

Lumsden, Charles J., and E. O. Wilson (1983) *Promethean Fire: Reflections on the Origin of Mind*. Cambridge, Mass.: Harvard University Press.

MacArthur, R. H., and E. O. Wilson (1967) *The Theory of Island Biogeography*. Princeton: Princeton University Press.

Macoby, M. (1981) *The Leader*. New York: Ballantine.

MacDonald, K. (1990) Mechanisms of sexual egalitarianism in Western Europe. *Ethology and Sociobiology*, 11, in press.

Mackie, J. L. C. (1977) *Ethics: Inventing Right and Wrong*. Harmondsworth, England: Penguin.

MacKinnon, J. (1974) The behavior and ecology of wild orangutans, *Pongo pygmaeus*. *Animal Behavior*, 22:3-74.

Madson, Douglas (1985) A biochemical property related to power-seeking in humans. *American Political Science Review*, 79:448-457.

Malthus, T. R. (1798) *An Essay on the Principle of Population*. London: Johnson.

Margolis, Howard (1982) *Selfishness, Altruism, and Rationality*. Cambridge: Cambridge University Press.

Marks, I. M. (1987) *Fears, Phobias and Rituals*. New York: Oxford University Press.

Markus, H., and R. B. Zajonc (1985) The cognitive perspective in social psychology. In G. Lindzey and E. Aronson, eds., *Handbook of Social Psychology*, vol. 1, 137-230. New York: Random House.

Marr, D. (1982) *Vision: A Computational Investigation into the Human Representation and Processing of Visual Information*. San Francisco: Freeman.

Marshack, Alexander (1979) Upper Paleolithic symbol systems of the Russian plain: Cognitive and comparative analysis. *Current Anthropology*, 20:271-298.

Marx, Karl (1964) *Economic and Philosophic Manuscripts* of 1844, ed. Dirk J. Struik. New York: International.

Masdon, Douglas (1985) A biochemical property related to power-seeking in humans. *American Political Science Review*, 79:448-457.

Masters, Roger D. (1982) Is sociobiology reactionary? The political implications of inclusive fitness theory. *Quarterly Review of Biology*, 57:275-292.

Masters, Roger D. (1984) Social biology and the welfare state. In Richard F. Tomasson, ed., *Comparative Social Research*, vol. 6, 203-241, Greenwich, Conn.: JAI Press.

Masters, Roger D. (1989a) *The Nature of Politics*. New Haven: Yale University Press.

Masters, Roger D. (1989b) Gender and political cognition. *Politics and the Life Sciences*, 8:3-39.

Masters, Roger D., and Denis G. Sullivan (1989) Nonverbal displays and political leadership in France and the United States. *Political Behavior*, 11:121-153.

Masters, Roger D., and Denis G. Sullivan (1990) Nonverbal behavior and leadership: Emotion and cognition in political information processing. *Institute of Governmental Studies Working Paper*, 90-4. Berkeley: University of California at Berkeley.

Masters, Roger D., Denis G. Sullivan, John T. Lanzetta, Gregory J. McHugo, and Basil G. Englis (1986) The facial displays of leaders. *Journal of Social and Biological Structures*, 9:319-343.

Maxwell, Mary (1985) Aesthetic feeling and the development of art: a case of gene-culture coevolution? Project for the Certificate of Advanced Study, Harvard University Extension Office, Cambridge, Massachusetts.

Maxwell, Mary (1990) *Morality among Nations*. Albany, N.Y.: State University of New York Press.

Maxwell, Mary (1991) *Moral Inertia: Ideas for Social Action*. Niwot, Colo.: University Press of Colorado.

Maynard Smith, John (1976) Group selection. *Quarterly Review of Biology*, 51:277-283.

Maynard Smith, John, and Gerard R. Price (1973) The logic of animal conflict. *Nature*, 246:15-18.

Mayr, Ernst (1961) Cause and effect in biology. *Science*, 134:1501-1506.

Mayr, Ernst (1982) *The Growth of Biological Thought: Diversity, Evolution, and Inheritance*. Cambridge, Mass.: Harvard University Press.

Mayr, Ernst (1988) *Towards a New Philosophy of Biology*, Cambridge, Mass.: Harvard University Press.

McCelland, J. L., D. E. Rumelhart, and the PDP Research Group (1988) *Parallel Distributed Processing*. Cambridge, Mass.: MIT Press.

McDougall, William (1913) *Social Psychology*. 3rd ed. London: Methuen.

McDougall, William (1915) *An Introduction to Social Psychology*. 8th ed. London: Methuen.

McEachron, Donald L., and Darius Baer (1982) A review of selected sociobiological principles: Application to hominid evolution II, the effects of intergroup conflict. *Journal of Social and Biological Structures*, 5(2):121-139.

McGregor, D. (1966) *Leadership and Motivation*. Cambridge, Mass.: MIT Press.

McGrew, W. C., C. E. Tutin, and P. J. Baldwin (1979) New data on meat eating by wild chimpanzees. *Current Anthropology*, 20(1):238-239.

McGuire, Michael T. (1979) Sociobiology: Its potential contributions to psychiatry. *Perspectives in Biology and Medicine*, 23:50-69.

McGuire, M. T., S. M. Essock-Vitale and R. H. Polsky (1982) Psychiatric disorders in the context of evolutionary biology, *Journal of Nervous and Mental Disease*, 170:9-20.

McGuire, M. T., and L. A. Fairbanks, eds. (1977) *Ethological Psychiatry: Psychopathology in the Context of Evolutionary Biology*. New York: Grune and Stratton.

McHugo, Gregory J., John T. Lanzetta, Dennis G. Sullivan, Roger D. Masters, and Basil G. Englis (1985) Emotional reactions to expressive displays of a political leader. *Journal of Personality and Social Psychology*, 490:1513-1529.

McKinney, W. T. (1988) *Models of Mental Disorders: A New Comparative Psychiatry*. New York: Plenum.

Mead, Margaret (1940) Warfare is only an invention—not a biological necessity. *Asia*, 40:402-405.

Meyer, Peter (1977) *Kriegs and Militarsoziologie*. Cologne: Westdeutscher Verlag.

Meyer, Peter (1981) *Evolution und Gewalt*. Hamburg: Paul Parey.

Meyer, Peter (1987) Ethnocentrism in human social behaviour. In Vernon Reynolds, Vincent Falger, and Ian Vine, eds., *The Sociobiology of Ethnocentrism*. London: Croom Helm.

Meyer, Peter (1990) Human nature and the function of war in social evolution. In J. van der Dennen and Vincent Falger, eds., *Sociobiology and Conflict*. London: Chapman and Hall.

Mills, C. Wright (1956) *The Sociological Imagination*. New York: Grove Press.

Muir, E. (1960) *Collected Poems*. New York: Oxford University Press.

Murdock, G. P., and D. White (1969) Standard cross-cultural sample. *Ethnology*, 8:329-369.

Murphy, J. (1982) *Evolution, Morality, and the Meaning of Life*. Totowa, N.J.: Rowman and Littlefield.

Nagi, M. H. (1983) Trends in Moslem fertility and the application of the demographic transition model. *Social Biology*, 30(3):345-362.

Namboodiri, Krishnan (1988) Ecological demography, its place in sociology. *American Sociological Review*, 53(4):619-633.

Nelson, Harry, and Robert Jurmain (1983) *Introduction to Physical Anthropology*. 3rd ed. St. Paul, Minn.: West.

Nesse, R. M. (1988) Panic disorder: An evolutionary view. *Psychiatric Annals*, 18:478-483.

Nesse, R. M. (1990a) Evolution and the explanations of emotions. *Human Nature*, 1:261-289.

Nesse, R. M. (1990b) The evolution of repression and the ego defenses. *Journal of American Academy of Psychoanalysis*, in press.

Nesse, R. M., and A. T. Lloyd (1991) The evolution of psychodynamic mechanisms. In J. Barkow, L. Cosmides, and J. Tooby, eds. *The Adapted Mind: Evolutionary Psychology and the Generation of Culture.* New York: Oxford University Press.

Newmeyer, Frederick (1990) Functional explanation in linguistic and the origins of language. *Language and Communication.*

Newton, James, Roger D. Masters, Gregory J. McHugo, and Denis G. Sullivan (1987) Making up our minds: Effects of network coverage on viewer impressions of leaders. *Polity,* 20:226-246.

Nicholson, N. (1986) Infants, mothers and other females. In *Primate Societies.* See Smuts et al. 1987.

Nicholson, N., and M. W. Demment (1982) The transition from suckling to independent feeding in wild baboon infants. *International Journal of Primatology,* 3:318.

Novikow, Jean (1896) *Les luttes entre les societes humaines et leur phases successives.* Paris: Alcan.

Novikow, Jean (1912) *War and its Alleged Benefits.* London: Heinemann.

Ouchi, William (1981) *Theory Z.* New York: Avon.

Packer, Craig (1977) Reciprocal altruism in *Papio anubis. Nature,* 265:441-443.

Packer, C. (1979) Inter-troop transfer and in-breeding avoidance in *Papio anubis. Animal Behavior,* 27:1-36.

Panskepp, J. (1982) Toward a general psychobiological theory of emotions. *Behavioral and Brain Sciences,* 5:407-467.

Parker, G., R. Baker, and V. Smith (1972) The origin and evolution of gamete dimorphism and the male-female phenomenon. *Journal of Theoretical Biology,* 36:529-553.

Parsons, Michael J. (1987) *How We Understand Art: A Cognitive Developmental Account of Aesthetic Experience.* New York: Cambridge University Press.

Pereira, M. E., and M. R. Izard (1989) Lactation and care for unrelated infants in forest-living ringtailed lemurs. *American Journal of Primatology,* 18:101-108.

Perrow, C. (1986) *Complex Organizations.* New York: Random House.

Peters, T. J. (1988) *Thriving on Chaos.* New York: Knopf.

Pfeiffer, John E. (1972) *The Emergence of Man*. New York: Harper and Row.

Pfeiffer, John E. (1982) *The Creative Explosion: An Inquiry Into the Origins of Art and Religion*. New York: Harper and Row.

Piattelli-Palmarini, M. (1989) Evolution, selection, and cognition: From learning to parameter setting in biology and in the study of language. *Cognition*, 31:1-44.

Pinker, Steven, and Paul Bloom (1990) Natural selection and natural language, *Behavioral and Brain Sciences*, 13:707-784.

Pitlo, A. (1981) Het Nederlandse Burgerlijk Wetboeken, Deel 4, Bewijs en Verjaring.

Pitt, R. (1978) Warfare and hominid brain evolution. *Journal of Theoretical Biology*, 72(3):551-75.

Plutchik, R. (1980) *Emotion: A Psychoevolutionary Synthesis*. New York: Harper and Row.

Plutchik, R., and H. Kellerman (1980) *Theories of Evolution*. Orlando, Fla.: Academic Press.

Popper, Karl R. (1959) *The Logic of Scientific Discovery*. London: Hutchinson.

Popper, Karl R. (1962) *Conjectures and Refutations*. London: Routledge and Kegan Paul.

Posner, Richard (1972) *Economic Analysis of Law*, Chicago: University of Chicago Press.

Posner, Richard (1981) *The Economics of Justice*. Cambridge, Mass.: Harvard University Press.

Price, J., and L. Sloman (1984) The Evolutionary Model of Psychiatric Disorders. *Archives of General Psychiatry*, 41:211.

Pulak, C. (1988) The Bronze Age shipwreck at Ulu Burun, Turkey: 1985 campaign. *American Journal of Archaelogy*, 92:1-37.

Quiatt, D. D. (1979) Aunts and mothers: Adaptive implications of allomaternal behavior of non-human primates. *American Anthropologist*, 81:311-319.

Raleigh, M. J., M. T. McGuire, G. L. Brammer, and A. Yuwiler (1983) Social and environmental influences on blood serotonin concentrations in monkeys. *Archives of General Psychiatry*, 41:405-410.

Rancour-Laferrier, D. (1985) *Signs of the Flesh*. Hawthorne, N.Y.: Aldine.

Rawls, John (1971) *A Theory of Justice*. Cambridge, Mass.: Harvard University Press.

Reich, R. B. (1987) Entrepreneurship reconsidered: The team as hero. *Harvard Business Review*, 65:77-83.

Reynolds, Vernon, and R. E. S. Tanner (1983) *The Biology of Religion*. London: Longman.

Richard, A. F., and S. R. Schulman (1982) Sociobiology: Primate field studies. *Annual Review of Anthropology*, 11:231-255.

Richards, R. J. (1986) A defense of evolutionary ethics. *Biology and Philosophy*, 1:265-292.

Rodgers, W. (1982) Bringing people back: Toward a comprehensive theory of taking in natural resources law. *Ecology Law Quarterly*, 10:205-252.

Roe, A., and G. C, Simpson (1958) *Behavior and Evolution*. New Haven: Yale University Press.

Rosch, E. (1973) Natural categories. *Cognitive Psychology*, 4:328-350.

Rousseau, Jean-Jacques (1964) *First and Second Discourses*, ed. R. D. Masters, trans. F. D. Masters and J. R. Masters (original, 1751-1755). New York: St. Martin's.

Rowell, T. E., and D. K. Olson (1983) Alternative mechanisms of social organization in monkeys. *Behaviour*, 86:31-54.

Rudwick, M. J. S. (1972) *The Meaning of Fossils*. London: Macdonald.

Ruse, Michael (1979) *Sociobiology: Sense or Nonsense?* Dordrecht, the Netherlands: Reidel.

Ruse, Michael (1982) *Darwinism Defended: A Guide to the Evolution Controversies*. Reading, Mass.: Addison-Wesley.

Ruse, Michael (1984) The morality of the gene. *The Monist*.

Ruse, Michael (1986) *Taking Darwin Seriously*. Oxford: Blackwell.

Ruse, Michael (1988) Evolutionary ethics: Healthy prospect or last infirmity? *Biology and Philosophy*, 1:27-73.

Ruse, Michael, and E. O. Wilson (1986) Moral Philosophy as Applied Science. *Philosophy*, 61:173-192.

Rushton, J. P., R. Russell, and P. Wells (1984) Genetic similarity theory: An extension to sociobiology. *Behavior Genetics*, 14:179-193.

Rushton, J. P., R. Russell, and P. Wells (1985) Genetic similarity theory: A reply to Mealey and new evidence. *Behavior Genetics*, 15:575-582.

Russell, W. M. S., and C. Russell (1983) Evolutionary and social aspects of disease. *Ecology of Disease*, 2:95-106.

Ryan, B. (1952) Institutional factors in Sinhalese fertility. *Millbank Memorial Fund Quarterly*, 30:371-372.

Sade, D. S. (1965) Some aspects of parent-offspring and sibling relations in a group of rhesus monkeys, with a discussion of grooming. *American Journal of Physical Anthropology*, 23:1-18.

Sahlins, Marshall D. (1976) *The Use and Abuse of Biology*. Ann Arbor: University of Michigan Press.

Saussure, Ferdinand de (1959) *Course in General Linguistics*. Trans. Wade Baskin. New York: McGraw-Hill.

Scarr, S. (1985) Constructing psychology: Making facts and fables for our times. *American Psychologist*, 40:499-512.

Schachter, S., and J. E. Singer (1962) Cognitive, social and physiological determinants of emotional state. *Psychological Review*, 69:379-399.

Schaller, G. B. (1972) *The Seregeti lion: A study of predator-prey relations*. Chicago: University of Chicago Press.

Schelling, Thomas (1960) *The Strategy of Conflict*, Cambridge, Mass.: Harvard University Press.

Schubert, Glendon (1989) *Evolutionary Politics*. Carbondale: Southern Illinois University Press.

Schubert, Glendon, and Roger D. Masters, eds. (1990) *Primate Politics*. Carbondale: Southern Illinois University Press.

Schubert, James N. (1983) Ethological methods of observing small group political decision-making. *Politics and the Life Sciences*, 2:3-41.

Schubert, James N., Thomas C. Wiegele, and Samuel M. Hines (1986) Age and political behavior in collective decision making. *International Political Science Review*, 8:131-46.

Schwartz, R. (1983) On the prospects of using sociobiology in shaping laws: A cautionary note. In M. Gruter and P. Bohannon, eds., *Law, Biology and Culture*. Santa Barbara, Calif.: Ross-Erikson.

Scott, J. P. (1980) The function of emotions in behavioral systems: A systems theory analysis. In Plutchik, R. and H. Kellerman, eds., *Emotion: Theory, Research, and Experience*, 35-36. New York: Academic Press.

Scruton, R. (1983) *Aesthetic Understanding: Essays in the Philosophy of Art and Culture*. London: Methuen.

Seyfarth, R. M., and D. L. Cheney (1984) Grooming, alliances, and altruism in vervet monkeys. *Nature*, 308:541-543.

Shaw, R. Paul, and Yuwa Wong (1988) *Genetic Seeds of Warfare: Evolution, Nationalism, and Patriotism*. London: Unwin Hyman.

Sherman, P. (1980) The limits of ground squirrel nepotism. In G. Barlow and J. Silverberg, eds., *Sociobiology: Beyond Nature/ Nurture?* Boulder, Colo.: Westview Press.

Sherry, D. F., and D. L. Shacter (1987) The evolution of multiple memory systems. *Psychological Review*, 94:439-454.

Silk, J. B. (1983) Local resource competition and facultative adjustment of sex ratios in relation to competitive abilities. *American Naturalist*, 121:56-66.

Silk, J. B. (1980) Adoption and Kinship in Oceania. *American Anthropologist*, 82:799-820.

Silk, J. B. (1990) Human adoption in evolutionary perspective. *Human Nature*, 1:25-52.

Silk, J. B., A. Samuels, and P. Rodman (1981) The influences of kinship, rank, and sex on affiliations and aggression between adult female and immature bonnet macaques (*Macaca radiata*). *Behaviour*, 78-111-177.

Simons, A. (1976) Psychic injury and the bystander: The transcontinental dispute between California and New York. *St. John's Law Review*, 51:1-40.

Singer, Peter (1981) *The Expanding Circle*. Oxford: Clarendon Press.

Slavin, M. O. (1985) The origins of psychic conflict and the adaptive functions of repression: An evolutionary biological view. *Psychoanalysis and Contemporary Thought*, 8:407-440.

Sloman, L., and J. S. Price (1987) Losing behavior (yielding subroutine) and human depression: Proximate and selective mechanisms. *Ethology and Sociobiology,* 8(35): 85s-98s.

Smith, Martin, Bradley Kish, and Charles Crawford (1987) Inheritance of wealth as human kin investment. *Ethology and Sociobiology,* 8:171-182.

Smuts, B. B. (1983) Dynamics of "special relationship" between adult male and female olive baboons. In R.A. Hinde, ed., *Primate Social Relationships: An Integrated Approach.* Oxford: Blackwell.

Smuts, B. B. (1985) *Sex and Friendship in Baboons.* Hawthorne, N.Y.: Aldine.

Smuts, Barbara, Dorothy L. Cheney, Robert M. Seyfarth, Richard W. Wrangham, and Thomas T. Struhsaker, eds. (1987) *Primate Societies.* Chicago: University of Chicago Press.

Sober, Elliott (1984) *The Nature of Selection: Evolutionary Theory in Philosophical Focus.* Cambridge, Mass.: MIT Press.

Solomon, R. C. (1983) *The Passions.* Notre Dame, Ind.: University of Notre Dame Press.

Somit, Albert O. (1976) *Biology and Politics.* The Hague: Mouton.

Sparshott, F. (1982) *Theory of the Arts.* Princeton: Princeton University Press.

Spencer, Herbert (1873) *The Study of Sociology.* New York: Appleton.

Srull, T. K., and R. S. Wyer, Jr. (1979) The role of category accessibility in the interpretation of information about persons: Some determinants and implications. *Journal of Personality and Social Psychology,* 37:1660-1672.

Srull, T. K., and R. S. Wyer, Jr. (1980) Category accessibility and social perception: Some implications for the study of person memory and interpersonal judgments. *Journal of Personality and Social Psychology,* 38:841-856.

Steinmetz, S. Rudolf (1929) *Soziologie des Krieges.* Leipzig: J. A. Barth.

Struhsaker, T. T. (1971) Social behavior of mother and infant vervet monkeys (*Cercopthecus aethiops*). *Animal Behavior,* 19:233-250.

Sugiyama, Y. (1965) On the social change in a hanuman langur troop (*Presbytis entellus*) in their natural conditions. *Primates,* 6:213-247.

Sullivan, Denis G., and Roger D. Masters (1988) "Happy Warriors": Leaders' facial displays, viewers' emotions, and political support. *American Journal of Political Science*, 32:345-368.

Sullivan, Denis G., and Roger D. Masters (1990a) Emotions and trait attributions in the evaluation of leaders: Experimental evidence. In Albert Somit and Steven Peterson, eds., *Research in Biopolitics*. Greenwich, Conn.: JAI Press.

Sullivan, Denis G., and Roger D. Masters (1990b) Nonverbal behavior, emotions, and democratic leadership. In George Marcus and John Sullivan, eds., *Reconsidering Democracy*. Submitted for publication.

Sumner, William G. (1911) *War and Other Essays*. New Haven: Yale University Press.

Surbey, M. K. (1987) Anorexia nervosa, amenorrhea, and adaptation. *Ethology and Sociobiology*, 8:47s-62s.

Suryabongse, L. (1954) Human nature in the light of the Buddha's teachings. *Journal of the Siam Society*, 42:11-22.

Sverdlik, S. (1986) Hume's key and aesthetic rationality. *Journal of Aesthetics and Art Criticism*, 45:69-76.

Symons, Donald (1979) *The Evolution of Human Sexuality*. New York: Oxford University Press.

Symons, Donald (1987) If we are all Darwinians, what's the fuss all about? In C. Crawford, M. Smith, and D. Krebs eds., *Sociobiology and Psychology: Ideas, Issues and Applications*, 121-146. Hillsdale, N.J.: Erlbaum.

Symons, Donald (1989) A critique of Darwinian anthropology. *Ethology and Sociobiology*, 10:131-144.

Takahata, Y. (1982) Social relations between adult males and females of Japanese monkeys in the Arashiyama B troop. *Primates*, 21:1-23.

Teleki, Gaza (1973) *The Predatory Behavior of Wild Chimpanzees*. Lewisburg, Penn.: Bucknell University Press.

Thaler, Richard (1985) Mental accounting and consumer choice. *Marketing Science*, 4, Summer.

Thayer, R.E. (1989) *The Biopsychology of Mood and Arousal*. New York: Oxford University Press.

Thornhill, R. (1980) Rape in *Panorpa* scorpionflies and a general rape hypothesis. *Animal Behavior*, 28:52-59.

Thornhill, R., and J. Alcock (1983) *The Evolution of Insect Mating Systems*. Cambridge, Mass.: Harvard University Press.

Thornhill, Nancy W. (1990) The evolutionary significance of incest rules. *Ethology and Sociobiology*, 11:113-129.

Thornhill, Nancy Wilmsen, and Randy Thornhill (1983) Human rape: An evolutionary analysis. *Ethology and Sociobiology*, 4:137-173.

Tiger, Lionel (1987) *The Manufacture of Evil: Ethics, Evolution, and the Industrial System*. New York: Harper and Row.

Tooby, John, and Leda Cosmides (1988) The evolution of war and its cognitive foundations. *Proceedings of the Institute of Evolutionary Studies*, 88:1-15.

Tooby, John, and Leda Cosmides (1989) Evolutionary psychology and the generation of culture, part I. Theoretical considerations. *Ethology and Sociobiology*, 10:29.

Tooby, John, and Leda Cosmides (1990) The past explains the present: Emotional adaptations and the structure of ancestral environments. *Ethology and Sociobiology*, 11, in press.

Tooby, John, and Leda Cosmides (In press) On the universality of human nature and the uniqueness of the individual: The role of genetics and adaptation. *Journal of Personality*.

Toynbee, Arnold (1935) *A Study of History*. Oxford: Oxford University Press.

Trivers, Robert L. (1971) The evolution of reciprocal altruism. *Quarterly Review of Biology*, 46:35-57.

Trivers, Robert L. (1972) Parental investment and sexual selection. In B. Campbell, ed., *Sexual selection and the descent of man*. Hawthorne, N.Y.: Aldine.

Trivers, Robert L. (1974) Parent-offspring conflict. *American Zoologist*, 14:249-264.

Trivers, Robert L. (1976) Foreword to R. Dawkins, *The Selfish Gene*, v-vii. Oxford: Oxford University Press.

Trivers, Robert L. (1985) *Social Evolution*. Menlo Park, Calif.: Benjamin/Cummings.

Trivers, Robert, and D. Willard (1973) Natural selection of parental ability to vary the sex ratio of offspring. *Science*, 179:90-92.

Turke, Paul W. (1989) Evolution and the demand for children. *Population and Development Review*, 15(1): 61-90.

Turke, Paul W. (1990) Which humans behave adaptively and why does it matter? *Ethology and Sociobiology*, 11, in press.

Turke, Paul W., and Laura L. Betzig (1985) Those who can do: Wealth, status, and reproductive success on Ifaluk. *Ethology and Sociobiology*, 6(2): 79-87.

Van den Berghe, Pierre L. (1981) *The Ethnic Phenomenon*. Westport, Conn.: Greenwood Press.

Van der Bij, Theo S. (1929) *Ontstaan en eerste ontwikkeling van den oorlog*. Groningen: Wolters.

Van der Dennen, Johan M. G. (1990) De primitieve oorlog in evolutionair perspectief. In J. van Hooff, G. van Benthem van den Bergh, and J. Rabbie, eds., *Oorlog; Multidisplinaire Beschouwingen*. Hoogezand: Stubeg.

Van der Dennen, Johan M. G., and Vincent Falger, eds. (1990) *Sociobiology and Conflict*. London: Chapman and Hall.

Van Hooff, Jan (1969) The facial displays of latyrrhine monkeys and apes. In Desmond Morris, ed., *Primate Ethology*, 9-81. New York: Doubleday Anchor.

Van Hooff, Jan (1988) Sociality in primates: A compromise of ecological and social adaptation strategies. In A. Tartabini and M.L. Genta, eds., *Perspectives in the Study of Primates*. Cosenza, Italy: DeRose.

Van Hooff, Jan (1990) Competition regimes and conflict, in particular intergroup conflict among animals, and war. In *Sociobiology and Conflict*. See Van der Dennen and Falger 1990.

Van Schaik, C. P., and Jan van Hooff (1983) On the ultimate causes of primate social systems. *Behaviour*, 85:91-117.

Vayda, Andrew P. (1968) Research on the functions of primitive war. *Peace Research Society International Papers*, 7:133-138.

Voland, Eckart (1984) Human sex-ratio manipulation: Historical data from a German parish. *Journal of Human Evolution*, 13:99-107.

Waldman, B. (1986) Preference for unfamiliar siblings over familiar non-siblings in American toad (*Bufo americanus*) tadpoles. *Animal Behavior*, 34:48-53.

Wallace, Albert Russell (1870) *Contributions to the Theory of Natural Selection*. London: Macmillan.

Walters, J. R. (1981) Inferring kinship from behaviour: Maternity determinations in yellow baboons. *Animal Behavior*, 29:126-136.

Washburn, Stuart, and C. S. Lancaster (1968) The evolution of hunting. In R.B. Lee and I. Devore, eds., *Man the Hunter*. Chicago: Aldine, Atherton.

Watts, Meredith O., ed. (1981) *Biopolitics: Ethological and physiological approaches*. New Directions for Methodology of Social and Behavioral Science, no. 7. San Francisco: Jossey-Bass.

Watts, Meredith O. (1984) *Biopolitics and Gender*. New York: Haworth Press.

Weatherhead, P., and R. Robertson (1979) Offspring quality and the polygyny threshold: The "sexy son" hypothesis. *American Naturalist*, 113:201-208.

Wenegrat, B. (1990) *Sociobiological Psychiatry: A New Conceptual Framework*. Lexington, Mass.: Lexington Press.

Westermarck, Edward A. (1891) *The History of Human Marriage*. London: Macmillan.

Whewell, M. (1840) *Philosophy of the Inductive Sciences*. London: Parker.

White, Elliott, ed. (1981) *Sociobiology and Human Politics*. Lexington, Mass.: Lexington Books.

White, Geoffrey (1980) Conceptual universals in interpersonal language. *American Anthropologist*, 82:759-781.

White, L. A. (1949) *The Science of Culture*. New York: Farrar, Straus.

Wiggins, J. S., and R. Broughton (1985) The interpersonal circle: A structural model for the integration of personality research. In R. Hogan and W.H. Jones, eds., *Perspectives in Personality*, vol. 1. Greenwich, Conn.: JAI Press.

Williams, George C. (1966) *Adaptation and Natural Selection: A Critique of Some Current Evolutionary Thought*. Princeton: Princeton University Press.

Willmuth, L. R. (1986) A retrospective evaluation—Darwin comes to American psychiatry: Evolutionary biology and Adolf Meyer. *Journal of Social and Biological Structures*, 9:279.

Wilson, E. O. (1975) *Sociobiology: The New Synthesis*. Cambridge, Mass.: Harvard University Press.

Wilson, E. O. (1978) *On Human Nature*. Cambridge, Mass.: Harvard University Press.

Wilson, E. O. (1980) *Sociobiology: The Abridged Edition*. Cambridge, Mass.: Harvard University Press.

Wilson, E. O. (1985) In the queendom of the ants: A brief autobiography. In D. A. Dewsbury, ed., *Leaders in the Study of Animal Behavior: Autobiographical Perspectives*, 464-484. Lewisburg, Penn.: Bucknell University Press.

Wilson, Margo (1987) Impact of the uncertainty of paternity on family law. *Univeristy of Toronto Faculty Law Review*, 45:216.

Wittenberger, J. (1979) The evolution of mating systems in birds and mammals. In P. Marler and S. Vandenberg, eds., *Handbook of Behavioral Neurobiology*, vol. 3. New York: Plenum Press.

Wolff, P. R. (1960) Hume's theory of mental activity. *Philosophical Review*, 49:289-310.

Wrangham, Richard (1980) An ecological model of female-bonded primate groups. *Behaviour*, 75:262-300.

Wrangham, Richard (1987) Evolution of social structure. In *Primate Societies*. See Smuts et al. 1987.

Wyer, R. S., and T. K. Srull (1986) Human cognition in its social context. *Psychological Review*, 93:322-359.

Wynne-Edwards, Vincent C. (1962) *Animal Dispersion in Relation to Social Behaviour*. Edinburgh: Oliver and Boyd.

Zuckerman, M., M. S. Buchsbaum, and D. L. Murphy (1980) Sensation seeking and its biological correlates. *Psychological Bulletin*, 88:187-214.

Zuckerman, Solly (1932) *The Social Life of Monkeys and Apes*. London: Routledge.

INDEX